DAVID & JANE

DAVID & JANE

The Fallen Sparrow

Bruce A. Burton

To order additional copies of this book, contact:
Xlibris Corporation
1-888-795-4274
www.Xlibris.com
Orders@Xlibris.com
24512

For Jaime

PROLOGUE

Between 1770 and 1773, after the
Great Ohio War between England and France,
Colonial legislatures and the English Parliament
struggled for supremacy over the Parliament's
right to tax the Thirteen Colonies. As
Parliament taxed, the Colonies boycotted
English goods—with the result that
Parliament stopped issuing land Patents.
Our story opens in the summer of 1770
on the Hudson River in Northumberland, New York,
only a few months after the Boston Massacre.

1

Summer 1770
On the Hudson River
Northumberland, New York

David watched Jane straighten her bonnet. His blood rose. His passion for her was always just beneath the surface.

—Providence had ripened his love for her following her father's death and his brother's invitation to come north to join his milling business. He was optimistic about his business prospects—so optimistic about the present he hadn't told Jane he would also be rich when he turned forty.

"What a view!" he said at how her brother's log house commanded the sweep of the bay. He wanted her to be less anxious about seeing her brother. "Don't worry, Jen," he leaned over and whispered to her. He touched her breast with his arm, but resisted kissing her in his mother's presence. For some strange reason his mother too had grown colder and more remote from him and Jane the farther upriver they came—He brushed the thought from his mind, thinking perhaps his mother's changed attitude was only in his imagination.

"David," Jane whispered at his hidden touch, pushing her arm through his.

"Ah, the Liberty Poles are behind us—" he continued, referring to John, "those poles are the last things John would think about up here. Look at his *land*—" he said so his mother wouldn't hear, pointing to the wheat-covered hill.

"I know John won't blame me . . ." Jane replied, casting her eyes on the deck of the bateau, "but what if he *should* find out about your brother helping cut down those *poles* in New York City."

David glanced at his mother. She hadn't heard Jane mention Thomas. "Don't mention it. If Thomas joins the British that's his business. It's not our concern, nor John's. Besides, factory workers set them up. *We're* beginning a new life up here—" Jane slipped off her bonnet and her long red hair fell over her shoulders. "Forget Golden Hill—" he whispered, trying to control his passion, knowing, however, that John *was* a Whig and that his politics caused his rupture with her father.

A child appeared on the steps of the house. Then a woman came out. David recognized Eva's blonde hair and the way it curved against her forehead. He drew his breath—

"Jane McCrea!" the woman called.

"Help me off the bateau, David," Jane said eagerly.

He took Jane's arm as she stepped toward the bow, then jumped off and reached up for her. He couldn't help notice how the pole men still looked at her. Guiding the twenty-five foot boat from the Troy falls they hadn't taken their eyes off her, and the unbroken woods along the river bank did little to relieve his agony at their stares.

"Oh, you haven't changed a bit, Eva! And how James has grown!" Jane exclaimed.

He watched her embrace her sister-in-law and then Eva's son. The boy's eyes were as large as blue halfpennies.

"Changed, Jane? How lovely *you* are!" Eva replied with a knowing light in her eyes.

"Oh, Eva," Jane stepped back, "you're going to have another baby!"

"Yes!" Eva laughed, brushing her sides with her hands, "in September."

"Jane has spoken often of you, Eva . . . and have you met my mother?" David came forward, looking back at his mother on the bateau behind him.

"What a pleasure, Mistress Jones," Eva said amiably.

"My back plagues me," Sarah Jones complained, her face cold, her not stirring in her chair.

"Oh, don't get down, Mistress Jones."

David recalled how his mother had refused to meet John and Eva for afternoon tea at the McCreas when they visited from Albany. He didn't like it when his mother blew cold like this. He began to suspect she harbored some deep feelings for Jane because of her family. It was a flash of intuition, which lit up the past without his thinking of it.

"And when will you wear yellow and take the leap, Jane McCrea?" Eva turned to her sister-in-law.

"After David's work is settled," Jane answered, taking David's sleeve.

"You are a millwright, aren't you?" Eva asked him.

"Yes, my brother Daniel has mills in Kingsbury," he explained, looking at Jane encouragingly, the thought of his prospects pushing thought of his mother into the background. "Didn't Jane write you of our plans?" He wanted Eva to understand that Jane wouldn't be staying with them for too long. He turned to her to confirm this—but Jane was looking over his shoulder. The July evening was close and she lifted her hair from her temples. He followed the direction of her gaze and recognized her brother's walk as he came along the riverbank toward them.

Jane brushed by him and met her brother a few feet away. John swept her off her feet.

"Oh, it's been so long, John!" he heard her say.

"Look at you," John said, setting her down and admiring his sister.

David could see that he was looking at her laced sleeves, high collar, and long hair flowing over her shoulders. He searched her face with his own eyes. How could he not do it, his remembering witnessing this same brother swinging Jane in the air when she was a little girl, her hair streaming, her eyes and laughter light and clear as running brook water. As Jane brushed her hair from her cheek, John had to see how the last two years had darkened her hair, and deepened her eyes . . .

"And are you engaged now?" John asked her.

"Yes," Jane answered, "Catherine gave me the quilting party before I left."

David knew that Jane had regretted not having written her brother because of her father. But as he had told her, John's quickness in answering her letter proved he loved his *only* sister.

"And what's your pattern, Jane?" Eva asked from where she stood.

"Butterflies and strawberries, Eva,—look, the quilt's right here on the bateau," Jane answered, turning to the boat as if to get the quilt.

"Oh, do bring the quilt up to the house so we can see it. Dinah will help us with your things," Eva said.

"Dinah?" Jane asked, turning back to her brother.

David saw Jane's hesitation. John hadn't said there was another woman in the house.

"The black woman who lives with us—" John informed her.

How odd John hadn't mentioned her, David thought. Having a black woman living with them opened a startling view of John McCrea. How could a Whig own a slave? He wondered.

"We can't visit with you now, John McCrea. If I get off this bateau, I'll not get on it again," his mother broke in archly. "It's been a long trip, and surely you remember my back, John McCrea."

"Yes, you remember mother's back, don't you, John?" David found himself saying to soften his mother's manner. "Are you still at Law, John?" he asked to shift the subject, wondering anew why his mother was acting this way.

"Yes, I am still at Law," John answered, smiling oddly at Sarah Jones.

"I've only seen you once since Princeton," David said awkwardly.

"Four years ago—but surely you can stay a bit longer?" John tried to persuade them.

"No, we really cannot stay, John McCrea," Sarah Jones turned to her son, "unfortunately, talking will only make it darker, David, and I had hoped to *get there* before dark," his mother insisted. "Talk, if you must, but pity me sailing on this bateau for four days, David!"

"I know John understands, mother," David said unable to hide her unmistakable rudeness. Did his mother seeing John here now remind her that he himself, her own son, hadn't gone to Princeton and sat at the Albany Bar? She had once told him that if John could study for the Law, he could as well. But he had never liked the idea of being cooped up in a law college despite the fact that he looked more like a lawyer in his Ramilles wig, embroidered waistcoat, silk stockings and satin breeches than John did dressed in his skin breeches. Or did Eva's speaking of her black woman now pique his mother's pride? "How thoughtless of me, of course, your back, mother," David apologized to conceal his own embarrassment for what she said.

"The Joneses are expected up river, John. David's mother has a new house waiting for her," Jane added unexpectedly to mollify the woman.

"Yes, a house Daniel built," David quickly added.

"And David's to work for him, John," Jane continued.

"On a *Dutch* mill," David said with scarcely subdued enthusiasm.

"Yes, you wrote of that, didn't you, Jen?" John asked.

David clearly saw that John accepted their attempts to slip the matter of their not staying.

David and John then lifted Jane's trunk off the bateau.

"I'm sorry about your father," David then said, suddenly flushing, immediately realizing his mistake. But Jane took his hand.

"David means we stopped in Pleasant Valley and Wheeler Case asked for you, John."

"Oh?" John asked with sudden interest.

David sighed with relief. Jane knew just what to say. How could he have been so foolish as to mention John's father knowing what he knew of their estrangement? But Reverend Case *had* tried to close the breach between John and his father three years ago. He searched for hard feelings in her brother's face in the faint light.

"And how are Catherine and the children?" John asked, revealing little of what he actually felt toward his father.

"I'll tell you later," Jane answered. She looked at Sarah Jones. "And it *has* been a tiring trip."

David reluctantly climbed back aboard the bateau. Given their intimate days on the river he had come to see Jane as his wife already. Leaving her like this, tore at him, and he could now see that Jane, too, actually felt something unpleasant toward his mother.

"Be careful, David," Jane said to him.

The sensuousness in her voice told him that she didn't want him to leave either—but it had to be now given the circumstances and even though she could see that he must be feeling like being torn up by the roots in leaving so suddenly.

"Oh, we'll be careful," he replied thickly.

The bateau edged away from the darkening shore. She blew him a kiss and waved. The bateau slipped out into the night. "Come, James, take Auntie to the house," she said over the pole men's splashing as they moved the bateau into the current.

2

The bateau inched along the western shore as a faint, white sky feathered the willows along the bank. The ripples of the river, the *whoosh* of ducks, and the whirr of an owl, resonating soft and clear in the quiet night—pure, full sounds, almost like her voice—echoes of the harp, the cello, and the violin, reminded him of the music he and Jane said they would someday have in their home. How often during an evening walk in Lamington had such music leavened their dreams? How complete he would now feel, if they were sailing together this instant to their new home.

"How much farther, David?"

"Not much," he answered, his mother's voice striking his ear like a cowbell. He hoped she wouldn't complain. The jostling wagon ride from Lamington to the river had ended, and a quiet day resting in Pleasant Valley relieved the barge sail. She *couldn't* complain, especially when she had just begrudged him those few minutes at John's.

But why had she barked like that when John had invited them up to the house? She knew John lived near them. He never understood his mother's feelings about Reverend McCrea and so didn't understand her rudeness. And she had to love Jane for her spirit and vision—nothing equaled the way she read THE TEMPEST by the fireside last winter, inspiring him with what awaited them here up north. The Hudson River valley had become an Eden for him. He had taken pains to tell his mother this—even to tell her Jane's brother's, James', marriage to Maria Hoyhing this summer in Ballston would precede their own. And surely his mother must have perceived Jane couldn't have stayed and lived with her stepmother, Catherine, after her father's death. Besides, he would not have left her to grieve for her father, *to sing like a bird in th' cage,* or to laugh at *gilded butterflies* as he perceived her grieving since her father viewed her as his Cordelia after his estrangement with John. He didn't understand what his mother had against Jane's father.

"That coot'll never sign."

David froze. The voice seemed to come from the bow of the bateau—not above them on the bluff.

"'Need ta think about it,' he says."

"Put him on the list."

The voices sank into the down river stillness, and, starboard, a raft of logs gurgled past them like the half-submerged hull of a schooner.

"Were those Non-associators?" his mother asked him in a frightened whisper. "I don't like the river at night."

"Don't be frightened. We'll be there soon, Mother."

He stepped back and put his hand on her creaking chair to still it, and looked back into the darkness to where the silhouette of the bluff melted into the blackness.

"Stay calm," he reassured her, "we've left New Jersey and the City behind us."

A year ago the Colony voted to boycott English goods in response to their excises. There had been violence at Golden Hill in New York City in January. Even his brother had been involved in that fracas—And people had been killed in Boston in March. But he told Jane not to worry about it with John, so why should he?

"You've got to expect some trouble. No place is without it," he reasoned with his mother, nonetheless. Yet, he hadn't questioned Daniel about such trouble. But if he had questioned his brother, would it have changed his plans? Daniel had still been able to build this house for his mother, and still offer him a partnership in his business.

"But I didn't suppose any trouble. We haven't even arrived yet," his mother replied sharply.

He didn't answer her, not wanting to say more within the pole men's hearing, but strained to see some light at the shoreline. Besides, what good would it do to debate her fears over idle talk?

His eyes followed the shoreline and a faint, star-like gleam appeared in the distance. He looked for one of his brothers as the bateau neared the light.

"How does Daniel expect us to find him without a light?"

"Hallo!" David called.

"Keep comin' . . ." a figure called back hollowly.

As the bateau neared the light, a man waded into the water and seized the bow.

"'Bout time, Solomon! My back's killing me. Had more nights on this river than I care to count!" Sarah passed her humor along to another of her sons.

"Well, hello, Mother!" Solomon pulled the bateau against the bank. "Can't think about the bateau now, when you're about to get off it, can you?"

His mother, speaking to herself, poked at the dark pile next to her chair and stood up. David took her arm and assisted her toward a plank lowered against the gunwale. Solomon guided her down onto the bank. As she reached *terra firma,* she adjusted her petticoat and squinted at a figure in the darkness.

"Thomas Yarns, Widow Jones, at yar sarvice," the figure said in response to her squinting, as he walked into the light. "My boys will move ya in." He wore heavy, ankle-high shoes, baggy breeches, and a loose shirt. A wide hat covered his eyes. "Cut yar standin' thare and help the Widow, Robert! Ca'mon, boys, get that stuff off!" he commanded, sending his sons into the water. "Don't leave that stuff out overnight. No tellin' who might filch it," he advised.

His remark made David pause in handing his mother's things over to Yarn's boys and Solomon—

—But the bateau unloaded, David paid the pole men, and the empty boat, low and black, swung back out onto the current and disappeared.

Robert, bent like a sapling under his load, picked up the lantern. Yarn's other sons burdened themselves with quilts and bedding.

"I'll take that," David said to the boy, taking both the lantern and a wooden bucket filled with candleholders from him.

"He can carry them things," Yarns protested.

David not answering, preferring to meet the man in the house where there was light, only said to Robert, "Follow me," and led the boys up the path. "Watch your step," he called back, as he picked his way over the roots and stones in the path until he gained the road. Behind him, Yarns' sons and Solomon followed with his mother. Across the road on the side of a hill, light streamed from the open doorway of a large house. David glanced back. Yarns in the rear carried what looked like balls of cheese. When his mother gained the road, he continued on up to the house. The smell of fresh lumber hung in the damp night.

When he reached the house, he helped Robert inside. White walls and wainscoting of red cedar reflected lantern and fireplace light throughout the room. As he stood there, momentarily overwhelmed, his mother went to a table and sat down, her fading damask petticoat falling over the side of the chair.

"Like these appointments?" Solomon asked, entering the house.

David read his mother's expression as she sat at the flesh-textured, mahogany table with its ball and claw-legged, yellow upholstered, Chippendale chairs. He smiled at her surprise with the unexpected elegance of the furniture as she rubbed the table's finish with her hand. None of her furniture brought from Lamington would suit this house with its large leaded-glass windows. Her farm-house itself had dry rot in the floor, cracked stones in the fireplace, and a ladder to the attic; but this house boasted an oak floor, brick fireplaces and a closed, hemlock staircase with turned balusters and polished handrail! A wag clock even graced the fireplace. He pictured Jane in black silk, her hair flowing over her shoulders, standing before such a fireplace in such a room. And she would have silver candleholders on the table, rugged floors and tapestries, gilded mirrors, and laced curtains. He shook his head as he took his mother's bedding from Yarns' sons where they stood holding it, hardly believing his own imaginings. What a dream! But his mother, rearing seven sons, had suffered for this house. How presumptuous she would think him, if she knew he wanted this for Jane. But his brother had built this house, and that alone made it more a reality than a dream for him.

"Nothing, but the best in this house," his mother said, breaking her silence. "Has Daniel built the barn yet?"

"No," Solomon answered, palming his sandy hair as he observed her.

"He will," she said with unexpected sharpness, as her thin hand glided possessively downs the arm of her chair. Her eyes glistened in the firelight, speaking her refusal not to forget or forgive the past, her smoldering anger or her husband's frustrations now that she had gained her due, long deferred by an unfortunate marriage.

"Let's drink ta the King and yar new house!" Thomas Yarns exclaimed, holding his housewarming jug aloft. "Get some water ta go with th' Widow Jones' rum, Robert. Ta the King and Widow Jones." The amber liquor splashed into glasses, and Yarns quaffed his rum and cleared his throat. "Yu've raised men and gentlemen, Widow Jones, ta honor King and country, as distinguished as summer from winter from the unnatural spirit of the country. Grants rabble, rioters, and thieves callin' themselves Sons 'a Liberty with their committees for N-o-n-a-s-s-o-c-i-a-t-i-o-n!" The stubble on his face gleamed like pewter filings. "Unnatural sons as needs horsewhippin'!"

"We heard something of that along the river," David hesitated, recalling the voices on the bank, yet not wanting to agitate his mother—it was enough that his brother had been involved with the Liberty poles and gone to Woolwich.—He watched his mother sip her rum and hoped, her reasons for celebrating notwithstanding, she wouldn't drink. Too often she gave over to the darkest boozy despairs and anger.

"A couple of 'em poked their Non-association paper at me. Put up to it by practitioners like Schuyler in the Assembly. Wants ta cut off trade with the parent state and print his own money. But the King won't allow it." Yarns took another swallow of rum and walked to the fireplace, where, in knocking the spent tobacco from his pipe, he shattered it against the bricks. "Damn!" he barked, looking narrowly at his son, who set a box on the floor. "No droppin' that stuff, Robert." He took another pipe from his pocket and worked a thread of tobacco into it. "Ya can count on me, if them rabble come again with their paper," he promised Sarah.

"I can count on my boys," she replied, her eyes hard and bright from the rum.

David touched her shoulder—"Don't drink on an empty stomach, Mother."

"No one needs to tell me about sons, Mister Yarns," she said, placing her hand on David's. "Look at this house! You've always taken care of me, haven't you, Davey?"

"Mother, please . . ."

"You and Solomon and Daniel!" she insisted. "Do you hear that, Thomas Yarns? These boys would do anything for their mother. But, oh, 'twad be 'sharper than a serpent's tooth to have thankless children' after what I went through raising them . . ."

"Mother," David said shortly, afraid she had already had too much liquor. But he had to give her latitude—. His stepfather, the long trip, her new house, her gray hair, and thin face compelled him to honor her feelings despite her boozing.

"Sarpents' teeth! My sentiments exactly!" Yarns exclaimed. "A heap o' thanks them mechanics in the City give the parent for gettin' the French off our backs." He swallowed more rum and dropped a coal into his pipe. Cocking his head, he puffed, and kicked the partridge hens. "Guess these'll wait. Can't get started too early. I'll intraduce ya ta Mistress Sary McNeil in Edward, a woman that knows the King's Law, David. Then I'll take ya on ta Kingsbury, knowin' ya'll want ta see yar brother, Daniel. Richer than Croesus!—Has real money! One o' th' big boys. Here, have another snorter, laddie . . . ."

David allowed him to refill his glass. Did 'Sary' McNeil know how to bend her elbow and booze like Yarns? If so, she wouldn't be good for his mother. Booze for angry people was like throwing whale oil on fire. And what if his mother fell back into her old unhappiness, and not yet in the house more than an hour? He hated the thought of Yarns' anger infecting her. Violence lay under his 'hail fellow will met' exterior—such make bates enticed neighbors. And what did he himself care about the French, English excises, or the Non-association? Not a thing! He had just wanted Jane and his mother out of Lamington and away from the City. What had happened with Thomas was enough—why should they have allowed themselves to be the targets of reprisals? The French war had ended six years ago, and his future with Daniel looked promising. He didn't need to meet anyone devoted to "the King's Law" either . . . yet . . . what of this Mistress McNeil? He asked Yarns about her, and, given his sea legs and the effects of the rum, the old man's form wagged before him in the light.

"Sary McNeil's a woman with land, Davey. Real land. Thousands o' acres. And she don't like what's goin' on," Yarns answered him, emptying his glass.

"Nobody likes what's going on, Mister Yarns, especially people from New Jersey. I'll have no 'Liberty Boy' activity, nor will I treat slaves like family," Sarah said, reminding David how Eva had spoken of her black woman, and coming too close to mentioning Thomas. "We are loyal subjects of the King without concern for excises or stamps. We have land of our own. And at my age, I want only my sons' companionship and peace. No one needs to tell me about hardship, Mister Yarns." She rose unsteadily to her feet, as David took her arm. "Now, you'll excuse me after this long day."

David led her to the first step of the stairs, relieved exhaustion prevented her from drinking more. He watched her climb the stairs while Solomon followed her with her quilts.

"Well, thare's a woman that knows her mind . . ." Yarns declared, raising his eyebrows and his glass to Sarah Jones' last footsteps on the stairs. "I rest easy knowin' yar belongin's will not be nimed in th' dark. Will send th' boys home tanight—but anytime ya need jackass-power, jest call!" he yelled after her.

3

In the morning while he waited for Yarns to get the skiff from the bushes where he had hidden it last night, David observed the house—It had a large central doorway and flanking double-sash windows, a masoned foundation, clapboard siding, two brick chimneys, and thick cedar shakes on the roof. And with it came one thousand, two hundred sun-drenched acres along the river! No question, he marveled, that Daniel's investments up here soon after the French war paid well.

He rubbed the damp morning air into his scalp and walked toward the house, liking the French path. Northward, he picked out a bluff, overlooking the river, he hoped his mother would deed to him for his house. He then decided, as he stood there, to make a rock path from the bluff to the river, build a yacht, and, maybe, even buy a slave to sail it. He turned to take in the river below the bluff and saw Yarns in the skiff. He didn't like the way the man waited and watched him without calling out to him to go.

"The boys left horses on the other side!" Yarns then called up to him.

David picked up his pack. When he reached the skiff, he flung it by the old man as though to tell him he hadn't figured out every angle about him as he sat gazing at him.

"Good idea—" David said curtly.

He instinctively disliked Yarns. His last night's potviolence, his ordering his sons around like a company of privates, his assumed familiarity, ready advice, and strong ideas about the "rabble," as he had called the rioting factory workers in the City, all reminded David of his stepfather. Yarns had continued to rant about the Colonies after his mother had gone to bed. The Grants people, wanting to move the boundary to this side of the river, made him particularly alkali. David had even begun to feel Yarns' anger as his own, until he caught himself questioning why *he* should concern himself with the Grants? He himself didn't like the English excises, or Johnny's inclination to use grapeshot on people—yet what of law and order? Still, he didn't approve of Yarns' language and putting thoughts into his head, which he should have for himself, if it came to that.

And he hadn't slept easily last night. Yarns' words continued to echo in the room like a drumbeat, and his eyes glowed like knife points in his semi-consciousness. The floor had rocked like the bateau, and suddenly his legs jerked. Boom! He felt the smack and saw his stepfather's flashing eyes!

"I like a thinkin' fella," Yarns commented on David's curtness, pulling his hat over his eyes and pushing the oars back to him.

Wanting not to think of him, David picked up the oars and began slipping the skiff across the river. He must settle his affairs with Daniel and establish himself. Yarns was only a temporary inconvenience he'd soon be rid of—but on reaching the other side of the river and gaining leather, Yarns renewed his last night's ranting and spooked his horse into the woods where he was knocked out of his saddle. He slugged from his jug, remounted, jerked the reins and shouted, "Any more o' this and I'll shoot you, you bloody varmint!"

As the horse reared and whirled in a circle, Yarns' jug came down with a gourd-splitting crack between its ears. He held the neck of the jug in his fist. "Damn!" he cursed, clinging to the animal before it suddenly sagged on the road with rum running down its withers. "Tannery, you sucker!" he screeched, driving in his heels.

A mile away, horse and rider stood at the edge of a swamp. Yarns' face was white as flour, though he jerked the reins violently as David approached him, declaring, "No horse is gonna rub my arse off under any tree!" His eyes burned into David's.

How often had David impotently witnessed his own stepfather's rage over some suspected insult uttered by a shopkeeper or a neighbor? How often, aflame with rum, had his stepfather threatened him with eyes like that, riveting him to the spot where he stood? He turned away from Yarns, barely able to stifle a counterurge to seize the man by the throat. . . .

But they continued on and crossed the swamp, and the crumbling walls of Fort Edward arose on their left. The Fort looked like a low eroded hill after being abandoned more than six years ago.

"Sary's under the walls of the Fort," Yarns pointed, "thank God for that. I never had such a dry ride."

A mantis, flying through the sunlight, silently landed on his hat and turned its head back and forth like a miniature cog-work. It held its green, sickle-like forelegs in the air above Yarns' hat. The angularity of man and insect merged in bizarre symmetry.

They approached a log house a few rods beyond the Fort, and, as they dismounted, a black woman appeared at the side of the house with an armful of firewood. "Massa Yarns!" she cried with initial fright. "Missis McNeil's inside and Polly's on her way beck fra' Argyle. Land, Massa Yarns, what an ugly thin' on yer hat! Missis McNeil! Missis McNeil!" she declared as she disappeared into the house.

Yarns reached for his hat, but not before the mantis fluttered off and landed on the roof of the house where it folded its wings into the shakes. "What ugly thing on my hat?" he snarled, still thick from his ride, turning the hat over and whacking it on his leg. "Jes' like a Negra, seein' things as ain't thare."

"Weel, Pap Yarns! An' wat e'er hoppen'd ta yer horse, bleedin' sae," a short fat woman about fifty-five said from the doorway.

"Had ta larn 'im by hand, Sary. Took it into his head to take Pap for a 'ride'," he answered, dismounting and holding his hat, "and yar Negra should avoid insultin' a free man with her observations."

David straightened his wig and tipped his hat to her.

"An' who's th' handsome gentleman wi' ye?" Sarah McNeil asked of him with a twinkle in her eye, preferring not to notice Yarns' reference to her slave and his odd preoccupation with his hat.

David beheld her kindly gaze and flushed face. She had soft, even affectionate, blue eyes, expressing compassion born of suffering. Yet, a canny stubbornness dwelled in her eyes too.

"David, younger brother of Daniel Jones," Yarns answered shortly, seeing she ignored his comments about what her slave might have said to him.

"Daniel, th' mill operator, aye. A pleasure lad. O' course, ye'll stay for tea, an' meet Polly." Gesturing to them to follow her into the house, she turned into the doorway.

David dismounted and followed her brown chemise and green bonnet into the house where a fire burned in the dark. To the left of the fireplace a ladder slanted in the faint light to a loft.

Mistress McNeil pushed a trivet and tea pot into the fire, then nudged a couple of chairs toward a rough-hewn table in the center of the room before sitting down heavily at the head of it and indicating that David should take a chair.

"Git th' cups an' pore th' tea, Eve!" she directed.

"A wee snort, Sary? Thare's nothin' ugly about a man's thirst with sech dryness out thare and with sech skin guts as that horse for transport!"

"Why o' course, Pap Yarns, nae trouble ae a'!" she laughed, adjusting her bulk in the chair, "bot spare me th' description of wot ye hae dane ta that poor animal."

"I'll take a sip then, if them skinners callin' themselves 'Non-associators' don't git their way," Yarns replied with exaggerated dryness in his throat, picking up on his sentiments of last night instead of laboring his horse any longer.

But Sarah said to David, "Hae same pigeon pie, David Jones . . . I was jest sittin' doon ta my tea," preferring to know about him this moment rather than the Non-associators which preyed upon Yarns.

She passed him a plate and sliced some bread. The knife gleamed in the candlelight and clinked on the dish. The pie, thick and cool, resisted the edge of David's fork.

"Well, ya have nothin' ta worry about yet from them Non-associators with yar property, Sary, which you'll keep by the King's grace," Yarns, nonetheless, continued, flourishing his fork and swigging the whiskey poured for him.

"Trew," Sarah sighed, giving in to his vein of talk since she had to, with the adjusted intention of telling David about herself and the problems Yarns referred to before questioning him about his own business, "my property in th' City goes weel wi' wot's an th' guid Lake George. A boon land, this—heels an' lochs like Argyle an' Inverness bought wi' th' bluid o' my kinsmen. An' food eneugh taa," she affirmed, beginning to eat her pie. "Mony a time my wee'un, Catherine, hadst tears in her e'e frae nae haen eneugh ta eat in bonnie Scotland. Isn't that sae, Thomas?"

"Right, Sary," he answered more content now with her attention and another swallow of whiskey.

"Bot we greeted gin we came owre seein' th' lochs an' th' heels for th' last. Ye ken th' sadness o' it, Thomas Yarns?"

"Indeed, Sary."

"My first husband, David Jones, was a Campbell. He died an' th' way owre," she explained, turning directly to him. "His kinsman, Duncan Campbell, fought th' French here in the last war. An' my second husband, Mister McNeil, is sarely, livin' in th' City. Gin my lassie, Catherine, died in th' City, she left me wi' her two-year-old bairn, bonnie Polly. We paid dear for gettin' here, didn't we, Thomas?"

"Ya paid real dear, Sary," he answered with another swallow.

"How long have you lived here?" David asked her, drawn out by the information she volunteered about herself.

"Couple o' years. Came up frae th' City ta leuk arter my land. Bot ye haen't spake o' yersel, David—" she said, coming to his situation.

"My brother has work for me at the Corners," he answered agreeably. "My mother and I came up from Lamington to Northumberland yesterday."

"Lamington, near Perth Amboy? Jersey's full o' Scots. Can ye dae a reel and blow th' pipes?" She smiled.

"No," David laughed.

"An' ye hae a hame in Northumberland?" she continued questioning.

"A new house for my mother."

"One caudna dae better than a new hoose, David! An' wark waitin' for ye! I wist ye luck, times bein' wot they're. 'Tis a wee hoose, this," she said, returning to her own situation and looking at the ceiling rafters before dropping her eyes to the room's two beds, its table and chairs, the mirror hanging near the door, and the trap door which cut a square in the floor. "I intend ta live here until Mister McNeil joins us frae th' City. We'el then build a proper hoose, supposin' we can git a guid price for owre land wi' these sluggish times," she concluded, looking at Yarns to bring him back into the conversation.

"But ya got the inn right across the road!" Yarns added for his part, reaching for the bottle. "Can't overlook the amenities. But ya're right about th' sluggishness, Sary. Hold on ta yar land until things settle down. No need ta sell for a linnet's chirp."

"'Tis nocht th' wee linnet which consarns me, Pap Yarns," she declared, looking intensely at him to elicit his sympathy, "bot people's fear o' buyin'!—Ah, Lord, bot wot do I know onyway, except ta watch my coppers ae th' moment?" she said self-deprecatingly. "Bot things *might* settle doon. Even Polly says sae. An', as ye say, Deborah Freel, bless her soul, in th' inn across th' road, adds ta my cabinet frae time ta time gin I run short," she compensated herself. "An' dinna leave yersel oot for splittin' cordwood for me, Thomas. An' th' wee dram we hae thegither on a caud day! I wad hate ta move away, an' nae hae th' pleasure o' yer company, man."

"This house has the best whiskey, Davey, boy," Yarns congratulated her with a wink at him, as he held his amber glass up to the candlelight. "Nope, ya jest can't get whiskey like this, except in Sary McNeil's comfy 'hoose'."

"Bot wat o' th' Fort, Thomas? Ye dinna suppose there'll be ony trouble arter New York and Boston? Seems ta me the fictin's a'ready startin'," she said with real concern, noting to herself that if the times were hard on her, then certainly David's prospects would be affected too.

"Ya must keep yar ear ta the ground, Sary."

"I suppose sae, bot I wist Polly's sodger wad marry hir," she volunteered. "I wad then consider sellin' land an' buildin'. Aye, wad build in Argyle near th' Allens—hae ye seen those rollin' heels, David? As bonnie as th' auld countrie."

"Next time I come, Sary, th' boys'll buck a stack of wood ta pop yar eyes," Yarns interrupted, still thinking of the amenities. He then pushed his tongue against his cheek and asked, "So, Polly's taken a shine ta a soldier?"

"Ye ken that, Thomas. Fell in luve wi' im 'afore we came up here. An' a handsome, stout lad wi' sparkling blue e'es. Tho' I maun say, he hase strang opinions," she said, glancing at David for some indication about how he felt about these troubled times.

"She wants ta marry him?"

"Hae ye ever hast a daughtir, Pap Yarns, much less a granddaughtir, ta ken somethin' o' th' ways o' a lassie's heart?" she asked, as though it was obvious people in love didn't think clearly.

"I had a ten years old girl who started sassin' me about my rum, Sary. A ten years old girl who couldn't work like the boys. A ten years old girl who I gave over to a neighbor lady."

"Nae, ye didna dae that!"

"I did, indeed, Sary."

Not wanting to delve further into Yarns' daughter's fate, Sarah continued speaking of Polly's soldier for David's benefit. "Bot Polly's sodger is a brae, quick-witted, strappin' lad. Th' kind o' laddie a lassie needs in this wild countrie. His last letter says he hopes for Adjutant. He's a laddie wi' ambition like you, David Jones! He's a guid lad for a Yankee, if ye dinna mind my sayin' sae, David. Tho'," she paused, "ye didna spak o' yersel. Hae ye a lassie, taa?" she came to the other point about him which she wanted to know about.

"Yes," David hesitated in answering.

"Solomon tells me she has long red hair, Sary. A lot of woman."

"A lot o' woman, aye. 'Re ye a Scot yersel, David, lad, or anither kind o' Britisher wi' th' name o' Jones?"

"No, I'm Welsh."

"Ye ken wot town?"

"No," David laughed, "can't recall any town. My people were here before William Penn, living in caves along the Delaware with the Swedes more than a hundred years ago—"

"An' is yer lassie livin' up here?"

"Yes, she's living with her brother a mile down river from us," he informed her.

"Guid, lad," she pronounced, satisfied she had most of his particulars.

"Her father was a minister in Lamington," he added, suddenly feeling that he wanted to make the best impression for Jane on this Mistress McNeil who thought plainly about things.

"David wants ta build her a new house, Sary," Yarns provided.

"A new hoose?" she exclaimed with renewed interest, raising her eyebrows. "Now that's wot I call a 'proper' purpose, David."

"Tho' I wouldn't wait ta marry her, the house, notwithstanding, Davey."

"Nae, Thomas. Th' lad maun provide for hir. She shudna marry lik I did ae anely fourteen, gin I hadst naught bot a loom ta blister my fingers and a straw pallet ta gie me a sare bak," Sarah advised, feeling that if she could reenforce this young man's purpose for his benefit, she would do it.

"Ya can roll in th' straw, Sary!"

"Anely a bundle o' sticks lik yersel wad want straw, Pap Yarns!" she laughed without being sidetracked. "An' wat's yer age, David?"

"Twenty. My hope is to start working right away, and, maybe in a year, build that house."

"'Tis a guid plan—an' how auld's yer lassie?"

"Nineteen," he answered, becoming embarrassed by Yarns taking in every word. Just as he found himself wanting to talk to this woman, he found himself equally constrained in doing so because of Yarns.

"I bet yer lassie is doin' th' thinkin'. Oney sodgers in hir family?" she questioned.

"Not that I know . . ." he hazarded, nearly certain that none of Jane's family had been military men.

"Weel, th' Scots need men o' th' clothe, taa," she replied of

Jane's father being a minister. "Frasers lik mysel, howe'er, 're military men. Ye say she lives wi' her brither?" she questioned more closely, searching for some hint as to how they might stand with the King. "A lawyer."

"Groused up here about th' stamps a few years ago, Sary," Yarns said sullenly, sucking on his pipe.

"A Yankee then, nocht a Scot . . ." she declared shrewdly, though without heat. But since she now knew Jane's brother's inclinations, her best advice to David on the issue was for him to know which side was the right side. There was no telling what errors might lay ahead for him, if he didn't see right away where his sympathies should be. "My people sodger'd in th' French war, an' receiv'd land here in Argyle and Salem. An' same hae pensions wi' Sir William Johnson an' his savages, tho' savages 're nae my cup o' tea. Bot I ask ye, David Jones, if this countrie dinna pay th' excise, who's ta pay for th' war, th' starvin' Scots ower in th' auld countrie? 'Tis a young countrie, this, as maun gie bak ta th' auld."

"I don't think about it," David answered, not only fearing that Yarns would crank up again, but unwilling to involve himself or his family in any way on either side of the dispute. He had concluded early on that, if he and Jane were to get ahead, it would be better to observe a strict neutrality.

"Th' King'll dress 'em in stocks and gibbets," Yarns weighed in. "John McCrea's a stamp man. Next thing ya know, he'll help those Grants squirrels move th' boundary across th' river onta us. Then they'll take our land and free th' slaves. How would ya like ta see Eve in the woods, Sarah? But McCrea will pay th' piper when th' King decides it's time."

"Do you own slaves, Pap?" David interjected, wanting to stop him before he slipped deeper into the bottle, sure he didn't have wealth enough to own slaves.

"No, I don't need ta own woolies, Davey. But tell me, what'll happen to them when the Grants rabble free 'em with no place to go? I suppose they'll have Injun tommyhawks in their skulls!"

"Maks me greet ta see sech gain's an," Sarah agreed with him. But perhaps it wasn't wise to dispute the issue, if the lad didn't want to be involved. It would be better to befriend his loved one. "Bot ye maun bring yer luve ta meet us, David Jones. She'll want ta meet Polly . . ." she concluded, abandoning the subject with a scrape of her chair and standing up. "Now finish yer tea an' eat these sweeties. Oh, dinna worry, Thomas," she turned to him, "th' King'll hae th' last word wi' these agitators. Th' history o' th' Scots tells ye th' King kens somethin' o' tommyhawks. Ye see wat he did ta th' French papists?" she, nonetheless, added for David's ears.

David stretched his waistband with his thumbs, straightened his waistcoat, and pushed away from the table. He had heard enough, and he wanted to get away from Yarns. Besides, he was eager to settle things with Daniel. But, he wondered, would Sarah McNeil be suitable company for his mother, and would Jane like her granddaughter?

"Tak a wee stroll, lad, there's a lovely spring an th' heel, or sit in th' chair by th' hoose," Sarah suggested, eager not to press him seeing his impatience to leave the table, if not the house. "We'll join ye in a bit."

David thanked her.

Outside the dark house, he shaded his eyes from the glare of the sun. He couldn't speak for what friends his mother or Jane should have, regardless of the opinions he heard expressed, but he would have to be careful of Yarns who wore his hostility toward John like a hirsute. Yarns was an opinionator for sure. For John's part, however, he didn't doubt that he probably had a reputation, given his principles. God knew he had given Jane's father enough grief because of them. He hoped, however, the strength of his principles had diminished with his father's death, and that they wouldn't affect Jane. And perhaps she would even like Sarah McNeil and her granddaughter. Despite her pronounced opinions, the old woman did have a kindly and generous way about her.

He looked up the road. North of Sarah's cabin a sign read, "Freel's Inn". Only a house with an extra room for travelers, he thought, shifting his attention to the 'lay of the land' up here. He looked north to where the ground rose to two hills beyond where the road entered the woods. At the top of the second hill, an enormous pine stood against the sky. Perhaps that was where the spring was that Sarah spoke of—A path to the left led to footbridges.

He walked past the switching tails of the horses and stopped on one of the bridges. It was a relief to get out of that confining house. The croaking of frogs and the hum of black flies filled the humid air. Brown cattails and yellow lilies grew near the river beyond the marsh. Up river, at the Corners, a clear river must rush from the mountains through steep gullies and tall timber. How ideal for mills! he thought, reminding himself of his purpose in coming here.

Wanting now to stretch his legs before going up to Kingsbury with Yarns, and curious about the spring, he followed the path over several footbridges and ascended the first hill about a quarter mile from Sarah's. He wiped the sweat from his face, and, though it was hot, decided to continue walking.

At the top of the second hill, the path joined the road near the tree he saw from Sarah's. The tree, at least five feet in diameter, had roots the size of the trunks of lesser trees. Even in a woods of large trees, this tree was huge. And there was the spring that Sarah mentioned. Before the age of settlers, he thought, the natives would have refreshed themselves here, for it flowed from a granite pool at the roots of the tree and ran under the corduroy road. The water gleamed clear and cold as winter pond ice. He kneeled and drank, letting the water numb the back of his throat. He took off his wig and rubbed the water into his scalp and face. This was God's country!

"God, what resurrection on a hot July day!" he said, unmindful of speaking aloud, while flicking the water, frigid and clean as January air, from his eyes.

Standing up and replacing his wig, he thought about Mistress McNeil telling him not to marry until he had a roof over Jane's head. It was true, Daniel, himself at twenty, had built mills and a house before marrying Deborah Wing last year, so why shouldn't he follow his example and her good advice? In a raw country like this, things would quickly favor him. But, God, how *could* he wait, especially if his mother deeded him the bluff! Yet didn't Jane deserve a completed home? Hopefully, it wouldn't take long, if Daniel had things set up for him, he thought.

"A cool spot on a hot July day," a voice echoed his comment. A young woman with hazel eyes and honey-colored hair leaned against the pine. "Grandmother said, 'David Jones wears satin breeches, a green waistcoat, an' a white wig.' Said. 'Leuk for a man wi' red hair.' I figured you'd make yer way up here," she said.

"Bonnie Polly, no doubt!" he replied with surprise, not noticing her approach from behind the tree.

"Polly, aye," she confirmed nonchalantly, coming to the spring with her bucket.

"Grandmother says ye hae a lassie," she said directly.

"Is that so?" he laughed, both delighted and surprised by her directness. It hadn't taken long for her grandmother to tell her all about him.

"How does she feel about havin' ta wait 'til ye get yer affairs together with yer brother?"

"Is that such a bad idea with guaranteed work and these up river mills churning out lumber?" he asked, at a loss at how else to respond to her, so obviously thorough had her grandmother been in rehearsing his situation with her.

"How long will you have work, tho'? Do you think the English care about us? This Non-association business might shut us all down. What will happen to business or land values, if we hae nothin' ta do wi' th' English? Prudence might dictate marrying now, and making th' best o' it before things get too tight," she more than suggested.

He had thought of that, but marrying now meant farming his mother's land. And though his mother insisted he live with her, there was no fast wealth in farming—he wanted a mill. His expectation was that settlers would continue to come up here, and they'd need lumber for homes. And hadn't he brought a new design for a high speed saw with him? He had it back at the house in his pack to show Daniel. But Polly, now so quickly mentioning this alternative of asking Jane to marry him now before he was ready, nettled him somewhat.

"Maybe you should marry your soldier," he countered, thinking that if she couldn't act for herself, yet was so ready to discuss his situation, then he could advise her.

"Go to th' City an' leave grandmother?" she answered nonplussed.

"Well, I can't inconvenience my mother either," he rejoined.

"Why can't yer luve live wi' her?" Polly pursued.

If he had the slightest hope his mother would approve, he would do it. But she held some grudge toward Reverend McCrea she seemed now to be carrying over to Jane. At least she seemed unusually reserved with Jane on the sail up.

"We can't live together," he answered, vaguely perceiving a tangle ahead of him on that issue, while at the same time amazed at himself that he was actually talking this way to this young woman he hardly knew. "Besides, Jane's living with her brother until I establish myself. You should know that we've thought about some of these things," he said, becoming suddenly very uncomfortable with revealing such intimate details about himself and Jane.

"Her brother's a stamp man, I hear."

"So?" he asked, growing alarmed at her directness.

"No matter," she said, sensing she had gone far enough with him, "I'd like ta meet yer lassie. She maun have character ta wait," she observed, backing up by way of complimenting him on his choice, and wishing him to know by her tone, as well, that John McCrea was of no real importance to her.

But David *was* caught on the issue of his mother and her 'feelings' for the McCreas, and *how* Jane might come to react to that. He knew *she* had too much character to force an intimacy with his mother. Of that he was sure. But how slippery was the ground between them? For a moment, he entirely forgot Polly's forwardness for what concerns she raised for him.

"You would like Jane, Polly," he said, feeling now that he really needed her advice.

But Polly seemed in no hurry to give it, but rather to continue complimenting him, having so successfully flushed him out. "I seem ta like you well enough too, and if yer Jane is o' a like mind,

I hae no doubt I'll like her. You appear ta be a man of character ta wait for yer luve—not every man would wait. It's ta yer credit," she said, smiling, secure that he couldn't now challenge her assuming such familiarity with him and his concerns.

"If you knew Jane, you'd understand she's worth waiting for," he found himself blushing—"Indeed, you're as pernicious as fire, going after me like this and speaking your mind the way you do—" He was now aware that he was actually reeling with the suddenness of this encounter and the problems it raised for him.

But Polly only answered: "Well, I could stay up here and talk ta ye all day, but not when people down below need tendin' ta, if ye know what I mean? I don't take too much time away from the hoose when grandmother passes th' time wi' Mister Yarns, less she starts floatin' like Noah's wife!"

"They booze together?" he asked, feeling somewhat foolish in asking so obvious a question.

"You said it, Mister David Jones," Polly answered, secure with his confidence and turning away down the road. "Well, are you comin'?" she asked, turning back to him before he had time to take a forward step, her honey-colored hair catching the sunlight beneath the trees.

4

When David returned to McNeil's, he found Thomas Yarns too drunk to show him the way to Kingsbury.

"I'll stay and have a wee bit more o' th' true stuff. Jest stay on th' road, an' ye'll come ta a big white house, Davey boy . . ." he said with a wave of his hand.

"Pore anither for 'im, David, 'afore ye leave," Sarah recommended, already in a similar way to Yarns.

"She's th' greatest lil' woman in th' world. Thare's no suckin' hind teat whare she's consarned. Wouldn't swap her for all th' tea in England."

The crapulous Yarns would no doubt return from the Afterworld as a spider clinging to the moist bung-hole of a rum keg, David thought, as he rode up the hill, feeling well-rid of the man's antics. He only regretted that Polly had to remain and contend with the man.

—A mile and a half beyond Bell's Tavern in Sandy Hill, he came to the Kingsbury Crossroads, a clearing of several log houses. He stopped at a white two-story house. A black boy, shading his eyes from the afternoon sunlight, opened the door.

"Yassum," the boy said.

"Daniel Jones at home?" he asked.

The door swung open to the smell of cooking, and, before he took a full impression of the hallway, a woman brushed into it from the other end.

"Who else, but David!"

"What luck, Deborah—the first handsome house I come to," he declared, taking her hand and kissing her on the cheek. "And what of the baby?" he asked quickly, not forgetting Daniel's letter and their brush with death.

"Bless Heaven, his fever's gone," Deborah answered, clasping her hands, and beholding him, before leading him into the parlor. Deborah had jet-black hair, dark eyes, and fine white skin. She was short, small-boned, and slightly stooped. She spoke quickly, catching her thoughts before they escaped her.

David stood against the cool parlor fireplace. A postscript about his son's fever to one of Daniel's infrequent letters had greatly alarmed their mother. Babies with fever usually died.

"What a relief Richard's all right," he said, further relieved this domestic crisis couldn't now also negatively affect his affairs. He observed the cool white walls of the room and the black strawberry stenciling near the ceiling. "An elegant house," he said, hardly audible for the impression it made on him.

"You like black on white?" she asked, following his gaze to the stenciling where the wall met the ceiling. "Daniel had nothing to do with it—I shall take the credit, David."

"An ominous pattern," David laughed at her artless admission.

"Ominous?"

"Tokening fruitfulness . . ."

"Yes, you're to work on the Dutch mill? Land, another one!" Deborah declared, more than content with her husband's prosperity.

"Daniel hopes to begin right away?"

"I suspect so."

"And where are Jonathan and the others?" David asked, going to the window and noting the sheep grazing beyond a thin stand of pines across the road. How pleasant it would be, he thought, to watch Jane tending lambs, to have someone like that door boy answer the door for her, and to have someone like Eva's Dinah help her keep such a house. And where the sun caught the tops of the trees west of the house, the expanse of pine, spruce and hemlock seemed endless. Yes, a mill operation buttressed by a farm with endless stands of timber—what else defined wealth and happiness?

"John and Jonathan work here in Kingsbury, but Dunham works with Daniel at the Corners," Deborah informed him about his other brothers. "You would think a mill here and two at the

Corners would suffice, but, oh, no! when Daniel and father confer, a new mill always comes of it . . ."

"Well, I'm here," he pronounced enthusiastically, ready to do his part.

"Does your mother like her house?" she inquired, coming to him at the window.

The declining afternoon recalled the rich lantern light in the house last night. "She loves it," he answered. "I could see she felt the wait was worth it."

"A house like that comes only once in a lifetime," she reminded him.

"Oh, I know. I hope to have one just like it," he revealed.

"Then Jane came?"

"Oh, yes. She's living temporarily with John."

"Daniel says she's very beautiful."

"Yes." Her statement made his legs tingle and his face reddened.

"Have you set the wedding date?" she asked, looking intently at him.

"Well, no, not yet. I must speak with Daniel first."

"Yes, I understand. I don't know what 'Tenty and I would have done without father's help. He built his first mill here six years ago."

"'Tenty?" he asked, uncomfortable with the comparison that she thought Daniel was 'helping' him. He wasn't up here to ask for Daniel's charity or favor—he had engineering to contribute.

"My sister, Content. Daniel didn't tell you she and her husband, Jacob Hix, and Daniel and I had a double wedding last year? And Content only fourteen!"

"Fourteen!" David exclaimed, thinking it odd that Daniel hadn't mentioned this—but then when it came to his own affairs, Daniel always had been 'close.' On their farm he was always willing to do things for him, if it benefited him. Deborah's talking like this shed light on his brother's closeness that he preferred not to recall.

"Father wanted her to wait, but a younger sister will not take 'no' for an answer."

"But only fourteen?" he repeated, reminded of Sarah McNeil mentioning her marriage at that age. He began to feel that waiting too long perhaps *wasn't* the best thing.

"And her husband is father's age. Jacob oversees father's mills."

"Oh," he said, focusing on Jacob's position. Of course, Content could marry young, if her husband had position and secure employment. "—I hope that Dutch mill will give me a start," he put in on his own behalf. "If your father built in 'sixty-four, he must be the largest mill operator in the valley. How grand." It comforted him somewhat knowing Daniel had this family connection, but it also raised new uncertainties, which made him uneasy. Daniel should have mentioned this connection. But his letters to his mother spoke only of his buying land and building mills. He now felt renewed impatience to come to terms on their partnership. He turned back to the window and noticed a turkey perched in a pine across the road.

At first glance, the bird appeared black. But as he looked closely, drawing Deborah's attention to it, it was an iridescent reddish-green, its lower body cinnamon with white-tipped tail feathers. A trace of red on the neck indicated a hen. It stood on long legs at an angle to the vertical line of the tree—then, surprisingly, the bird fell through the branches, and two Indians appeared. Seeing the bird fall like that, followed by the Indians' plucking an arrow from it, startled him.

"I wonder what they think," he stated, feeling their appearance vaguely challenge his interest in land and business.

"They're father and son," Deborah provided, turning away from the window. "The boy is Eunice Williams' grandson."

"Oh, the Williamses of Massachusetts?" All New England and New York knew of the raid on the Deerfield settlement in 1704. "What is he doing up here, or should I say down here?"

"He comes down from Kahnawake outside of Montreal with his father. Eunice Williams married a Mohawk Indian up at St. Regis," Deborah amplified.

"Remarkable." He had often heard of white people choosing to live with the Indians, but had never actually met or saw such a person.

"She didn't return to Deerfield when they ransomed the family."

"Is that so?" he mused.

Deborah then lit two lamps on a nearby table, as her door boy began bringing in the table settings. Night had nearly fallen and the glow of the lamps reflected off the inside of the glass. David continued to look out the window and at his misshapen reflection in the glass. Could he, two years ago, have predicted standing in his brother's house, Jane enshrining his every hope, discussing joining Daniel's milling business?

"Everything has design, I suppose," he said more to the glass about himself than to Deborah about the Indians and Eunice Williams, though he thought of them, too.

"Father says Providence governs all, David."

"Is that what he said about Eunice Williams marrying a Mohawk Indian?"

"Well, yes . . ." she began.

"I feel the same way," he interrupted her, "with my receiving Daniel's letter, it coinciding with Jane's father's death as it did. It's the same with these Indians—it all seems to go together, and for the good I hope!" he confessed. And how odd it was that these Indians appeared at such a propitious moment, obliquely challenging his purpose!

"You think about such things, don't you, David?" she asked, observing him, just before he turned away from the window.

"Well, it's hard not to," he admitted, feeling again, more powerfully, that the sudden appearance of the Indians and how they took that turkey did seem to challenge his claim to land and a home. Thought of this challenge filled him with vague superstition.

"Everything will work out, I'm sure," Deborah said, noting his unusual expression.

Just then the door opened.

"David!" Daniel greeted him.

David spun on his heel, but before he could speak Daniel turned to his wife.

"No reason to wait on dinner, Deborah. The others are on their way."

David noted Daniel's round face behind his spectacles. He had grown fat with the years. His jacket hung loosely at the sides of his round stomach.

"Ready to begin work?" Daniel asked him, smiling and rocking back on his heels in an appraising, almost lordly way.

Daniel's appraisal of him put David immediately on the defensive. "Why, yes, if there's work," he replied, responding to his brother's appraisal of him, feeling as uncomfortable as an exotic vegetable.

"The dinner's ready," Deborah stated, gesturing to the table behind her.

"Okay—let's eat," Daniel said, compressing his lips and leaving David for the table.

David registered his brother's expression. Was he annoyed with him already? perhaps he should have been more instantly deferring to his brother for his status as mill operator and businessman. "'Rich as Croesus!'" Yarns had said of him. "'One of the big boys!'"

—But was it proper for Daniel to make him feel this way? Daniel was, after all, his brother, not a Lord he owed *feu duty*. The unpleasant undercurrent he experienced recalled their struggling years together on their parents' farm. Had wealth changed Daniel? David questioned himself, going to the table and sitting down. The table had a finish like glass and the thin spindles of the chair sprung against his back.

"Yarns show you the way?" Daniel asked distantly, even indifferently, as if inquiring about the weather in Ford Edward.

"Before he fell into the whiskey jug at McNeil's," David answered. "But aren't you going to wait for our brothers?"

"Oh, they'll be right along—" and as Daniel spoke, they came into the room.

David stood up and shook their hands. They were pleased to see him.

"You found your way through the wilderness!" they laughed.

Daniel held up his spectacles to the light, and observed all of his brothers, save Solomon and Thomas, seated together.

"Understand Thomas left for Woolwich," he said casually, "—

was involved with the Liberty Poles in January, Mother wrote," he stated, rather than questioned.

"That's right," David confirmed. "Upset Mother, though she's strong on the King."

"As she should be. But it doesn't take much to upset her, even if our older brother set the right example. I half expected you to join the army too, David."

"Why, when there's work up here?" he replied, wondering how Daniel could think that he would join the army in light of his invitation to come up here to work.

"Yarns is a muckworm," Daniel then observed, dropping back to him, "but at least he got you as far as Edward."

His brothers laughed in agreement.

"His sons unloaded the bateau," David informed them, suggesting that though Yarns was what he was, his sons were not the same. But how could he account for that? Was Yarns married? he asked, though it really didn't matter to him, especially as Daniel expressed surprise he hadn't joined the British army.

"His wife and his old mother died," Daniel answered dryly.

"I heard him tell Sarah McNeil he gave a daughter away?"

"It killed his wife, David," Deborah explained. "'Little' Melanie Yarns lives with the Tuttles down from your mother's."

David then thought it odd that Daniel hadn't once asked about their mother and her liking of the house—Should he bring her up or focus on Daniel's accomplishments?

"Where did you buy your appointments?" he decided to ask, thinking the chairs came from Philadelphia or New York because of the Non-importation Association.

"Philadelphia. Paid Pounds Sterling," Daniel said bluntly, leaning back in his chair with the air of a man who understood such furniture represented intricate and important issues of business.

"Father gave us these chairs," Deborah mildly corrected him

"Hard to get English stuff, but the Non-importation and the depression makes them dog cheap," Daniel waved his wife off, beginning to slice the turkey.

David accepted a silver plate with gravy on his stuffing. The turkey melted on his tongue, but a lump formed in his throat.

"The Non-association hurting you?" he asked, finding it hard to accept Daniel could escape the depression, which brought hardship to so many. Yet, hadn't he himself told Polly, or at least thought it, that there would still be business up here with the arrival of new settlers?

"No, the King's Navy buys our trees. We'll always have a market," Daniel answered.

"But what about competition? Surely other mills sell to the King."

"The Jessups up river have forty-eight thousand acres, but their Patent hasn't gone through yet . . ."

"Forty-eight thousand acres!" David didn't know whether to rejoice or be offended at anyone owning so much land. Such huge amounts of land owned by so few meant that either there was great expectation of settlement, or that there would be a glut of lumber. And how did the Law allow anyone to buy so much?

"'Paper' men bought from the Mohawks through Johnson, if you want to know how they got around the Law. But the Crown hasn't issued them their Patent yet. The Jessups will need currency, and I want that island below the falls after the Dutch mill is finished," Daniel revealed. "You have to take advantage of opportunity to get ahead," he lectured.

David was taken back. Daniel spoke of land deals and currency. He himself had no hard currency—"How do I fit in?" he struggled to get out, wondering whether his saw was an opportunity or an impediment to Daniel.

"You'll work as Jacob Hix's millwright," Daniel stated.

David put down his fork. He saw his partnership bound away like a deer.

"Where is the mill going?" he could hardly ask, fearing to even mention his saw.

"Show you tomorrow," Daniel answered, his shoulders low and elbows high as he ate. "Eat," he said, wiping his mouth and laying his linen by his plate, "you must be hungry after your ride."

"A raft of logs went down last evening," David said, losing his appetite in his refusal to drop his place in the business. But how should he raise the issue of his saw and his partnership?

"Our logs."

"You expect me to work for wages?" he then asked straight out.

"Have you capital for the new mill? By the by, does Mother like the house?" Daniel answered just as directly.

"Loves it," David answered, the blood rising to his face.

"Put real money into that house, but will get it back in the end."

"Daniel!" Deborah exclaimed.

"Fine, Daniel," David declared shortly, furious with his brother.

"It's *business,* David."

"But I thought I was to be your partner," he stated openly.

"I only have work," was all Daniel answered

"But I've got a *circular* saw. I wrote you about it, remember?"

"But only on paper."

"I brought the design, yes."

"Everyone has ideas."

"It's a sure thing. We'll divide the profits."

"Impossible. Did I ever say anything about dividing profits?" Daniel demanded, suddenly very serious.

"I assumed when I wrote you . . ."

"Remember what the 'old man' said, 'Never assume a damn thing.' You'll work like your other brothers. Now eat, your supper cools."

David looked at them, then back at Daniel. "You talk like him," he said in a low voice, restraining his mounting fury.

"Too bad he didn't see how his raising paid off. Listen, I did this myself," he asserted with an odd smile.

"That saw is *my* capital, and you know it. Yet, Mister Wing helped you, didn't he?" David clutched at Deborah's disclosure. "Everybody has to get their start."

Daniel smiled, ignoring his comment about capital. "If you're hot on that saw, put up the money and smelt it, then we'll go fifty/fifty."

"You know I have no money. Why are you doing this to me?"

"I don't either. Look at the times."

"But you're rich."

Daniel smiled. "Because I know how to use other people's money."

"Mister Wing's, you mean—" he said bitterly. "That attitude got you thrown off the farm," David challenged him out of desperation.

"You never mentioned this, Daniel," Deborah said.

"My father doesn't matter," Daniel replied, his family concerns and David of little importance. "By the way, has John given up Law, and how is Jane taking her father's death? And what of your wedding?" he asked indifferently.

"It depends on the mill!" David repeated, returning to his situation, unable to control his anger. "That's why I'm here."

"Well, don't take the momentary pleasure."

"What do you mean! I brought my design—right here in my pack!"

David pushed away from the table and walked to the dark window, not bothering to retrieve his design from his pack. How often had he experienced a similar impotence with Daniel? How could he have thought he had changed, that his brother would be fair now that they were men? Bitterness overwhelmed him.

"Okay," he said calmly, everyone's eyes at the table on him as he returned to the table.

"What did you think of Sarah McNeil and Polly Hunter?"

David didn't answer, but drifted on a sea of resentment. He had tied to a drifting raft of logs, not the wharf he expected.

"Sarah remembers Culloden, but she's propertied and will side with the King on the Non-association. Introduce her to Jane. Sarah's officious and mothers," Daniel advised, not the least affected by David's anger.

David returned to his chair as though he had been cudgeled, wondering how he could explain this turn of affairs to Jane.

5

The next morning he and Daniel took the Bay Road past old Fort Amherst and crossed Butler Brook toward the Wing's tavern at the junction of Bay and the Military Road from Fort Edward. They passed Wings' tavern and approached the river. They had spoken little.

When David saw the river and inhaled the soft, damp air and the green milled lumber, he felt annoyed with himself for having lost his patience with Daniel; for what did he know of Daniel and his business? Perhaps the Boston and New York City troubles, widespread unemployment, and falling land values, made money tight—perhaps he was lucky to work at all. What Polly warned him of yesterday about the Non-importation shutting business off gnawed at him. Did Daniel actually fear losing money on his saw? Did he have wealth or not? He thought so—his house and Deborah's perfumed sheets indicated wealth. Yet prudence required he not push Daniel too hard.

But as he tempered his expectations, he heard the rumble of the falls and saw the river's power. It flowed below the road beneath the gray mist of the falls in flecks of gold, red and silver in the morning sunlight. These falls were the pot of gold at the end of the rainbow. This river had power, and power meant mills, and mills meant property. David's dream of success turned him in the saddle toward Daniel, forcing him to abandon his prudence.

"Fourteen saws for this Dutch mill is a Trojan horse requiring a dozen pitmen, Daniel. My circular saw will do the work of twenty saws. I'll give you the Patent to the saw, and we'll split fifty/fifty!" he exclaimed passionately.

"No," Daniel said irritably, "you either construct it yourself or forget it. Too many people want handouts."

"Belt-driven," David pressed, ignoring the insult. "If you put the money up, I'll repay you from my inheritance."

"No," Daniel repeated emphatically. "The time isn't right, except for a sure thing, your inheritance included. Besides, Abraham will not risk it."

David's chest tightened. "If it's his capital, he should decide."

"Look, the answer's, no."

"You brought me up here on false pretences."

"Mother wouldn't come without you—besides, I can't gamble."

"You wanted the money from her farm."

"She's better off, isn't she?"

"But you have a sure market."

"Nothing's sure."

"Look at my design."

"No."

"Why won't you cut me in?"

"The saw's not forged, and I don't have venture capital for that—"

"That's not the reason!" David hissed unhappily, feeling he was butting his head against a wall.

They reached the mills. Boiling with exasperation, David looked down at them. Their pitched roofs below the bank to their left glistened greyly in the morning shade. The light flutter and low rumble of the wheels only sharpened his disappointment. The pungency of sawdust and the sweetness of flower drifted up the bank. The headrace between the grist and the lumber mills would have to be enlarged to accommodate the Dutch mill. David noticed an island in the river.

"That what you want from the Jessups?" he asked tortured, a new mill on that island his last hope for his saw assuming he could finance it himself.

"Yeh . . . this road goes to Jessups'."

David looked to his right. The road, rutted from logs drawn over it, wound into the woods. He turned in the saddle, hearing voices behind him. A man in brown vest and jacket, and a girl in white petticoat and green bonnet approached them.

"You beat my rooster this morning, lads," Abraham Wing greeted them.

"Please, meet David, Abraham. Showing him the new mill's location," Daniel said affably, as if no disagreement separated him from his brother.

"Good morning, Mister Wing," David said, concealing his bitterness.

"Daniel spoke of you, lad. Have a big job," Abraham replied kindly. "Has David met Jacob, Daniel?"

"You'll need to enlarge the headrace, Mister Wing, to push fourteen saws . . ." David said, deliberately not looking at Daniel and hoping to interest Abraham in his saw.

"Speak with Jacob, son. He has great mill experience," the older man interrupted him, his gentleness deflating him completely. "Go see Jacob. He and Daniel know the job. Then come to the tavern and meet the family."

David's eyes rested on the girl's face. Her girlish youth stunned him—and her husband was his Overseer!

David watched Abraham and his daughter walk away, feeling if he could only talk to them he might convince them. How desperate he felt! But rather than riding after them, he followed to the mill where he would work as a millwright, not as partner and inventor.

As they neared the mill, the light flutter and low rumble of the wheel, the falling water and working saws filled him with anguish. He heard the 'burr' of a missing cog on the crown wheel.

"Hear that?" he asked Daniel almost acidly.

"What? There's nothing wrong with that."

David didn't reply, but simply observed with dejection the uncut timber high along the bank and the ground around the mill torn up by the hoofs of oxen. Confident in his skill and hearing that missing cog only embittered him the more.

Through the open building parallel saws moved slowly up and down in the shadows. A thin man came out of the building.

"Wasting no time, Jacob," Daniel greeted him.

"Lumber for the new mill, lad," Jacob drawled. He had long gray-streaked hair. "We'll finish in six weeks."

How odd Content married such an older man, David thought. It also seemed unnatural that he answered to the younger Daniel.

"Brought David to help you."

"A brother of yours is a brother of mine," Jacob said good-naturedly.

"Cog missing off the crown wheel," David nearly assaulted him, feeling the man's well-intentioned remark about brothers like a bayonet in his groin.

"Yeh, needs a new tooth. Limpin' along with her, though. Teasin' her along," Jacob replied agreeably, unmindful of David's tone.

"Let's look where the new mill's going," Daniel prompted.

They walked through the building to the new mill site. The water flowed between the stonewalls of the headrace to the gristmill. Widened and deepened for an undershot wheel, an expanded headrace could serve a third mill, especially an efficient, circular saw, David observed. But his design evaporated like the mist off the falls in the hot sunlight. It would be another mill of tedious construction. It would take a long time to save for his house on wages, even if his mother gave him that bluff tomorrow!

6

David saw Jane's clothes on the bank as she swam toward him, her full breasts and white curves beneath the water, her head above the dark surface of the river. As she came to him, his feet in the sand, he pulled her warm and ample to him. Her breasts came against his chest, and he encircled her buttocks with his arms. She moved against him, her skin soft as rose petals. He kissed her neck hungrily and held her. Having her in his arms made him forget his trip to Daniel's. What did his brother matter when he had his beloved in his arms?

"Jenny," he said, sweating in the humid air.

"Shush," she whispered, clutching him, her eyes shining, her ears protruding slightly from her head. "I should not have come," she teased.

"Don't say that," he said unevenly.

"You compromise me . . ." She put her fingers on his lips and laughed lightly. But how could she deny the urgency of his summons? He had returned from Kingsbury and brought news with him. And she could come and go with perfect freedom at John's. Life seemed suddenly very delicious to her as he held her in the cool water, and she pressed her fingers against his lips.

How their legs intertwined took his breath away. "Will John know?" he stammered, thinking of her wet hair.

"We are engaged, aren't we, David Jones?" she asked softly, kissing him. "I can come and go as I wish. Isn't this what we wanted?" she whispered.

"Partly, yes," he answered, tightening his embrace and feeling the fullness of her body against him as he held her in his arms. How could life be so good to him when the news he had for her was so disappointing? She was the only thing he had in life, and he held her as though his life in the moving current—caught in the current of the river—depended upon her. What Daniel or anyone else said was of small importance when he had her in his arms.

"Look at the stars, David," she urged him, "the whole sky is open before us—we're like two mariners in the stream of the world."

"Yes," he choked, looking upward, his feet in the soft river bottom, the warm points of light and the dark ripples of the sky exciting him and making him dizzy while holding her. And how her hair encircled his waist! Desire itself informed the firmament and the heavens!

She felt his heart pound against her as his hands slipped below her hips. His urgency drew her to him, and she began to melt in the water when hot temptation struck her through his fingertips. She slipped from his arms and pushed away from him.

He watched her retreating form rise white and full from the water at the bank. He followed her, as dark and lusty as Pan.

"Don't dress," he breathed heavily, huskily, pulling her gently to him and enfolding her in his arms, wanting to be *that* close again.

"The mosquitoes!" she protested weakly, her breath coming in short gasps, fearing his lightening touch and what would come of it. Her body ached for release, but his husbandry wasn't complete. It would be a premature harvest. She resisted gently, reminding him again of the mosquitoes.

They bit him everywhere. He reluctantly released her. "Damn," he said, slapping his arm and beginning to pull on his clothes. The sight of her body gradually being clothed tortured him, and by the time he adjusted his wig, she had dressed. When she spoke to him he was out of breath.

"What did Daniel say?" she asked.

She stood back a little way from him and tried to see his face in the soft, faint light. She needed to be secure in the reality of a future. Making love by the river was divine, but, like the beauty of clouds, only the glory of a moment.

He had avoided telling her, hoping his love for her would temper his disappointment and bitterness and inspire him with the right words. Her question, however, coming now as it did, though he should have expected it, startled him.

"I missed you, Jen," he whispered, his hand sliding under her wet hair. How could he tell her that the hopes he had nurtured in her were shadows?

"Did he like your idea?" she persisted, ceasing to brush her hair. "Did you show him your design?"

"Abraham Wing is financing the new mill," he answered half-truthfully, hoping to evade having to admit he hadn't shown Daniel his design, or that his brother refused to even look at it. "But we'll have lumber for our house."

He turned from her and slapped his hat on his thigh.

"Lumber?" she asked. "But your saw and your partnership?" Was it too indelicate of her to press this on him now? She felt momentarily sorry for what looked like pain on his face, then felt confusion.

David saw her reading his expression in the dark. He wiped his forehead with his handkerchief, loathing the truth. But they had read Daniel's letter together, hadn't they? *She* believed Daniel meant them to be partners.

"I'm not a partner," he confessed, unable to keep the bitterness out of his voice.

"Not partners? Tell me, David, what's wrong?" She drew close to him and put her hand on his arm. "What aren't you telling me?"

He had cast the best light on his relations with Daniel, failing to disclose, however, those snatches of bitterness, long dormant, which so often spring up in childhood among siblings. His love for her created possibilities in response to his own longings without regard to those feelings, and what was now plainly the ambiguity of Daniel's correspondence with him.

"We always want to believe something and to ignore what's there," he said ambiguously of Daniel as a boy, trying to explain the reasons for what he was about to tell her.

"What do you mean?" she asked, perplexed, "didn't you show

him your plans, didn't he favor you?" She saw his foundering, and braced herself.

"No, I didn't show him my plans. Oh, Jen, you read his letter," he appealed to her, as if they had both misread Daniel's intentions, and that it wasn't his fault, "but he wants an island for another mill, and Abraham . . ." he continued, growing confused with not wanting her now to know the truth.

"But tell me . . ." she said, her voice falling in the darkness as she realized what he was trying to say.

"—But I have work. We'll only have to wait," he half-apologized, half-excused softly, searching for the words, trying to keep the bitterness out of his voice, and hoping she would accept what he said without probing for the reasons for their abridged dreams.

"But he's buying land . . ." she pursued, drawing close to him again. "That means there's opportunity for you, as we believed." She tried to avoid the reality, which lay behind his attempts to explain what happened.

"I didn't expect it . . ." he interrupted, ashamed and impotent, the victim of false hopes and poor judgment. "But the risk is such . . ." he feebly justified, knowing he had not misperceived Daniel, and didn't want his brother's behavior to reflect on himself.

"You're saying he refused you? That he's not interested in a partnership or your saw, as we thought?" She resisted pulling away from him, so obviously did he need her understanding. She sensed his unspoken condemnation of Daniel without knowing the reasons for it. She dropped her hairbrush into her handbag. "Did our hopes blind us to trouble up here? Did he say why things had changed?" she asked, seeking a clearer explanation, uncertain as to what Daniel actually said to David.

"No. Daniel said he had a market for his lumber—" he hesitated, knowing she asked for a fuller explanation.

"Then what is the problem? If there is lumber, then there's a chance for your saw. But it's not that, is it? It's Daniel, himself. Tell me, David, please . . ." she paused, wanting to help him, seizing on the thought of a correctable misunderstanding between them she didn't know about.

"He's afraid . . ." he began, shying away from the truth of how Daniel used his mother's property. He knew of a similar case in Lamington where Widow McCallister's daughter and her penniless husband not only nimed her property, but the rightful inheritance of her other brothers and sisters as well. The widow had given them a parcel of land (their making themselves indispensable to her) and money to build, expecting to own that part of the house they built for her; except that they extended the deed to all her land and kept total ownership of the house. Daniel was doing the same thing. But how could he tell Jane this, aware that she wouldn't be satisfied with his present explanation?

"What is he 'afraid' of? That doesn't sound like Daniel," she persisted, though she didn't know him that well.

"He's miserable," David then confessed.

"Miserable?" she repeated.

"He brought me up here because of Mother. Her assets from the farm, her house—well, it's like the Widow McCallister in Lamington nimed by her daughter and that fast talking vagabond she married! But maybe he'll change," he suggested, hating to leave her without hope.

"Widow McCallister? Yes, and her house?" she asked in disbelief.

"He owns the land and the house. Though she still promised me land!" he began.

"The land, too?"

"Yes . . ." and Daniel would have told him that he had a new house to live in too—even as he nimed his mother's property and his rightful inheritance in her estate. But recognizing this choked him, and he couldn't give words to it.

"Didn't your mother say anything to you? Didn't you ask her?"

"Yes, but she just said to talk to Daniel—but why did I have to talk with him, if I assumed that her money would give her title?" he asked, desperate for vindication.

"But why should he do this when he has his own business,

and you have a saw to contribute?" she grasped, trying to reconcile why, when a person had so much, he still wanted more.

"I don't understand him, either, Jane. Wealth has changed him," he averred, perfectly aware that, if this was true, Daniel wouldn't change, "but I should have known . . ."

"Don't blame yourself, David," she stated, trying to understand the consequences of this for them. But why did he do it? Was it simple greed, or didn't Daniel approve of her? "Is it because you are engaged to *me?*" she continued, forcing back her resentment, if that was true, but having to ask, nonetheless. She couldn't deny Sarah Jones' unexplained aloofness toward her—or how she might have affected Daniel. Was he doing this because he didn't want David and her, after their marriage, to share in his mother's property! The thought paralyzed her.

"How could you think that, Jen!" David protested, clasping her arm. "They know how we love each other." Thought of what she referred to sickened him. He was sure his mother, for whatever she was feeling, had nothing to do with Daniel. But how could he be sure?

She let her eyes rest among the stars. A warm breeze brushed the bank. David's tone almost convinced her of the truth of his denial, but she couldn't be certain. She sighed with doubt. "I'm sorry to have mentioned it," she said, looking up at him and kissing him. "There's no doubt things will work out, David. This is a temporary set back. Since we don't know what Fate has in store for us, we shouldn't despair," she continued, trying to raise his spirit, by minimizing the impact of his revelations. "It's not for me to question your family like this," she concluded to help him save face.

"Oh, it's all right, Jen." He looked into her eyes, which were as open and giving as the river. "Has John spoken of your father?" he asked, shifting to her family, feeling she had given him underserved grace.

"John has no ill-feelings. He's only happy I'm with him and Eva," she said, allowing the tension and disappointment, for his peace of mind, to temporarily leave her voice.

"You have a dependable brother," he joked awkwardly.

"John would do anything for me," she said without complacency. "He is the best of brothers, and he always was." Her comment made the comparison with Daniel unavoidable.

"No brother in his right mind would do anything less," he said, kissing her gently, confirming that it was her goodness, which required such treatment of her.

"I should return home now. I don't want them to worry," she replied softly, reaching for her handbag, though, if he asked her to, she would spend the night out here with him, so badly did she feel for him and herself, and so suddenly yielding did the night consequently make her feel with the softly flowing, dark river, twinkling stars, and mild breeze brushing the scent of flowers and pine over her.

"I'll take you to meet Sarah McNeil and Polly Hunter before I begin work at the Corners," he whispered, forgetting that he hadn't told her about them.

"Oh? You didn't mention them." She didn't know whether thought of meeting new people made her feel better or not.

"A widow and her granddaughter I met at Fort Edward," he explained, not speaking of Yarns. "Polly is engaged to a soldier in New York. She and her grandmother are waiting for him to come up from the City, so they can build in Argyle." How hollow that sounded after what he had told her! "I think you would like Polly and her grandmother. They are Scots," he concluded weakly.

"James is marrying in a few days," she said as she acknowledged what he said, also indicating when they would next be together.

When they returned to John's, he watched her go inside. She was like ripe fruit, ample and yielding, as she went out of reach through the open door like that—. He swallowed against the pain of her leaving, wishing that he had been able to stay with her. Yet how understanding of his disappointment she had been!

But what would excessive waiting do to them? This was catastrophic! he gasped, as he began walking back to his mother's. He had to accept the finality of Daniel's action, given his deliberate intent and his mother's current, unaccountable disposition, and comfortable situation. If he fought this, she would cry that he was killing her! What could he do? Alas, he and his half brother were joists held together by pegs of felt, if not actual enemies. As he walked, he blamed himself for misjudging. He should have had an alternative plan and not built Jane's hopes up so. Yet, he never expected such a maneuver! And he had wanted Jane to think he had judgment, could accomplish for himself, that he had a future and could provide for her. Now, her forbearance and giving nature deepened his anger and shame, and the darkness didn't hide the flush upon his neck and cheeks.

And what of his inheritance? Should he have told her about that? No, that was twenty years in the future, if then—his mentioning that to her now would be a lame compensation, fatuous and unrealizable because of the very distance which separated him from it. He had to swallow his rage. He would have to struggle as best he could; his love for Jane and his own self-respect required it.

7

The implications of David's unexpected disclosures made Jane toss on her bed all night.

How could Daniel do such a thing! What between the two brothers explained it? The implications were devastating, if David had no access to land, their whole future was 'up in the air.' But, perhaps, it wasn't animosity between the brothers, but a defensive move on Daniel's part because of the Non-association. But what did she know? She just hadn't expected this of Daniel. Though brief, his letters had encouraged them. 'Bring Mother and come to Northumberland. I have land, and you can come into the business with the rest of us,' which David said meant his other brothers. Wasn't that a promise? Didn't David then write him about his saw? And though Daniel hadn't specifically answered about the saw, he repeated his mother should sell her farm, and he would build her a house. What was David to think, if Daniel had not rejected his saw? And how could he have foreseen that Daniel would also own his mother's house! She had agreed with David this was his opportunity—and it was clear to them his brother had wealth enough for his saw. But what a deception, and why?

If she feared anything might go wrong, it was that the Colonies' problems might abridge David's prospects, not a personal difference with his brother. But how could it be other than a personal difference, if, as Daniel said, he had a market for his timber, unless it was simply greed?

This transference of wealth after what his mother promised him, plagued her, even to birthing a tainted, sub-conscious counter-desire in her for property.

And how could she explain Sarah Jones' aloofness? Did her new house change her feelings toward her, as David suggested wealth had changed Daniel, making him manipulative? Did Sarah's coolness mean that she had nothing to give to her son and his new wife? Or did she have some agreement with Daniel to keep her and David from Daniel's property? But hadn't his mother promised David land before they came up here?

When Jane finally fell asleep, she awoke confused and depressed. She slowly dressed in the light of the small window by her nightstand, her eyes burning from lack of sleep. Perhaps washing her hair at the river would lift her spirits. At least, if Eva washed her clothes at the river as she was accustomed to do in the morning, she could ask her about the Non-Association which *had* to affect Daniel in some way.

Jane took a folded towel. The hot sun, flooding the hill in front of the house, nearly blinded her. She squinted from the steps and saw Eva at the shore with the wash. Redbreasts chirped in the nearby pines.

"Eva!" she called, leaving the steps for the river.

"Down here," Eva called back.

The sloping ground in front of John's house was covered with flowers, and the hem of her petticoat brushed wild clover, chickweed, blue chicory, and black-eyed Susans. David had promised her bright days like this—'Summer's hymns to Penelope,' he had called them. And even if John and Eva didn't live in an imposing house like Philip Schuyler's, which she had seen on the bank of the river in Albany, the broad swept of the bay fronting it painted Eden in its own colors.

"Did you sleep well?" Eva asked when she reached her.

"No," Jane answered truthfully, "but this summer morning relieves me somewhat."

"Oh?" Eva said, rinsing a pair of breeches in the river. "Was it the bed?"

"No," Jane replied, suddenly at a loss, now that she said she hadn't slept, on how to broach what bothered her without mentioning David and his brother. She lifted her petticoat to her knees and waded into the river and let her hair fall into the water, "Your bed is every bit as comfortable as mine in Lamington—"

The water was so cool and refreshing she had to resist the urge to hang her petticoat on the bank. She soaped her hair, and it foamed as she washed it before drawing it toward her through the water. "Such gorgeous hair, Jane!" Eva observed of it, rich as a skein of red yarn.

"It isn't too long?" she asked, rolling and squeezing it.

"It's a gift from God."

"Oh, Eva, you always say the right thing—" Jane replied, struggling with weariness.

"But, why didn't you sleep?" Eva asked again.

"Will John return today?" Jane evaded, pressing the water from her hair and walking to a chair. "I mean, that's part of what kept me awake," she half-apologized for not answering Eva directly. She picked a snarl with her comb, trying to gain time to be more specific without Eva guessing her question related to David. "I mean, did John go to Albany?" Again, Jane wanted her question to appear idle, but not evasive. She didn't want to draw Eva's attention to John's stamp activity four years ago and his resulting problems with their father either. She suddenly felt confused and awkward, and realized her tiredness affected her thinking. "I'm too tired," she stated, "to think straight."

"Did you hear John leave early this morning?" Eva asked, wringing out a frock, not at all concerned at her sister-in-law's distracted manner.

"Yes, I heard him leave," Jane answered, welcoming Eva's smile as it minimized her awareness about what she really wanted to know. "But is he returning today?"

"Yes."

"Will he give up Law because of the Non-importation?" The question came of itself.

"Come to the line." Eva nodded toward the house and picked up her basket, Jane's manner clearly indicating she had difficulty speaking about something.

Jane swept her hair behind her neck and followed up the hill to the clothesline stretched between the house and a post. She took a ribbon from her pocket and tied her hair, leaving it long to dry, and picked a chemise out of the basket, snapping it gently before hanging it on the line, thinking it best to let Eva speak.

"Judging by what we read about the trouble down country, we'll feel it here. That's what you want to know, isn't it?" Eva fronted the issue. "And, yes, it worries me John might give up Law. At least, he tells me, they'll not back down on the Non-Association. But it's not just John, is it, but David you're thinking of?" Eva smiled. What else would keep her sister-in-law awake all night, and account for her uncharacteristic obliqueness?

"Both of them," Jane admitted. "I am worried about David, that's true. But also about John. Please, don't think I'm only concerned about myself and David."

"I know," Eva assured her, "we all think first of the one we love. There's no harm in that, Jane. But John's even more involved than two years ago. The Non-importation is his principle concern."

"You support him, then?" Jane dropped her eyes. The question was awkward because she didn't want Eva to think she opposed John because of her father.

"Yes, I support him," Eva answered. "And it shouldn't be a problem between you and your brother, or between you and me. What happened between your brother and father is past . . ." Eva hesitated, sensitive to intruding, unsure of how Jane was taking what she was saying.

"I understand it's past, Eva—" Jane held Eva's eyes, respecting her wish not to intrude. "But do you have reservations about what John is doing?" she elicited, thinking that Eva was possibly ambivalent about John's activity.

"Life would be easier, if the times allowed it."

"Yes," Jane replied, understanding her. "But what happened to them?" she asked of John and her father.

"Your father insisted he study for the Ministry," Eva informed her simply.

"It wasn't the stamps, then?" Jane asked surprised, clasping the clothesline with her hand, ready to know that one of her heartbreaks might end as she fronted another.

"The stamps had something to do with it," Eva turned to her.

"But John never felt ill toward me for not writing?"

"No, because he loves you so. Of course, it must have been difficult for you between the two of them," Eva sympathized, touching Jane's outstretched hand.

"Yes, especially their not being reconciled before father's death. But what could *I* do? I was too young!" And what could she do now for David?

"Yes—but it's over now, and we can't change the past. You and John need only love each other." Eva searched for the effect of her words in Jane's eyes.

Tired as she was, fronting the unexpected from Daniel and all that it meant for her and David, and standing in the hot sun, what Eva said suddenly brought tears to Jane's eyes. Eva didn't avoid delicate issues. And she must have to explain to her! Jane even loved her for that—what other woman could she hope for, for her brother?—She looked sadly across the acres of wheat beyond the clothesline. "You worry about him," she said, unable to keep her voice even, trying to find a way to bring her into her confidence.

"Especially with another baby coming—yet, men like John must act."

"You suffer, don't you, Eva?" she asked, thinking also of herself, her father, John, and now of David's rejection by his brother and possibly his mother.

"Don't we all? Yet, we are stronger for it. If John gives up Law, it will be because the Law stands for what is wrong.

"And David is having trouble at the Corners, isn't he?" Eva shifted, "though I don't want to pry, if you don't want to tell me."

Jane looked down. "Yes!" she almost cried. Even in Eva and her declaring themselves to each other, she still found it difficult to admit David's abridgement, their having come here with such hope. "Daniel refused to accept him as a partner."

"But he can farm . . ." Eva offered her.

"His farming *his* land is not what we want."

"'His' land? What's happened?" Eva pressed alertly.

"Yes, Daniel's land. And he owns the house, too, and only

wants David as a wage-earning millwright. And he didn't even look at David's saw," she stated abjectly.

"But I thought his mother owned the land and the house," Eva observed, alert to Sarah Jones' unmistakable manner on the bateau the evening Jane arrived.

"And so did we, until yesterday, when David found out otherwise from Daniel."

"And the saw? Did he bring it with him on the bateau?"

"No, he didn't smelt it, or whatever they do, but it's a sure design, even so."

Eva nodded.

"Is Daniel doing this because of John?"

"For John's stamp activity?" was the only thing Eva could think of—

"Yes."

"Not if Daniel invited David up here since then, Jane. Besides, he would have worked out the house with Sarah."

"Could it be, though, that he can't sell his timber despite what he told David?"

"Possibly," Eva answered, not fully knowing, "but I doubt it since he hasn't signed the Non-Association."

"Then why is he doing this?"

Eva shook her head. "Property."

"There must be some other explanation."

"Isn't that enough?" Eva picked up her basket, and held it poised against the largeness of the baby she carried. She started to speak, but thought better of saying anything negative about Sarah Jones' uppishness, if she was going to be Jane's mother-in-law.

"Yes? Property?" Jane pressed her.

"I've seen this before, Jane. Someone in a family becomes rich, and for that reason he steals from the others. Or someone in a family senses an opportunity, and he does the same thing, though this often requires an outsider. Wealth can be a cancer, feeding on and destroying others as it destroys the one who has it."

"John wouldn't approve of that," Jane declared defiantly.

"No."

"Do you think that's what Daniel's doing?"

"Probably, though I don't know his family."

"And with his mother's approval?"

"If she's never thought for herself—everything a woman owns becomes her husband's property when she marries."

"And so she just went along with Daniel without telling anyone . . ." Jane concluded. "But why would she do that to her other sons? Sell her farm like that and give all her money to Daniel for him to end up owning the house as well as the land?"

"She is probably not a woman accustomed to thinking for herself, for whatever reason. Or she is a mother who felt Daniel cared more for her."

"But that's not true. She dotes on David. He's done everything for her. He kept her alive on that farm when his other brothers came up here and her husband died."

"Then I can't explain it, Jane. You'll have to see what happens."

"But it already *has* happened—" she cried.

"I don't know what to say to you, but look . . ." Eva paused, at a loss of what more to say at present to her sister-in-law, except to try and make her feel better.

"What?" Jane went to her. "What should I do?" Her face revealed her helplessness in the face of a such deception.

"Promise you won't tell?"

"About what, Eva? Don't play with me at a time like this," she appealed to her, not knowing what Eva was saying.

"I'm not playing with you, Jane," she answered, dropping her basket and gently kissing her, "only John's bringing you a gift."

"A gift?" Jane questioned, stunned.

"And you mustn't refuse him. This is not an extravagance, but something necessary—"

"Oh, Eva! You mustn't, and isn't because of this, is it!" Jane implored, indicating that even a trifle would spoil her.

"No. Not because of this."

Jane looked at the ground and then toward the sky, her still wet strawberry-colored hair glistening in the sunlight. Her eyes sparkled with tears because she hadn't written her brother in two years, and because he loved her and didn't hold her not writing him against her. Because her sister-law was kind and generous like her brother—and maybe too because their generosity even frightened her because it would tie her to them the more when she feared the future.

"He loves you," Eva said, noticing her tears and touching her arm as she held the basket. "I hope those are tears of joy. It's something, frankly, that John wants to do because he *is* your oldest brother."

"I don't know what to say." Jane wiped the tears from her cheeks, struck at how Eva so easily gauged her feelings and eased her pain.

"Don't you want to know what he's bringing you?"

"Oh, yes, please," she answered quietly.

"A horse."

"How could he, with the baby!" Jane returned, struck by the largeness of the gift.

"Don't think it, Jane McCrea."

"I don't know . . ." but the significance of the gift overwhelmed her.

"We all have dreams, Jane. We know what it's like to have a dream—and we want only what is best for you."

"Oh, you do, don't you, Eva!" Jane cried, throwing her arms around her sister-in-law's neck, feeling in a rush a lightening of the weight of her disappointments.

8

That afternoon, sight of the bateau bearing the horse across the bay toward the house made Jane breathless with excitement. When the boat touched the shore and she watched the horse led off it, she thought she had never seen such a creature. And if a silver gilded horse didn't overwhelm her, John handed her a package containing a new riding habit! She looked helplessly at Eva, only too self-conscious in accepting such a gift, but Eva's eyes approved as Jane left for the house to dress.

—Now John held the tether line. Jane stood in her Saxon blue riding habit, tightly laced at the waist with cuffs turned back at the elbow in yellow butterfly-like wings, the skirts of the jacket flowing out over her petticoat with David beside her in his green waistcoat. She also wore a cocked hat with an ostrich feather arching over her long red hair.

How conspicuous she felt dressed like this! Though she might have, at weak moments, dreamed of such elegant apparel, she felt out of place dressed in these clothes in this setting. John and Eva were dressed simply; only David's green waistcoat made her feel less pretentious. But it wasn't proper to refuse. Refusal to wear these clothes and accept this horse would have insulted John's sensibilities. His and her own dignity finally required she accept these gifts.

The light gray filly turned in a circle, her head and white tail high—her hoofs striking the ground crisply. With strong back, wide and deep chest, and square rump, the mare took the circle. Over the moving body of the horse a schooner appeared on the river. Jane squeezed David's arm as the horse and the boat followed one another like the lines of a lyric.

"Don't you love her?" Jane asked him self-consciously, urging him to accept that the beauty of the filly and her personal adornment only enhanced the natural scene.

David agreed he had ever seen a finer horse. "And you look just beautiful," he said, responding to her disposition and need for approval. Yet, it was not difficult for him to approve of her, or to say how striking she was, for to him she had always had 'breeding,' his own ambition for her acknowledged that. But had she ever ridden before?

"May I ride her, John?" she asked, impatient for some activity to relieve her lingering self-consciousness.

"Are you sure, Jen?" David asked. "She's a young horse—" he added, indicating he knew she had little horse back experience.

"Oh, I think I can, David. I have to try, and when, if not with you and John here?" she asked nervously, while at the same time welcoming the effort.

John brought the horse in and Jane raised her palm, pricking the filly's ears forward. She stroked her nose. The filly's eyes were deep and rich as black agate. Jane brought her other hand up to her white, linen-like mane. The animal seemed gentle.

"Charlotte's a good name," she said spontaneously, hardly aware that she choose the name of the King's consort. "Will you help me up, David?" She leaned on his arm and he helped her onto the saddle where she arranged her petticoat over the filly's back.

"Take it slowly," he advised, aware of her need for confidence.

"I have ridden before," she laughed, "though I'm not overly experienced."

"Let her go," John said to her, confident in her quick ability to ride.

They stepped away as the filly took several short steps and stopped.

Jane urged the horse on, and with two, and then three quick steps the filly began to trot. Jane brought her to a canter, and the breeze against her face brought tears to her eyes, making the trees seem to float along the riverbank.

At the end of the field where it met the woods and the wheat field on her left, she neck-reined. The filly sidestepped across the road into the wheat, and the wheat snatched at her petticoat.

Jane stroked the filly's neck and straightened her hat in a single gesture. Then something reddish-yellow jumped in the wheat and her heels came back against the horse. The filly jumped and flattened out beneath her, breaking the wheat by in waves. Above the running filly's flat ears, Jane heard John call to her from the house as the horse quickly closed the distance between them. She hung on, imagining herself sailing over the horse's head into the wheat before John intercepted her.

"Rein in!" he shouted, reaching for the reins and stopping the horse, jolting her back against the back of the saddle.

He held the bridle as the bit ground between the frightened filly's teeth. "She has spirit," he said, holding the bridle, while stroking the horse firmly, stilling the wild agitation in her eyes.

"Are you hurt, Jen?" David asked, as she slid from the saddle into his arms, her legs shaking.

"No, I'm not, but that cat!" she cried, more alarmed than hurt, straightening her hat and smoothing her habit with shaking hands. "If John hadn't stopped her, she would have gone by the house and over the hill to the river!"

"Ah, it's all right for the first time. You'll get on to it," John minimized, as he slipped the saddle off the mare and handed his sister a brush. "The bateau ride made her edgy . . ." he said, relieved she wasn't hurt, "Just curry her."

She took the brush in her hands. "Though I have only myself to fault. I should have just walked."

"The cat spook her?" her brother asked.

"Yes!" she exclaimed.

"Maybe she doesn't like her name," John winked at her.

"But Charlotte is such a pretty name, isn't it, David? Don't tease, John, she could have thrown me," she rebuked her brother, though her voice still quavered.

"You hung on . . . *jumped in with both feet*," John laughed, seeing how quickly she recovered, and taking her elbow to be certain.

"Yes, though my legs are like sand," she admitted, smiling.

"But how did the horse feel! Is she right for you, does she run well?" Eva asked.

"Smooth as lightening! And see how sure-footed she was going through the wheat! She frightened me to death, but she stayed on her feet.

"She really is such a beautiful animal, John. And I love you both for giving her to me. Yes, and we will get to know each other, won't we, Charlotte?" she continued, pulling the brush through the filly's long mane as the strength returned to her legs.

—The sparrows stirred the lime-colored leaves of the cool poplars when, later that day, Jane and David walked along the river to Sarah Jones' house. Jane especially loved the clean-smelling ferns and the willows trailing their branches like hair in the amber current of the river.

Ahead, at an elbow in the road on their right, a bluff overlooked the river. David strode toward it, leading the filly with a surveyor's bounce in his step, his red hair visible at the edges of his wig. Jane slid from the filly into his arms and, with his waistcoat soft against her cheek, they walked hand in hand toward the edge of the bluff.

As she looked down at the water, Jane found herself wondering how she and David could still have their home and land given Daniel's refusal and his financial chicanery—If he still had a market for his lumber, why should David settle for just that, given his skills? Perhaps, he could build his own mill incorporating his saw. They could then buy all of what they needed for their home.

Jane's eyes rested on the flowing river and the current. David's mother's property fronted the river, so why couldn't he have his saw on that property, if he could get her on his side? If she consented, Daniel would have to agree.

"Why can't you build your own mill, David?" She faced him, imagining a large wheel turning here over the edge. "Couldn't your mother demand that Daniel honor her promise to you?"

"The river's too slow here, Jen. You need moving water, steep land, a falls, not water that flows like molasses," he answered, turning away from the edge. "This is not good water for a mill."

"But what of the land for our house? Can't we at least get that?"

"I can try, and maybe even start a ferry business there . . ." he tried to buoy her, though his enthusiasm waned, knowing how long it would really take to save, even if he could get his mother to agree to the land.

"Is there money in ferrying?" she asked.

"Some."

Jane felt his anguish. How long would it take for the home they dreamed of? A house with a separate kitchen and closed stove, a dining room and parlor, and rooms upstairs for the children— something like Philip Schuyler's The Pastures which they passed in Albany on their way up from Lamington. How the Schuyler house crowned the hill on the west bank of the river! She had drunk the sight from the deck of the schooner. The red brick, Georgian mansion had massive windows, white shutters, and sloping lawns, an orchard and barn. And inside the house she imagined cool rooms with high ceilings and walls painted in soft blues and greens, a parlor with a dining room, a ballroom upstairs over a galleried central hallway, and bedrooms with canopied beds. The laughter of Schuyler's daughters in their wide hats and white petticoats as they sat in front of the house in the shade of a large tree, oblivious to her passing on the schooner below them, had also sharpened her yearning to possess such a house. It was natural for her to imagine owning such a house, coming as she did with David with such hope.

But those were wild imaginings! Something grand, which a part of her had said wasn't realistic. But now Sarah Jones' new house, as an example, and Daniel's chicanery, prompting her counter-desire for property, had rekindled those imaginings.

"I could wait for something like the Schuyler mansion," she said half-seriously as she took his hand.

"Knowing we couldn't have it overnight?" he intoned half-seriously himself, given his changed circumstances. But how could he even ask the question, aware the Schuyler family owned land and businesses for generations. That house cost a fortune. He looked at the ground, thinking that he had a mushroom's chance to be a mountain.

"I can't imagine owning a house like that," he confessed, "Schuyler has thousands of acres, saw, grist, and flax mills; a store, tenants, a fleet of sloops and schooners; even a herring fishery here on the river, and he trades as far away as Antigua and the West Indies. And he has an estate at Saratoga . . ." He hoped, however, that what he said might temper her dream rather than tarnish it.

His look arrested her imagination.

"We must begin somewhere," she answered meekly. "Daniel did, and look at what he's done."

"He cheats and steals."

"We needn't do that, David!" she laughed, taking his hand and beginning to walk back to the road. But she did inwardly question why some people succeeded and others didn't. Luck certainly played a part, if skill and hard work alone couldn't make it happen.

"I wish that conniving brother of mine . . . damn! That saw would have given us property," he exclaimed, wiping his face with his handkerchief. "But how can I convince him?"

"He *might* change his mind, if he smells money in it."

"Are mushrooms lilies? I don't want to get our hopes up again with him."

He looked up through the trees. The air had turned muggy.

"I don't mean to make you unhappy, David. You didn't deserve this," she consoled him.

"Especially since the value of Mother's Lamington farm derived from my efforts," he agreed bitterly. He helped her onto the saddle. She took the reins, leaned over and kissed him. "I know Daniel doesn't care. Business has hardened and isolated him from me. I've thought about it, but it would be like taking water from a frozen well to try to change his mind about my saw," he said.

"Such a brother!" she stated.

"If I had a brother like yours, I'd have no problems! He bought you this filly just like that." He snapped his fingers. "Well, Daniel and I never agreed, and, as I thought he might have changed, he was manipulating behind my back."

"Is he the same way with your other brothers?"

"Yes."

"Will your mother talk to him?"

"It would upset her."

"But what about you? Doesn't your grieving about this mean anything to her?"

"When I brought it up to her, she said *he* had the experience. She said only that she would think about it."

"Does what he is doing have to do with your father?"

"I don't know. It just hurts me more for you, Jen, after our plans," he said, looking up at her and pressing her hand. "Oh, Jen . . ."

"Let's not talk about it."

"Will you always say that?"

"Will I always love you?"

"I love you, Jen . . ." his voice dropped off, as he found the words inadequate.

9

"Why doesn't Peter come, what's keepin' him?" Polly whispered a few hours after Jane and David had arrived at Sarah Jones'. The rain beat off the roof, and the fire danced at the back of the fireplace making the orange wainscoting glow.

Jane's wine twinkled like stars in her glass. She had met Polly now for the first time and, instantly, they related like sisters.

"Peter must have a reason for staying down there, Polly," Jane answered absently, thinking of the wait ahead of her after her talk with David by the river in the afternoon. It didn't seem as important to her Polly's soldier, Peter Tearse, had not come up from the City yet. She didn't want to pet, but now at Sarah Jones' the rain affected her. Did Polly really have cause to complain? After all, she had much to look forward to, given her grandmother's land. Sarah McNeil could easily sell some for the home Polly wanted.

"You're not very cheerful, Jane."

She noticed Polly's gray eyes narrow in the soft light as her friend touched her arm. Polly pressed her honey-colored hair behind her ear, urging her to speak. Jane sighed, annoyed for letting her mood show. She moistened her lips from her glass.

"I want to be cheerful, Polly, but the rain depresses me," she said, touched by Polly's concern. "But you shouldn't worry about Peter," adding to make Polly feel better, "he'll keep his commission, regardless of what's happening in the City, and he'll join you before you know it. You've much to look forward to," she pressed earnestly.

"But somethin's troubling *you*—"

"It's nothing," Jane replied, unconvincingly "—it's only . . ."

"Daniel and David's new saw?"

"Abraham Wing controls their property . . ." she evaded.

"Send David up ta th' Jessup brothers. They hae plenty o'

land an' timber. They could run Daniel out o' business with that new saw o' David's," Polly encouraged her. "Business isn't so tight yet, that ya canna do that."

"Polly, please . . ." Jane glanced across the room at Sarah Jones and Sarah McNeil talking by the fireplace, not wanting them to hear.

"Don't worry about them," Polly whispered, drawing her chair closer to Jane's. "Ye must think o' yer own interests," she continued, gesturing with her glass toward her grandmother. "Take a tip frae her—two marriages, an' each time she comes out with a chunk o' property. 'Tis no great fun losin' yer husbands, but she thinks on her feet."

'Maybe she could give us some of it,' Jane thought, recoiling at the impropriety of her own thought.

"Maybe, if the Jessups had their Patent, David should go to them, but I'm too confused to think about it, Polly." She wanted to shift Polly's attention to Peter and away from David and herself, fearing Sarah Jones would catch how she felt and ruin any chance of her correcting her treatment of David.

"Well, lass, I'd move tomorrow, if Peter came up. Grandmother haes land in Argyle that brings tears ta her eyes . . ."

"We have much in common, don't we?" Jane asked.

"Aye, dependents and foundlings both. A lassie needs a mother."

"I was two when my mother died, and can almost remember her—"

"My mother died soon after I was born. Every lass needs a mother, or, at least, a grandmother . . ."

Jane pressed her hands together in her lap. "And I miss my father, more than anything," she confessed softly.

"All th' more reason ta look out for yersel," Polly said firmly, drawing her breath and looking up at the ceiling as if the rain might seep through it. "When it rains like this, it reminds grandmother o' th' auld countrie'."

The flames retreated in gray wisps behind Sarah Jones' chair. No doubt a crofter's cottage in the 'auld countrie' didn't have the perfume of fresh lumber like this house, which sent shivers up one's back, Jane thought. The combination of the rain, the fire, and the wine, and her feelings for her deceased father made her sad.

She felt David's hand on her neck as he came behind her. Jane looked up into his eyes just as the door flew open and the rain pushed a man through it.

"What a night! Brought ya some real good eatin' while the boys fix the harness for ya, Widow Jones. And h-e-l-l-o, Sary!" Thomas Yarns exclaimed.

"Who is that?" Jane asked David.

"Someone who helped Mother move in," he answered uncomfortably. "He'll probably not stay." Though he knew otherwise.

"Looks like you fell into the river, Mister Yarns," Sarah Jones declared, while Solomon took his hat and hung it by the door.

"Wet, yes, but a damn sight better'n any river," Yarns laughed, eyeing Jane. "And is this David's loved one with the long hair?"

Jane turned in her chair and looked at David.

"Yes, Thomas," Solomon answered.

"An' wat a lad walkin' o'er ta th' neibors on sech a night. Probly croonin' th' whole way," Sarah McNeil intervened, shaking her head and moving closer to the fire.

"Man of action, I am! Brought ya some things for the table, not that ya can't provide for yarselves, mind ya, but a little something would go well with the festivities," Yarns declared, shifting his attention from Jane to the room. He pulled a jug of rum and beefsteaks, wrapped in burlap, from a sack he held in his hands. "The boys dressed her this morning, jest for this housewarmin'."

"Calls himsel a man o' action an' th' rum cames oot o' th' sack first."

"Now, Sary, yar not denyin' a man a bit of cheer on the occasion of this housewarmin'!" Yarns protested, his voice booming throughout the room.

"Nae, I wadna deny ye a guid time or a wee bit o' cheer, Pap

Yarns," Sarah McNeil agreed, waddling over to David and Jane. "Right, handsome David Jones?"

"David was always the handsome one, people said," his mother declared from her chair, looking at Jane.

Jane held the woman's eyes for a moment, wondering just what she meant by that. Did she mean that she would do anything for her son, or did her look mean that, with her husband dead, she would possess her son and resented her? How else could she interpret what she had done to David? And what mother would say such a thing in the presence of another son, even if it was true?

"We don't care much for good looks at a time like this," Solomon reacted on his own behalf, amicably enough on the surface, referring to the rioting in the City.

"Ah, lad, ta th' deil wi' those doon countrie, City folk. Let's jes enjoy this bonnie hoose in th' presence o' young luve," Sarah McNeil said of Jane and David.

Jane noticed his mother's lips tighten and the color rise in her cheeks.

"Furgit them mechanics, Sary! Ya think the King'll furgit 'em? Not on yar life, little woman. He'll come down on 'em hard, and when I say hard, I mean hard!" Yarns rolled up his sleeves and put his hand on Solomon's shoulder. "Right, Solomon?" he asked, weaving where he stood. "If ya got a bad tooth, horse it out, and them down there is a bad tooth!"

"Bluid'll flow," Sarah McNeil agreed.

"The King'll spin and weave 'em in both Boston and New York, mark my words," Yarns continued, swigging from his jug, "and I'll watch 'em. Ya bet I will."

Jane drew back before the man's growing anger.

The heat rose to David's cheeks.

"Th' man ne'er haulds bak 'is opinion."

"Thieves and skinners formin' committees! And whare's yar brother, Jane McCrea, if not at this housewarmin' o' yar expected in-laws?"

Yarns' eyes suddenly glowed in his flushed face as though he stood over a forge.

Jane recoiled from the man's sudden assault on her—David hadn't even spoken of this man—Why should he speak like this to her? She shivered, disgusted, feeling something horribly fateful about him.

"Doin' Committee work, huh, is that what yar brother's doin'?" he demanded of her.

She set her glass on the table. David put his hand on her shoulder and Sarah McNeil interrupted before she could reply.

"Dinna start on my lassies, Pap Yarns, or ye'll find yersel in th' river."

"I don't even know you," Jane said sharply to him.

"Well, I know ya!"

Someone then knocked on the door, and Yarns' son Robert stood in the doorway with the rain pouring off the roof behind him.

"We fixed the harness," he reported.

"Come in out of the rain," Solomon drew the boy forward into the room.

"My brothers are waiting for me," Robert answered, observant of his father.

"Close the door, boy, didn't I larn ya better'n that!" his father barked.

Robert turned and called out into the rain for his brothers who appeared holding their hats. The water, dripping from their hats, shimmered like splinters of glass on the polished floor.

"Look at them. Raisin' men, not thieves nor skinners," Yarns said drunkenly. "Finish the harness?" he demanded.

They answered they had, and he waved them back outside where their forms passed in the rain beyond the window.

"Th' lads canna ga bak ta Kingsbury in this weather?" Sarah McNeil protested. "At least gie th' lads same warmum tea, Pap Yarns."

"Ah, ya coddle 'em ta much, Sary. I want 'em tough, not pretty— which reminds me, Davey, when 're ya and Jane tyin' th' knot?"

Jane recoiled at the man's question as if it foreclosed on any idea of their marriage.

"I been wonderin' about that, and let me give ya some friendly advice. If ya love that girl, marry her. What does Daniel, yar big brother, matter next ta true luve? Property ain't everything, though ya know what he's after," Yarns declared, rubbing his fingers together in the air. "Pounds! Could 'a told ya that that first night I met ya, comin' with yar mother ta this new house, preened like a Christmas turkey. But, Davey, me lad, ta hell wi' Daniel. If ya love this buxom girl, marry her—though I must say that family of hers will give ya nothin' but trouble, Davey," Yarns laughed, pushing his face toward the couple. "Mark my words, you'll have trouble with that McCrea, if you marry her, Davey," he repeated.

Jane stood up and walked away from the table to the other side of the room. Polly followed her.

"Don't talk about my son Daniel like that," Sarah Jones said angrily. "Talk about anyone you please, but you have no right to speak of my son like that."

"Dinna mind his boozy overcrowin'."

"Say what ya want, Sary, but I bet pence ta puddin' Daniel Jones, the prodigal son, owns this place. Git it after the widow is gone. Daniel's a big man, wheelin' and dealin' on other people's property. Suckered in old man Wing. I know Daniel Jones, sucker his own brother up here and then serve him only chicken feet—I see it all comin'. Daniel's a muckworm."

"Yarns!" Solomon shouted suddenly, taking the man's arm.

"Take yar hands offen me, Solomon Jones. Or has Daniel got ya brain-rummelled too?" Yarns sputtered.

"You're drunk."

"Ya ain't heard nothin'!"

"Stop your damn shrieking!" David yelled at him.

"Open yar eyes, Davey. Ya been had. Otherwise whare's the weddin' bells and yar dear-luve's quilt ta lie under? Ya come up here expectin' property ta float on the river! And that brother of yars, lettin' ya believe it! God, boy, yar so green behind the ears sheep can graze there."

Jane pressed her back against the window and looked across

the room at the man. Her knuckles turned white as she gripped the sill behind her.

"Boys! No more of this after your f...." Sarah Jones cried, clutching her breast.

"Take yar hands offen me, ya two river rats!"

Yarns' fist caught David on the ear and knocked off his wig. Solomon pinned the man's arms. Yarns threw Solomon against a chair and kicked out at David. The three of them scuffled like wrestlers trying to get holds. Yarns fell on his back with a dull thump with Solomon on top of him. Yarns thrashed wildly. David's fist came down on him with a hollow crunch. He dragged the bleeding Yarns to the door and threw his hat out after him.

Jane turned around and looked at the dark window. The rain ran down the glass in silver streaks.

"I love John, Polly. That man is hateful," she said, wiping her eyes and pressing her burning forehead against the cool pane.

"Don't pay him any mind, lass."

"I don't care about John's committee work. That Yarns man had no right saying those things about him." But she couldn't deny the truth of what he said about Daniel, especially as it made the truth of David's changed circumstances more painful to her.

"Don't take it so hard, lass. I've seen him like this before. The morning will see him humble as a lamb—besides, David and Solomon gave him the turnip."

"How long will we have to wait, Polly?" Jane asked under her breath.

"Ye wadna rather stayed in Lamington with yer stepmother?"

"At least she announced my engagement," Jane answered, adding, "unlike this family of quiet enemies." Jane barely spoke above a whisper as she turned toward Sarah Jones. "Is it all luck, Polly? Do I have only a future of disappointment ahead of me?" She wrung her handkerchief.

"Lucky for Thomas Yarns he didna get his neck wrung, muddled like that. His mind is blawn away by th' dram." Yet, Polly was at a loss as to how to console Jane for her unhappiness.

"Our Trinculo," Jane said despondently of him.

It continued to rain into the night.

Jane's eyes, deep blue and dark-edged, searched the low fire. The faint firelight made her hair a chestnut red. David didn't care about Daniel, John, Yarns, or the sleeping women upstairs. He didn't care about tomorrow, only to drink from her eyes and lips and hold her very soul on his tongue . . . and she responded, gentle as wine, smelling of roses.

"Jenny," he breathed heavily.

He wanted her, and though her mood threatened to block his desire, it couldn't stop the flow of his passion as he caressed her warm breasts and raspberry nibbles in the dying firelight.

"Do you love me, David?"

He couldn't help it.

"David."

"Just say, yes, Jen."

"We can't. Not here . . . not in this house."

He kissed her breasts.

"This once, Jenny." His hands found their way.

"David . . ." she whispered in weak protest, "please, not here." She pulled away. "It just doesn't feel right. It doesn't. I want to, but I can't. I know you understand. Please help me to bear it. I feel different . . . please."

10

The evening at Sarah Jones' threatened to color the remainder of the summer for Jane. What Thomas Yarns had said about John and Daniel webbed her every thought, tying her prospects for an early marriage into hopeless snags. The certainty of a long wait filled her with a gloom even long and frequent rides by the river on Charlotte couldn't lift. She tried to keep her feelings from David, not wanting to discourage his efforts to change Daniel's mind about their partnership; but, after they had reached Ballston for her brother's, James', wedding, she revealed them.

John's remarks, outdoors at lunch after the ceremony, about the Ministry's interference in Colonial commerce sunk into Jane's ears like molten lead. Across from her Beriah Palmer listened with the intensity of a convert. And yet, how she had wanted to identify with Maria Hoyhing's look of possession when James slipped the ring on her finger, but was prevented from doing so by this very talk of politics!

"Schuyler has also affronted the excises in the Assembly," Beriah said in the glare of the glass-like Long Lake behind him.

Tortured, Jane listened to him. The Non-Association guaranteed business would come to a standstill, just as Eva had forecast, and David's millwork might end for all Daniel's assurances to the contrary.

"Three times the size of the United Kingdom, and with nine-hundred miles of coastline to trade from, the Colonies can easily sidestep the Ministry's policies. We don't need England's trade—we can trade with the French—nor do we need to tolerate the three months it takes the Ministry to make decisions for us," John said in support of Schuyler's efforts to rally the Assembly against the Ministry.

"We all feel that way, John, including Eliphalet," Beriah agreed, referring to Reverend Ball who had just married James and Maria. Beriah sat back and acknowledged Jane's brothers' nods. "But what about the Grants people squatting on Schuyler's and Van Rensselaer's lands? Will they weaken New England's commitment to the Non-Association?"

The only good thing about this trouble was that it brought John and his brothers together again after John's break with his father. But how this talk confined her! The specter of Yarns loomed before her.

"No, the Ministry's responsible," John answered.

John had told Jane that the Wentworth Grants Patent overlapped the New York Patent between the Connecticut and Hudson Rivers and that the Ministry had not resolved the land dispute.

The sun oppressed the afternoon. The cool lake invited her to swim. Let Eva follow the men's talk, she wished to leave the table. She took David's hand, urging him to come with her.

"Let's walk by the lake," she whispered.

They excused themselves.

"Why so unhappy?" David observed of her, as she stopped to free her petticoat from the raspberry bushes, which lined the path to the lake.

She snatched her petticoat free and breathed the sticky air without relief. Deer flies snapped against her bonnet. She slapped one on her arm.

"I haven't seen my brothers in several years and they *must* talk politics," she said, wishing anything but this had reunited them.

"But Philip has come up from Lamington," David pointed out.

"Not Catherine, Robert, or Gilbert," she retorted irritably of her stepmother and other half-brothers. It wouldn't surprise her, if they opposed this Non-Association business. She couldn't make sense of any of it; she was at six and seven with it.

"Jane, did you really expect Catherine to bring little Catherine and Creighton?" David asked of the youngest of Catherine's children.

"I don't know, the happiness I expected here eludes us . . ."

"Would you rather not have come, or stayed in Lamington?"

"No," she answered, vainly trying to keep the petulance from her voice, "but at least we had friends there." She thought of her engagement party. Every woman in town had come to it, and when she had announced her intention to leave for Northumberland they all said they would miss her. Now Lamington didn't exist for her except in memory. And her hopes for David's partnership had been so high!

"Then what?" he repeated.

"Everything just seems wrong." She watched the high yellow grass at the lakeshore ebb in the hot breeze.

"Forget what happened at Mother's. Brooding over Yarns won't help."

"It's not just him, everything seems closed to us." She didn't mention it, but she harbored real fears his mother opposed his marrying. Her behavior toward John and her looks at her housewarming gnawed at her.

"You don't mean that, Jen."

"Look at John. What will come of that?" She pulled at the long grass and it cut her fingers. John's activity, following her like a dark cloud, threatened to stifle her again. And yet she understood why Eva would encourage and support her husband.

"Don't make so much of it . . ." David said, looking at the lake in frustration. "I could be out of work."

"And when will that happen?" she asked, fearing the worst.

"Forget about Daniel and John, Jen. We must lay our own cobbles."

David took off his hat and wiped the headband.

"How?"

"Look, we only came up this summer. Even Schuyler has problems. You heard them talking back there."

"Yes, that's true." But then she thought that Schuyler was rich.

"And I work," he pleaded for understanding.

"For pence." It hurt her to say that.

"As much as I can—it's the times."

"No," she then declared angrily, growing desperate to blame someone or something for their situation. "Daniel's at fault!" she struck out.

"Well, what can I do about him?"

"How about the Jessups? Will they give you a chance?" she asked, seizing on Polly's idea.

"And risk Daniel knowing . . ."

She retreated from the possibility of Daniel's retaliation. She glanced at the lake and yearned to loose herself in the cool water.

"Don't think about it, Jen." He took her in his arms. "Enjoy James' wedding at least."

His kiss and his mentioning the wedding began to dissolve her disappointment.

"We have each other, don't we, Jen?"

"Yes." She looked at the ground.

"You're only nineteen."

"Nearly twenty," she corrected him gently, touching his face.

"But your brother James is twenty-four," he sought to encourage her.

"Older than Content at fifteen," she rejoined, realizing that he was right, though it hardly made her feel better. Her feelings were as divided as fall from spring.

"Have it your way," he said to humor her, sensing the return of her usual good spirits.

His caring eyes appealed to her. She realized she gained nothing by comparing herself to others, though she couldn't resist it. It would be wonderful not to compare—to live each day! But they had had a predicate, hopeful feelings from which the future would spring. Expectation had informed their lives. "If others can have a life of their own, David, so can we."

He had never thought much about Content or Polly, but he had thought about Daniel and Deborah. He agreed with her. He wouldn't give up either, but as long as she loved him he could wait . . . . But they should not make themselves unhappy by looking at what others had. He consoled himself by thinking the other sex mostly thought of these things.

"If women didn't think of a house and family, there wouldn't be any life at all," she said, breaking in on his thoughts, making sure he understood her. But she didn't press him. She didn't want to discourage him. Her own youth and inexperience cautioned her against a rash insistence. As with her brothers, she should encourage him.

"No one's going to deny us, Jen."

"Daniel has," she couldn't help saying.

"Maybe I can convince him," he said without real conviction.

"You know best," she let off, giving him the lead.

"He might budge . . ." his voice trailed off.

"And your mother?"

"What about her?"

"Has she mentioned our marriage? She should have said something by now."

"She hasn't mentioned it."

"Don't you think she should?" she asked, implying that if she hadn't said anything, he should speak to her.

"She's only just settled."

Jane bit her lip. She didn't know how far she should go with David. She didn't want to risk deepening her problem with Sarah. She had begun to suspect his mother wanted to keep David for herself after her husband's death. But she couldn't impugn the woman too quickly because so much depended on her. "Yes, maybe she's still settling in," she said, concealing a return of her despondency.

"Give her time, Jane."

He drew a bottle of wine from his waistcoat pocket and set it in the grass and made a place for her to sit. He went up the path and returned with raspberries in the bottom of two glasses. The wine tumbled into the glasses and the raspberries floated to the top. He handed her a glass.

"Stop worrying, Jenny."

She held the glass of wine in her slender fingers.

He felt responsible for a vision as he beheld her sitting beside him holding her glass to her lips.

"To our home?"

A surge of desire came with his swallowing the wine. He then kissed her, tasting the wine on her lips.

"I'm sorry, David," she said quietly, sighing, and resting the stem of her glass in her lap. "Is it really wrong of me to have these feelings?

"No."

"And your mother not saying anything after our engagement?"

"Nothing's more important."

She wanted to surrender to him with the wine and his kiss on her lips. If she surrendered to him and bore his child would that force the question and change their situation? She had known other women who had done this—What was more important than children and a family?

"Where shall we marry?" he asked.

She now faulted herself for allowing herself for insisting with him. He wanted the same thing she wanted. "Albany," she answered without hesitation.

"And our honeymoon?" he continued, reliving their dream.

"London." His questions suddenly opened the matrimonial horizon to her again. The sunlight transformed her wine into liquid gold. His questions made her dreams more vivid than ever. She looked at him. But how sad he looked, as though her answers now filled him with a swimmer's despair on reaching a ship miles out to sea.

"I guess Albany and London," he agreed quietly, trying to keep alive what brought them up here.

"I've dejected you," she said, sensing he too had real doubts.

"I only want to come home to you."

"David Jones!" she cried, leaning over and kissing him. If he faltered and the flame waned, what would she do! "And that's what I want!"

She did not feel materialistic in her desire for a home and property, or in wanting an Albany marriage, except that she had always imagined life in these terms. And if she didn't continue to hold the possibility out to him, what then? His ambition might languish. And why should she settle for a penthouse? The whole world stood before her. If she dared to think, to love, then she dared to dream. And if she dreamed, why not of their full life together? She had grown up with him. (She had no liking for his father or for Daniel for that matter. She disliked boozers, hypochondriacs, hypocrites, and misers.) David had youth and energy. She couldn't let their dreams die. And why should she sit by like a wallflower or a mute? She wanted a real life, wanted to hear the trilling of birds, wanted to rejoice in the gentle blessing of summer breezes, have the bushes breathe on her, feel at peace. Her own youth and purpose pressed upon her—surged within her— she wanted life and compass, yearned restlessly for it. What was more natural than to feel this way at her age in this new country? Life itself fired her dreams and impelled her forward!

"Let's go for a swim!"

"Now? Here?" he asked with disbelief.

"Of course—we can swim behind those bushes," she said, pointing up the shore to where sumacs hung out over the lake.

Thought of swimming with her made his heart thump.

11

As summer passed to fall, however, Jane's dream remained snagged against Sarah Jones' silence and Daniel's unchanged decision to only employ David at wages.

Jane paused in her bundling and tying. The dry stubble of the cut wheat caught at the hem of her petticoat and pricked her ankles. She wore leather gloves to protect her fingers and hands. The autumn day, which had begun cold, grew hot in the afternoon. The men paused only at noon to eat and now worked on in the heat, never seeming to tire as they swung their scythes into the long brown wheat, their scythes catching the sunlight like the silver bodies of schooling fish and the men's wide brown hats swaying with the motion.

Jane gazed across the bay at the river where a schooner passed south to Albany. She imagined Schuyler's Saratoga estate from the river. She wondered why, when she walked the same ground, breathed the same air, and watched the same river flowing south in the sunlight the land could not bear for her too . . . .

She felt impotent. If born a man, perhaps things would have been different for her. She might have grasped life, rather than lose herself in the poetry of the colors of grass and leaves, the blueness of the sky, the scents of fall, or in brown-eyed Susans growing in the fields. She struggled against her cheated feelings and her unrealized longings, made particularly sharp for their being unfulfilled by people so close to her, and glanced at Eva deftly raking the wheat. She had complained of pains in the morning, but had insisted on coming out into the field—how little dreams affected Eva! She was a model of forbearance and patience!

Eva straightened up and held her sides.

Jane raised her eyebrows and slipped off her gloves, expecting

Eva to speak. When she didn't speak, Jane asked, "Is the baby moving again?"

"This work, this bending over has helped, but the baby's close now." Eva blew lightly between her lips, her face glistening with perspiration. "Come back with me to the house, Jane," she said, kicking the lose wheat from her shoes and turning heavily away.

"Should I go to Fort Edward for Doctor Smythe?" Jane asked with some alarm.

Eva stopped. "I've got Dinah."

Jane watched her sister-in-law, heavy with child, walk away from her. The men didn't seem to notice her leaving, and the bay lay placidly nearby them, yet Jane felt Eva's footsteps as surely as if they made the earth tremble. Her own preoccupations vanished. She could think of nothing else but Eva having her baby now! "You're having the baby!" she called, throwing down her gloves.

Only half-turning, Eva's words drifted toward the bay. "Someone must be with James."

Jane hurried after her, and when they reached the house they found Dinah scrubbing the stones of the fireplace. Eva went wordlessly through the room to her bedroom.

"I guess that baby's camin," Dinah quickly observed, reaching behind her and piling more wood on the fire. She picked up a large kettle. "James is atakin' his nap," she informed Jane without hurry.

"But what about Doctor Smythe?" Jane asked, at a loss of what to do as the black woman went for the door. "Doesn't Eva need a doctor?"

"By the time that doctor gits here that baby'll be born. Now go in an' make Missus Eva comfortable."

Jane then heard the kettle clank against the stones of the well outside. She went quickly into Eva's bedroom.

Eva lay in her nightgown on her bed with a pillow behind her head, breathing deeply and regularly. She rolled over on her side.

"Are the pains coming? Do you want me to rub your back?" Jane asked, going to her and beginning to rub the small of Eva's back with her palms. Her own disappointments, aspirations, and

desires amounted to little next to childbirth! The obstacles Daniel
and his mother had put in her way paled in importance to children,
a family, and a loving husband! As she massaged Eva's back and
recalled 'insisting' on an Albany wedding with David last summer
at James' wedding, the color rose to her face—how ashamed she
felt recalling that as she stood before the drama of birth. This
didn't cost a farthing! And hadn't she come to David without a
dowry, or freehold land or paraphernalia of her own, but with only
one hundred and seventy pounds?

"Shall I find John?" she asked, feeling she would do anything
for Eva at this moment, short of throwing herself under a runaway
carriage.

"No," Eva answered huskily, her face flushed.

Jane took her sister-in-law's hot hands into her own.

"I'll get water."

She returned with a jar and a washcloth. "Would you feel better
lying on your back?"

Eva's face tightened and she began breathing shallowly. "Yes,
on my back," she answered, turning back over with difficulty.

Jane gently washed her face with the cool cloth. She took her
hands up in hers and washed them too. "Do you want this pillow
under your back?" she asked calmly, comfortingly, reaching for the
pillow.

"Yes."

She pushed her palm under Eva's back and slid the pillow
under her. Eva took a deep breath and closed her lips. The pains
came regularly and she groaned.

A wave of pity swept over Jane. She wrung out the washcloth
and brought it to Eva's face again. "You must relax," she said. She
recalled the posts on Catherine's bed, but Eva's bed had no posts.
"Do you have something to push against?"

"Give me that sheet," Eva only answered, half-nodding toward
the dresser against the wall to her right, "and fold the corner of it
between my legs." Her body rose up and she groaned.

As Jane spread the sheet over her sister-in-law, Eva seemed to
rise off the bed. Jane felt dizzy. Where was Dinah? She reached for

the comb on the dresser. The quickening succession of Eva's pains frightened her. The way Eva looked at the ceiling frightened her. Eva's eyes, deep and opaque, were half-closed, and half-focused. Her own hands trembled, as she wrung the washcloth—"Dinah will be right here," she said just above a whisper.

"I feel sick."

Jane slipped her hand behind Eva's neck and held the bowl. She wiped her mouth, folded the washcloth, and wiped her forehead. She then plunged a clean washcloth into the jar, wrung it, and laid it over Eva's forehead. "Oh," Jane whispered, readjusting the pillow and brushing her hair, "it'll be over soon."

"Yes."

Dinah brought the hot kettle into the bedroom.

"Bring the nightstand o'er chile," she said to Jane.

Jane's fingers found the edges of the table as she brought it to the end of the bed. The bottom of the kettle smoked on the wooden table. Dinah dipped a cloth into the hot water, and Jane felt the heat on her own hands.

"Shut the door," Dinah said quietly, calmly. "Are yer legs hurtin', honey? Are yer legs hurtin'?"

"Yes," Eva moaned, half-consciously.

"Breathe deeply, honey, breathe deeply."

Pressing her palms against the soles of her feet, Dinah raised Eva's knees. She then lifted the corner of the sheet and her hands went quickly back and forth to the kettle.

"Oh!" Eva cried, reaching for the sides of the bed.

Jane rubbed Eva's hand—her own legs like bread dough. "It's going to be a lovely little girl," she said.

Eva closed her lips and held her breath. She braced her feet and held the sides of the bed. She bore down.

"Breathe, honey, breathe.—Gie me those cloths on the dresser, chile," Dinah said to her, pointing to the dresser behind Jane and dropping the cloth she used on the floor.

Jane reached behind her and put the bundle of cloths at the foot of the bed. she noticed the fluid and dark blood on the discarded cloth on the floor at her feet.

Eva cried out and her legs shook.

Jane reached toward her stomach.

"Don't touch her stomach, chile. She's tender there," Dinah said softly, not raising her eyes to her.

"It's all right . . ." Jane said, stroking Eva's arm instead. She looked down over the sheet at Eva's distended body and the baby's dark head appeared.

"Bear down, honey, this baby's crowning."

Eva groaned and bore down, and the baby's head turned in the black woman's hands. Jane gulped as Eva pushed, and then there it was in Dinah's hands! Dinah quickly wiped the baby's nose and face with the cloth and held the breathing and crying baby.

"It's a little girl, Eva!" Jane exclaimed, "a beautiful little girl." Breathless with the sight of the baby, she washed Eva's face with the cool cloth.

"A girl?" Eva repeated after her—"Let me have her, Dinah." Her arms came up off the bed. Limp from the effort of the birth, Eva took her baby in her arms.

As Eva held the baby, Jane washed her with a warm cloth. She felt the urge to take the baby to her own breast.

"Oh, she is darling, Eva, so darling . . ."

The baby's eyes opened—the clearest blue Jane had ever seen— and her little tongue came out onto her lips. Her face wrinkled up and she shut her eyes, making a sound like a small animal.

Eva turned the baby against her breast.

"Thank you, auntie Jane," Eva said.

"Oh, Eva, a little baby girl . . ." Jane said so gently, she herself might have borne the child.

During the following winter when Eva suckled the child in the rocking chair by the fireplace, the need to take the baby in her arms nearly overwhelmed Jane. She could even feel the small eager mouth closing over her nipples. So obvious was her passion when she made small talk, or folded linen, Eva would hand the infant to her and Jane would take the baby in her arms and hold her against her clothed breast, tenderly cradling her neck and head in her hands. At such moments, she held her own future, and the terror of childbirth she experienced in watching the baby's birth vanished. Or when the baby slept, her tiny blonde head on the small pillow, Jane would gaze longingly at her and feel her every sigh and movement beneath the small blankets, the baby's sighs and movements echoing her own heartbeats. A miracle lay within the cradle—and how painful to resist taking her up and covering her with kisses! She was Eva's baby, John's baby, and, for Jane, she was also *her* baby, especially on the very coldest winter nights when she longed to have the infant in bed with her, envying her parents their child lying between them.

And during the following spring, summer, and fall as the baby grew, Jane bathed and dressed her, leaned over her and let the child pull at her hair—how those tugs brought her lips to her neck, making the baby smile! Those innocent eyes quickened the mother-urge in her, turning her thoughts to David and the same miracle awaiting them. What color eyes, hair, what shaped nose, and how light would *their* baby's eyebrows be? And the shape of the budding mouth would be the same because she and John were sister and brother, and because David had red hair like John, and because her own father had light hair like Eva's—Wouldn't *her* baby have auburn-colored hair?

And then in fall, Eva bore a little boy, and James had a little brother, little Eva two brothers! And the house seemed only a little small.

Then John observed her when the third child came, evaluating her as a mother with many children. Did he think her love for their baby girl, for little James, had lessened because of a third child? Could one tire of diapers and feedings and the care an infant required when David waited for her a couple of miles up river? Did the work of caring for babies gradually dampen her passion to bear them? prompting John to ask in late fall while the family sat by the fire, "Do you want a large family, Jane?"

"Oh, yes, John . . ." she answered, welcoming, however, because exhausted by her attention to little Eva, a day up river alone with David. But she clung to her answer, feeling her carefree girlhood only bespoke a flickering desire to momentarily escape. Though as time passed, her forgotten concern with Sarah Jones' silence and her own desire for a family inevitably stirred within her again.

12

Christmas

1771

It turned warm, and snow floated over the hill and the bay. When the wind came up, it swirled dizzily and the roof made small creaking sounds under the weight of it.

Jane lifted her niece and tapped the window to draw her attention to the falling snow. The child looked quietly, her fine blonde hair curving over her ears. Then as darkness curtained the window, she squirmed. How quickly darkness falls, Jane thought putting her niece down on the floor.

"On summer evenings the sun lingers on the far shore, then dallies at the back of the house—but it leaves without notice in winter," she observed, turning around, only to notice Eva looking at the empty tree frame across the room. "They'll be back soon, Eva, don't fret," she said, as she left the window and paused by the table and the small, finger-shaped candles. "It takes time to select the right tree." But the house did seem empty.

"I shouldn't fret, but James will be soaked."

Something struck the windows. Jane glanced back at the black pane as though someone tapped there.

"Sleet," she observed.

"We'll jes hang this line for the chile's clothes," Dinah declared, coming from her room with a clothesline which she looped over hooks on the far wall.

A stew simmered over the fire and the light flickered off the log walls. The aroma of baking bread and the scent of evergreen wreathes filled the room.

"Isn't it better to be inside, Dumpling?"

Eva laid her sewing aside and hugged her daughter. The little girl curled her legs up and snuggled against her mother. She looked with large blue eyes at the fire as the sleet hissed and crackled against the windows.

The sight of Eva and her daughter filled Jane with renewed longing. She rolled a candle from the table between her fingers and her eyes darted to the mantel and the maple sugar wrapped in a small box.

"Can she have a piece?"

"Yes."

She took the box wrapped in green paper and red ribbon and handed it to the child. She opened the box and took the sugar in her small fingers.

Jane picked the paper off the floor. "A present from uncle David."

The child tentatively closed her lips over the sugar.

"Good?"

The child smiled.

"Don't forget the bread," Eva said.

Jane opened the oven door at the side of the fireplace and slid in the peel, lifting first one loaf and then the other.

"These are baked."

"A little longer—Oh, it would be so hard without you, Jane," Eva declared, lifting her strained knee and re-positioning the pillow.

"You'll walk soon," Jane said sympathetically, though Eva's needing her kept in abeyance the inevitable thoughts winter brought.

"You haven't worked on your pillow-set . . ."

"We haven't set a date. It's not as though my carriage is at the door."

Jane didn't want to think about David's not working with the Dutch mill completed in the fall, nor did she wish to think of his mother's continuing refusal to speak of his land. Her silence had piqued her into laying her pillow-set aside and to take up knitting and sewing for her niece and nephew. She had knitted a cream-white sweater for little Eva, mittens for James, and scarves and hats for them both from wool Eva had spun since they bought no English yarn.

"Should I bring out the presents?"

"Let's wait," Eva suggested.

No sooner did she speak then the door opened and James scrambled over the threshold, hopping from one foot to the other.

Ice rattled in the doorway as John pushed the tree, smelling of sap and snow and covered with small brown cones no larger than incense sticks, through it.

"James found the tree," he said, setting it in the stand.

James wriggled out of his wet coat and dropped his hat on the floor.

"It's lovely," his mother said. "Dinah has dry clothes, James." Suddenly Eva was radiant with the return of her husband and son and the boy running to her.

John hung his hat on the peg near the front door. He walked across the room to a chair. "We met David. Asked him to come with us, but he said his mother waited for him," he said non-committedly as he lit his pipe and sent blue smoke into the room.

"Oh," Jane said, feeling a pang.

"I asked him," John repeated, as though now finding it odd David would not return with him.

She picked up the candles.

"Did he speak of the island?"

"No . . ."

Jane turned to hide her embarrassment. "What's holding it up?" The three of them knew future work for David depended on it.

"The Crown won't confirm the Jessups' Patent until sure of what side of the Non-Association they're on."

"Then Daniel would favor the Non-Association," Jane said, aware of the contradiction and skirting David's not coming back to the house with John. She started to clip the candles on the tree.

"Sure Daniel can wait since he sells trees to the King."

"Should the bread come out, Jane?"

Jane clipped her last candle on the tree, and her feet seemed to stick to the floor as she went to the oven.

She laid one loaf on the cooling stand behind Eva and took another to the table, the loaf as heavy as cordwood in her trembling grip. Of course Daniel could wait, not having anything to lose. And hadn't she lived a year and a half with John and Eva? Hadn't they supported her halting progress to the altar when the understanding was that she would only live temporarily with them? Hope so long deferred now made her sick at heart.

"I don't know what this struggle is about," she declared, "but it hangs about us like chains. And how long can I live with you? This was only supposed to be temporary."

"You may live with us as long as necessary," John answered. "Daniel will grab that island as soon as he can, don't think he won't. And the Jessups will have to make up their minds soon. They must ship timber." There was no mistaking John's censure.

After dinner, Jane held little Eva. Her niece pointed at the tree which burned, though was not consumed, reminding Jane of the Burning Bush. Her great-grandfather had come to Perth Amboy nearly a century ago, bringing his dreams for the land 'flowing with milk and honey' with him. Dreams for a better life had imbued her family with hope eternal, but how remote her own dreams now seemed!

She glanced at her brother. She loved him, but couldn't resist connecting his rupture with her father over the stamps and his going to law with the current troubles and David not working. When would he work again? Daniel still milled lumber and floated logs to the City, but he didn't need David for that, only for building. She excused her brother because she loved him, but nothing had excused Daniel for giving David false hopes.

The lights on the tree faded. 'Better is a dinner of herbs where love is than a fatted ox and hatred with it', she thought, comparing John to Daniel's and his mother's practices.

But why hadn't David returned with him and James before dinner? What had his mother demanded of him? Did his not coming to the house signal a refusal not to come for Christmas dinner tomorrow?

The following day, however, David did come to dinner. She and David walked by the wheat field. Jane pushed her hands into her muff. The oaks and maples, and the pines and hemlocks on the hill and along the river shimmered in the armor of last night's storm. The pines titled like chandeliers. The dinner, David holding her arm, the crystal under her shoes, and the amber light and crisp blue sky made the afternoon a hymn. Jane breathed the cold air. Her present contentment allowed her to question him as to why he hadn't returned to the house with John last night.

"I didn't want to explain to mother," he only answered, pushing his hands into his pockets.

His answer pricked her—She thought the day's radiance and her present mood might buffer his answer, shield her with indifference toward his mother. But his reply irritated her—Why had *he* to explain to her after what they endured from her?

"Why does she stand between us like this?" she asked openly, unable to conceal her wounded feelings.

"She's not standing between us, Jen," he shrugged evasively.

"Then why must you explain to her? *Her* silence requires an explanation." She looked at the sky, which seemed to lose its color. The branches of the elms clawed the air. Discussing his mother made her brittle and harsh. "Explain, David." She now realized her last night's humiliation had ripened to bitterness overnight.

"My father's ghost haunts her."

"His ghost?" Jane asked incredulously.

"But he's dead, and its over," he stated.

"What's over?" She felt some malignancy stalked her.

He waved his hand.

"That time you visited John at Princeton, father said you were with child."

"With child!" she flushed.

David threw up his hands.

"—Mother told me yesterday. But he's dead and it's over," he insisted, taking her arm, the sickening nature of the accusation evident on his face.

"And you didn't come last night because your mother told you this?"

"I would have come."

"You believe her?"

"No, it's slander!"

"And your family believes this?"

"I don't know what they believe!" he exclaimed with exasperation and anger.

"How cruel," she said, looking at the icy ground. "So this explains her and Daniel . . . ."

"I spoke to her last night."

"And?"

David shook his head.

"And you talked with her.—'The words of the wicked lie in wait for blood, but the mouth of the upright delivers men'. I'm innocent, I tell you!"

"I *affronted* her, Jane," David said in anguished self-defense. "Believe me, I did."

"The Lord hates 'a false witness who breathes out lies; and a man who sows discord among brothers,' David Jones. Your family drinks from a poisoned well . . ." she said, feeling physically sick. "And what else have they laid up for us?"

"Father estranged them."

"And nothing will change that as long as we both live!" she cried with shock and horror at his disclosure, the future seeming to crack like the ice crystals under her clogs as she turned away from him back to the house.

"Jane, please," David implored after her.

*   *   *

After knocking, James entered the room with a cup of mint tea. A gray silhouette stood by her bedside.

"Auntie Jane?"

"Put it on the table, please, James."

"Are you feeling better?"

She smoothed her hair back and looked at the ceiling rafters. "Yes," she answered, feeling weak, but no longer feverish, as a bluejay announced dawn. "Have you eaten breakfast?" She looked sadly at the young boy's tender, caring face.

"Yes," he answered. "'Uncle' David came last night . . ." he innocently volunteered, wanting his Auntie to be well again.

Jane thought she had heard David's voice at the height of her fever, half-perceived him standing by her bed, flushing her delirium with Sappho-like passion: "'If I meet you suddenly, I can't speak— my tongue is broken; a thin flame runs under my skin; seeing nothing, hearing only my own ears drumming, I drip with sweat; trembling shakes my body and I turn paler than dry grass. At such times death isn't far from me.'"

She closed her eyes. "How long have I been ill?"

"Three days, Auntie."

She turned her face away. Why had Thomas Jones slandered her? Because of her long hair, the way she walked, for some unsuspected pride in her manner, or because David loved her? Or because of her father, or her brothers, or Thomas Jones' own guilt for appearing naked and drunk behind her that night after his wife had gone to bed and David had gone outside? She had dropped the plate she washed when she saw him unexpectedly standing behind her like that. Or was it because her own father, on returning from a neighboring parish, had found Thomas Jones visiting Catherine? Had he slandered her for these reasons—not even telling his son until his mother said this now, a more heinous crime than the slander itself?

Her guiltless shame gave way to anger, and she raised herself on her elbow in the growing light. Why should she question the motives of a dead man! Rather she should confront his wife, show her the non-existent *prima brava* lines on her abdomen!

She pushed her legs over the side of the bed, and her hair fell thickly over her knees. Her nephew stood holding the tea, innocently bearing her cup like her second. Seeing the boy and beholding his unconditional innocence and loyalty to her made her want to cry. And what would result from affronting Sarah Jones, except further hardening the woman toward her? She took the cup from her nephew and kissed him. She then sipped the tea and it soothed her aching soul.

Before she left her room, she couldn't help but overhear John and Eva beyond her door guessing at the cause of her illness. What could she tell them? If they doubted David, wouldn't she have to expose his father to clear him?

She opened the door. John turned toward her at the other end of the room.

"Jane!" he exclaimed, coming anxiously to her.

"I'm well now, John," she replied, self-consciously accepting the close way he looked at her.

"What's going on?" he asked.

"John," Eva intervened from her chair.

"I can talk, Eva," Jane said, sitting at the table. "I must speak." She had to speak. She rested her arm on the cool planks. She paused, looking at her outstretched fingers. "It's David's father."

"His father?"

"David didn't come Christmas Eve because his mother told him I went to Princeton to bear a child."

"What?" John demanded angrily.

"*And* it's his mother," she said helplessly.

"His mother!"

"And yet I have done nothing!" Jane exclaimed, rubbing her fingers on the table, the tears rushing to her eyes. Then it came to her, *that* day when she and David walked—The images flowed as the scene came to life: the reds and oranges, the *potpourri* scents of fall, the black shadows against the back of the Jones' barn, the blending of grass and bushes, Sarah's half-rising figure—and she and David had walked on, her not knowing if he saw his mother, not knowing what she saw meant anything, until her suspicion grew to certainty when she saw them together—Sarah's anxious survey of the tinker's wares on her front porch when she and David returned to her house. Yes, she had seen her that day! Jane clenched her fist. The color rose to her cheeks. "I saw Sarah Jones with someone. I had forgotten it." She wiped her cheeks.

"You saw her with someone?" John asked.

"With a tinker behind the Jones' barn after Princeton," she answered, ashamed of mentioning it.

"Did David see her?"

"I don't know. But why should *he* repeat to me what she told him, if he loves me?" she cried with anguish unable to withhold from them the depths of her pain and grief.

"Oh, Jane . . ." Eva said, rising from her chair and clasping her daughter-in-law's shoulders. "It can't be that."

"And if it is?" Jane sobbed. "We have no future."

"Let me talk to him," John nearly demanded of her.

"No," she refused him softly, rubbing the back of her hand across her eyes. "David has to love me—you can't make him love me. Something's happened—" but she was at a loss to say what had happened to him.

"If he loves you, he'd challenge his own mother," John insisted.

"Maybe he doesn't know about her," Eva pointed out.

"And how can I find out without telling him myself and having him hate me for it?" Jane nearly sobbed.

"If she knows you know, she's gambling on your saying nothing."

"Talk to him," Eva counseled.

"He's close to her!" Jane confessed.

"You are not certain of him, then," Eva observed. "And if you're not certain . . ."

"Oh, don't say it, Eva," Jane implored her with despair in her voice. "I can't think that he doesn't love me. But how can I be certain?" she asked wretchedly, not wanting a commitment from David because he was only angry with his mother, if he didn't know about her. She wanted him to love her for herself. *He* had to feel certain, had to be constant as air. "I must tell him I was only ill," she said. "But I'm sure he loves me," she affirmed, while yet wondering how she would know.

13

1772

Jane didn't avoid Sarah Jones that spring or summer. David came to John's house, and Jane visited David at his mother's. She even let David believe no problem existed between them, and she never revealed, by word or gesture, to Sarah Jones any knowledge of what her son had said to her at Christmas. Nor did John or Eva speak to David about his mother's slander—with the result, the lovers' hopes and dreams sprouted again like spring flowers. But a flower doesn't sprout without the promise of blooming, and Jane never lost sight of pressing David about his mother, and, so inevitably, his mother's silence about his land, with its promise of marriage, arose again.

David, himself, remembered when Polly questioned him at Fort Edward the day he first met her at the spring about why he and Jane didn't marry and live with his mother. He never thought what his mother had said at Christmas had anything to do with her making him wait. He thought, rather, that it had more to do with Daniel's hold on her and her property—Or even that his mother felt insecure about his marrying now and leaving her.

"I understand now," David said abruptly, when he and Jane took James fishing. Taking the line from James, he pulled the baited hook off the bottom of the river. "Don't let it rest on the bottom, James."

He glanced at Jane sitting a few feet from him on the bank, half-hoping she hadn't heard what he wanted to admit. Yet how beautiful she looked with her hair plaited and layered in a French braid, which glistened like linen rope in the sunshine. How could he have thought the trouble between her and his mother happened because of what his mother did and wanted to keep hidden?

"You refer to Christmas . . ." Jane said softly, hoping he would declare himself to her now.

"Yes, Christmas . . ." he answered.

"I never had anything against her," she said so quietly and diplomatically that he might not have heard her. She watched the line slacken, as the current made a question mark of it on the surface of the water.

David coughed, holding James' attention on his line, "See, you've let it hit bottom again."

Jane looked away. Did he know about the incident behind the barn? She had the feeling that he did know.

"Tell me, you knew about her," he himself suddenly revealed.

"Tell me first whether you believed her—whether you doubted me at Christmas." Jane's low whisper left her lips like a razored prayer.

"I didn't doubt you," he said firmly, looking at her with fleeting pain in his eyes. "But I had forgotten . . ." he paused. So completely had he blotted what he saw from his memory that he hadn't even recalled it when speaking to Polly.

"Then you know . . ."

"Yes," he answered, beyond the boy's hearing. "I had hoped that you hadn't seen."

"And I of you," she said, relieved, but also tight with the expectation that he would declare himself anew to her.

He left the boy's side and went to her. "So you don't hate me for it . . ." he whispered.

"Not if you've chosen," she answered, ready to absolve him for his ambiguous reaction to her that day of telling her and his silence up until now.

"I chose *you* long ago." He took her hand and pressed it to his lips.

"And can she still say nothing about our property?" Jane couldn't resist challenging.

"She's my mother . . ." David answered abjectly.

"Then you *haven't* chosen," she said, pressing him and resisting pulling away from him, seeking to hold him to a commitment to her, if he really loved her. "How can you say that after what you know about her? I'm going to be your wife. What do you expect of me?" she then asked bitterly.

"I can't affront her with what I know. It would kill her. Surely you understand," he pleaded with her.

"And so I should suffer and accept this?" she challenged again.

"She's suffering for what she has done—"

"I don't believe it." Jane pulled away from him. She wanted to believe Sarah suffered, but she couldn't believe it, for it wasn't natural to suffer without changing, and Sarah Jones hadn't changed . . . but, if she had suffered, would that make it any easier for her and David with her continued silence? "Maybe I could live with it, if I knew she suffered," she said, nonetheless, without bitterness, not wanting to be spiteful because it wasn't in her nature. "Maybe then I could endure her."

"Jane, you're stronger than her—Please, understand."

"To what advantage am I stronger?" she asked, not wanting to let him off easily. "Maybe she wants you to believe that to burden me with it, to keep me silent, to keep me from insisting with you that she do something about the land she promised you for our home before we came up here."

"I can't change her, and you understand things."

"Understand what? That she hasn't relented?" Suddenly she felt sorry for him. She wanted to rise above his mother, yet also wanted to hurt her, to make her feel the pain she had inflicted on them. Her sense of justice cried out for it.

"So I should forget, turn the other cheek, because she's your mother and because you've always done that? I could do it, and let her have her way. But what would that do to us?" Yet, did she prefer indifference to the woman rather than hatred? Wouldn't that hurt her more? And hadn't David said he had chosen her— didn't that close the issue of his mother between them? Did she need his love demonstrated beyond the admission his mother lied and acted immorally? Perhaps she could forget the injury done her as long as they both knew the truth about her. Couldn't she mistress this new attitude, carry on as though Sarah could do nothing to her? That what she did, didn't matter? David *had* declared himself—and he wanted her to help him, had asked her for understanding. But she recoiled, not admitting to herself that David was weak in the face of his mother. Her love for him in his situation blinded her—in a burst of passion in waiting for so long for him to speak, she capitulated to him.

"We're not going to let her hurt us, are we, David?" Looking into his eyes she grew confused and lost sight of her object.

"No—she'll see she has no influence, that she can't do anything to us, or change us," he agreed passionately, seeing her suddenly relent toward him.

"But your mother won't change, David," she sprang back.

"You can do this for me, though, can't you?" he pleaded with her again. "I'm afraid of killing her."

His pleading eyes dissolved her. How helpless she felt when he looked at her that way! She truly hated the idea that he would suffer more than he already had because of his mother. For a moment, nothing but his happiness mattered to her—not even her own.

"It is *our* future, not hers, and we're still young, aren't we?" she exclaimed, grasping at least for some shred of support from him. "We understand this, don't we? At least we know her, don't we? And it's for you, not her," she said firmly, needing him to at least affirm that she did only what he asked of her because *he* asked it.

"Yes, I *knew* you would understand, Jen," he said, taking her hand with relief, only too aware that they were both caught by Aphrodite even when neither of their interests seemed to be favored.

"And you love me more for doing this, David? Tell me," she said, wanting to cry at what her love for him had wrung from her. "It's only because I love you," she said, near tears.

"And, I love you the more for it, Jen. God, Jen, I do, and I hardly know what's happening when I'm with you."

14

July approached.

Since spring when David declared himself anew to her on the riverbank while fishing with James after his mother's accusations at Christmas, Jane realized that her love for him had come as unexpectedly as the scent of strawberries that day three years ago in the fields of Lamington. Love had come without reason or explanation in his leaning against the tree and looking at her. Up to that time, he had been one of many boys among her brothers and among his, and, then, when they had all left home and her father had died, there *he* was. They had seemed at first to share their loneliness from a distance—he was the boy left by *his* brothers to work the neighboring farm, and she was the lonely and bereaved girl down the road, the youngest and only sister of her brothers. Then it happened between them among the strawberries. Their future dreams together had naturally followed the leap of her heart that day.

And so for David's sake, alone on the farm living with his mother and father, she now truly resisted resenting his mother, lest her resentment hurt him and also disfigure her own feelings for him, making her love hard and brittle, defiant and grasping. And so now too since Christmas, when Sarah Jones turned her head a certain way, or refused to answer a question put to her, she reminded herself of David's love and what they shared. She reminded herself of his truthfulness and his present suffering because of her. And if she needed additional strength to resist showing resentment toward his mother for her continuing silence about their marriage, she found strength in his face and yearning eyes, and in her feeling that the future belonged to them, not his mother. And so, recalling the nature of their love and its beginnings, she attended the auction in late July at Patrick Smythe's house in Edward with renewed hope.

The bidding opened on a sideboard. Daniel hadn't bought the Jessups' island and David had no work, though he earned some money from the ferry he had built in the spring. He even looked prosperous beside her in his high boots and wig. But could they afford the sideboard? Or could they *not* afford to try to buy it, to live without the inspiration of owning it to place in their new home when that time came? If they could buy it, it would inspire them toward their new home. In the *lange strahlers* of the afternoon, which pierced the yard in front of Pat Smythe's house like orange columns, the mahogany sideboard glowed with oriental richness, and she longed for it as though the very shape of her imagined house had transformed itself in miniature into the shape of the sideboard.

"Twenty pounds, who'll give twenty pounds?" the auctioneer called.

Jane recognized people at the auction: The Tuttles and the Hiltons, who lived between John and the Joneses; Hugh Munro, Adam Ramsey, and the Freels, who lived across the road from Sarah McNeil. There were also people from Kingsbury, the Corners, Argyle and Salem whom she did not know. Deacon Shepard, another of John's neighbors, joined the bidding.

"Thirty pounds!"

David nodded.

"Forty pounds!"

Jane listened, her a hair a golden red in the slanting light, holding David's hand, only too aware that forty pounds was considerable for them.

"Fifty pounds!"

She gasped. Fifty pounds sounded like a sudden musket shot! If the sideboard went higher than that, what of their house itself? Suddenly she feared the sideboard *would* elude them; even drag them penniless after it—She turned to Content and Polly and said, "Fifty pounds for one appointment? How can anyone build a house when appointments cost so?"

"Oh, th' cost will shoot up," Polly answered simply, as though knowing of auctions and the value of furniture, for hadn't she often predicted the cost of all things would spiral?

Surely they couldn't buy it, Jane thought. She and David had saved only three hundred pounds, and here the sideboard was at fifty!

One of the Jessup brothers spoke up.

"Sixty!"

The auctioneer looked at David and he nodded.

"David, we can't spend anymore than that. Stop bidding," she said, growing frightened at the prospect of parting with more of their money. But was there a chance he would soon begin work on the bridge? But what chance?. Daniel had not bought the island yet, and the three hundred pounds they had already saved included the one hundred and seventy willed to her by her father.

"It is seventy."

The sandalwood inlay of the sideboard gleamed. Its allure masked impoverishment, the price continued to climb. Jane was at once drawn to it and repelled by it.

"Ye're in deep, lass, think o' th' other things ye'll need first. Appointments come last," Polly said.

"Oh, I know, Polly!" she said.

"Eighty pounds."

"Do you want it, Jen?" David asked turning to her, but not seeing her for being caught up in the bidding.

"Ninety pounds."

"Look at it, Ladies. Not another from here to the City!"

David held the bid at ninety pounds.

"Who'll give one-hundred? One hundred to Mister Jessup. Now One-ten, Mister Jones, do I hear one-twenty?"

"No more, David!" she cried, suddenly grasping his arm, terrified by his expression. "Stop." She tried to conceal her insistence from the crowd in only squeezing his arm harder. But he didn't look at her. His face was set—she could only think that he was mistakenly doing this for her, that he could clear all their disappointments in his buying it.

"One-thirty, one-forty. Do I hear one-fifty, two-hundred pounds?"

"We face ruin," she pleaded, certain of disaster.

"You should have it," he answered, not really hearing her.

"No," she half-cried, "it's too much. Listen to me!" The attention of the crowd checked her from grasping his other arm and directly facing him.

"Two-hundred and fifty pounds . . ."

What began with simple hope and longing became nightmarish. Tears hung on her lashes. She wanted to rush to the auction block and to stop the merciless chant of the auctioneer who stood over them like an executioner.

"Three-hundred . . . do I hear three-hundred, Mister Jones?"

"Four-hundred, four-fifty . . ."

The auctioneer looked from David to Ebenezer Jessup.

"Five-hundred. Five-hundred pounds, Mister Jones."

"David!" she cried desperately, clutching his arm with all her strength.

"Five-hundred . . . five . . . five . . . sold! to Ebenezer Jessup for four-hundred and fifty pounds Sterling!" and the gavel came down on the block.

"Damn!" David exclaimed, clasping her wrist, seeming to recognize her presence for the first time.

She held his arm for support, her legs like pudding.

"How could you?" she gasped, feeling faint, glancing over at Ebenezer Jessup who lifted his notes for the sideboard from what looked like a stack of table napkins in his hand. "Take me away from here," she said, the color gone from her face as though she stood before the gates of a gaol. And who could believe for a moment that Ebenezer Jessup had no money, and that he needed to sell the island? She found herself pushing David from the crowd.

The strength began to return to her legs as they made their way through the people. James Higson stood before them as they made their way.

Jane looked at his friendly face, his expression doing little to relieve the bitterness, which followed her mortification at not only having nearly lost their savings, but having risked indebtedness.

"Don't mind it, David," he declared, gesturing disdainfully toward Jessup, unmindful of David's circumstances, "appointments don't make the man."

Jane caught her breath.

"I should have the house first," David replied irritably, seeing him, still seemingly unconscious of how close he had come to utter ruin.

"Lucky he didn't stick ye with it, David Jones, after driving up th' price," Polly said pointedly.

Polly's remark strickened Jane, for she knew that Polly fully grasped the consequences of a five hundred pound indebtedness. "Maybe there was a chance at fifty pounds," Jane said weakly, trying to convey to Polly not to say more.

"It won't ruin Jessup, but, I say, what's happening back there?" James asked, looking back at the crowd.

Jane turned quickly, noticing Content hadn't followed them. She clasped her neck with her hand when she saw Content kneeling in a circle of people clutching her breast—

"Get Doctor Smythe!" someone called.

Jane involuntarily turned toward the auction stand where Doctor Smythe jumped from it. She looked quickly back at Content—Jacob Hix lay on his back at her knees! James Higson rushed by her, back to where they had stood. David followed and Polly took her arm.

"Come, lass."

When they reached the spot, James was pushing on Jacob's chest—his pushing sounding like breaking straw. Jacob's face turned white, then gray.

"He's gone, James," Doctor Smythe said, standing up.

"No!" Content cried.

"Yes. A heart attack," the doctor confirmed.

Jane tried to reach for her, but had to make way for the men lifting Jacob's body. "Oh, Content!" she wanted to cry as James and David carried her husband toward the shaded doorway of Pat Smythe's house.

Content then rushed by her as the crowd moved mutely toward the house.

Jane followed into the house and saw Jacob lying on the parlor table. Someone passed her into the room.

"God willed it, Content," Abraham then said, clasping his daughter in his arms.

"And with our anniversary tomorrow . . ." Content sobbed.

Dark fumes coiled snake-like from the lamp on the table where Jacob lay. Jane twisted her handkerchief in her hands in the dim light. Like a fickle wind, God had taken her father like that. She touched her bobbing head and leaned against David. She seemed to float in a measureless darkness in response to her father's calls, 'Jane! Jane!' Then before she knew it, she was lying on a sofa with the salts stinging her nose and Polly chafing her wrists.

"Jane . . . Jane?"

The room swam into view. The dark ceiling threatened to fall in on her. She lifted her arms. David stroked her cheek. She sat up slowly.

"Ye fainted, lass."

"I want to go home, David," she said, the damp smell of the house making her sick.

Later, David held Charlotte's bridle as they walked along the road toward the ferry. For an instant, as the sun sank beyond the trees, Jane felt terrified and alone. A shadow hung over her.

—David had taken off his wig in the July heat. They had been spared ruin at the auction, and he had carried his friend's body into Pat Smythe's house. Her fainting had been like a brush with death. Yet how innocent he seemed, still walking with a spring in his step! The events of the day seemed of little consequence to him. Did they matter only to her—did her reminding herself through out the summer that his mother's ill opinion didn't count also only matter to her? What of *him*? Hadn't he seen how fragile and uncertain life was! and how quickly 'Tenty had become a widow?

"We must promise each other, David, never to lose sight of what we are to each other," she said, caught between wanting to rebuke him for what she perceived was his indifference since leaving the Smythes, and wanting to clasp him to her breast because he was all she had and she knew fortune had spared them.

"I felt the madness," he confessed, thinking she spoke of the auction. "But I wanted that sideboard for you more than anything."

"I meant Jacob . . ." she said, leaning over the horse, filled with dread at sinking into an early night, like Content, before life dawned for her.

"He was good," David admitted, catching her urgency. "I know, I know, how easily we forget. Oh, Jen . . ." he stopped and turned up to her. "Let me hold you."

They stood motionless on the dark and empty road, holding each other, further words unnecessary. She drew even closer to him and shuddered as that terrifying shadow she had just felt so near her left her to his embrace. She then sat upright in the saddle and wiped the perspiration from her forehead, his admission also absolving him, and freeing her of the terror of loosing him.

—At the crossing, the ferryman's cooking fire across the river gleamed beneath the hulls of crimson-edged clouds in the west.

When they boarded the ferry on the dark river, a dog's howling floated down the valley. Standing at the rail, she pressed against him and let the dog's howl sooth her as though it was a kind of threnody, reminding her this moment would always be theirs. What dominion did death hold, if David loved her? Did she need Psyche's penny and the beauty of Venus, that sideboard or even a new house, if she had him? How would she, could she, ever forget this day?

15

In the fall after the auction, Jane and David frequently went a
mile from John's to view the Tuttles' farm down by the river. There
they dreamed, even imagined, the Tuttles' property as their own,
demonstrating the truth that, regardless of the obstacles, young
lovers will still cling to their dreams.

The path glowed with bright fall leaves under the cool trees
and morning yellow bathed the woods before the harshness of
noon as the small wagon left the road.

Jane stroked her niece beside her on the seat. They carried a
basket of ham, cheese, bread, pieces of cold chicken, and wine.

Little Eva kneeled on the seat and looked down at the basket
behind her as the wagon tilted up the hill.

"Hungry?" Jane asked her, filled with a sense of completeness
and joy because, as with after the auction in July on the ferry with
David that evening, she had again experienced a profound newness
this very morning outside John's house as she sat watching the sun
rise over the bay:

—The new Jerusalem had presented itself in a gold reflection
off the water. In the flickering colors of the trees on the water, she
saw herself as a bride adorned by heaven for David; saw herself as
his sanctuary and truth in the water given to the thirsty without
price; and saw herself as his temple with floor and foundation of
pure gold, clear as glass, adorned with sapphire and carnelian and
all the precious stones of the awakening. "'Behold, I make all things
new!'" she inspired from the BIBLE in her lap, placing her hand
over the line, letting the sensuous Mediterranean longing, and the
morning's *natura Americana,* which adorned her, deepen her love
for him. "'It is done! I am the Alpha and Omega, the beginning
and the end.'"

"Oh, sacred September, cousin of July! how you affirm my love, how you lift me from 'the sea that is no more, the lake burning with fire and brimstone, that second death suffered by all liars,'" she declared of his family. "—How the ongoing seasons and the consolations of antiquity strip me of their poison-dyed garment and dress me in bridal gold!" she prayed as she sat there, feeling the fulsomeness of life, poetically enhanced by the BOOK in the very depths of her nature, guarded her from all mishaps.

But, then, as she intensely relived her morning communion, Charlotte stopped at the top of the road—Jane saw two Indians talking on the hill in the sunlight! One of the men was shorter than David—and younger, perhaps by a couple of years. The other man was taller, dressed like an Indian, but as black as a slave.—He wore a wig! Seeing the man wearing the wig blocked her reverie and following impulse to turn the wagon around.

She nervously flicked the reins and the wheels crushed the fallen leaves. Sight of the wig itself drew her forward like the silent tolling of a bell. She couldn't take her eyes from it, as the mare pulled the wagon toward a bush.

She stepped from the wagon, terrified by what impression her own carnelian loops in the sun might make on them. She had a deep, almost uncontrollable fear of Indians engendered in her by the French War, which the wig stirred. She tied the reins to the bush with trembling fingers. Yet not wanting to show the fear and horror in her eyes, she turned and faced the dark, almost black, man who wore the wig.

Where was David! What had happened to him! She verged on panic.

She reached for the blanket in the wagon and looked over her shoulder, seeing the fold of the wig and the unmistakable strawberry stains. Her gaze drifted over the glowing leaves, the bleached roof of the Tuttles' barn, and the silver river beyond. She put her arms around the child, and, hardly conscious of doing so, took the blanket and lifted the child from the wagon.

She walked toward the Indians and felt her legs turning to sand. She fought the impulse to turn and run. Her niece pulled

away from her. She was powerless to go after the child, or to even
call to her. She laid the blanket on the ground as though some
action in a dream she was watching. Little Eva ran down the hill.
Jane looked at the wig. The man stood up. Speechlessly, she
watched him walk deliberately down the hill. She lifted her arm
as if to beckon the little girl back to her—but the man approached
the child and spoke to her. He took her by the hand! Jane looked
with terror at the strawberry stains and the Indian's black face as
he turned back to her, bringing the child with him. Grief and
horror seized her—tears splashed in her eyes when he approached
her.

"Don't be frightened," he said. "You don't want to lose her."

"Indians don't wear wigs!" she cried, clutching the child from
him.

"No," he agreed, "but the white man had no need of it," he
answered matter-of-factly, unconcerned by her reaction to him.

"What white man!" she exclaimed, drawing back and stepping
away from him with her hand on her neck as she noticed the black
horse hair stitching which closed the tear above the right temple
where David often lifted it with his thumb. She imagined the
Indian plying his needle at the wig. "Did he have red hair?" she
gasped.

"Over his ears . . ."

"What happened to him!" she cried.

"He didn't want to part with it," the man only volunteered,
turning away from her and speaking to the other Indian.

She watched him walk back to the other Indian. Their strange
language filling her with inexpressible fear and shock. "Didn't want
to part with it!" she cried, unable to keep from rushing after him.
She didn't care for herself, didn't care even about her niece so filled
with anguish was she in wanting to know.

"Jane! Louis!" David waved, suddenly appearing on the hillside.

She stopped: "David!" she cried, falling headlong toward him,
"oh, David!" She threw herself on him.

"Why what is it!" he exclaimed at her manner. "I'm only late,"
he said, catching her.

"That man, your wig!" she gasped, trying to control her voice when she knew they watched her from the hill.

"What?" He felt her shaking in his arms. He shook his head. "I *sold* the wig yesterday. The man's come to pay me for it." He held her chin up and looked at her. "Oh, Jane . . ." he said, realizing what she feared before she interrupted him.

"I didn't know . . . seeing him like this . . ." she brushed at her tears.

"He's a friend. I thought I would be here first. I forgot to mention it. It's all right, Jen," he tried to explain, holding her by the shoulders.

"You can't imagine, David!" she said against his shoulder. "You didn't tell me," her voice was plaintive. As she held him the fainting spell she had had at Pat Smythe's threatened her again. She felt the same dizziness with her head against his shoulder. She allowed him to press and soothe her with his arms—she turned her face up to him and breathed deeply, dispelling the dizziness and the sickness of her fright, but she still trembled and her heart still pounded as she walked up the hill with him.

They approached the Indian. He still seemed not at all concerned at her reaction to him, but merely invited David to speak. Jane tried to fathom those black eyes, but they were as unrevealing as pitch. She shuddered with David's taking her by the elbow—

"This is Louis Cook and Thomas Williams, Jane."

She glanced up at the men and wiped her cheek with the back of her hand, having no words with which to reply. She had never been this close to Indians, never known such fresh and sharp fear of them as this.

"Jane lives this side the bay, Louis," David explained to him. "You gave her a fright," he half-laughed, looking at her, his eyes seeking her forgiveness for this imbroglio. "We hunt together, Jen," he added, hoping that she would say something, hating himself for not having told her he first met these men at the mill the fall following seeing Thomas and his father shoot that turkey at Daniel's the summer he had arrived. If only he had told her about them, he could have spared her this! "They're from St. Regis and

Kahnawake," he said awkwardly, noting that though she now nodded, he could see this pitiful bit of information meant little to her.

"On the St. Lawrence River and near Montreal," Louis clarified.

"Did you bring the money?" David then asked, wanting to be done with his business so he could explain to her.

"Ten pounds," Louis nodded, taking the bills from his pouch.

Jane's glance involuntarily fell on the notes the man took from his pouch. The man's long fingers clasped a roll of paper and peeled them away. He handed them to David. The strangeness of seeing this Indian handle money displaced her earlier shock and fear. The transaction now made her angry. Hadn't David worn that wig when they first declared themselves in Lamington? Hadn't she arrested his strawberry-stained fingers when he tried to adjust it on his head? How could he sell it without telling her? And why to Indians? She had to resist turning away from the transaction.

David folded the notes and looked at her. "We can add this to our savings, Jen."

She glanced at the ground without replying.

"Louis wishes to impress Johnson!" Thomas Williams laughed.

Jane looked at him. His voice was almost boyish, belying his muscularity and almost cat-like appearance.

"If he dresses like an Indian, I can dress like a white man," Louis retorted.

Jane recoiled. The man's intention insulting her wounded feelings. She felt disgraced and pre-empted, as though what she felt about what David was doing with these men scarcely mattered, as it mattered not at all to them.

"Oh, don't sell it, David, I can sew it, and take the stains out . . ." she said suddenly, making herself feel even worse with having to appeal to him like this in front of these people.

"It's a joke, Jen," he said. "—I'll buy a new one. You can pick it out after we start the bridge!" he declared, his clear effort to save face vanishing in the instant of remembering his good news.

"The bridge?" she asked, not fully grasping what he meant, even half-thinking that he only evaded her.

"Yes, Daniel's bought the island! Solomon just told me. That's why I'm late."

"You have work then?" The full meaning of what he was saying washed over her.

"Yes, Daniel and Abraham plan another mill. We'll have lumber," David continued to declare with unchecked enthusiasm. "Look, Jen, I needed a new wig," he added half-apologetically.

The news lifted Jane from the tangle of feelings this incident excited in her. How long they had waited for this news which she thought would never come! Suddenly she was lifted.

"Look," Louis said, interrupting him.

Jane followed his pointing hand to where smoke churned slowly over the Tuttles' barn scooping large patches of blue out of the sky. She stepped back. She looked at David for an explanation—she even glanced at the Indians—

They gazed at the barn as though rooted to the hill. They then turned wordlessly away from both her and David for the path, which led over the other side of the hill.

Jane turned back to the smoke. Flames licked the eves and crawled up the white shingles. She watched speechlessly when a scream came from the building.

"Oh, my God, David," she exclaimed, chilled by the unearthly sound.

"A horse, Louis!" David, turned from her, calling to the departing Indians as though for help.

But Louis only waved as he kept walking.

"Do something, David!" she cried, clutching his arm. But what could he do! They were helpless bystanders; the barn was a volcano of flame! Red sheets rolled up the roof to the ridgepole.

"The barn's going like a lamp—there's nothing I can do," he said.

The fire raged like wind, and smoke blew over the hill. Shingles and boarding dissolved, leaving a glowing and cracking skeleton of timbers. Then the building fell, sending sparks and smoke over the river.

"How could that have happened?" she asked, feeling in the

air beside her for her niece without taking her eyes from the sight.

"That's no accident," David only said, half to himself.

Jane observed the void below the trees where the barn had stood. It wasn't only that an emblem of their dreams, a fantasy of her's and David's had gone up in smoke, but Mister Tuttle often came to the house to accompany John to Albany for their committee meetings on the Non-importation. If this barn burning was no accident, then what real violence threatened her brother for what he was doing? She was filled with a new dread. "*Who* would do this?" she asked.

"Let's go," he only answered, backing quickly away from the smoke and the sweet smell of burning horseflesh. "This is no place for us . . ."

Jane stared blankly at the void where the barn had been below the line of the hill. "Who *could* eat?" she asked, thinking David still stood next to her. It seemed to her they only responded to events, stood on the sidelines and suffered only what chance offered them. What would come next? She looked to David for an answer as though, beside her, he read her thoughts, but he was lifting Little Eva into the wagon. With the burning of the barn, she had even forgotten his good news about the bridge.

She walked back to the wagon and saw herself absently reaching for the basket behind the seat, though she had no appetite. He blocked her arm as she lifted it.

"Not here, Jen—"

"Of course not," she replied.

She let him guide her onto the seat. She drew Eva to her. Who could predict the future? How vulnerable and helpless she felt watching the barn burn. Everything that happened resembled a strange puppet show that she watched with odd irrelevance. Her meeting the Indians who seemed so indifferent to her; David's selling his wig; the spectacle of the burning barn; even the transaction of the island and the promise of the coming bridge occurred irrespective of her presence or existence. And yet how dedicated she felt this morning; how dedicated she felt that night on the ferry—as if she was David's 'foundation' by special reservation! And yet not a word to her about his intention in selling his wig. But how could she be reserved especially for him without her being given influence, without her existence being relevant to anything, which happened around them?

As the wagon rocked down the path through the woods, she then questioned the 'dark leap' marriage really was—Fate or Providence clearly strewn the path of love with thorns of pain and dashed hopes which finally made an uncertain dependency of her sanctuary. Yet she loved him all the more for this! But what was there for her, if she couldn't rely on David's judgment, and nothing gave her the slightest influence on events?

"You sold your wig before the sale of the island, didn't you, David?" she asked of his impulsiveness, his recklessness at the auction impressing itself upon her anew, lacerating herself with her own question.

"Yes," he reluctantly admitted.

"But you didn't really want to sell it, did you?" She was almost frantic with wanting to know that he had thought about her before selling it.

"I guess not—"

"And you thought of me, even in such a small thing?"

"Do you forgive me?" he asked, without actually realizing what she was asking.

"Yes," she answered, looking at the bobbing head of her mare as she tugged the wagon along the road, wondering whether he would ever understand her feelings. "We must trust each other," she found herself repeating what she had tried to convey to him that night while walking along the road after the auction when she experienced such terror and emptiness. But how close could two people really be? And did she really know David? She had the sense with him now that she fumbled in a dark chest looking for something she could only locate with her hands, knowing it was there, but not finding it. And why had she felt, by contrast, so complete and significant this morning? What was it in Life that held out two closed hands to her, each concealing mysteries that she found herself constantly having to choose between, hoping that she might choose the right one? She was baffled by where Life was leading her—yet her father had always told her that nothing happened without design.

They gained the road toward John's.

"Let's go to *our* place," she said, referring to where they swam that first night after arriving from Lamington, almost desperately needing the reassurance of some spot to affirm that she still had a voice that someone responded to. There, at least, surrounded by warm leaves and yellow fall grass with the sun on her face, she could still smell the river and glittering leaves and forget herself, even once again lose herself in David's caresses even if he didn't understand her feelings.

She observed him next to her manipulating the reins and guiding the wagon off the road along a barely visible path toward the river. She felt the movement of the wagon and the pressure of her niece's small body against hers as though the flicking of the reins and the pressure of that small child's flesh were the only tangible things in life. She then surrendered herself and her cares to the glittering, irresistible warmth of this fall afternoon, as though it held the only balm that life offered.

When they arrived at the spot and David left the seat beside her to tie the mare, she paused and let the sunlight and the scent of fall cleanse her skin and hair. For all of what she experienced today, life ebbed back upon her and filled her with new calm. She reached for the blanket behind her.

She spread it on the bank, almost religiously sensitive to the river ebbing shallowly at the shore grass. Scarlet sumacs concealed them from the road. She sat on the blanket, expecting David to retrieve the basket. A thick loop of her hair came loose. She tied it back. He then unexpectedly leaned over and kissed her when he brought the basket. For a moment she lost herself against his warm lips. She then gave Eva some bread and the child toddled off toward the water.

David lay next to her, supporting himself on his elbow, and encircled her hips with his arm.

"I would like a child," he said, gazing at the little girl.

She felt his hand on her breast and the other stroking her leg under her petticoat. His touch affected her like the sun opening the pedals of a flower. What else was there to care for in life besides this?

"Not here, David," she, nonetheless, breathed heavily, her eyes on the child, as the heat rose in her body.

"She's too young to understand," he answered thickly, swelling with purpose, drawn on by the moist folds of her skin and the drawing warmth of her thighs pressing against his hand.

"You will never understand anything else but this, will you, David?" she said, letting him have his way with his hand beneath her petticoat, mindful of the child, but allowing herself too this bliss . . .

16

November '72—October '73

Jane and Content stood in the falling snow and watched the men work. The gray November air and the rushing river didn't muffle their words, but rather echoed them with striking clarity.

"Robbie's bringing the beams now," Jane heard David say to James.

"Drop them on the bank," James' reply came from behind the barely visible stone abutment.

In his floppy hat, work jacket, and loose fitting breaches, David moved confidently, unaware of anything but his work. The team blocked Jane's view of him as Robbie guided the animals past her, the beams furrowing long black gashes in the earth. When Robbie brought the oxen around and approached the abutment, David then waved to her through the falling snow. Standing on the bank of the river holding the oxen by their yoke with the giant trees of the island behind him, he assumed Heraclean stature. And how hugely the animals steamed and glistened in the gray air!

Snow seeped into her cloak. As she and Content watched, she knew Content must feel as much a part of building the bridge as she did. It had been a full two years wait.

"How are they going to lift those?" Content pointed at the beams the oxen dragged to the site.

Jane shook her head. "They're monstrously long and heavy," she agreed.

"How will they support them with nothing in the middle?"

Jane remembered the drawing of the bridge David showed her describing its supports. "They'll use king's posts." Her answer sounded very knowledgeable, she knew, but she didn't want to give Content *that* impression. After all, it was Content's father who owned the bridge.

'King's posts', Jane McCrea?"

Jane hesitated, but marked a triangle in the snow with her toe. She really didn't know how such supports functioned—David had only briefly explained them on a bit of parchment—but she had to show Content at least something of what she knew.

"So it won't be a stone bridge," Content commented, both disappointed by the idea of a wooden bridge and resentful of what Jane seemed to know about it.

"With all these trees?" Jane couldn't help but point at the woods. David had told her these pines measured two hundred feet high and thirty-six feet around. A single tree contained enough lumber for the whole bridge. "He says stone is too costly. Besides, this bridge has to have a roof for the oxen to cross it," she added, deciding that if Content chose to misunderstand her interest, then there was no point in acting as though she didn't know what was going on.

"Well, *what* do I know, Jane McCrea?" Content replied archly.

Jane caught her unmistakable tone. Content was behaving coarsely. And what did the cost of the bridge matter to her, protected as she was by her father's wealth? This bridge really didn't mean much to her. Yet it meant so much to her and David! especially as a new mill would follow on the island.

"I'm returning to the tavern," Content announced shortly, turning away.

"The men have to work in this weather," Jane replied, unable to keep the censure out of her voice. It was not hard to justify her reaction to Content, if Content couldn't see how much harder the falling snow made the men's work. They needed encouragement under such conditions. But was Content acting this way because she gave the impression in answering her questions that she had some possessive interest in the bridge, or was it because of her grief over Jacob's death only four months ago?

"You'll not know how they get the beams across the river, 'Tenty," Jane called after her.

"It's too *cold,* Jane." A protected girl's complaint marked Content's tone as she retreated into the falling snow.

Jane watched her walk away, suddenly keenly feeling the unmovable melancholy of November. Inclement weather and the changing seasons affected her greatly. As the seasons passed, she had the sense of the river flowing by her bearing others' lives to unknown horizons while she only watched from the riverbank like a rooted tree under rain-filled clouds. Yet she valued Content's friendship, knowing she hadn't experienced true loneliness. Content's situation held out the same possibility for her, and Friendship was a glimpse of Heaven, wasn't it? And who could better understand this than she herself who had lost her family and endured the censure of David's?

As she stood in the falling snow watching the men with her back to Content's retreat, however, she didn't want to dwell on thoughts of loneliness. For what if a beam slipped and David fell? The river thundered in her ears. The oxen's chains clanked dully over the ground as Robert Yarns led the swaying team to the mill to her left. She feared an accident in the dark. In the near dark, her clogs slipped on the snow.

"David!" she called, walking across the soggy ground toward him. "Shouldn't you stop work now?" she waved to him as he levered the end of a beam toward the abutment. She could hear him straining as the beam turned against the black and white earth.

"Let's call it a day—have Robbie put up the team," David said, hearing her approach and jamming the iron lifter he held into the ground. "You'll catch a qualm out here, Jen," he stated as she came up to him. He then turned away from her as James came up over the bank toward them.

"We'll lay these tomorrow—" James said, raising his hat on reaching them and half-turning toward the river. "Still think the bridge is high enough?" he asked David.

"We're thirty feet above the river," David answered as though repeating what he had already assured James before.

"How are you going to get the beams across, David?" Jane asked, the sight of the surging river making her almost dizzy.

"We'll pulley them up on the other side and use the oxen to haul them into place," David assured her. "Ca'mon, Robert!" he then called to the boy. They then walked to the road.

Slush clung to the hem of Jane's petticoat as she walked. "Can you work through the winter?" She had divided feelings about that—if he couldn't work, it would take that much longer, but it was more dangerous to work in the snow.

"Sure," David laughed. We'll finish in no time."

Even after his long day, he seemed happy. Not working after work on the Dutch mill had ended, had made him unhappy. He had told her the second mill would produce their lumber. He had decided to season it in one of Abraham's sheds, then float the load to his mother's house on a raft. Once she saw it stacked on the knoll, she would give him the land, he told her. "So how long will it take to build the bridge?" she asked.

"Couple of months, if we can keep Robert."

He joined them on the road, splashing through puddles of slush.

"Gave 'em hay—" he said breathlessly of the oxen.

"Good," James replied, slapping the boy on the shoulder.

Jane glanced at the tavern, barely visible in the falling snow. Smoke curled from the chimney down the roof and swept across the woodshed; the icehouse, the horse-barn, and the blacksmith's shed huddled together in the waning light. Strangely, despite David's assurance he would finish the bridge quickly, the dark afternoon suddenly oppressed her. Dusk came like a thief. Uncertainty on their getting home in this weather stole upon her. As the sound of the falls had died away, the wind now howled high in the trees.

"—Listen to that wind! A blizzard for sure," Higson observed.

David and Jane looked at each other—she had come only for the day. She always returned to Northumberland at the end of the day.

"Well, we can get back . . ." David guessed.

But she didn't want to risk it in the snow. The wagon might break down. And she feared wolves. She looked at him and shook her head.

"Ah, don't worry, Jen," he stated.

When they reached the tavern, Abraham opened the door for them.

"Do you think we can get home in this weather?" she asked the man, needing additional reassurance.

"No—I've seen these storms. We'll have eighteen inches before morning," Abraham contradicted David.

"Oh, no," Jane said as the wind buffeted the chimney and sucked the fire against the fireplace. She spread her cloak across a chair. The wind roared and the heavy logs of the tavern creaked. "What shall we do, David?"

Abraham went behind the bar. "We have rooms," he said, overhearing her. "You lads want something to take the chill off?" At the fire he ladled mulled cider spiked with rum. The liquor steamed against the black stones. He pushed the kettle back. "—How does the bridge look?"

"We'll put the beams across tomorrow," James informed him.

"Each day's the Lord's gift." Abraham picked up the tray of mugs and came from behind the bar. He offered Jane a mug.

She sipped the drink. Abraham's words comforted her, and suddenly, stranded here for the night didn't disturb her. It wasn't worth the risk, trying to get home in this weather, and this house was always cheerful.

"Here's a toast!" Abraham stood before them holding his mug aloft. Everyone drank, and he sat in his chair by the fire. He looked judicial in his suit and vest. He always dressed in suit and vest, even when he shod horses. "Where's Robbie ? An honest man, working in weather, needs something warm," he added, noticing the boy at the back of the dark room.

"Don't mind," Robbie said in a budding, agreeably manful way.

"Down on the Oblong, we worked from an early age. Now, not so young," he explained with a laugh.

His wife, overhearing him, came down the stairs into the taproom with Content. "Oh, you're not so old," she scolded him affectionately. "But you men must be hungry enough to eat chair-legs, land!"

Jane stood up to help set the table, but Antis stopped her. "Content and I can manage, my dear."

"Oh, Mother!" Content exclaimed, welcoming Jane's help.

"She's been in that storm," her mother contradicted her daughter.

"Oh, no," Jane protested, privately pleased for what Antis said about her being outside while Content had returned to the warmth of the tavern.

"Speaking of storms, let's take Manchester. The Ministry overlapped the boundary and took money for two charters on the same land!" Abraham exclaimed.

"Not that again, Father, please!" Content declared, going to the pantry and disliking even more to hear talk of politics after her mother's refusal to let Jane help her lay the table.

"People need homes, my dear!" her father called after her.

In October, Manchester had declared that 'no person on the Grants should accept or hold any office under the civil authority of New York.' And the town's people had exchanged shots with the Albany sheriff.

"Damn the Ministry!" James said, leaving the bar, which he had been leaning against to poke the fire to a fountain of sparks.

Jane glanced at Content where she placed dishes on the table. She noticed how she and James looked at one another. She was certain now that love had budded between them. This surprised her so soon after Jacob's death. But why should *James* hold back? she questioned. He had a smooth path before him.

"Damn the Ministry for sure, but who owns that wedge of green mountains between the Connecticut and the Hudson?" Abraham queried him.

"Allen's ruffians," Content only objected to gain James' attention.

"I don't blame them—" James mildly replied to her.

"Oh, James Higson, boundaries, mills, bridges, and business is all you think of . . ." But light, not argument, played in Content's eyes.

Jane observed their interplay. This first cup of hot cider, the warm room, the fire, and her association with this family made a Mozart of the howling wind on the roof, and she forgot about the propriety of Content's lack of continued grieving for Jacob. So then, why was Content short with her at the river a few hours ago? Was it simply that she had wanted James to stop work and come to the tavern? Had she hoped that James might follow her? Or was she short with her because she herself hadn't gone, thinking that David would follow her too? But what difference did it make now that they were inside the tavern?

"How lovely you look, Jen," David said aside to her.

She looked warmly and givingly into his eyes understanding now better than ever how he felt about his work—understood, too, Abraham's words to Robbie Yarns about a man's honest work. Talk of Manchester didn't disturb her. And how much greater their future joy when David could finally build their house! She pressed his hand.

"Do let me help, Antis," she offered anew as Antis brought a platter of meat to the bar.

"Shall I cook these?" James interjected.

"These first," Content intervened, handing him another platter piled high with sliced potatoes and pointing coyly to the skillet hanging on the fireplace.

"Oh, James, you've worked all day.—I'll do the cooking," Antis countered her daughter. "And look, Content, since Jane insists, bring the table linen."

"Isn't there land enough for everyone?" Robbie asked from where he stood just beyond the light.

Jane looked at him, surprised that a boy his age thought of such things.

"Our history is a struggle over land, Robbie—first with the French, and now, with this Proclamation business, likely more trouble with the Crown. Everything comes down to land. As much as in the Grants as with the conflicting land claims of Virginia and Massachusetts and the King's refusal after Pontiac's uprising to allow settlement beyond the Alleghenies. How much land isn't the issue, but who owns it. Overlapping of ambiguous charters is the problem.

"My, father, you always said the Indians were entitled," Content chided him.

"That doesn't change peoples' feelings about being cheated."

"And what about the Indians?" David asked, thinking of his first impressions and hopes at Daniel's the second day of his arrival. Though he didn't have any strong feelings about Indian land, somehow it seemed connected with his own deep desire for property denied him until now.

"Lord, father, you make it sound like the Colonies will fight the English next," Content continued.

"And why not, if the Ministry closed the frontier? Anyone can see, child, that that would be resented after the sacrifices of the French War. People feel they have the right to settle beyond the Alleghenies. And Pontiac just hardened their feelings. Things can boil pretty hot in six years," he then explained, turning to David.

The wind broke the stillness of the room. It surprised no one Abraham could say such things. He always spoke the hard truth. It was just that what he said was particularly disturbing—

Jane, for her part, saw the Tuttles' barn burning in the howling fireplace. Some one had burned down his barn because of the Non-importation aggravated not only by taxes, but the Proclamation of 'sixty-three. English policy had divided neighbors. Some thought that anything the Crown did was within its rights even though they didn't agree with its policies. Others, reacting to its policies they didn't like, challenged the Crown's authority to not consult the Colonies. She didn't know where it would end, and she shuddered to think David's bridge might span a burning abyss.

"What good came of the war, if the English keep the frontier closed? It's fine to regulate the Indian trade and protect their land, but the Ministry never consulted us after the war. It's like the Grants—old boundary lines are moved and new ones drawn without consultation . . ." Abraham reasoned and explained simultaneously.

"Mister Tuttle lost his barn," Jane murmured. "I hate to think where this might lead."

"We could have civil war in a few years," Abraham imagined for them. "And if that happens, it will take the Ministry by surprise because they have always undervalued the strength of the Colonies—they've always viewed us as errant children. They don't see the power we have here. They don't see what's under the surface. They close their eyes to it—the simple truth is that if one side has no respect for the other, it will end in a fight."

"Good lord, Abraham!" his wife exclaimed.

"I'm only trying to explain, Antis."

"It's an appalling thing to think."

"We can't stick our heads in the sand like our brethren in Pennsylvania, thinking nothing will happen because of these excises and the Allegheny prohibition. English policy is likely to produce more violence. Not everyone loves the King, you know. Do you think those Scots from Ulster living along the Connecticut river in the Grants came over here to be closer to the King? Do you think the Dutch right here in New York feel any differently, regardless of their conflict with the Grants? Or the Puritans in Massachusetts, either? Or the Germans along the Mohawk? Or the Swedes? So, as Friends we can't keep our heads stuck in the sand either. We may not like violence, but that doesn't mean it's going to go away. Isn't that what Franklin told them in Pennsylvania? There's going to come a time, if these problems aren't settled quickly, when we're going to forget our own differences and unit against the King."

"Really, dear!" Antis protested sharply.

"Well what's the difference between English and French policy, if the result is the same, my dear?"

"But gracious, my dear, you're talking of something much worse than disagreements among neighbors."

"Of course I am."

"And what about the Indians?" David asked.

"They're likely to get caught in the middle," Abraham answered, sadly. "You can see with Pontiac's reaction to the English beating the French, they got left out of the Treaty."

"So, what do we do?" James asked.

"The country needs flour and lumber, doesn't it? Always will, won't it? Yet, I think we should support representation in Parliament. We can't certainly be inactive like our Pennsylvania brethren Doctor Franklin tried to and failed to organize on the Ohio when the French came down. English policy has already provoked a reaction. The Non-importation gathers strength daily, and we can't afford to underestimate the strength of it."

David's news in September about building the bridge had brought fresh hope to her. Now what thorny strands did Abraham's words weave into her hope when their prospects now looked so much brighter! The firelight even cast a halo over David where he sat. Yet he didn't even have property. In a small way, which seemed very large to her, they shared in the larger grievances of the Colonies over land questions. How then would what was happening now affect them?

Antis, spreading sliced potatoes on a skillet before the fire, blocked the light and David's halo vanished. The fat on the skillet hissed. The wind howled, and the door suddenly blew open.

"My! Close it, son," Abraham waved at Robbie.

"We have guests," the boy answered.

"Let them in, let them in, lad!"

An Indian emerged through a swirl of snow in the doorway.

"Louis!" David said, standing.

"The storm bends the pines—" Louis answered, as two women and another man followed behind him into the tavern. The women had calm, dark faces.

"Welcome, friends—" Abraham was on his feet to assist them with their coats.

"We smelled your smoke," Louis laughed.

"Come by the fire." Abraham motioned Robbie to push chairs up toward it. The Indians came forward. The women took off their cloaks.

"Coming from Kahnawake?" David guessed.

"And a merry trip! And Atsitsina coming from the Great Sault . . ." Louis introduced the other man.

Antis brought the women cider.

"The Great Sault? That's a long way," David said with amazement.

"And why from the Sault, Louis?" Abraham asked.

"Lot of trouble and no trade up there," Louis answered him.

"Don't the Frenchmen trade any more?" Abraham sought an explanation.

"Not the French King. Only the English."

"And what of the frontier? Trouble there too?" Abraham continued questioning him.

Louis then turned and translated the question for Atsitsina who answered.

"He says the Indians never made peace with the English after the French war. He says feelings are still hard toward the English and the Confederacy who enforced the English peace after Pontiac. The Winnebagos near Mackinac and many Frenchmen remain hostile to the English—he says St. Luc la Corne stirs things up. Atsitsina fears another Michilimackinac."

"See, what did I tell you?" Abraham asked, turning to the group. "I was just speaking of that. If there were any Frenchmen still up there, which there are, I would say the French War will start up again."

"Abraham!" his wife again exclaimed. "You are exasperating me, dear."

Atsitsina referred to the massacre of English soldiers the summer of '63 after the war ended with the French. The French had outraged the Lakes' Indians by ignoring them in their treaty with the English. Several hundred Sacs and Chippewas gathered to play la crosse outside the gates of the newly garrisoned fort at Michilimackinac. Only one English trader, Alexander Henry, lived to tell of the massacre. Pontiac's uprising followed and all the English forts in Canada fell to the Indians. The war only ended when the Iroquois and Sir William Johnson intervened on behalf of the English before Pontiac's murder.

"Will there be another flare-up?"

For a moment no one responded to Abraham's question and Jane took the opportunity to observe the Indian women's striking black hair, clear skin, and fine features. It amazed her that they would travel in such weather with their husbands. Atsitsina then said something, which made the women smile and look at her.

"He speaks of your hair," Louis said to her for them. "The lake sand where they come from is that color. They want to know your name."

"Jane McCrea," she answered self-consciously, uncomfortable with such familiar talk from Louis.

"These are Falling Sparrow and She Trails Her Feathers," Louis then told her. "They want to know what your name means?"

Jane considered saying she didn't know because 'Crea meant 'sheep-stealer' in the Highlands. But certain that no one in the room knew that, she answered, "Shepherdess."

"'A pretty name,'" Falling Sparrow, Atsitsina's wife, replied when she heard it translated.

Atsitsina nodded when his wife spoke.

"Do you have children?" Jane asked her.

"Two boys left with the Grandmothers at Kahnawake. My husband will return for them in leaf-sprouting."

Jane momentarily envied these women their mobility, freedom and community, leaving their children even with other Indians they apparently didn't know before coming down from the Sault. She tried to reconcile this generous practice with her accustomed fear of the Indians. She even felt Falling Sparrow's pain of separation from her own people, and regretted the fears she carried toward Indians resulting from the experiences of her New Jersey childhood.

The lamb chops hissed behind her as James laid them over the orange fingers of flame that reached through the grill.

"Falling Sparrow would like to know, if *you* have children," Louis said to her. "And is your husband here?"

"I am not married," Jane answered," touching David's arm. "We wait for our house."

Falling Sparrow nodded. She was out-going and not at all afraid to speak, as though she knew white people well.

"When Atsitsina came to my father, my father asked about his ponies," she explained. "Atsitsina had only the one and thought my father would give me to him for that one. That pony had one blue eye. But my father asked for several ponies! 'But I would take several with only black eyes,' he said. Atsitsina had no other ponies, but spoke radiantly as spring clouds: 'I will give you horses of any colored eyes you wish, Father.'

"'I didn't see him again until late summer when he handed the leathers of a string of painted ponies to my father. Knowing my mother approved, my father asked me, 'Would you like one of these, Falling Sparrow?' I pointed to one. Atsitsina led the pony away with me on it. That's how I became Atsitsina's wife. I asked my husband how he got those ponies. He said, "I am an active warrior."

Atsitsina laughed softly.

How simple! Jane thought. How different from Daniel who had only to take David into his business that first summer—surely their house would have happened as quickly as Atsitsina's returning with a string of ponies.

"'Now we look for a home,'" Falling Sparrow continued. "'It is sad to hear the Elders speak of the old days when land and beaver were plentiful and no teepee wanted. But the French and the English brought war. We women and children have no place to live . . . '" she ended sadly.

"Starvation drove us from our homes across the sea," Jane justified uncomfortably, yet sympathetically.

Falling Sparrow and She Trails Her Feathers looked at each other and nodded. "'Men should not fight,'" She Trails Her Feathers said without bitterness.

"Why not go beyond the Mississippi?" Abraham asked.

"'No Indian wants to leave his homeland,'" Atsitsina answered with simple dignity.

"And what about the trouble between the Bostonians and the English? Won't you get caught in the middle down here?"

"How can they understand our problems?" James interjected.

"The Oneidas live close to the Bostonians, and, as Atsitsina said, the Lakes' Indians are bitter after the French had the hatchet taken from them. The united Iroquois attract Atsitsina."

"But do the Iroquois know the difference between Bostonians and Englishmen?" James noted.

"Disputes between brothers can be settled," Louis replied, indicating that he possibly knew more about the problems facing the Colonies than he voiced. "And I told him that they had been counseling the Bostonians and the English for a long time—ever since the Chain of Friendship between them after Quidder." He continued to explain, referring to the Dutch, before translating what he said to the others.

Jane wondered if any one in the room understood this cat's cradle of politics and disappointment that seemed to tie them all together. And what if fighting broke out?

"Why didn't you stay at Kahnawake?" she asked, knowing nothing of the place except its location near Montreal.

"Village rivalry between French and English interests make Kahnawake the same as the Lakes," Cook answered.

Jane didn't know that the French had started Kahnawake with Mohawk converts seventy years before Sir William Johnson established himself among the Mohawks down here thirty years ago. Nor did she know that many Kahnawakeh Mohawks hated the French as much as others hated the English. She merely saw French and English interests had divided the Indians. Any wonder then why Atsitsina and Falling Sparrow came to New York to live among the Iroquois? Rarely did people think, unless politicians or land speculators, in terms of these New York Iroquois as Mohawks, Oneidas, Tuscaroras, Onondagas, Cayugas, or Senecas, except that they were united Indians who had long had a Chain of Friendship with the English.

"So the people of Kahnawake fought the English Colonies in the last war?" she asked to explain what sovereignty divided the Indians at Kahnawake, now that the French no longer controlled them.

"Mostly," Louis answered, "except for those who kept close ties with Johnson's Mohawks."

"And what of you, Louis?" Abraham asked, steering the conversation back to where it had begun.

"I have grown up near the Bostonians," he answered simply without revealing more.

The bridge construction continued slowly into the winter. Progress faltered, however, because much of the lumber for the new bridge was redirected for homes at the Corners; or often the weather prevented work.

During the long winter, Jane would spend evenings alone near the fire thinking of the future while the children, and Eva and Dinah slept. She frequently remembered Falling Sparrow. Dislocation had stalked her family too, except that other Indians helped her. Her gentleness contradicted her fears of Indians. Yet she wondered if she would like to move like Falling Sparrow, and if the Indians hated the settlers because of the loss of their lands. Clearly Falling Sparrow almost said that when she said that, 'white people gnaw at the bank and Indian women and children have no place to live . . . ' But was she any different from Falling Sparrow who was also at the mercy of events?

When she thought about such things, she often thought of John's future too, and how he and the other Non-importation people continued to resist the Ministry and the King's 'tyranny', as he termed it. He called the earlier English and Colonial war with the French a "war of kings." But what did he think of the Indians? 'They are not a people of kings', he often said, 'but like us, their victims.' The Ministry created the depression that forced people onto Indian lands, "though there are plenty of knaves making fortunes by swindling the Indians. I would only fight Indians if I had to, if the Crown forced us to."

Then John gave up law during the winter, and his future was as unpredictable as hers.

In January, Abraham's mills froze and David's work on the bridge stopped. The cold continued throughout February, and heavy snow in March prevented his drawing logs to complete it. Then in late spring, Abraham continued to mill lumber again for homes, which further delayed construction of the bridge until summer.

Finally, during the summer of 'seventy-three David found

himself working alone on the bridge. Robbie Yarns was tied to his father's farm, while James couldn't leave the other three mills because summer also saw an increased demand for flour and lumber. Jane thought summer would never end, and that David would never see the end of long days.

She would ride to the Corners and watch him work in the hot afternoon. He often worked without his shirt and sweat dripped from his very hat brim. Her heart bled for him when he fell asleep beside her on the seat of the wagon with Charlotte tied to the back of it on their way back to Sarah Jones'. And some nights he never left the Wings, but slept in one of the mills.

But the bridge, nonetheless, neared completion. In early fall when the roof rafters went up and the shakes went on, it looked like a house. Watching him work on the bridge, she imagined him, high in the gables, building their own house on the knoll.

In October, he completed the bridge. In mid-afternoon the high pines along the river nearly blocked the sun, casting the bridge in half-shade. David had nailed the last length of siding to the bridge. He threw down his hammer and wiped the sticky gum from his hands onto his breeches and walked through the leaves to the road where he sat against the bank.

"Done!" he exclaimed, looking up at the sky, his hands behind his head, not even looking at the bridge.

In the cool fall air, she lifted his hat and wiped his face.

"Aren't you going to look at it!" She exclaimed, turning toward the bridge and the yawning river filled with its own thunder. The opposite end of the bridge ended abruptly in the uncut wilderness of the island. The beautiful bridge, with intermittent latticework on its sides to allow enough light for the oxen as they crossed within it, went to nowhere! "Look at your bridge," she urged him with tears in her eyes when she thought of how much more effort the new mill would require of him.

"I don't want to," he said unexpectedly, the long months of hard work etched into his face. "Look at that bank. Rock! How can I build a headrace into that!" he moaned. "The effort will flatten my bones to the thickness of sheet metal!"

"But you always said working made you happy," she said pathetically, too aware that it wasn't the right thing to say as he lay exhausted before her. "But don't think about the other mill then, darling," she quickly continued, her last fall's and winter's broodings about the troubles in the Colonies and the Indians a distant memory now that the bridge finally did stand completed before them. She raised her hair off her neck and let it slide down off her elbows. She slipped down next to him. "It's beautiful. Think only of that," she sighed gently, "and how happy I am with you."

17

"Threw the tea into the harbor! Dressed as Mohawks?"

"Listen!" Antis Wing said, hearing her husband outside the door at the top of the stairs. Downstairs the tavern had fallen quiet, and the snow fell as softly as a cat walking on the roof.

Abraham, David, and James Higson entered the room.

"What do you expect with their keeping the tea excise? They'd repeal paint and paper and glass after the Boston Massacre—but not tea!

"Well, Ladies, the Bostonians dumped it into the harbor."

A clamor began downstairs. James closed the door.

"Just as things were settling down," Antis exclaimed with vexation. People applauded the repeal of the excises Abraham mentioned; everyone expected the tea excise to be repealed next. But since November, a year ago, when work on the bridge began and Abraham gave his gloomy prediction on the Colonies' troubles, no further crisis had erupted—

"Settling down? This villainy is ten years old!" Abraham moaned with uncharacteristic heat. "So, Ladies, you thought I was wrong last year? Licensing the Indian trade, not allowing settlement beyond the Alleghenies, restricting our commerce—as though some small island could absorb what three-and-a-half-million people can produce—and then adding taxes to the depression that followed the French war to pay for the war! My God, you could only expect smuggling, rioting, boycotts of English goods, and committees springing up like mushrooms. And now this."

"But why did they dress like Indians, Father? That's not fair," Content protested.

"To conceal their identity, obviously, 'Tenty," he answered.

"Or to show our defiance—if they are not going to treat us

like true English Subjects with the rights of Englishmen then what better way to show them our difference from them?" James added, while reflecting on the grievances Abraham listed. "But you forgot to mention how worthless they've made our currency, Mister Wing, and our having to quarter their soldiers with no mind to the fuel, candles, vinegar, cider and beer we're forced to provide them."

Abraham pursed his lips.

Jane dreaded his declaring the impossibility of building the new mill, even though last year he had implied he would continue to build mills and mill flour and lumber. And hadn't David said he would announce the new mill on the island tonight! They expected enough lumber after next year to build their house, and once his mother saw the lumber on the knoll, she would deed David his land. And, so what, if Daniel charged them for transporting it, if their house became a reality? But with what was now suddenly happening in Boston, she dreaded Abraham might change his mind on the mill.

"The devil will demand payment for the tea. And how will people pay for lumber—and how can we profit from the general suffering?" Abraham asked them.

"If you sell to the British, your money will be worth something, and you'd have the capital you need to build three mills." David colored, realizing he had broken his neutrality. He didn't intend to say this, but the words came of themselves. He feared more than anything the new mill wouldn't be built, that he wouldn't have the lumber for his house. That was all he meant to say—he really didn't know what resources Abraham had. He knew he was out of place in saying this, but he couldn't help himself. He looked at Jane wanting her to see this in his eyes. But then how could he back down now, having declared his thoughts?

"I'd rather fight, dressed as Indians or not—If we don't have a voice in Parliament, what do we have to lose? Let the devil take them!" James opposed him vehemently.

Jane caught the look in David's eyes and tried to tell him with her own not to say more, not to lose his temper. He had already disagreed with James, and, if James married Content and became his Overseer, what would prevent him from terminating David's work? Hadn't they already spoken of this? And didn't David appreciate that James himself supported building the new mill?

"Where does the English Constitution state we have a right in Parliament, James?" David asked, however, turning from her to meet James' hostility.

"David's right. We are the child of the Board of Trade and Plantations without a voice," Abraham unexpectedly agreed with him.

"With all due respect, Mister Wing, we *are* English Subjects," James, nonetheless, pointed out to him, arguing that in being Subjects of the Crown the colonists *had* voting rights in Parliament.

"No, we answer to the *Ministry*, James, and the Ministry represents us to the King. We can only appeal by Petition to the King through the Ministry."

"That's scandalous! I could agree with that, if we were small, but you said yourself we are a population of three-and-a-half million people! A Ministry can't govern us as if we were some mercantile. Well, then, if that's the way it is, then only the boycott can change it. We must continue to support the Non-importation. If we are only a business of the Ministry, then they shall have no business of us until we have the rights of Subjects."

"And who will pay us for our lumber, then, James?" the older man asked.

"We'll take grain from the people in exchange, Mister Wing. Surely we will not be hurt as much as the Ministry which grows fat off our productions."

"Yes, we must keep the mills running," Abraham admitted, his nod indicating that he had long thought of this. He looked curiously into a corner of the room. Had this Boston Tea-party actually changed anything? his look seemed to say. "We must assume the worst, that the English will close the port of Boston. Yet, we have timber, people arrive daily, and we must eat. That mill must be built," he finally stated.

"And my wedding, father?" Content quickly followed.

"A Tea-party can't prevent it."

Jane was filled with bitter-sweetness. Fortune blessed everything Abraham Wing touched despite what seemed to happen around him to prevent it! He only had to say the words to assure Content's future. Business and family were complimentary for him. Business enlarged him, rather than isolated him. And who could ask for more loving grandparents than he and Antis who cherished grandchildren as the *crown of the aged*? What a contrast to David's family! And what deeper reason, in addition to that tinker, had set Sarah Jones against David's marrying her? she was unable to keep from asking herself. And how could a simple childhood antagonism between David and Daniel, held over into adulthood, only explain Daniel's stifling his brother's ambition?

The snow fluttered like moths against the black pane. Jane sank into the outside darkness, letting the night envelope her with the certainty of more waiting and the gloomy mystery of Sarah Jones. And her children would never know grandparents like the Wings. If only her father had lived! She drew her shawl higher on her shoulders against the outside coldness—but Abraham *was* going to build the mill. That offered her some consolation.

A sudden shriek rattled the window.

"How can his bloody lungs take it!" James exclaimed.

"He would ruin a Christmas dinner," Abraham agreed as he walked, frowning, toward the door.

Jane averted her face and looked at the floor.

"*THEY SHOULD STRING THOSE SCUMBAGS UP ON THE STEEPLE OF THE NORTH CHURCH FOR DUMPIN' THAT TEA AND PUTTIN' IT OFF ON TH' INJUNS!*"

"Can't you do something to keep Munro and the Jessups from encouraging him, Abraham? Caleb Baker wouldn't stand for this in his alehouse at Sandy Hill, and neither should we. I deplore such violence, dear. I just can't endure Mister Yarns and those stamp troubles again," his wife declared.

Jane flushed. Yarns had seen her and David come into the inn. She had always avoided him when she found him potulent here at the Wings'. And hadn't David said that he had seen him near

Tuttle's barn before it burned last fall? The sound of breaking crockery and scuffling came from downstairs.

James started for the door.

"Don't go down, David," she whispered to him as he stood up to follow James from the room. She searched his eyes telling him that the mill would be built, that Yarns didn't concern them.

'YA DAMN LIBERTY BOY, HIGSON!"

A muffled curse floated up the stairs. The man's horse-like scream chilled her despite what her eyes conveyed to David. She couldn't help seeing imaginary flames in the darkness outside the inn.

"Leave him alone, Higson!" Hugh Munro could be heard shouting.

'HE WAS ALWAYS THE BEST LOOKIN' O' MY SONS!'

David's face turned white. "I'll pound that barn-burner to a cooking paste," he hissed, looking at Jane. "That's the only way to deal with him."

"No," she whispered, gripping his wrist.

"BUT HE WON'T MARRY HER!"

She froze at those words. Then heard the door slam. She looked out the window and saw Yarns foundering in the snow. He raised his stick to her.

"This tea thing will blow up like the stamp troubles, Abraham. Mister Yarns will be certain of it," Antis observed unhappily.

"Now, dear, don't mind him." Abraham walked to the window, his eyes revealing memories of burning barns and fisticuffs brought about by the Stamp Act. He turned back to the room. "This tea business will bring the English to a boil. If they close Boston, they'll provoke rebellion."

His words fell fatefully on the room conjuring up burning mills for Jane. She shuddered, imagining David's lumber on the knoll rolling in smoke above the flowing river.

18

Spring 1774

But through winter and the following spring Abraham's mills didn't burn, and Daniel and Abraham drafted their plans for the island mill. Since completing the bridge in October, David took his wages for building it in lumber for their house and succeeded in milling and stacking what he needed in November. In late spring when the river cleared of ice, and before work began on the island mill, he floated his lumber to his mother's.

Daniel had agreed to transport it. He would provide David with four men, but David had to pay haulage for the rafts and bateaux. David argued, however, that since Daniel floated logs to Albany anyway, he should not pay the full fee, if he loaded the beams and rafters on short rafts and unloaded them at his mother's. The resulting smaller rafts of logs would then go on to Albany. David would pay half. Daniel reluctantly accepted his terms, though he argued hotly he would have to pay for another trip to make up a full load to the English Navy. Higson overheard their dispute, and, to save his brother's face, David remarked that 'Daniel was under pressure'. 'An interesting way to describe him,' Higson had replied under his breath. David had little choice but to repress his embarrassed resentment with a smile.

David hadn't told his mother he would deliver his lumber on her 'doorstep,' and, though encouraged by his determination and his arrangements for transport, Jane feared his mother's reaction. He had asked her to come to his mother's after stacking the load on the bank. They would then tell her together about the lumber. How could she refuse him after enduring his mother's slander that Christmas two years ago and his declaring she couldn't change their feelings for one another? Surely Jane's being there would blunt her resentment toward his mother for denying them for so long.

The musk perfume of milled oak beams, planking and rafters, and the resinous scent of pine boards and cedar shakes filled the spring air on the knoll.

"Well, Jen, there's our 'house'!" he said proudly, as he surveyed the knoll and explained how the house would front and command the river, what stone he needed for the foundation and chimneys, and where the well house would go—

Jane listened, but her eyes rested on Sarah's door some distance from them. She followed David's pointing. The curve of the knoll had only the sky behind it. Near the top a rock jutted up, and they walked to it. The rock was rounded like the smooth bottom of an unused kettle. A shrub bearing tiny purple flowers and small dark leaves grew near it. As they turned and faced the river, she noticed Sarah's door open.

"We have a mile view of the river, Jen. We'll build right up to this rock. This bush will grow at the corner of the house—looks like an ivy," he said of the nightshade. "That maple tree will give shade . . ." he paused, as his mother walked toward them.

Jane watched her. Sarah seemed to roll on wheels like a thin mechanical doll with her knees punching against the pleats of her petticoat.

"Well, dear, you've brought the lumber for the new barn." Out of breath as she reached them, Sarah's words came through pinched lips in the soft afternoon. She spoke only to her son, not looking at Jane.

"Mother, this is Jane's and my house."

The pupils of Sarah Jones' eyes dilated.

Jane's gaze rested on the leaves of the bush near the rock.

"Daniel spoke of the barn . . ." Sarah's said quickly, her face flushing.

"No," David laughed uneasily, "this is my house. Weren't you waiting for this, Mother? I mean, my getting the lumber and setting up, before you gave me the land?"

"Daniel didn't say that, dear," Sarah replied with a hot voice.

"What about the animals? We need a barn first." Her eyes grew wide and hot. She rubbed her throat, never taking her eyes from her son. She seemed to have difficulty breathing. "Daniel promised . . ."

"No, mother, Daniel has nothing to do with this. This is our house, Jane's and mine," David insisted.

"I can't give you the land, David. You can't have it, yet . . ." Sarah's voice failed.

"Why?" he asked, alarmed at her reaction.

"Daniel, knows . . . he promised—I can't give you the land now—God!" She clutched her throat.

"What's the matter with you!"

She leaned against him.

"You promised. I've built mills and bridges . . ."

"Don't . . ." she said, turning away. "Do you want to kill me?" she moaned.

He clasped her gently by the shoulders and searched her face. She pulled weakly away and walked down the hill. He shook his head as he watched her go. "She acts as though I've poisoned her."

Jane mutely witnessed her reaction. "I know why she's sick!"

"She thinks this is for the barn. She's going to talk with Daniel!" he exclaimed with disbelief.

"She can't make you. The lumber is yours. She can't take it away from you."

"Ours, you mean!" he declared with anguish. "Maybe McNeil would sell us land," he said almost desperately. "But it would kill her. Oh, Jesus, why?"

"She won't let you go, David."

Tears of anger welled in her eyes. How could she allow him to give up his pitifully small inheritance, allow Daniel to take everything from him after what he had already promised and taken from them and after his efforts over these last four years? Would they just have to leave their house here in the weather? Was it possible his mother would never change, that she could witness their lumber rotting before her eyes, could witness her own son's unhappiness?

David slapped his thigh, stricken at seeing her tears and flowing red hair as she looked across the river. He didn't know what to do, so certain was he his mother would agree to letting him build—

"I guess we'll just go to Content's wedding this summer, David."

"Whatever you say, Jen." Defeat and bitterness tailored his reply.

"Were you going to have a root-cellar in the house, David?"

"Below the pantry . . ."

"Will the wood rot?" Thought of that crushed her.

"If the boards touch—"

"Could you sell it?"

"Oh, God, Jen!"

"I would hate to see it ruined."

She wiped her hot eyes. The roof of the house she imagined David building appeared upside down like the bottom of an ark to her. Her dream sank in the sunset on the river with the root cellar yawning toward the sky and the nightshade David saw at the corner of the house growing on the bow in the dying light.

19

Mid-summer saw Content Wing and James Higson marry. As the couple held hands in the log church, Content's brown eyes glistened in the candlelight.

"Bless them in this Eden," Abraham prayed.

"Amen," the congregation replied.

The couple embraced, turned from the altar and walked down the short aisle through the sunlit doorway.

Jane followed Content's sisters, Deborah, Patience and Mary, keenly feeling the understated nature of Content's wedding. She caught David's eyes which said, 'Why should we wait longer, when we can also be husband and wife as we leave this church?' But her eyes answered he knew only too well after his mother's refusal last spring. Yet, the waiting had ground upon them both and produced in Jane a counter longing for the kind of wedding she imagined in Ballston four years ago. Now that she endured the obstinacy of David's mother, a short, simple wedding would not satisfy her—she would have hills of flowers, hallelujahs, the rapture of hymns, and a long yellow gown hooped like a tulip. Justice required such a wedding. And when had she decided this? When her dream had floated away that spring afternoon when his mother refused them their home. If Sarah blocked her dreams, then nothing required *herself* abridging them. And why when David continued to work long days should a fine wedding not also inspire *him*? Passion for him and injured justice fused in her heart, making such an understated wedding as Content's unacceptable.

As she waited for David outside the church with the June sun warm on her face, her resolve, however, began to melt. The thorn that pressed against her heart began to soften. The Friends congratulating the bride and groom under the pines appealed to her forgiving instincts. Yet even a simple wedding eluded her! And how enraptured Content looked, so small and bird-like in her yellow petticoat and green ribbons! In desperate self-defense, she imagined the garden reception of her own wedding with fountains, trimmed yews, lilies and tulips blooming in edge-cut plots with silver on the tables and gentlemen in swallowtail waistcoats, expensive wigs, and ruffled sleeves speaking in English accents. Observing Content made her imaginings burn the hotter.

"Now th' knot's tied, lass, 'Tenty maun work ta keep her husband," Sarah McNeil said, reading Jane's face and balancing the demands of matrimony with its bliss. The older woman had encouraged Jane's desires for a proper wedding, but to allow them too great a rein risked plunging Jane into despair. One had to limit expectation, when the prise gleamed fitfully from too great a distance.

"And they'll have children," Jane remarked absently, not mindful of the older woman's intent. Rather she associated Sarah with what she sought to possess herself. "And a husband and a home to care for . . ." she continued, forcing a smile and fingering her hair beneath her hat.

"Aye, everythin' in season. Dinna dae onythin' o' that sort yet, Jane McCrea. Ye'll want siller in yer hame, tho' James hase a guid start as o'erseer." Sarah downplayed what Jane witnessed as a way of encouraging her.

But talk of silver and James' work made Jane's dream and David's work more remote, yet intense. It gave her the sensation of chasing a shadow in the declining light—the longer one chased, the greater one's desire to possess it, until it finally disappeared leaving the passion for it unquenched. Happiness depended on property, which Content brought to James. What did the British closing the port of Boston or stripping Massachusetts of its government matter when Abraham still gave his daughter a wedding and built mills? Nor what did it matter that the Non-importation Congress met in May, or that last week the Ministry extended the Canadian boundary to the Ohio river, blocking the land claims of Connecticut, Virginia, and Massachusetts? The Adirondacks protected the Wings from events. In fact, all that happened since the Boston Tea Party also favored Polly in Peter Tearse's orders to come to Fort Edward.—No, nothing Sarah McNeil said made her feel better because nothing changed for her. It made her feel worse. Discord and confusion only intensified her longing.

"Did yer fither mention th' King in his sarvices, lass? Abraham Wing didna spak o' th' King," Sarah said, focusing on something more tangible and less complex than what Jane felt.

It seemed only yesterday to Sarah that she first met David Jones four years ago on his way to his brother's. She had expected everything to fall into place for Jane. But work and a quick marriage hadn't happened, and Jane's friendship became one of shared confidences. Noticing the way Jane glanced aside and drew Polly away after Sarah Jones' housewarming, Sarah concluded the problem lay with Daniel.

And hadn't she given Jane motherly love, the friendship of her granddaughter, and shrewd counsel? Conversely, Jane made her feel needed in her widowhood, though gaining Jane's confidence took time. Jane retreated when she spoke of her own ill-fated marriages. And Jane never spoke of John's activities. At first Sarah thought this merely the slight of the generations. Then she attributed it to Jane's 'Yankee streak,' a tension in her character she couldn't read.

"Did yer fither mention th' King in his sarvices, lass?" she asked again, hoping to draw Jane out.

"Father always said, 'God save the King'," she answered with mixed feelings about the wedding not having pageantry, flowers, or hymns. Her father delivered sermons, interpreted God's words, and led the congregation in prayers and hymns which floated upward . . . he led his flock like a shepherd or a parent. How different from Abraham who responded to his Congregation's spirit when it moved them. Yet the ceremony did not lack religious fervor, and a marriage did happen! Her vision of marriage with the couple looking upward through the minister and the steeple toward God even adjusted itself to one in which the couple stood in an open field with the minister in his round hat between them, and their log church low in the distance. (What would Jane have given right now to have taken Content's place because of what had happened with David's mother!) A king with scepter hovering above them at the knees of God in that setting seemed incongruous, she reasoned, so desperately did she envy Content's marriage.

"The Friends don't need to mention the King. Nature needs no extras."

"Th' weddin's wi' oot sanction then," Sarah flatly stated. "Th' Minister a'ways mentions th' King." Sarah's eyes narrowed, Jane's answer defining her 'Yankee streak' for her. She spoke without reverence, givin' o'er ta impulse. She disregarded th' sacred—yet, th' lass pined for wat she didna hae. "I wonder if Abraham Wing supports th' Boston people?" she asked pointedly.

Jane half-wanted to humor her, not wanting to talk of the wedding now, or the Boston troubles. The wedding gave her pain, and she couldn't entertain a rebuke from Sarah. Besides, she liked the Wings. She answered Sarah McNeil's question honestly, but not to offend her.

"Abraham dislikes what the Ministry does."

"I see," Sarah replied, sensing Jane wanted a cool distance between them.

"Auntie, several days travel separates us from Boston," she said, touching her arm. "What do Abraham's politics and religion matter?"

"We're nae sae far frae Boston, lass," Sarah replied in a leading and heavy way. "Bot I'm for gettin' oot o' th' sun."

Jane watched her walk into the shade and sighed with relief. Sarah would have begun speaking of John. He spent much of his time in Albany, and Eva worked like a man threshing wheat and grinding flour as a result. This wedding brought Jane herself relief. Did it's simplicity or its not having the sanction of the King, as Sarah said, matter? What did James' and Maria's wedding four years ago in Ballston lack?

As she observed the table with its rolls, pastries and punch and the smell of roasting lamb, she weighed her life and the people she knew with her inclinations and wounded feelings. Why had she to choose between simplicity and city elegance? They both required property and the promise of a livelihood, or else principles, which inspired John and Eva. But sheltered by her father, she had no such principles which might have sustained her and allowed her to accept something less. So her imaginings and the idea of possibilities guided her. Her readings of plays, fairy tales, and even the BIBLE inspired her. And where her culture and her education gave her certain expectations, the nobility with their clothes, horses and carriages, music, fine manners and speech shimmered before her. She simply couldn't turn her back on the nobility—one grew up with the desire to possess! Yet how sensitive she was in not wanting to give that impression to people—to John and Eva, even to David. Yet, hadn't Sarah McNeil herself declared that a proper wedding needed the sanction of naming the King, and that included everything associated with royalty—the pomp, glitter, and refinement that constituted ceremony? She had been raised to want that. Not that it was something that her father had insisted upon for her, but because it was in her Highland heritage! And what was the alternative, but to be dressed in homespun, and to toil day after day for the rest of her life? What was the alternative but no marriage at all—the very barrenness of that prospect called up the opposite with its attendant pomp and ceremony.

She found herself tossed in a chop of choices, so thoroughly had David's family and the Wings' success complicated her feelings. Sarah McNeil's and John's opposing views, and even the conflicting inspirations of Nature itself frustrated a clear choice for her. The unadorned beauty of a day even evoked a desire in her for refinement. A schooner in the bay, with its gentle lines complimenting the curves of the shore, only completed a sunset. Nature herself begged that adornment which she found herself frustrated in possessing.

And what of her love for David? He excited her and brought out feelings in her that, at moments, made other desires shallow. He made her forget wanting anything except that final surrender . . . but allowing herself that now, wouldn't she hate herself, if it left her unfulfilled? So many women endured the drudgery that followed surrender. She didn't want a home and family David couldn't support. She wanted him to always feel new, not to hate her for giving in to him, though he said he wanted that. No, she wanted a more complete life with him. She insisted upon this. Justice itself now insisted upon it for her. Yet, wasn't she obliged to accept the happiness that favored Content, if only that small consolation for her waiting and suffering was held out to her?

Unable to reconcile some of the contradictory feelings the wedding caused in her, she felt alone. Yet she was not beyond thinking of other's happiness. It was, after all, also important she favor Content in her happiness, rather than dwell on her own lack of it—and Polly's happiness, too, she thought, seeing her friend come toward her through the groups of people.

"Have you had any news from Peter?" she asked.

"He's coming, an' Grandmother, topped off wi' th' weight o' that headdress o' hers, will sit on him when he arrives," Polly answered, though not loud enough for others to hear.

"Polly!" Jane laughed because it was more seemly than to cry, looking over at Sarah sitting in the shade of a large maple tree. She had twisted her hair around a ball of hay into a foot high beehive and had stuck bluejay feathers, sprigs of pine, and flowering strawberries, for her maiden name of Fraser, into the sides and the top of it. She did her hair, she told everyone, "'Arter th' latest fashun o' courtly people." She sat under the tree, a pastoral, rather than a courtly, composition of bee's nest, feather and field. Viewing her offered Jane a trinity of a rebuke, farce, and despair.

"Amplified like that she'll hae ta honor her promise o' givin' me a wedding and a parcel o' land—"

"Polly, you are a scandal."

"Eggs, honey, and a whiff o' incense when it all comes apart."

"But tell me of Peter?" Jane half-cried with tears in her eyes.

"His coming has something ta do wi' th' British closing Boston—" Polly said, compressing her lips.

"What does Fort Edward have to do with Boston? The fort's

only mounds of dirt," Jane declared, suddenly feeling that the Boston trouble was closer than she thought.

"I don't know, except what his letter said."

"What letter?" David asked, bringing them glasses of punch.

"Peter's coming to Fort Edward," Jane answered.

"His company is being sent up from th' City."

"It probably has to do with the Grants," David suggested. "You remember Manchester and Arlington declared their independence of us last fall? But it will only take a few soldiers to settle the boundary."

"I'm in th' dark about it, David Jones."

"Peter's company will settle it," David stated, passing the matter off.

Jane and Polly exchanged glances. The boundary dispute with the Grants would affect everyone on the east side of the river, including Sarah McNeil, Daniel, and even the Wings. And what if squatters succeeded in taking Argyle? A company of soldiers would provoke fighting which might involve David. There was an awkward silence.

"Don't worry about it, Jen," David repeated what he had told her before.

She looked at him, allowing his eyes to reassure her that this event couldn't possibly affect them. They had only to think of themselves, their love and their marriage. She saw the return of his expression in the log church—she thought that he might even now take her by the arm and ask Reverend Abraham Wing to marry them.

"I guess there is nothing to fear, Polly," she then said, turning her eyes away from her lover, saddened that she couldn't say to David, "Yes, it's time—I'll be your wife."

On their return to Northumberland, the lovers stopped along the road. The moon moved above the steeple-like pines, making the needles gleam like glass threads against the dark sky. The river turned black and turquoise in the moonlight.

David could smell her perfume—her hair had the scent and tint of clover blossoms. He pressed his lips against hers, as he brought her off the saddle.

"Are we wrong to wait so long, David?" she asked, as though they had a choice once they had abandoned their house on the riverbank. She stood before this moment of surrender, and felt the more uncertain because of the temptation.

"Jen, it doesn't matter to me how long I have to wait. I'll work forever, pile lumber like Ferdinand, as long as I know you love me," he whispered passionately, as he held her in his arms.

She slid from his embrace and laid a blanket on the grass where the overhanging branches softened the moonlight.

As he returned to her after tying Charlotte, she held out her hands to him and he came beside her. His fingers loosened the buttons of her bodice—

"Oh, David . . ."

Her breasts fell into his hands. He kissed them and felt her lips on his ear—

"David . . ."

Her thighs yielded, firm and full under her petticoat.

"—No."

She sat up. Her hair covered her shoulders like red earth in the turquoise light.

"Oh, Jen!" he said, drawn by love of her—

"Don't ask it of me, David. I want to, but I can't." She folded her petticoat under her. "I want you when we're married. I have to save for you. Kiss me."

She kissed him long and deeply, and he tried again, and her resolve melted.

In his palm she was as round and full as a large peach—gentle at first she pushed slightly and yielded, then pulled away, virginal and heady, leaving him with only the feeling, the scent and the moisture, and talk had no place between them—

She wiped her cheeks and arranged her petticoat hoping she hadn't upset him. She knew it tortured him—and how she wanted him! It tortured *her* to block their desires and needs . . .

"I wish my father could have lived to marry us—give the bride away and say the words as Abraham did for Content today," she said, trying to hold back her tears. "Now, he'll never see his grandchildren." The salt of sorrow reached her lips—how she wanted to have those children, but she was caught, suspended in time without her father to comfort her children, without a husband to give them to her. Like a pine unable to bear cones she tossed in adverse winds, growing alone with David beside her among others bearing cones, as Content would, beneath the paternal branches. She pushed her face against his shoulder. "I miss my dad."

How helpless he felt holding her, feeling her sobs! He burned, unable to possess her, to give her the home she dreamed of, the home he had promised her, the home that lay in lengths of beams and boards on the knoll. Yet how near! Why couldn't he uproot these trees, mill them, and build her a house right here on this spot? He pulled her closer and felt her heart beating against his. He only needed the chance.

"Oh, Jenny . . ." he said pathetically, tears in his own eyes.

"We should have been happy today, happy for 'Tenty and James, but we watched them sail away from us . . . and with Polly's Peter coming. I don't want to be left on the shore, David. I don't."

"You won't be . . ."

"Is it wrong of me? Why do I vacillate so? Only for you . . ." she said, begging him to understand her.

"We'll get our break . . ." But he wanted to say that they should yield to each other. He didn't have the strength for denial. Yet he said the opposite to comfort her, to show her he understood the wedding and home she wanted, even shared this with her because he thought it pleased her. But inching toward his goal like this made him desperate, and at times he felt violent toward his mother.

"'All things come to those who wait,' father always said."

"I love you, Jane," he replied, his passion not cooling, only the flames of it retreating into the coals of desire. His lips tightened sadly and resignedly as a laborer's when confronted with a seemingly endless future of working days without hope.

"And you'll never leave me, David?"

The tears flushed in his eyes—he looked into hers, deep and wide as the sky. "I would harness the moon for you," he declared, his voice cracking.

"How patient," she sighed, touching his face, putting her fingers on his lips, and kissing his eyelids.

20

But the time needed to save the money the lovers needed for their wedding required more than David's patience. For in response to the British Intolerable and Quebec Acts, which followed the Boston Tea Party, the First Congress, which met at the time of Content's wedding, requested every county, city and town to have a committee to enforce the Non-importation. So, in early fall the market for Abraham's lumber began to fail, and David faced unemployment on the island mill.

The lovers consoled themselves that the general suffering might end the Non-importation. If not, David should press his mother, even though this might harden her to keep her land. But he had to build their house before the mills completely stopped! And if his mother still refused him? The couple could sell their lumber, or go to New York City and open a forge—alternatives which only deepened their gloom. When their future seemed darkest, however, David received a communication from the Jessups. After waiting for six years, Governor Tryon had finally approved their Patent, and they were celebrating the event!

"Imagine, forty-eight thousand acres!" David had exclaimed, his eyes alive with the possibilities for him.

"Have they invited you?" Jane's mind spun. Such rich men would need millwrights!

She drew her tartan around her and breathed the sharp, red and yellow scents of fall hardwoods woven into the fabric of spruce, hemlock and white pine as their carriage rolled up the mountain toward the Jessups'. She pressed his arm and felt the carriage tip as Sarah McNeil shifted her weight on the back seat. At David's request, the Jessups had invited her and Polly to their celebration too. Jane felt more at ease having them with her, knowing other

Adirondack landowners would attend the Jessups' party. She also felt her friends would shorten the ride, but, in reality, her own expectations lengthened it. How could it be otherwise after all this time going to Zion and the turquoise lake set among the gold, emerald and carnelian-tinted mountains she had heard spoken of so often? Her thoughts flew ahead and her sighs vibrated on the leaves.

A wolf with black-tipped ears and black mask appeared on the side of the road before vanishing in long leaps into the woods.

"How like black flame!" she exclaimed, delighted at seeing it and thinking David's fortune might change with equal quickness. How long had they waited for this chance? She recalled the years, Daniel's reneging on his promise, David's mother's silence, then assault on her, David's efforts on that first mill, and then the bridge—now all that promised to change as the woods opened up at the top of the road, and the Jessups' lake presented itself on her left. The trees on the far shore wore imperial red, and the water, a cold military blue, ribboned with green and unyielding as glass, invited her onward.

"Can ye see th' hoose?" Sarah McNeil questioned.

"There, I think, ahead," Jane answered excitedly, pointing at a low house, half in shadow, stretching along the shore ahead of them. Orange and black butterflies covered the partially sunlit road leading to the house. The butterflies floated like leaves around the carriage as it bounced in the ruts of the road. A butterfly as large as a small bird flew up at her.

"That hoose is brae eneugh ta stop a winter wind," Sarah observed soberly, taking in the size of the logs of the house.

Jane laughed and waved off the large Monarch.

The carriage stopped at the house and David gave her his hand. The low long building with its overhanging roof of thick cedar shakes was as stolid as a barracks. She could hear music within— then Ebenezer appeared like a nightingale in the doorway wearing a brown wig, soft boots, and a long velvet waistcoat over his satin breeches. Jane gave him her hand and he pressed it to his lips.

"Charmed . . . though I have seen you at the Wings, I've never had the honor of meeting you, Miss McCrea," he said in a fluted voice.

She blushed as he kissed her hand, unaccustomed to such attention. And how different an impression he made on her after the way he had egged Thomas Yarns on at Abraham's tavern just before Christmas last year!

"So pleased to meet you, too, Mister Jessup," she said, withdrawing her hand.

"Thank you for your invitation, Ebenezer," David said with a bow.

"You have ideas, I understand," Ebenezer pronounced, rather than asked.

"For a new saw, yes," David replied quickly. "Something I've no doubt you'll be able to use."

"Well, we must talk of it, young man." Ebenezer turned to the other women. "Welcome, Ladies . . . come in, please."

Talk of David's saw excited her. He had told her that he thought Ebenezer had learned of his saw from Hugh Munro, who had stopped at the island in the spring. Though David guessed that Peter Freel, living next to Sarah McNeil, might also have spoken of it to the Jessups. Their telling the Jessups about David's saw might have been because they knew that David didn't support the Non-importation; both welcomed David working for the Jessups. But did the politics of these two men concern David? No. Ebenezer's interest in his design is what interested David. How often he assured her something like this would favor them!

"We must talk," Ebenezer repeated, showing them the open door.

Inside the house people dipped like swallows to a minuet of French horns and bells. A butler offered them champagne, and Jane tasted its bouquet on the rim of the cold glass.

An Indian stood on the other side of the room beyond the dancers wearing a knee-length red cape, arching feathers, skin breeches, and moccasins. The colors of his dress mocked the October firelight. He looked almost feminine. How different he dressed from Atsitsina and Louis Cook, Jane thought.

"Joseph Brant, Colonel Guy Johnson's Secretary," David said, noting her interest. "Louis mentioned him. He's the deceased Sir William's brother-in-law."

"And the other?"

"Sir Guy Johnson."

Jane recalled Sir William Johnson had died of a heart attack while hosting an Iroquois congress at Johnstown in July, and Sir Guy had inherited his Iroquois Superintendency. The valley buzzed on whether the Johnsons would oppose the Non-importation.

"Let's freshin' oursels 'afore dinner," Sarah said, setting aside her glass.

The women followed a butler down a lantern-lit hallway lined with imposing portraits. At the end of the hall he ushered them into a room with canopied beds.

"Ach, lassies, th' Jessup brothers live lik lairds!" Sarah declared, dropping her shawl on a chair and beholding the room. A fire burned in a field stone fireplace. She rinsed her face from a basin of water.

"Did you see that Indian?" Jane asked, brushing her hair in a wall-length mirror.

"Aye, who could hae miss'd 'im, lass?" Sarah answered, drying her face. "Who'd a thought a savage could hae sech deportment? Bot I guess they can strut wi' a million acres—aye! gie me America wi' a million acres an' a army o' savages ta do my biddin'. Sir Guy and 'is Highlanders ken wat livin's aboot. I hear he inherited 'is father-in-law's Superintendency owre th' savages—aye! an' a bodyguard o' three-hundred stout Highlanders at Johnson Hall taa."

"That was Sir Guy standing near Brant," Jane informed her, in awe of their power and possessions.

"Aye, he hase the Indians behind 'im. Ne'er count oot the canny ways o' an Irishman."

"Can yer cousin, Simon Fraser, get some Mohawk land too, Grandmother? Hasn't he already petitioned th' King?" Polly asked.

"Aye, for 'is sarvice in Spain he wants land here in America. Thare's no place lik America for a fresh start!" her grandmother answered enthusiastically.

Listening to Sarah, Jane almost wished David himself had joined the British army for the land officers received for their service. Hadn't his oldest brother, Thomas, gone to Woolwich? Recalling that fact was like finding a forgotten handbag in her trunk. But if David had joined the army six years ago like him, instead of doing millwork, he would have land today. She hoped he would speak without delay to Ebenezer about his saw.

She surprised herself. If John knew what she was thinking now, it would shock him. But even so, the Crown might still settle the Non-importation. She, of all people, knew things could change suddenly.

"Ye seem preoccupied, lass." Sarah clasped her hands, her eyes soft as blue cloth in her round face. "I ken wat ye fancy. Leuk a me. Mister McNeil ne'er saw th' land he own'd up here, dyin' as he did," she said sadly, "bot I still hae land. An' gin David works for th' Jessups, ye'll hae yer land an' a hame. Dinna fret aboot yer brither, either. We a' hae ta mak owre own way in this warld."

"I know, Auntie," Jane said, Sarah mentioning land and a home raising goose bumps on her neck.

"Polly an' I luve ye, lass, an I maun spak lik yer mither."

The older woman's words reenforced the effect a painting above the fireplace had on her, and Jane's heart beat quickly. Would she ever wear elegant clothes like that Lady in the painting who had two pretty daughters and a slave to carry her umbrella? Would she, in fact, have the property her birthright as a British subject promised her? Standing in this house gave her hope—yet, might she question her desires? She didn't believe in slavery. Looking at the painting she couldn't help but feel some impurity in her desires.

"One day, perhaps, Auntie," she assented mildly, squeezing the older woman's hands, so close to real property making her shiver, nonetheless.

But her ambition threatened to sink her. Was this what she really wanted? And what of a husband and children? Property didn't compare with true love, a family, brothers, and friendships. This house, and what it contained, now seemed less important to her. Her coming happened casually, just an unexpected written invitation. It seemed no time at all had passed when Polly first mentioned David working for the Jessups at his mother's housewarming. And Polly heard Ebenezer speak to him about his saw. The quickness and casualness of events bred a certain superstition in her about the impermanence of all this.

"Am I *rushing*, Polly?" she asked, turning away from the painting.

"*One in th' hand is worth two in th' bush,*" her friend advised.

"I *must* stay calm," she reminded herself, being so close to realizing the beginnings of her dreams filling her with a sudden fear of them escaping her. She should take Polly's cautioning her seriously. Polly loved her!

Later, a butler in high collar and tails ushered them into the dining room. Jane slipped her arm through David's, aware of the men's eyes and the women's voices like the songs of birds.

She wore her hair in a combed roll, rich as finished cherry, with a dress cap of silk gauze and green ribbon with a loop of pearls inherited from her mother. She wore a cinnamon-cream gown, open and formal, with treble lace ruffles, tight sleeves, and scalloped flounces. A rosette of red silk adorned her bodice, and a tear-shaped pearl on a thin black ribbon hung from her neck. The pearl accented her skin and framed her neck and face. As she walked into the dinning room through the glow of the chandelier and the gleam of Queen Anne silver, she touched the pearl. The most beautiful woman in the room, she glided over the oriental carpet toward the end of the table.

Ebenezer toasted the King, Governor Tryon, Sir Guy Johnson and Joseph Brant, pointing out what honor the Royal Patent conferred on him and his brothers.

Jane sipped her wine and glanced up at the chandelier. Its two transparent globes, linked by gold chain, held six curved crystal arms with gold candles. Did that chandelier hold the bowls of god's wrath for what she was thinking! Why did such a thought force itself upon her now? Was she guilty of desiring to grow rich with the 'merchants of the earth'? Had Ebenezer tainted her passion? And if she glorified herself and played the wanton, sitting like nobility, no widow mourning, would her deeds repay her double and burn her with fire? Would an hour and these toasting men and women, and the silver on the table and the gold lights waste her because of her pride?

Fear of God made her tremble. How could the daughter of a Presbyterian Minister desire such things! Surely having no role in making this wealth made her chandelier inspired fears groundless. She chastened herself for basking in these lavish surroundings, and for pridefully thinking of her own beauty. She meekly asked David about his speaking to Ebenezer.

"I haven't spoken with him," he answered, clinking his glass against hers as Ebenezer finished his toast.

After the onion soup, the quests had the choice of suckling pig, pheasant with apricots, or broiled lake trout. Jane forgot her anxieties as she chose the pheasant. She then noticed the mahogany sideboard across the room, which Ebenezer bought at the auction three years ago. How fateful to see it in the very room where she now dined.

As her eyes rested on the sideboard life seemed circuitous to her. How often when one reached for something, what one reached for flew from one's grasp; yet, if one pursued a tangent, how unexpectedly what one wanted fell into one's lap! Such *coups* defined life. But wasn't chance really Providence in another guise? Her father always said life had design, whether we understood it or not. Things didn't happen by chance alone. She and David had not succeeded in possessing that sideboard, but they 'possessed' it here, now, three years later, nonetheless. Perhaps what they suffered meant they must exercise appreciation before obtaining what they desired. Her past anguish had to have some reward for it to have meaning. She had never been taught to believe that suffering was empty.

She declined the whipped syllabubs and accepted the candied rose petals for dessert.

After dinner a quartet played, and the men talked. Jane observed David's and Ebenezer's expressions on the other side of the room. David's face expressed the certainties of the cello, and Ebenezer's the thoughtfulness of the violin and viola. Sir Guy, standing near them, blew gray cigar smoke at the ceiling.

Then suddenly he shouted above the strains of the music at a man next to him!

"Lewis' attack on the Ohio means war, John! And you can bet Massachusetts and Connecticut will also try to roll back the Ohio boundary."

"Won't the Shawanese fight for their land?" Butler asked.

"They'll cut Lewis to pieces. But half the people supporting the Non-importation claim Ohio land. Massachusetts and Connecticut, not the least. You know what this means, don't you?" Sir Guy demanded of Ebenezer.

"Of course," Ebenezer answered, breaking away from David and Joseph Totten and Stephen Crossfield who stood at his elbow.

Jane looked among their faces that plainly bespoke shock—

"Damn the speculators," Butler hissed.

"That politician Schuyler has deeds to Indian land up there too, and he'll drag New York into this—"

And what did this sudden news mean? Could this effect their Patent with the King, which must follow Governor Tryon's approval? Did they fear Lewis' attack on the Ohio would freeze all land transfers?

Jane noticed Brant, in his cape and feathers sip his brandy with a cloudy expression. Another Indian then entered the room and spoke to him. Their language resonated in their chests. Brant's face darkened. He set down his glass. The other Indian stepped back.

"Peter now tells me the Shawanese sue for peace at Kanahawa," he declared thickly to Sir Guy.

"Impossible!" Sir Guy bellowed, throwing his cigar into the fireplace. "They would have cut the Virginians to pieces!"

"You underestimate them. Peter says Lewis defeated the Shawanese and a band of Cayugas at Kanahawa yesterday," Brant insisted.

Sir Guy smiled bitterly.

"Well, since the Virginians won't accept the Canadian boundary that means *we* must do something," he said, referring to the inconclusive Iroquois congress in July.

Brant's face was like a gray calm over water.

"The Confederacy will let the Shawanese settle their own differences with the Virginians. We fought the last war side by side with them. Virginians are not Frenchmen. The Longhouse doesn't understand this quarrel with the King, and Sir William counseled neutrality," Brant reminded him.

"But the Virginians struck first!"

"Against the old allies of the French," Brant pointed out.

"But the Cayugas—"

"So much the worse for them for not listening to Sir William and the Elders."

"Hang it, man, Lewis struck with the hatchet! These Virginians won't distinguish among you Indians. Land is land. They'll beat on the doors of the Longhouse of the Six Nations next."

The music stopped.

"The Cayugas acted alone. The Confederacy will not fight the Virginians," Brant repeated stubbornly.

"And what of Molly?" Sir Guy demanded, referring to Brant's sister and Sir William's widow. "Listen, Joseph, your influence depends on her now that Sir William's dead. If the Americans have their way, there won't be any more land deals like this one. And what of Kirkland?"

Jane had heard of Kirkland, the Boston missionary who lived with the Oneidas. The Catholic Johnsons deeply resented his influence among them.

Brant didn't answer. Everyone could see that he didn't like Sir Guy mentioning that his influence among his own people depended on his sister's marriage to Johnson. But did he want a war with the Americans? All knew that the Confederacy had suffered in the French war, had fought alongside the Colonies. The Confederacy had even counseled the Colonies to confederate among themselves to fight the French. And now this Congress opposed the King! A bitter division burned for all to see on Brant's face, yet if Kirkland maneuvered, this Congress might split the Confederacy itself. He turned to Peter.

"Get the horses."

Having won his point, Sir Guy turned on Ebenezer.

"If you want your land, you must now publicly oppose the Non-importation."

"The Ministry will insist upon it," Governor Tryon agreed.

Ebenezer Jessup's face turned white.

Sir Guy and Joseph Brant left the room.

Jane looked in shock at David. John had said the Quebec Act would provoke the Virginians, but who could have foreseen it would affect the Jessups? And what retaliation would be taken against them, if they opposed the Non-importation? And if they refused to oppose it? Their Patent wouldn't be approved and they would have no land, and David no opportunity. What was within reach just an hour ago took wing! Why did every road they took end in a *cul de sac*? What annulment would come next?

Jane walked across the room to David, oblivious to the women's eyes on her. She took him by the sleeve. "Does this mean that the King won't approve their Patent, David?" she asked, scarcely above a whisper.

He nodded—"Unless they come out against the Non-importation."

21

Winter '74-Spring '75

David's missed opportunity with the Jessups proved, however, over the next eight months less a concern for Jane than her fear that he might be conscripted, given the increased hostilities which broke out—The Ministry's moving the Canadian boundary to the Ohio River through the Quebec Act affected the land claims of three Colonies, and every Protestant objected to the Ministry's recognition of French civil law in Quebec, and its guaranteeing the property of the Roman Catholic Church.

The Virginians' attack on the Ohio, and actually learning about it from Indians at the Jessups, immediately stirred her childhood memories of Ohio Indian warfare during the time of Pontiac after the French war. Her Presbyterian neighbors in Lamington served in the war, and those memories haunted her. How could she avoid remembering her own father's pulpit exhortations on every man's duty to his country? Every family in Lamington had experienced the loss of a son, brother, or father.

Further, the Yorkers' boundary dispute with the New Hampshire Grants made her fears even more immediate. If Peter Tearse's Company was being detailed from the City because of it, according to Polly at Content's wedding, what did that mean for David? How could he avoid being mustered in? Surely, the Colony would need soldiers. So the Ohio boundary issue coupled with the Hudson River dispute with the Grants filled her with foreboding on the carriage ride back from the Jessups.

And that wasn't the worst of it, for when she arrived home she learned that the First Continental Congress had directed every county, city, and town in the Colonies to choose a committee, by qualified voters, to enforce the Non-importation association, an action later approved by the Albany County Committee in December.

She spoke with John whenever she could get the chance over the following months. Active on the Albany County Committee, empowered by the Congress to enforce the Non-importation, he would know if open defiance of those asked to sign might follow reporting them when they refused to sign. He would also know if the Committee, rather than the Albany Assembly, had the authority to raise soldiers to deal with the Grants. And if the Committee intended to conscript David, she hoped John could prevent it.

She did not mention David when she spoke to her brother, but focused on the Committee's authority, not understanding how people could change lawful government.

"Qualified voters chose the Committee," John answered her.

"But do most people support you?" she hazarded, trying not to challenge him personally with the question, fully realizing that many people now openly questioned Governor Tryon's royal authority expecting that the Albany Assembly would dissolve in favor of the Albany County Committee.

"If the Assembly dissolves in favor of the Committee, Tryon can't govern. If all Assemblies throughout the Colonies dissolved, then the Congress of Committee representatives will govern. Our grievances demand this," he anticipated her.

"Will there be conscription then?" she asked fatefully, unable to conceal her real worry from him.

"Yes, if there's more fighting. I see little alternative after Lewis' attack and with Massachusetts being stripped of its government."

Her respect for her brother did not blind her to his arguments or his commitment to the Non-importation. Yet his commitment chaffed her, and she found herself wishing he would withdraw his support for it. She even momentarily glimpsed what her father must have felt toward John over the stamp riots.

"The British use strong measures. Look at Boston. If they try to disarm Massachusetts, bloodshed will result. And what of the

Johnsons, their armed Highlanders, and their Mohawks who oppose the Non-importation? We will probably have to conscript."

She knew that he could see the fear in her eyes when she asked him who would be asked to serve.

"Men fifteen to fifty," he answered her, though she thought he intentionally avoided what he knew was in her heart about David.

The Albany Committee gained strength in the Assembly throughout that winter, and, as John predicted it would, the Assembly dissolved itself. But before it dissolved, the Assembly passed a Militia Act which, given its timing in early April and the events Jane witnessed, had more to do with the Johnsons than the trouble in Massachusetts, for in March, Sir John Johnson, the deceased Sir William's son, sponsored a resolution in the Tryon County Court of Quarter Sessions condemning with 'abhorrence all measures tending to alienate the subjects of the crown, or to draw the inhabitants to dangerous and rebellious opposition to the parent state.' He had complained to local magistrates that the Bostonians threatened him with 'seizure', which he announced to the Iroquois, fanning fears in Albany of an armed confrontation.

The Albany Militia Act of April required all males in the province between 'fifteen and fifty enroll in the militia under penalty of fine.' The Act only exempted 'Quakers, millers, furnace men, firemen, colliers, professional men, civil and royal officers, and slaves.' Exemption, however, could be bought, 'dependent on assessment in proportion to the conscript's estates of not more than $10.00 nor less than $1.00.'

John had brought a copy of the Act home, and Jane gasped with relief when she read the list of exemptions.

"David's exempt as a millwright, isn't he, John!" she exclaimed, clasping her brother's arm, impressed anew by the truth of what Abraham Wing had said about the importance of mills even in these troubled times.

For the first time, John looked directly at her when he spoke as though to emphasize that over the course of these several months with her repeated questions and her unhappy attempts to allay her own fears, he had to tell her there might not be a guarantee for her: "He might be exempt, depending on how many millwrights Abraham needs. You must understand what is involved, Jen."

"And what is involved, John!"

"Nothing less than a mustering of the country. Lists and exemptions like this are not made up unless the danger is overwhelming," he answered to the point.

John's response about David's status made her doubly anxious. For the first time she had to admit to herself that The Act only specifically mentioned *millers*, not millwrights, which included James Higson and not David. Assuming then that David wasn't exempt, her only hope lay in her brother who had served on the Committee from the very beginning. If Abraham chose his son-in-law, then John had an equal claim on her behalf for David, she reasoned. She then had no choice but to pursue him—but she had to be careful, she thought, because John was already critical of David's family and she didn't know how he might react to her efforts to have David avoid service.

She knew John loved her, but she also knew his evenhandedness and the strength of his convictions. He would resist using his influence. Yet surely, he understood her interest. But what arguments could she use to justify his intervention? First, Abraham had four mills and needed millwrights. Second, Daniel could claim David for his Kingsbury mills. And, third, for the first time in five years, she felt Sarah's evil selfishness in requiring David to live with and care for her might work to her advantage.

David, for his part, watched the events in Massachusetts with alarm and anger. No matter how often Jane stressed the possibilities of exemption, he feared conscription. He knew Abraham preferred James, and convinced himself Daniel wouldn't lift an eyebrow for him. As for his mother, Daniel might argue he *himself* could provide for her, and she always bent to his opinion. And John? He sacrificed for the country, and would undoubtedly expect the same from him. If he shared anything with Daniel, it was his dislike of John McCrea's politics. David, consequently, felt isolated from his own family and resentful toward John.

His increasing gloom distressed Jane. But she held out hope he would not be enrolled. Even when news of Lexington and Concord, when the British army finally attempted to disarm Massachusetts, reached the Colony of New York in mid-April, David had still received no notice from the Committee. Events took a more ominous turn at the end of the month, however, when Lexington and Concord prompted the New York Committee to call the First Provincial Congress with powers to govern, conduct war, and 'execute the recommendations of the Continental Congress.' She watched with increasing alarm as this Congress assembled in May, and a Second Continental Congress convened soon after. Then when fighting broke out with the Johnsons, and Allen from the Grants and Arnold from Connecticut captured Fort Ticonderoga, fighting seemed to erupt everywhere, and district committees collected weapons and ammunition, and began disarming Non-associators. The question then became *when* the Committee would come looking for David.

June arrived. In mid-month Massachusetts asked New York to request the Congress to prevent Guy Johnson from inciting the Indians against them, and General Gage declared Massachusetts in a state of rebellion, citing Hancock and Adams as 'rebels and traitors.' Had the Committee sufficient enrollees to assist Massachusetts and contain the Johnsons? Or had David in not signing the Non-association escaped their list of enrollees? Jane secretly hoped John had intervened on his behalf, but she feared the worst. Keeping silent she would not alert the Committee to David's having been possibly forgotten. And if she kept silent long enough, and the Committee did nothing, British soldiers might restore order. She refused to think what would happen to John, if soldiers occupied Albany. She trusted in her brother's resourcefulness. Given the quick ascendancy of the Committee system and the power of its Congress, *David* worried her more than John did. For, as she favored herself with thinking David might escape conscription, opponents of the Provincial Congress began arming. The Provincial Congress brought Angus McDonald, for example, before it on the fourteenth and he confessed to recruiting forty men for a battalion of Highlanders. Jane feared this might prompt a search for non-signers.

22

June 1775

Jane rode north to meet David because he hadn't wanted to meet her at John's.

What did he want to tell her? That he no longer worked at the Corners? That the Committee had enrolled him? Or that he had even decided to take up arms against it?

She shivered with dread, particularly because her last night's dream wouldn't leave her. It subdued the day, made the crows silent and the river gray and indifferent—each hill along the road offered her a cold shoulder, and the redbreasts flew coolly the other way.

She didn't want to ride any farther, only sit and sort things out—

She sat against a willow and watched a cormorant through the orange trumpets and green spears of tiger lilies dive off shore. As the bird disappeared beyond the flowers, a dizzy lifetime, not eight months, seemed to have passed since the Jessups' October party with its clink of silver and glint of crystal. How the initial possibilities of that evening had buoyed her before the news of Lewis' attack on the Ohio had annulled them! Now the Johnsons skirmished with Albany, tried to muster the Iroquois, and even ordered Samuel Kirkland, the Bostonian Minister, away from the Oneidas where Atsitsina and Falling Sparrow had gone. But even worse, the Jessups had received their ultimatum to disavow the Non-importation Sir Guy had spoken of that evening as a condition of the Ministry confirming their land. The conclusion that David had no opportunity with the Jessups, if they didn't have property was inescapable. And if the Jessups only hired him under those conditions? his working for them would force him to oppose the Non-importation himself, something unthinkable to her given her loyalty to her brother. But what were the alternatives? Hadn't David and James already nearly come to blows at the Wings over the Kingsbury celebration after the capture of Fort Ticonderoga in early May? Did David's pride now require him to stand up for what he had already declared to James?

That warm night she and Content, David and James had visited outside the Wings' tavern when news came of an attack on a Whig bonfire in Kingsbury. Word had come that Whig homes had been burned, and James had shouted for his horse. David had tried to stop him, and they might have come to blows if she and Content hadn't intervened. That moment had ended any friendship between the men—coldness reigned between them ever since. And, so, was David now coming to tell her he no longer worked at the Wings because James had terminated him? And was the Committee now enrolling him because of that?

She feared the worst because the Congress was now raising an army to invade Canada to draw the British out of Boston after the fighting at Lexington and Concord in April. Soldiers from the City, far more than Peter Tearse's Company, had already passed up the river across the bay.

The cormorant bobbed to the surface with a fish sticking from its beak.

"Jane."

"David!" she cried, jumping up as he came toward her and handed her a letter. Instantly the words, *COMMITTEE OF CORRESPONDENCE,* jumped out at her.

"I've no estate to buy this off," he said angrily before she could reply.

"My God," she gasped, feeling as though she was now drifting down river. She recalled her last night's dream of being in her Lamington garden as she weakly held the letter in her fingers. Her garden was strangely canopied with red willow leaves and thick strawberries, roses and peas. The strawberries seemed to bubble, and the peas intertwined like English lace. Someone came to her and she turned, offering him the plants to look at. He smiled wryly and she looked at the peas again. They were no longer lacelike, but large, bulbous, and misshapened. David had then entered the garden and a hole opened before him in the ground. She stepped toward him and screamed, and, when, she was about to fall through it, he took her in his arms. She had awakened terrified with her eyes hot from crying. The letter she now held between her fingers affected her like her dream.

'I planted them for you,' she now wanted to say to him as she had in her dream when he took her in his arms. But the letter was real and there was no waking up from it to find that it wasn't true. Their hopes and their dreams themselves seemed now to have brought them to this juncture.

"What am I going to do, Jen?" he asked, kicking the jack-in-the-pulpit that grew near his feet.

Her eyes wandered over the blue-green lichens which covered the trees, the soft earth, the rounded stones, the elms, the oaks, and even over those wisps of lichen which hung from the willow she was leaning against, adorning the tree like hair, as though Nature herself might provide her an answer to his question. And the very way he rubbed his scalp with his hands after asking brought tears to her eyes. His dejection and despair then colored her soul and she thought she would rather die than not be able to answer.

"Don't answer it," she said as firmly as she could with the words working themselves against the back of her throat because his hand found her neck under her hair. "John will help us," she swallowed, throwing her arms around him.

"But he's on the Committee . . ." David protested, feeling the weight of her body against him. He took her head in his hands so he could see her face.

The tortured expression in his eyes shocked her into defiance—why were they always given the oblique angle—first by Daniel; then his mother; then Jessups' land going out of reach; then his rupture with James; and now this summons! her eyes responded to him—But John had influence!

"He can help," she said, not even naming her brother, slipping her hand desperately into his.

He could see that she struggled to make sense of what he had brought her to—he could only kiss her by way of telling her what she thought was possible was less real than a mirage.

"He can't help," he then replied, sickened by the futility of begging the very Committee that sought to enroll him. "Maybe I should join Johnson. He's having a council with the Six Nations at Johnstown. He's forming a battalion . . ." his words left him like thieves.

Jane shrank away from him and turned her face away. "What are you saying about a council? You know where the Johnsons and Brant stand. You know of their court resolutions, their armed Highlanders, their skirmishing with Jacob Sammons, their banishing Kirkland from the Oneidas, and their efforts to muster the Iroquois! Your working for the Jessups is not the same as joining the Johnsons and their Indians!" she exclaimed

"And why not after what Lewis has done? And what if the Iroquois attack the frontier because of it . . ." he tried to reason with her, while at the same time regretting even having mentioned the Council given the shock it caused her.

"Is that why the Committee is summoning you?" she asked, pinning him down, not distinguishing between the Iroquois and the Lakes' Indians of the French war. "You don't want John to help?" she continued in disbelief at his intention.

"Whigs got us into this," he answered feebly, his mistake for not first taking her through this alternative plainly evident on his face.

"Whigs! It's not Whigs. How could you ever think to join Johnson and his Indians in any attack on our frontier? You won't join Johnson!"

"Jane, listen. The Johnsons won't let the Indians stand idle— millions of acres are at stake. The Johnsons will not harm us, they're on the Jessups side," he protested, "and if I don't join them, what am I to do!"

"You will not join Indians to fight your own people!" she cried, horror of such a prospect redoubling the hideousness of her dream. "I know it hurt you with the Jessups, but—"

"I should have joined the army years ago like my brother, Thomas," he persisted, unable to extricate himself.

"Of what value is that kind of hindsight now?" she asked, remembering, herself, that at the Jessups the same thought about David joining the British army had crossed her mind when Sarah McNeil had said that her cousin, Simon Fraser, had petitioned for land as an officer.

"And he's a Captain now."

"Why didn't you tell me?" she found herself asking, though the question bore its own futility.

"It was back in 'seventy-one and it didn't matter then. Now Lewis has started a war."

"But John can help. Listen, David," she now pleaded, returning to the real problem of his conscription.

"How, if he's one of them?" he appealed to her, angry at his own clumsiness.

She left his side. The river flowed full and quiet. At least now she had an opportunity to change what she most feared he might intend. She thought back to Lewis and wondered that his attack would lead to this—that David would actually consider joining the Johnsons! Certainly she was right, for Johnsons' Mohawks wouldn't or couldn't distinguish between Whigs and Tories. It was madness to think she, much less John and Eva and the children, could expect protection from Sir Guy. She had witnessed his rage. What civilized man would turn Indians against his own people after the horrors of the French war? She began to tremble—her childhood memories of the massacres in neighboring Pennsylvania filled her with horror and panic. A sickening emptiness formed in her stomach. "Not Indians!" she cried, losing breath, and helplessly losing her opportunity at calm with David's rashness. She then felt his arms around her.

"Very well," he said quietly.

"Promise me, you won't think it again . . ." She clutched him in her arms.

"I promise."

"Jane." She turned suddenly and saw John standing on the road. He came from behind the madness and fear she had just glimpsed like a savior. "Eva's looking for you," he said.

"I . . . Oh, John, you have come—" she wiped her nose. "Show John the letter, David," she said, turning to him quickly, not knowing that maybe John would vanish before she could control her voice.

"I know about the letter."

"Tell them he can't. You must do this for me, John . . ." she requested, hurriedly going to him.

"I can't . . ." he replied, taking her gently by the shoulders.

She stepped back from him. "But I'm your sister. Surely, you can . . ."

"But it's like I told you, Jen—the threat is there and there is no choice. David's not a miller."

"He's a millwright!" she pleaded.

"Abraham chose Higson," he informed her regretfully.

"Am I a traitor to still ask then?" she asked, not fully realizing how close to the truth her question was.

"No, of course not. But the Committee offers him a Lieutenancy with the Thirteenth, Jane . . ."

"And if he doesn't go?" She searched his eyes for some fissure of sympathy and understanding. She even sought in the lines around his mouth the familiar favor of his aid. But the lines at the sides of his eyes were tight in saying what he thought must be said to her. Her hand came up and touched his red hair in an effort to fend off the inevitability of what his look conveyed. What was happening fell upon her like an axe.

"They'll put him on a list with the others who refuse service," he answered gently but evenly, taking her arm in his hand.

"What in God's name is happening?" she murmured, looking at one and then the other of the two men. "How is it that things have come to this? How is it that things have stolen upon us like this without our knowing? This can't be happening to me, John."

"But it is, sister—" there was no mistaking the regret in his voice.

"And you saw it all coming? And you tried to tell me—" she said, as though everything she had seen happening up to this point had moved, during all those months when David seemed safe, with a sinister slowness and sureness that at times made it remote and impossible—but she had been fooling herself. She saw that now. Events had stolen upon her as surely as the night—yet, hadn't she with the other part of her mind been alarmed at the speed at which things happened? Could she deny that? No, she couldn't deny that either. Somehow what was happening had come slowly and all at once and she was bewildered by it, and for a moment sickened by it because John was caught up in it too—

"By whose authority will my name be put on a list?" David flushed.

"By the authority of the Congress," John answered, turning to him.

"Which has taken the Law into its own hands."

"If the Law was ever granted us, except in bloodshed," John replied evenly.

"John, listen . . ." Jane cast for the words, trying to anchor herself in the reality of the present while the past and future swirled around her, threatening to suck her under.

"I will not serve—"

"An army is on its way to Boston, David. Surely you know Concord and Lexington aren't going to go unanswered. They've killed innocent people."

"Don't tell me about innocence, John. Lewis opened it up, and how can you call that rabble from the Grants under Stark an army? We Yorkers won't go."

"You're mistaken."

"We only want to be left alone, John," Jane pleaded with him, fearing what might happen between the two men. "Surely, John, you know we have never taken sides in this . . ."

"David's an able-bodied man and I can't cover for him, Jane. What do you think is happening? Where have you been when I've been trying to tell you what's been going on? They are stripping us of our rights and shoving bayonets down our throats."

"Can't or won't, cover for him, John?" she asked pitifully, seeing his anger rise to the roots of his red hair.

"Don't plead with me like this, Jane. David can't remain neutral—don't you understand this? It's like a fire. You either have to put it out or be consumed by it—you can't stand and watch."

"You can't cover for me and you won't cover for me," David stated harshly. "And I don't want you to do either." He looked away to keep from glaring at John.

"If you loved my sister, you'd defend your country, David," John pursued him.

"Have pity on me, John! It's not his fault. I don't want him to go—"

"You haven't a cause, John McCrea."

"You don't think shooting people in Boston, or denying us the right to trial, or suspending our charters is cause enough, David?"

"We only want to be together, John. Listen to me."

"They'll hang you, John McCrea."

"Then they'll hang the whole country," he answered.

"Please, John."

"David's *not* a miller, Jane," he declared, turning to her. "listen, I suffer for you, feel for you, but there's no way out of it. He's a healthy man, and the country needs him. Look, you can't hide any more. There's nothing else to say."

"But this is lunacy!" David exploded. "I have never had any part in this affair!"

"You're either for us or against us." And then John looked closely at David, trying to find where the real man was—"And what have the English done for you, David?"

"They are not impressing me!"

John then turned to leave, but stopped and spoke. "I will do anything for my sister, David—but for you, there is no excuse."

"Oh, John, then you don't hate me!" Jane cried. "And you can do something!"

John looked at her. "How can you still say that? You see the position I'm in, you see what's happening to the country, and you see the position he's in—"

"You know what this will do to me. You're destroying everything for me . . ."

Her lips quivered as he walked away.

She stood on a precipice.

The June foliage hung over the opal darkness of the river.

Through her tears a yellow swallowtail stitched its way in the air toward the purple heads of chives growing on the bank. She wanted to reach out and press the insect between her fingers, but she wiped her eyes and watched it fold out its wings, exhibiting its yellow eyespots and twin tails like black bonnet ribbons.

How could John do this to her? It was heartless of him to pluck her wings!

"Maybe the Committee will leave us alone," she said between hope and despair, turning to David.

"They'll put me on that *list*," he reminded her, repeating in his own turn what John himself had said. "Your brother is of no use—he always hated me."

"That's not true," she defended John vaguely, unable to provide any other answer.

The butterfly tumbled one blossom after the other. Hadn't chance put that chive in the swallowtail's way? Its eyespots and curving twin tails caught her like the eyes and fangs of a snake. John was not her enemy. He only spoke of what was happening—he would never hurt her. It was the Committee. It was all the Committees! There was a sickness, a fever in the Colonies. But for them, whatever it took, they must keep that predatory Committee from them.

"I'll talk to him, again," she said, barely finding hope in her own words.

"But you heard him. I must do my duty!"

She shook her head. "Who is to say what Duty is, David, unless only our love—nothing else matters," she said as though she was praying.

As she looked at the ground, she then felt him touch her neck, suggestive of how he had touched her that first night when they swam together after his return from the Corners. She didn't remind herself of what depressing news he had had for her then, only tilted her head back and let her agony and fear, mounting depression and flashes of hope rush out of her in the passion she felt for him.

The swallowtail fluttered off.

"I won't lose you to them, I won't . . ." she said, pushing her cheek against his hand. She felt as weary as though she had climbed a steep hill.

23

John left for Albany that night to receive the new recruits for the army for Canada, and, during his absence, Stark inflicted severe casualties on the British on Breed's Hill in Boston on June seventeenth. Jane hadn't thought, few did think, that farmers could fight the British army—but they had fought it, and to a standstill. Further, a man named Washington besieged the city in early July, and her hope faded the British army would quickly gain control of the Colonies, insuring David's escaping enrollment.

When John returned two weeks later, he reported people were starving in Boston, and that Congress *had* to send an army to Canada to draw the British out of the city. Schuyler would command it, if the Grants did not resist his command, given his role in their dispute with New York over the boundary. The Committee planned to disarm Guy Johnson and other Non-associators in Albany County. Jane gave up hope John could do anything for David.

"The Committee received a letter from John Graham this morning, saying David refused his commission," John then informed her.

"He said he wasn't going to answer the Committee! Someone informed on him," Jane cried.

"It doesn't make any difference. The Committee would have found him anyway—"

"Will they send him to Canada?"

"Or keep him here to disarm the Johnsons. Either way, he can't avoid the field—"

David's earlier intention made Jane flush. James Higson *must* have informed on him because of the Kingsbury bonfire affair! He was now certainly on the Committee's list.

Jane rubbed her hands in anguish. "Can you assign him to Albany?" she repeated.

John shook his head. "The Congress needs officers, not clerks in Albany."

"And you?"

"I shall wait and see."

In August Sir Guy Johnson, unsuccessful in uniting the Six Iroquois Nations, and learning the Committee's intention to disarm him, fled to Montreal with Brant where Governor Carleton approached the Mohawks of Kahnawake and Saint Regis 'with the suggestion that they provide warriors for the royal service,' and where Sir Guy addressed sixteen hundred Indians about the *ill usage* inflicted on them by the Americans. Afterwards, some Mohawks who had fled with Johnson returned to Johnstown carrying war belts. Indians were then assigned to patrol the Richelieu between Saint Jeans and the Canadian frontier against the Americans.

In September the army of the Congress marched on Saint Jeans where it was intercepted by this Indian force under Tice, Walter Butler, and Peter Johnson, the half-brother of William Johnson Junior who had informed Brant at the Jessups' party of Lewis' victory over the Shawanese and the Caygugas, where it was forced to retire to Isle Aux Noix. The army suffered badly from malaria, and, given its losses, John himself joined the army on October twentieth, the day after Governor Tryon fled Albany to a British warship. John's leaving made Jane realize David would not escape hostilities, if detailed in Albany—for the struggle took the Committee itself into the field! She had two worries: David's detention; and John facing sickness and death in Canada.

She and Eva lived from week to week for news of John.

Events happened quickly over the following months. It was the longest fall and winter she and Eva had ever lived: on November twelfth Montreal fell to Montgomery (his having taken command from Schuyler who had fallen ill), and he captured the famous Canadian partisan, St. Luc La Corne allied now with the British after the fall of Canada, who had led the French Indians against

the Colonies in the last war. In December, the Committee captured
Johnson Hall and took Lady Johnson into custody; and news arrived
that Montgomery had been killed and Arnold wounded in the
attack on Quebec City. She and Eva trembled for news of John.
Had he fallen to sickness, been wounded or killed? They tried to
comfort each other and endured the childrens' questions about
their father. Winter deepened, and Congress ordered all Non-
associators disarmed. Jane feared soldiers would come for David,
that he would be impressed to drag cannons through the snow
from Fort Ticonderoga to Boston to force the British out of the
city. The first week in January, not having seen him for two days,
she abandoned the house.

She hung on events like the snow on the trees she passed.
The air rubbed her face raw as she rode along the road with
Charlotte's hoofs squeaking on the cold snow. Why hadn't David
come to her? Had they come for him? She urged Charlotte to a
canter, but the wind cut her face like a razor and she slowed to a
walk.

As she followed the frozen, pewter-gray river, the ice rubbed
smooth and shiny by the wind, she rode by the Tuttles' farm where
she saw Mister Tuttle splitting cordwood with an ax by the house.
His having no sons, Melanie Yarns carried wood in her arms into
the house. The cold air bent the smoke from his chimney against
the roof. Only the very coldest days bent the smoke like that. The
leather of the saddle numbed her legs. She waved to him, and he
waved back—Melanie dropped her wood when she waved—but
out of sight of the house she heard his door close with a crack from
the cold when he went to help her.

Nearing David's mother's, her eyes fell on the snow-covered
lumber on the knoll. One saw that abandoned pile the first thing
coming up the road. Nature itself urged a house on the knoll. No
matter where one stood, that knoll, with the large maple tree,
attracted the eye like the focal point a painting. How like Daniel
to build his mother's house below the horizon instead of
commanding a view of the river. Daniel's devious motives burned
in Jane's breast, and she grieved anew for those abandoned snow-

covered beams, shakes, and boards. How her Ferdinand had piled those logs for her!

She rode up the curved drive in front of the house.

Just then David came out of the well house.

"God, Jane, you're riding on a day like today? Even the well is frozen—" he exclaimed, his breath coming in a cloud.

"You didn't come—" she said, dismounting, her legs numb and stiff from the cold.

He took her in his arms and kissed her. "Let's go inside . . ." He led the mare to a nearby shed and forked out some hay. "I'm half-inclined to build that barn," he said from the small shed as he leaned against the open door.

"Never," she replied, feeling she would never capitulate to his mother on the barn. She was locked in silent war with Sarah.

"No, of course not," he agreed, explanation unnecessary.

Jane had a sinking feeling as they walked toward the house. She had avoided Sarah Jones since the day she denied them their home. As they neared the door, the curtains at the window moved and Jane regretted coming.

She took off her scarf and cloak inside the door. As her eyes adjusted from the outside brightness, Sarah's shadow passed into the kitchen.

"Have you heard from John?" David asked.

"Nothing," Jane answered. "Eva's sick about him. The children torture us with asking for him."

"A lousy affair, their rushing at Quebec—though, if he had been with Arnold or Montgomery, you would have heard something. A bad blizzard that night—only a few got through the gate into the town."

"How do you know that?" she asked, taking her eyes from the kitchen door.

"Robbie Yarns, returning from Albany, told me this morning. The Whigs in Albany should know."

"Then John's alive!"

"They should know in Albany," he repeated.

"Has Robbie Yarns enlisted?"

"He's too young. 'Next year,' they tell him. Higson fills his head with Whig stuff."

"James should talk, exempt because of his marriage," Jane said bitterly, thinking that much of what happened to people depended on either luck or who hated you—for a moment she thought she herself would have preferred going to Canada than struggle with Sarah Jones who plagued her like a nightmare.

"I don't mean anything against John—but I agree about James," David said, thinking how callous he sounded about Whigs after telling Jane what he guessed of John.

"John's doing what he must . . ." Jane sighed.

"That's enough talk of Whigs in this house!." Sarah Jones declared, coming into the room, "even of John McCrea. Your concern for him surprises me, David, after his attempt to impress you."

"He's Jane's brother, Mother," David defended himself.

"If his father could see him now, he'd sit up in his grave."

Sarah's bold assault took Jane off-guard. What right did she have to speak of her brother and father like this? "My father may not have approved of his going to Law, and I may not approve of John's politics, Mistress Jones, but they are my family."

"Who carries the wood and feeds his family then?" Sarah asked acidly.

Jane looked at David.

"Mother . . ."

"A man should provide for his family. Do you see my sons up there in Canada?"

"Each of us must do what we must," Jane replied shortly.

"Do tell me about it, dear."

"Does it bother you to see our house rotting on the hillside, Mistress Jones?" Jane asked point-blank.

"Not at all."

Jane wore her composure like armor, but her bitterness and resentment toward the woman burned beneath her skin.

"It's of no account to me. But we speak of John and your father," Sarah thrust icily.

"And what of them—?" Jane asked, breathless given her knowledge of Sarah.

"John must suffer his Princeton ways. But I confess, he is not suited for the ministry."

"John never claimed more rectitude than he has—though I think my stepmother's husband, my father, had rectitude, don't you agree?" Jane returned, scarcely veiling her reference to Thomas Jones' attempt to seduce her stepmother.

"Not so upright as to control his son, unfortunately."

"But upright enough to provide for his family, Mistress Jones. Upright enough to honor his wife and children," Jane maneuvered, thrusting closely at the cancer of Thomas Jones' slander and Sarah's infidelity. She wanted to catch and expose her. Suddenly her personal nightmare with this woman became vivid—the enemy stood naked before her. If only she could deliver the death stroke! Lance the corruption that brought such pain and unhappiness upon her . . . "He never had an ill-word for his son," she said, thinking of how Thomas Jones had split the sons of her own household against each other.

Sarah turned away, picked up a stick, and turned it lightly in her hands before laying it on the fire. "And how could your father speak ill of your brother, my dear, if he didn't really know his son's ideas?"

"But that was before the stamps . . ." Jane stopped, Sarah's political smoke screen blinding her.

"No, that wasn't before the stamps, but in the thick of it," Sarah cut in, sensing she now steered the exchange.

Jane felt the woman slip away from her. "But you can't say the same of yourself," she declared, trying to regain her advantage.

"Meaning?"

"You knew your sons so well. And now they live right next to you—they don't have the luxury of distance to keep you knowing them. You watch their every step. Get what you want—the barn. How can you speak ill of your sons, if they give you what you want?" Jane now regained the advantage she thought she had lost.

"No, I've already told you, it doesn't bother me to see the barn deferred," Sarah countered.

"But what of your self-respect? You have this land . . ." Jane saw a fleeting opportunity.

"I have nothing to complain of. It pleases my sons to do for me," Sarah came back, avoiding mentioning the land she withheld.

"Yes, how well they turned out . . ." she replied, trying to maneuver the woman back to that fall day when she and David saw her with the tinker.

"David knows the necessity of waiting," Sarah said, emphasizing the duty of sons.

"He's more dutiful than you know. He remembers one fall . . ." Jane began, on the verge of disclosing what she and David knew about her and the tinker.

"This has gone far enough," David intervened.

"Well, your mother wants to know what you know, David," Jane asserted, trying to convey to him she would now affront her with her past, not wanting him to take this opportunity from her. "Your mother says my father didn't know anything about John, but surely you know your mother better. And of course your father too. That's a decided advantage, isn't it?" Jane thrust, hoping he didn't miss the chance that offered itself, desperate he understand her intention.

"I don't know what you mean, my dear," Sarah broke off, seizing David's intervention. "But David is not in Canada, and he provides quite well for me, wouldn't you say? Now don't you have something better to do. A ride outside, some winter air to cool you off, perhaps, dear?" Her tone became the elder woman's, the mother of sons, and the mistress of the house. "Do give my regards to Eva. I never see her." She then left the room.

How could she have escaped? What could she say now with her out of the room? Jane smoldered in her chair, feeling the sting of their unchanged positions. Sarah held the high ground, succeeded in maintaining their frozen polarity. If only David had come forward, they might have exposed her, at the very least broken cleanly from her—and who knew what might have opened up from that? Had he intervened intentionally? Couldn't he see how she had evaded them? Hot and intense as never before, Jane sat in her chair. She listened for Sarah in the kitchen, hoping she listened.

"Why didn't you speak?"

"Of what?"

"I wanted you to tell her what we know."

"I couldn't do it," he confessed.

She looked at him. "You couldn't do it?"

"No."

"Shall I tell her myself?"

"No—" he answered, dejection and disappointment for Jane, even fear of his mother ambivalently expressed in his eyes.

"Our house might have been within reach—"

"I couldn't."

"Are you helpless?"

The door to the kitchen slammed shut.

Jane looked across the room. Sarah had listened from the kitchen, yet perhaps heard only the tone of their voices, their disappointment, the sound of differences between them. If she listened, she would fly out of the kitchen. Jane retreated. She had lost her opportunity. She took up her cloak and scarf.

"I can't bear it here—this house is a crypt."

Her new house was as distant to her now as if the logs never floated down the river—her objective as distant as John's up in those frozen Canadian stretches.

24

1776

Jane sat with the pamphlet in her lap. She had never seen such a cold January—the cold seeped through every crack in the house, numbing her hands and feet. The snow, inviting and sinister, glistened like diamonds in the pale moonlight.

She slipped her handkerchief from her marten muff and dabbed her nose. The maple trees, cracking in the cold night, brought her attention back to the pamphlet, and she thumbed through the pages to the ticking of the clock.

'Youth is the seed-time of good habits, as well as in nations as in individuals,' she read. 'No man was a warmer wisher for a reconciliation than myself, before the fatal nineteenth of April, 1775, but the moment the events of that day was made known, I rejected the hardened, sullen-tempered Pharaoh of England forever; and disdain the wretch, that with the pretended title *FATHER TO HIS PEOPLE* can unfeelingly hear of their slaughter, and composedly sleep with their blood upon his soul.' ' . . . many submit from fear, others from superstition, and the more powerful part shares with the King the plunder of the rest.' Jane read the last few lines, ' . . . until an independence is declared, the Continent will feel itself like a man who continues putting off some unpleasant business from day to day, yet knows it must be done, hates to set about it, wishes it over, and is continually haunted with the thoughts of its necessity.'

Jane dropped the pamphlet as though it burned her fingers, stinging her into wakefulness. *INDEPENDENCE!* She had lived a tortured dream since her father's death, a soul seeking happiness through the darkness of grief. Bereft of the paternal nest and fending for herself, wouldn't this national independence, which Paine called for, set her further adrift? Hadn't what led up to his call stymied her efforts to have a home, adding disappointment to pain, redoubling her loneliness and grief? As with her own father's decease, what would her hopes finally come to without a king?

She had always honored the King as her father. Even when she teased Sarah McNeil at 'Tenty's wedding, saying nature needed no royal adornment, she merely reacted to what she herself couldn't possess because of these troubles. Hadn't the Non-Association prevented David from working with the Jessup brothers? And hadn't the uncertain times added to Daniel's breaking his promise to David? And because of the trouble in Boston and the invasion of Canada, didn't separation from David threaten her now? A father and a king did adorn and improve upon nature, sanctifying life. Hadn't 'Tenty's father married her to James Higson, and hadn't not having her own father marry her and David grieve her after 'Tenty's marriage? With what finality Paine's words shut out the past! How absolutely he assaulted the paternal tree and its protective branches, laying waste what gave security and meaning to life— What future lay before her? This call for independence threatened to extend her orphanhood. She might never marry; never have the completeness and happiness that came from having the family for which she yearned.

As she sat thinking, her future merged with the indefiniteness of the Colony's future, and both took on a cold and silent January character. A country without a king and a home without a father made the one hostile and the other cheerless and empty. How could she find happiness when both conspired against her and David?

Eva's clogs rapped against the floor in her bedroom. It was one o'clock. Jane shivered and tucked her robe under her legs as Eva entered the room.

"I can't sleep," Eva said.

She felt Eva's cold hand against her cheek. How could she explain to Eva how she felt without mentioning John and her father and risk arousing those dormant and twisted feelings for her father and John again, and without mentioning Eva's slave-owning which contradicted the independence Paine called for and she favored?

"Why did John go?" she simply asked, unable to keep the anguish from her voice. She yearned for the family peace of childhood when she watched her brother work, rolling hay and pitching it onto the wagon, and feeling his strong arms when he carried his only little sister home. Yet his huddling against a snowdrift outside the walls of Quebec City drowned her in sorrow. They had a common father! were of the same blood and family— Oh! to relive those days of childhood, to have life as it used to be!

"He went to fight that accursed king," Eva answered, withdrawing her hand, isolated by her own principles and fear for her husband.

Jane stared at the fire, but didn't see it. She saw only John leaving last October three months ago; saw only his dark silhouette retreating through the dusk toward the shore of the bay and the waiting boat. She had cried when he had stepped into the boat because he had denied her his parting words before going off to war. The pain of his leaving her flung her back to their estrangement when he had left their father's house before their father's death. And would she ever see John again? And why, for what cause? The very perversity of his purpose now sharpened her love for him— and now what cruel messenger would fate send against him because of this evil rebellion he so heedlessly supported?

She thrust the pamphlet at Eva, hardly able to express the anguish Paine caused her.

"This is parricide . . ." she gasped.

Eva looked aside at the burning logs and sat down, not taking the pamphlet from her. "You must understand its inevitability. The old ways don't work in this country. We will not wear the King's harness. What can be more obvious?"

"Oh?" Jane asked bitterly, Eva's words transforming the flames of the fire into cold, yellow knives. "You speak of Independence when you own a slave? You speak of Independence trapped by John's absence like this? And how can you know the pain of the estrangement between fathers and sons, between a sister and her brother?" She found herself unintentionally giving voice to Sarah Jones' sarcasm as she interjected her own family sorrows.

"Sons have wills of their own, Jane. Husbands have wills. And if they are good-willed men, they will not stand for wearing any harness. This slavery you speak of is only because of kings. John has his own future. This country has a future—it is like a young man. That King is no longer father to this country. The old laws don't work here. We came to escape kings. Your brother is still a shield and protector, only you don't see it. If your brother, and my husband, is not free, then we women are not free either."

She clutched at her former hopes as though intervening time had never dimmed them for her. The very coldness of the room sharpened her hopes: John left during the royal colors and crispness of fall. She recalled the burgundy stencil winged monarchs like newly fallen leaves on the road in the cathedral of the woods on her way to the Jessups'. Their guests, in their capes and petticoats, had mirrored those colors. The word 'King' had evoked color and vitality. Her childhood had been a bombazine of warmth woven by the paternal hand and nurtured by mild and deferential brothers. What did Eva know about brothers? Independence brought only estrangement. The fire waved dizzily before her eyes.

"My brother is making a terrible mistake. It isn't natural to do what he's doing—What gives John the right to bring this kind of unhappiness and suffering upon us?"

"He has the 'natural right' of a human being before the God that created us all. He has the obligation to tear away the rotten mask of kingship which disguises the tyranny that oppresses us."

Dinah then came into the room.

"I heard you talkin', Chile. Haven't ye told her, Missus Eva?" Dinah asked her. "That your husband bought my freedom, and that I live here of my free-will?"

"But John might die!" she half-cried, reacting to their common front and curling her fingers against her palms. How did she know that John had bought Dinah's freedom? They had never told her. But it didn't make Eva any less cold to her. John was still in danger of losing his life! "January has fathered you, Eva. Your indifference to John's suffering is harder than the nature you speak of. He should have remained here to keep you safe. Oh, I wish he hadn't gone! If only I had been able to talk to him." Oh, if only John had spoken to her for just a moment before he had left! "What have you done to him, Eva, that he didn't even speak to his sister before he left?" Why had he only stood there outside the house observing the soldiers across the bay before he had gone—why hadn't Eva said something to her? Why didn't she understand what John meant to her?

"Your talking to him would have changed nothing, Jane, except that you would have made him suffer all the more. You are thinking only of yourself. If you loved your brother, you would have said something to *him since he is the one making the sacrifice.* But I do love him, and he will return *stronger* than before."

"I would have spoken to him, Eva, but you prevented it. You knew I wanted to—How terrible of you, Eva," she replied in her own defense, her lips barely moving, the cold touching her spine like a knife. She had struggled to live here after David refused his commission; struggled to live here with Eva after John had left. But now, Eva's rebuke left her hanging like an apple in winter. Her last supports were being denied her. But she would have answered Eva with a fugue, if the cold in the room and Paine's words hadn't iced her soul. And where could she live, if she broke from her sister-in-law? Nowhere. Sarah Jones' hatred had trapped her here with her brother and family, and now they were turning their backs on her. She wanted to reach across the field and through the woods to David and feel the protecting warmth of his hands and body. He was all she really had in life.

"You were silent toward your brother after David's refusal to answer that commission, Jane. You clung to that silence. That's what was terrible for your brother. Only you can soothe your own regret and pain. And do you think I would see him sacrificed to a meaningless cause? Do you think it is easy for me to imagine him up there in those frozen wastes? He and our children are my world. How can you not understand that?"

Eva brushed her loose blonde hair from her face and without

another word walked back to her bedroom. "You can't deny me knowing that."

"But a family and children are *everything!*" Jane called after her as her sister-in-law closed her bedroom door.

How had they come to this pass? How had she and Eva become estranged like this? It was because of David and John. Because David had refused that commission from the Committee, because John hadn't helped her when she had asked him to, appealed to him, even beseeched him to help her that day by the river. What alternative had been left her, but to show her wounded feelings and the pain she felt except by keeping silent? And Sarah Jones had also treated her harshly a few days ago, and because she had been unable to speak to David about his mother further hardened her silence. She had felt cut off by John and David's mother, and how could her feelings for Eva, who encouraged her husband, not be affected by this as well? Eva had chosen her side, so how could she expect any warmth from her? Couldn't Eva see this? But she wasn't as selfish as Eva had said! And she didn't want people, especially her family to think this of her. She had never wanted to be involved in this quarrel—Oh, why couldn't Eva see that? She had only wanted for her and David to be left alone.

25

April, 18, 1776

"Any sign of them?" Content asked, untying her apron and coming to where Jane peered through the window at the rutted road outside the tavern.

"No," Jane answered, wondering why Content had invited her here to the tavern to meet these Commissioners. She hoped Content thought she would learn of John from them, rather than suggest to her the rightness of their action and casting a rude light on David's differences with James. She preferred to think that. Or, if not that, Abraham might have suggested the idea of her coming, his knowing her concern for John. But Content acted all in the world as though this was just an ordinary April day. But was it? She seemed particularly fidgety at this moment.

"It'll take 'em a wee bit at this time o' year," Polly observed, pushing a chair up to the table behind them. She wore a long blue gown,

"Oh, don't fuss with the furniture, Polly!" Content then exclaimed irritably. *"They* would travel in a gale. Weather doesn't determine what they do."

Content's reply clearly indicated she had dropped her political indifference and had become a Whig since marrying James. So, Content had invited her here to see for herself that she supported that Congress of Committees. But she cared more for John's welfare than Content's 'patriotism'.

"The Yankees should hae expected starvation and sickness running at Quebec. And they pin their hopes on a priest to save 'em at th' last hour!" Polly retorted. "'Twill take more than a parcel o' Commissioners ta face th' gale they've brought on themselves."

Jane didn't know whether the army's failure to take Quebec irritated Polly, if she voiced Sarah's Loyalism, or, if this priest, accompanying the Commissioners, offended her Presbyterianism. Or had Content's refusal to identify these Commissioners by name, other than to say a priest was with them, provoked her? Either way, Polly's sentiments with Peter out of danger at the fort annoyed her.

"It's easy to dismiss the suffering of these Commissioners on such a journey with Peter at the fort, Polly," Jane said, supporting their efforts to bring the Canadians in on the American side because of John. She favored anything that would ameliorate the army's condition. If this priest, or any priest, could help, then she supported him too, though she hadn't time to give much thought to whether the French *habitants* now supported, or would support, the rebel army.

"The Quebec campaign *did* draw the British out of Boston, Polly" Content emphasized. "I agree with Jane, if this priest can help, so much more our gratitude for what he's doing."

"Who is with this priest, by the way?" Jane asked her.

She had endured the suspense of not knowing. Yet, would she have come, if Content had told her more than that she should meet them? Content had written, 'I can't tell you. If the Tories knew of their coming, they would try to kill them. I can only tell you a priest is with them.' Jane had to accept Content didn't know.

"And what about th' rascals stealin', Content? Not seein' a penny for what they take. A blue petticoat o' all things!" Polly asserted of Captain Lammar's requisitions of the Wing family in mid-March.

"Don't pick, Polly," Jane said. "Your fencing is purposeless and you can't influence what's happening."

"Don't forget the shirt, handkerchief, pewter basin, and the fowls, Polly," Content continued to dispute Polly, however. "Besides, Captain Lammar signed for everything, and it's to aid the sick at Lake George."

"It's still filching . . ." Polly began, stopping abruptly. "Look . . ."

Two riders galloped toward the tavern. Mud spattered up

against the window as they quickly dismounted at the door and came into the tavern.

"Is this Wing's tavern?" one asked, bursting into the room, his eyes darting.

"I am Content Wing."

"And your father, where is he?" the officer asked abruptly, his eyes stopping at the pantry. He then walked across the room, looked into the pantry, and spoke to the other soldier—"Ask those women by the well, if they've seen anyone." He came over to Jane. "Have you seen men outside the tavern?" He had penetrating gray eyes. He was not unkind, just very anxious in his duty.

"No, I have seen no one, but ask Content. Those women are helping with lunch," Jane added, turning to footsteps on the stairs.

"Colonel George Elrich," the officer introduced himself as Abraham came down the stairs and across the room to him.

"How many are you, Colonel?"

"Three Commissioners, Father John Carroll of Baltimore, and ten horsemen."

Abraham raised his eyebrows and waved at his daughter. "Inform your mother, Content."

"And how far are they goin' ta get in that?" Polly declared, still at the window where she sighted a wagon approaching.

The wheel ruts in the road jostled the wagon as it neared the tavern. A troop of riders stopped in front of the door. An old man sat in the wagon.

Antis then came into the taproom. "Content, have the women drawn the water?" she asked.

Colonel Elrich quickly went to the open door where the April sunlight fell narrowly onto the floor.

Jane watched two men assist an old man from the wagon. His gray and wispy hair fell to his shoulders as he walked stiffly by the window. She turned to the door as they entered the tavern.

"How lovely a reception!" The old man said on seeing them, nothing of weariness in his voice. His glance made her agreeably self-conscious because she wore her flowered muslin with long sleeves and ruffles and had arranged her hair in a tilted knot.

"Misses McCrea and Hunter, and Content, my daughter . . ." Abraham introduced the younger women, "and my wife, Antis. Ladies, Doctor Franklin from Pennsylvania . . ." he paused in his introduction, not knowing the other men.

"Charles Carroll, his brother, Father John, and Samuel Chase, all from Maryland," Doctor Franklin finished for him.

Jane immediately understood Content's invitation to her was to receive Doctor Franklin. She was there to lighten his journey. She was not offended by this, but suddenly felt she would do anything to assist this man delivering John, for all knew Doctor Franklin succeeded at whatever he attempted. She would gladly lighten his journey, if she could.

Antis reached for his cloak, and the old man's fingers fumbled at the clasp.

"General Schuyler said you had little time," Abraham apologized, fronting his visitor agreeably.

"Indispensable man," the doctor replied, allowing Abraham to lead him and the other Commissioners to the table prepared for them. The neighborhood women, who had volunteered to help Antis, entered the room, followed by the escort whose boots sounded heavily on the floor. Content seated them, and Colonel Elrich and four others sat at a table close to the Commissioners.

Doctor Franklin sat down and sipped his ale with a hint of fatigue.

"And how has your trip been thus far?" Abraham asked, genuinely concerned for the elder man's health and safety.

"Brutal," Samuel Chase answered for him, "though Doctor Franklin endures better than any of us."

Jane noticed how Doctor Franklin smiled with an unmistakable hardness. She had no way of knowing that he had told the others of his party that he did not know if he would live through this trip.

"Only know, Sir, that your tavern is an oasis. But if the truth were known, I thought I would die before reaching Montreal. Now, I know I will get there," he said.

Jane pitied him the mud on his boots and stockings. He also

appeared to have fever. Suddenly this most extraordinary man, who had such a reputation in the Colonies, seemed very human.

"I hope we don't inconvenience you, but General Schuyler voiced concern about Tories in Kinderhook and the King's district of Albany. General Washington sent one of his personal bodyguards. You met Colonel Elrich?" Samuel Chase asked.

"Moments ago," Abraham answered, nodding at the table where the Colonel sat.

"But we've encountered no Tories," Charles Carroll went on to inform them.

"I would have felt better if you had come with twice the number of men—but, I suspect, the secrecy of your visit will have the desired result. No one knows of your coming," Abraham declared, confident of having preserved the trust General Schuyler had placed in him.

"But you could have told your own daughter, Father," Content objected with self-effacing petulance.

"I couldn't have betrayed General Schuyler's confidence, could I have, dear? Now, tell us Doctor, what are your chances? Will the Canadians join us?" her father answered, coming immediately to the point of the Commissioners' purpose.

"If we can get them before General Burgoyne arrives in May. Father John will interpret for us. The French Catholics are not happy," Doctor Franklin answered of the *habitants,* but avoiding prematurely mentioning, however, his desire for them to join the Congressional union as the fourteenth Colony.

He began eating his soup. The town's women served ale, and plates of lamb and potatoes.

"Is reconciliation impossible then?" Abraham asked.

"I fear so. We cannot negotiate with the Howe brothers holding pistols at our heads in New York, and Congress is determined to save the army. General Washington will also enter Boston tomorrow. And, of course, Burgoyne will rattle his sword when he steps on land," Doctor Franklin answered him.

"Mister Paine spoke for us. The issue is no longer reconciliation, Sir, but separation," Charles Carroll affirmed.

Jane looked blankly at her plate, recalling how Paine's
COMMON SENSE had frozen her that January night when she
had first read it. Her relations with Eva hadn't, at least on the
surface, thawed either since that January night. But beneath their
hard exteriors both women had unspokenly recognized their
common concern for John. Now, Charles Carroll's statement about
separation made her dreams as cloudy as April puddles, reminding
her of Catherine's shroud-wrapped pronouncement that her father
had died, news that had ended her childhood. And why, now,
must such news be repeated in spring, the time of birth and
nurturing? Why, as new shoots grew from the ancient tree must
they now be cut at the roots?

The conversation grew fainter, and she drifted like a moth
toward a dark light as she momentarily forgot about John in the
larger mission of these Commissioners.

"We must save the army. The struggle will grow hotter," Sam
Chase reiterated their purpose.

"What an abridgement," Abraham sighed as he witnessed the
truth of his forecast, which had come to commit him to the
Congress.

"Pride and power curse mankind," Father John Carroll
observed, blotting his lips with a napkin.

Jane made a conscious effort to understand what she was
hearing, tried to understand something of Doctor Franklin. Old
and revered, the author of POOR RICHARD'S ALMANAC,
everyone respected him. For Eva, he embodied her cause. Something
of a Jesus and a Socrates, he evoked reverence, even love. But he
was mild and affectionate, and ill! How could he save an army? She
found herself torn between pity and respect for him and abhorring,
if that was not too strong a word, his cause.

She looked at him. The April light framed him across the table
from her. His face, though lined with fatigue, was rather youthful
for his seventy years. Yet, riding in a wagon to Montreal would
probably cripple, if not kill him. And what, but a barren landscape,
would remain to them after his death, if the Colonies succeeded in
separating from England? Sincere and open, he had no air of

possession, culture or power that distinguished a gentleman. For all he was trying to accomplish, she might have known him all her life. But the Colonies *were* English!

"Why do you favor separation?" she asked him, frightened for him, as much as for herself, by his dark leap. "We *are* Colonies. Isn't it important to keep the empire unbroken—" she pursued him, seizing the words as they rose to her lips, "to keep our language, civilization? What will become of us adrift from the parent state?" she concluded desperately, overwhelmed by the thought that the Colonies would be lost in limitless seas, if they separated from England.

"Civilization will not stop with separation, my dear—We will have new literature, inventiveness, a culture breathing freedom," he answered her gently and patiently, taking his napkin from his collar and wiping his brow as he looked curiously at her.

"The King divided us and kept us weak," Charles Carroll supported him.

"And we're not an island, but a continent. Inevitably after eight generations, we are Americans," Doctor Franklin continued, looking at her across the table as though not aware that Charles Carroll had spoken.

"But didn't the King defeat the French?" she almost pleaded with him, trying to remind him that the English and the Colonies had suffered as a family during that desperate war.

"We drafted a plan for our own defense at Albany which the King rejected. He sent us regiments we didn't need, and taxed us for them. Now he contends with us instead of the French," the doctor answered simply, though his expression indicated that it was not such a simple matter.

"Americans?" Polly questioned somewhat scornfully, "the *savages* are the only real Americans."

"Polly Hunter!" Content exclaimed at such a rude assertion.

"Well, it's the truth," Polly defended herself shortly.

"No, we're Americans too," Doctor Franklin smiled, correcting her.

"What do we share wi' savages, Doctor!" Polly persisted.

"My, Polly, you speak so!" Content declared.

"Well, this affair isn't th' simplest thing to comprehend," Polly shot back at her.

"I must agree with that, Miss Hunter. But let us say over the years we share their 'thinking', and that we are something of brothers," the old man averred.

The other commissioners became silent as the old man talked.

"Is there any hope for the army, Doctor?" Jane asked, not wanting Polly to hold him in such futile discourse when she had to know of John.

He shook his head. "It's in a sad state. We shall meet with the Canadians. Father Carroll will assist us."

"Do you know my brother, Colonel John McCrea?" she asked him.

The old man shook his head. "No."

"But will you ask for him?"

"Indeed, I will, Miss McCrea—and tell him I met you."

"But th' *savages*, Doctor Franklin, what about them?" Polly insisted.

Jane wondered if this man would find John in Montreal, or on some swampy island in the river near St. John's.

"The savages . . . yes . . . our survival always depended on our relations with them. We have come to behave something like them through our negotiations and alliances. How else have we survived?" He wiped his forehead. "Our Assemblies recognized, indeed the Iroquois Indians stressed during the French War that our defense depended on a colonial confederation. We used the Iroquois model for our plan at Albany in 'fifty-four," the old man stated, looking at Polly with good-humored circumspection, clearly revealing he didn't expect this kind of questioning taking refreshment.

"Don't tire yourself, Doctor," Father John Carroll said. "You have fever."

"On the contrary, I feel invigorated now, John. I don't often have such pleasant company," he assured the priest. "Now Weiser, a fellow Pennsylvanian," he went on, "spoke of Iroquois government during those dark days on the Ohio, Miss Hunter. You should know that. The Mohawks had made Conrad a Pine Tree Chief. He and an Oneida, Schikellamy, kept our alliance with the Iroquois together. We discussed the make-up of their Grand Council, and we used the term in our Albany plan," he paused. "European government provided no model of confederation. Adopting the Iroquois' was as natural as breathing. So, you see, we are all Americans, and we share certain thinking with the Indians."

"I suppose ye'll make the turkey your national bird," Polly quipped under her breath.

"What is the *difference* between us and them then?" Jane asked, caught by the man's explanation when he might just as easily have evaded Polly's questions with aged privilege. "For surely we are different."

"Difference? None in our desire for free government, which is why the King rejected our plan as too democratic."

"'Democratic'?"

"Electing our assemblies, having a Council that would determine our policies, raising our own revenues—Yet, even so, we gave the King veto over our actions. Still, he rejected it, and so did our legislatures because of the veto granted him."

"Election is the Indian idea of freedom," Abraham added. "Mister Paine's 'natural rights' come from John Locke who cited the Indians in his *SECOND TREATISE ON CIVIL GOVERNMENT,* justifying the Glorious Revolution. My 'Quaker' forebears with William in the Netherlands handed down the story. It's something of family history . . ." he continued to clarify.

"Quite so," Doctor Franklin agreed, pleased with his addition. "The great John Locke knew the natives had real government. He had read Sagard and the *JESUIT RELATIONS.* But we had known *all along* what he attested was true. The Ministry, however, will never accept this except at great suffering to us all," he sighed. "Such is the folly and pride of princes."

"The Indians are ignorant savages, for all you borrow from them," Polly declared.

"Ignorant? Perhaps. But we are a continental people like them and don't always know the ways of Providence, my dear," Doctor Franklin concluded, looking at her.

"You think the Indians wretched beggars because they don't live like us, Polly Hunter—" Content challenged her.

"'Tis plain they don't live like us," Polly hastily agreed with her.

"Like peasants?" Doctor Franklin then asked.

"Worse, sir . . . *savages.*"

"Savages, 'people of the forest'? Certainly not peasants who are European," he gently guided her, "who must bear the taxes and oppression of a king."

"What should one think of people who live as they do?" Polly persisted.

"Have you seen their villages, Doctor Franklin?" Abraham asked him.

"Yes, I have. They have log houses, orchards, and fields. Do our frontiersmen live as well? But it is their civil relations, their *government* that we are borrowing, Miss Hunter. Our desire for real government inspires us to resist English tyranny. We don't see the Indians as children of the forest as the English do, but as brothers . . . And are we better than them who have the gift of government because they live in log houses? They don't have universities, it is true, and so much the better, since even universities have perpetuated ignorance. And so *we* struggle, as a result."

"And what about the Iroquois in this struggle, Doctor?" Jane asked, the very idea of them joining the conflict filling her with horror, yet holding out hope they would not fight the rebellion given what Doctor Franklin just said about them and their freedom. But who could overlook how they fought the French in the last war? The French not only committed atrocities against the Colonies.

"It is our ardent wish that they remain neutral, though their 'father the King', through his surrogates, is doing everything in his power to raise them against us."

"And what is to prevent it?" Abraham asked.

The old man shook his head. "Their *chain of friendship* was always with the English. The English surround them and have taken the place of the French. Who is to say—will the appeal of their brothers in the Congress be as strong as the appeal of their 'father'? Will they see the difference between us, you might ask? We can only hope that a wise council among their elders will prevail over the new class of warriors who have arisen among them out of the French war . . . But I fear the influence of Brant and the Johnsons.

"But as delightful as this is, Lake George comes no closer for my talking, I fear," he said regretfully, pushing away from the table, the subject of the Iroquois seemingly prompting him to the business before him. He stood up slowly.

Abraham went for his cloak. As the Commissioners put on their coats in the streaming light of the doorway, the soldiers left the tavern. Theirs was no gradual parting—

"I will not forget your brother," he said, turning to Jane.

As he then turned and spoke to Abraham, Jane stood beside her chair filled with sudden hope that he would rescue John. She might not have understood what the great man said, nor even agreed with him, but she believed he would find her brother.

The door closed. His plate and napkin remained on the table. How quickly he had come and departed! What he had said of the Indians now left her feeling strange and awkward. She had felt the same way when Falling Sparrow and Atsitsina had come to the tavern during that November blizzard. Such strangeness was frightening now, however, for in the new world that this old man perceived hung her own and her brother's destinies.

"Imagine, th' savages," Polly remarked, returning from the door.

"He's a visionary," Abraham replied, hearing her. "Oh, I don't mean just about the Albany Plan and the Indians, but the idea of Unity and Law! Swedes, Englishmen, Dutchmen, Germans, Scots, Irishmen, Welshmen, and Frenchmen—" he counted them off on his fingers, "all with different religions, making up the different Colonies. Think of people knowing only war coming to these shores. Think of them united, not by a King or religion, but by Law! Think of them as Americans. That's Franklin . . . . That's the Indian Confederacy Franklin acknowledges. Imagine our own confederation stretching across the continent from sea to sea, stretching north to south!" He rocked on his toes possessed with the idea. "The man is daring. He brought Thomas Paine over here—America will give us the peace and unity Europe always denied us, a new Union governed by Laws."

"My, dear!" Antis said.

"Aye, Mister Wing. How are th' Indians themselves going to fit in? much less Highlanders, slaves, and people with different speech, dress, and station . . ." Polly asked. "Th' rascals are already taking all their lands . . ."

"All nourished by common boundaries and the shared idea of free government," Abraham went on, seemingly oblivious to Polly's interjection.

"He held a key to the heavens and understood the thunder of Princes," Antis half-mocked, referring to Doctor Franklin's electrical experiments. "And now he applies himself to this war—"

"And government. Besides," Abraham continued, "all people who come here crave peace and unity. And this unity will abolish slavery as well . . . You can't tell me Doctor Franklin doesn't see that, too."

"Aren't you expecting too much, dear?"

"We must suffer, must sacrifice first, must give our lives if need be . . ." Abraham said with sudden sadness. "But he *will* get to Canada! And he *will* find John, Jane!"

"Oh, I pray for it, Mister Wing, with all my heart," she declared, turning away from him for what he said of sacrifice and all that the old man had said cloaking her thoughts in a vague, uneasy dusk of the spirit. This encounter seemed dream-like to her. But she yearned with all her heart that the old man's promise to find her brother wasn't a dream—that this remarkable man would find him . . .

Later when she and Polly returned to Sarah McNeil's house, she rebuked Polly for her assertiveness with Abraham and Doctor Franklin to which Polly replied, "How else are we ta know what's goin' on, if ye don't make 'em speak up? Peter never tells me anything . . . At least now I've seen the great man and hae some sense of what's goin' on, though it's still somethin' o' a muddle where th' savages and his talk o' government are concerned. 'Tis a wee bit early for talk of government, isn't it?" she tested, making Jane acutely conscious that the rebel army hadn't gotten out of Canada yet.

26

May 1776

David stood outside of John's log house, awkwardly waiting for Eva to ask what he knew she would ask him. Why else would she guess he was here unless out of work after the events of the last few weeks?

He thrust his hands into his waistcoat and turned toward the voices and pole banging across the bay. The soldiers he watched marching, beneath a milk-splashed sky, went to Fort Edward and Lake George. Arnold had abandoned the siege of Quebec and Burgoyne had occupied the city. These soldiers moving north were receiving the remnants of the army and preparing for the British advance. They had just requisitioned Abraham's saws for Lake George, which had shut down his mills. David questioned why the rebels didn't transport the finished lumber to Fort George—but then, it wasn't his war.

Eva withdrew into the house and closed the door.

He questioned Jane with his eyes as to why Eva had said nothing. He noticed a mantis crawling at the hem of Jane's petticoat and flicked it off with his fingers.

"She's concerned about John, the sick and wounded," Jane answered. How odd, however, that they had heard nothing from John, especially since Robbie had learned of the disaster at Quebec in Albany in January. John should have sent word, if the Committee had information. She supposed him lost. The condition of the army returning from Canada the last two weeks alarmed them: more ghosts than men, many straggled behind the army. Had John not written for that reason? Was he lying wasted and sick somewhere, or was he dead? The very thought of his dying strickened her—but she had to cling to the hope that Doctor Franklin had found him.

"Of course, Eva's concerned about her husband," he replied, the clanking of poles and oars on the bateaux across the bay fading beyond the tree line. "I shouldn't have come, but I had to tell you about Wing's saws."

Indeed, Jane insisted he come, rather than her go to his mother's. Her anxiety about John demanded this. And, not the least, if she didn't wait for John should he come home unharmed, it would seem like desertion to him. David's news of the saws came as no surprise to her—like an expected death, the news only numbed her.

"Come live at Mother's. At least we would be together," he whispered.

"No." She shrank from the very idea. Had he forgotten his mother's words in January?

"Solomon's there. It wouldn't be just the two of us living together," he pleaded, annoyed she wouldn't even come to the house when he requested it. And what did he care of John? He would return. The rebels always managed to hang on. What else could they conclude about him when no word of his being sick, wounded, or captured had reached them? And he had his words with him last June on his duty. And hadn't Jane made her decision then? He didn't have to consider John. This war disgusted him.

"Have you forgotten your mother?" she asked him, in disbelief of what he wanted her to do.

"We'll be Methuselahs by the time we marry," he answered, avoiding reference to his mother, preferring to think if she shared her house his mother would change.

"Don't say that, David." She hated witnessing these years dissolving like spring snow. She had looked in the mirror at twenty-six and heard the clock ticking. He need not remind her of her age. "Do you think it's easy for me to see John and Eva with their children, Content and James, Deborah and Daniel? I'm not so old, David!" She said, hurt and frustrated enough to cry.

"Waiting's killing us."

"She's killing us!" She didn't remind him of how they had sidestepped the Committee, which, if they had not been able to do, would have meant impressment or prison for him.

"If I had gone with the Johnsons . . ."

"You would be in Quebec or Montreal."

"I'd be paid for my efforts like Thomas. Johnson and Brant are with Burgoyne now."

"Thomas is safe in England." 'And Johnson and Brant are doing their best to stir up the Indians against us,' she refrained from saying, insisting instead, "But we've stayed together, and Polly and Peter must wait."

"I should have pried the land out of her when we arrived."

"Yes! You should have. And now maybe you see that what I wanted was not from selfishness, but from love and desire for a family, only—"

"Oh, Jen, I know that—"

And still, it hadn't happened. Their house only rotted in pieces on the knoll. She thought of Franklin in April forcing the issue of understanding. The Ministry would not concede anything to the Colonies—and David's mother would never move an inch toward her son's happiness. But it still could happen, if he demanded it of her. Her hottest thought was David would affront his mother. Living like this was a slow death.

"When this war ends, insist with her," she found herself saying, surprised that she had already accepted that the war now governed the present.

"When will the British get here? Hasn't Sarah McNeil said anything? Her cousin, Simon Fraser, is with the army, isn't he?"

The past year they had lived with fear of his detention, but David not having taken up arms against the Congress, and his work at Abraham's had saved him. But, now, his neutrality without work might not save him from conscription or detention.

"Simon Fraser wrote from Cork on April fifth he was sailing with six regiments. Polly told me yesterday." Revealing this to him was like outlining the moves in a British game she had up until now, given her worry over John, only an abstract interest in—

"Did you see his letter, or is this more of Sarah's cricket chirping about *Fraser the schoolteacher?*" he asked.

A week ago Sarah McNeil had mentioned that another relative of hers was 'organizing' resistance to the rebels in the valley. She had mumbled he was a *schoolteacher.*

"Polly read the letter," she confirmed. But what use was it to dwell on this? It was John she was anxious about. She only faintly perceived British efforts to put down the rebellion—

"I'll believe those regiments when I see them, letter or not," he said with undisguised disgust.

Jane knew that Sarah McNeil stretched the truth, but the letter *had* come from New York City and it *had* coincided with Burgoyne's arrival.

"The letter is real. Don't you think that there might be a reversal?" Suddenly the prospect of it sprang like a flame of hope.

"Maybe they'll get here by fall," David only answered her, having found little in events to give him hope. He looked up into the sky where a turkey vulture made desultory circles in the sky.

A skiff knocked against the bank. Jane turned toward the shore. The sound startled her like someone touching her unexpectedly in the dark. But she couldn't see in the glare off the water, and, suddenly, Eva rushed from the house. She then saw John throw his haversack on the bank. Her throat went instantly dry and she swallowed against it.

"I don't belong here," David said abruptly. He wanted to clasp Jane's shoulder and turn her away.

"Come with me!" she said short of breath, taking his arm. Her petticoat caught in the grass and she nearly fell as she started down the hill pulling David after her. "Thank god, you're safe!" she exclaimed, rushing up to her brother, oblivious of Eva's attentions to her husband. "We've had no word from you," she cried, throwing her arms around him. Then she recoiled, feeling his hard and brittle arms around her and his bones through his shirt.

"Shall we unload, Colonel?" the soldiers asked, unconcerned with the greetings occurring in front of them.

"Yes," John answered them, picking up his haversack, his unsmiling eyes drifting beyond Jane to David.

"I asked David to come," Jane urged upon him, pressing his arm.

Eva picked up his coat. "Come to the house, John."

"Camp by the well." John pointed it out on the hillside.

John and Eva walked up the hill. Jane stood back, looked at David, then took him by the hand and followed. Eva's words came to her confidential and softly consoling: "We heard about the Cedars . . ." Everyone knew of the Indian attack on a retreating contingent of Arnold's army, which, on faulty intelligence, had surrendered to the British and Indians, though an inferior force, near Montreal.

"St. Luc poisoned the Canadian Indians before his capture. The Kahnawakes warned Washington in February about him. But what could Washington do? After Butterfield surrendered, the Indians started in . . ."

"I can't go up there," David said, stopping. "I didn't take the Commission, and you can see how he feels. No telling what happened up there—one thing will lead to another. Look at him."

"Maybe he's not himself," she admitted. John was hollow cheeked, his eyes gray as smoke.

"What do we care what they're fighting about? I only love you."

"It hurts me to see him like this . . ." She didn't know which way to turn, whether to follow John or go with David.

"Come to the house tomorrow," he said.

"But John might need me, look at him . . . ."

"He has Eva," David insisted.

He then kissed her and slipped away from her.

She watched him go, his leaving tearing something inside of her. David stood in the meadow with the tree line behind him— she waved wretchedly and watched him walk slowly away.

If John's absence from October to May, or the events preceding and including the publication of *COMMON SENSE* calling for American independence in January, or Jane's meeting the Congressional Commissioners at Abraham's in April didn't convince her of the seriousness of events, then John's condition convinced her. Troubles like Golden Hill six years ago, involving David's brother, Thomas, in New York seemed small and remote compared to how John was ravaged. He was no brother, husband, or father of a Lamington neighbor who brought the effects of war into their house, but her own brother!

"John, what's happening?" she asked inside the house, trying to grasp events.

The suffering on his face expressed ice with cutting edges, fires that wouldn't warm, food that wouldn't nourish, disease that thrived in fever, headaches, and stomach cramps. She saw amputations, bullet wounds, bearded men screaming. She saw the gray of death in the dark lines under her brother's eyes.

"This is not a war of words, but the old way reasserting itself. What have you done since I've been gone?" he asked.

What was he suggesting, that her non-involvement challenged his cause, his suffering?

"We kept the fires through fall and winter. We fed the children," Eva answered.

Jane watched the children with their father. James stared at him. Little Eva sat on his knee, looking strangely at him. Her sister-in-law, two months from delivering her fourth child, held the youngest baby.

"Let me hold him—" John wrapped the baby in his hands, seemingly forgetting his sister. "Could you take another campaign, Eva?" he asked, turning to her with steel in his eyes.

Eva bent over and kissed her husband. Jane noticed the tears streaking her face. "Only, if I have word from you."

"I had no 'secretary'," he lamely joked.

"We can do it again, if you can."

For the first time, Jane felt completely alone—how could she feel otherwise? Her brother seemed a thousand miles from her. His cause possessed him, the way he stalked it, like some unfeeling wolf, filled her with dread.

"We shall continue to fight. Necessity dictates to us," he stated.

His defiance now stunned her. She couldn't condemn him alone now either, for too many people were struggling and dying. He reminded her of Paine's words about a man hating to set about a task, but haunted by its necessity had to undertake it. She tried to balance 'parricide' with John simply resisting something he could not accept. Perhaps she stood in the same relation to Sarah Jones whom she would never accept either. Maybe the same steel-like thread of anger held them together despite their differences.

"But you both need to know . . ." he continued, stopping—

"James, we need firewood—" Eva said, sensing the importance of what he was about to say, sending her son from the house.

"*They* will swarm for their 'English milk'. And the Johnsons, Brant, Butler . . ."

"Because of Lewis two years ago?" Jane interrupted him, feeling anger, bitterness, and panic in his bringing up the Indians.

"No, not Lewis, only. It's the old war still. A nice pirouette, isn't it, with our kindly 'father' and his Ministers?"

Jane turned into the sunlight streaming through the open door so that John couldn't see her face. Atsitsina spoke of the Lakes' Indians' hostility. David said he should have joined the Johnsons! She wanted to follow James from the room, to run after David and tell him they must escape this hydra of war.

*   *   *

"You can't live with them, can you?" He clasped her elbow.

"He's my brother! I Can't leave him! The alternative is unthinkable."

Their voices echoed the scolding chirps of nearby redbreasts the next day by the river. How lovely the quiet spring sky and the flowing river, yet how ragged their feelings! How fresh and alert the redbreasts, skipping for wisps of grass; how refreshing after the cold winter when snow, falling from a tree branch, only told where a bird flew. She brushed her hair with her fingertips.

"Don't ask me again to live with her."

"Burgoyne will end all this."

She wanted to believe it, but the Canadian campaign put a simple solution out of reach. John spoke of other campaigns, and Doctor Franklin had spoken of a new country. Dreams like that didn't die easily. This struggle would continue. How would her leaving John's house solve anything? Events immobilized them.

"We must wait," she said.

"That's all we do!" he shouted.

"And love each other," she tempered him.

"Like you always say. God, I wish I had your patience, Jane."

"We have election! We count, David!" Her eyes conveyed deep faith. What else was there for her to draw on, but her deepest faith? If she lost that she would go mad.

"You're a Minister's daughter."

"I want what's best for us." She leaned against his chest, saddened and reduced by saying, *no*. She dreamed of some winged shape taking them into the sky away from their torment.

"Nothing I say helps," he said, dejected. "And what of Sarah's *schoolteacher*? I could secretly join . . ."

"Join them without a commission?" she answered wearily, growing accustomed to his returning to the idea of his resisting the Congress.

"That Congress isn't legitimate."

"And Daniel?"

"He's riding this out . . ."

"Sensible," Jane laughed with bitter and weary mockery.

"He'd suck water from a stone."

"We can get through, somehow," she said.

He gently touched her face. His eyes melted her and made her feel hollow inside. The urges of spring pressed her against him. The turmoil around her increased her passion. Strife held a sacred compensation for her.

27

Late July

Jane listened, but she didn't hear any sounds down at Fort Edward or on the road. She slipped her feet into the spring, hoping the cold water would calm her agitation. She had hoped to find quiet with Sarah and Polly, but Sarah's anger with the *Declaration* made it impossible to stay at the house. Now when she wiggled her toes in the water and the humid night became bearable, she recalled her own reaction to the Congress' *Declaration* read in Albany on the nineteenth. She was stroking James' hair to keep him from crying:

> *Why can't I play outside, Auntie Jane? he had sniffled.*
> *You must have supper.*

She would have gone to the shore with him, rejoicing in his wondering eyes as he looked at the bay. But Eva had said not to go because of the activity of people returning from Albany.

She had watched James go to the door with the sound of Eva's cooking fire falling on her ears with the regularity of rain.— Then a light appeared in the doorway, and John tousled his son's hair. John had gained his weight and strength back over the two months since his return from Quebec. He gave her a handbill that she held like thin flame between her fingers. *When in the course of human events . . .* she read in the lantern's glow, her eyes flying over the page. Her hand shook when she handed it to Eva.

The Colonies' *Declaration of Independence* shocked her, and she made her way to a chair, pulling James with her, thinking her dream of a house lost forever. The *Declaration* would protract the struggle and also involve David! John noticed her reaction.

"They tried to assassinate General Washington. The Hickey Plot convinced even the wavering," he said. He then told her that Congress had needed something more to unify them when support for the cause waived after Quebec. The threat to Washington's life had given the Congress and the people that unity. The *Declaration* expressed it.

The water of the spring numbed her to the base of her spine. She rubbed her feet. Congress had declared what Paine had called for in January, and the news of the Declaration had entered her breast like a sliver of ice.

"It's not safe up here at night," David exclaimed, coming out of the darkness.

"I knew Sarah would tell you I was up here," she said, slipping on her shoes and straightening her petticoat.

"God, Jane, the place is crawling with rebels. Please, come to Mother's." He picked up her bucket.

"Don't walk so fast, David. We can't meet except here, since you don't come to John's." She caught his arm and shook a pebble from her shoe.

After John returned home in May, David had refused to see her there. And though John didn't forbid his coming, she sensed he would have, eventually, if David persisted in coming. His avoiding coming in the first place had added to the tension between them. Meeting him at Sarah's remained their only option.

Voices floated up the hill.

She could barely make the soldiers out in the darkness. As they approached the soldiers, the soldiers stopped them as they began to pass.

"Miss McCrea? Adjutant Tearse sent us . . ."

"I don't need looking after, Lieutenant," she interrupted him, not wanting David to speak to them. It annoyed her that Peter had asked this Van Vecten of the First New York to look out for her. His thinking Polly and Sarah needed watching and protection with so many soldiers at the fort didn't mean that she needed the same attention. She feared their watching her would also compromise David when he came to Edward to meet her.

"Hallo!" someone then shouted behind them.

A lantern swung back and forth as Yarns came up to them.

"Who are you?" Van Vecten asked.

Jane pulled at David's sleeve in silent effort to draw him away.

"Jest a minute," Yarns said, outflanking her, and turning on the Lieutenant. "And who 're ya ta ask who I am?"

The smell of stale rum permeated the air.

"What's your name?" the Lieutenant then demanded, looking closely at Yarns in the lantern light.

"No one," Yarns answered sourly, pushing his wide hat back and exposing his white forehead in the light.

"Take him along," Van Vecten said flatly to the soldiers with him. "Cool him off in the fort."

"Take yar hands off me!" Yarns shouted, jerking his lantern from a soldier's reach. "Look, ask them . . ." he said, pointing to Jane and David.

"Who is he?" Lieutenant Van Vecten then asked them.

"Thomas Yarns," David answered, "a Kingsbury farmer."

Jane squeezed his hand. As much as she hated Yarns, she feared what he might say about David.

"Go with them, or come with us," Van Vecten directed him.

"I'll go then," Yarns sputtered, pulling at his hat and staggering.

Jane and David walked on, and Yarns' wheezing pursued them.

"Wait up!" he shouted acidly.

David clenched his fist.

"Don't, David," she said.

"Now's my chance to let him have it."

"No, you will both be taken to the fort," she cautioned him, shrinking from such violence.

"I've got news from Bell's," Yarns said hoarsely, hurrying up to them.

"What news?" David asked harshly, turning on the man.

But Yarns pushed obstinately by them. "When we git ta Sary's!" he taunted.

"I could kill that son of a bitch!" David hissed.

Having to see Yarns at Auntie's now made Jane sick to her stomach. The smell of rum in the air made her ill.

"I can't go in there," she said emptily, barely able to press back a strand of her hair. "The man makes me ill."

"Here, have some water," David said, setting down the bucket and handing her the ladle.

The cold spring water washed away her nausea. How could Sarah abide the man? How often had decency demanded she speak to her—yet how often had she just held her tongue because she was in Sarah's house?

"That polecat."

"Ca'mon!" Yarn's hollow voice graveled up the road to them.

"Let's hear his news, Jen. Maybe he *does* know something."

Getting land for a house and a mill, or a farm from the Jessups still hung about David like an aura. Tired with resisting him, she consented to go to the house.

When they reached Sarah's, Yarns was sitting at the table with a glass of whiskey in his hand.

"Leuk ae th' man racin' doon th' hill!." Sarah said of Yarns as they entered the house. "Had' ye a moment thegither, luves?" she asked, making Jane feel even worse for consenting to come with Yarns there.

"The rebels almost took him," David informed her. "He thought he would lip those rebels."

"Nae, he wadna be sae foolish wi' the fort infested wi' 'em."

"If those skinners think they can push Thomas Yarns around, they've something comin', Sary!" the old man cut back. He then exploded with indignation. "Robert even joined 'em! Imagine, Sary! Used ta wash him in th' tub and shake 'im off like a little rat," he raged, holding out his hands and snapping them to show how he dried his child. "But I disown 'im, d-i-s-i-n-h-e-r-i-t him! No more of him comin' back ta headquarters!"

"Nae, twas a guid lad!" Sarah reacted with shock at hearing that Robert had joined the rebels.

"No respect for his father! Can ya believe that?"

"Nae, I say. Wat didye dae ta th' lad, Thomas?"

"Nothin'," the old man sulked. "He was always a scamp ya had ta larn by hand."

"Ye dinna mean ye beat th' lad!" Sarah asked shocked.

"Na."

"What's your news?" David asked, not caring to hear any more from Yarns.

"A little thing," Yarns then answered with drunken confidentiality. "A guy at Bell's gets it from Headquarters, if ya get me, Jones. Sary, how about another touch?" He held out his glass. "The Big Boy," he continued after swallowing and wiping his mouth with his sleeve, "says Friends o' Government are ta 'stay put'. 'Stay put.' Them were th' words."

"What 'Big Boy'?" David asked.

"Come on, Jones, 're ya that stupid?" Yarns snapped at him. 'Who do ya think?"

David's color rose.

"*CARLETON*! The royal Governor o' Canada, ya dang charlie horse!" Yarns then looked over at Sarah, knowing he was safe with her for the way he spoke to David.

"Burgoyne's not leading the army then?" David asked in disbelief because everyone had expected that Burgoyne would pursue the rebels retreating from Canada.

"No. Burgoyne's not leading the army, but th' Governor himself."

"What about Arnold's navy at Ti?"

In the wake of his retreat from Quebec, Benedict Arnold had begun building a navy at Skenesborough on Lake Champlain twenty miles north of Fort Edward to impede the British pursuit.

Yarns guffawed. "What navy! A real outfit, a real navy is comin'. Trust Pap, Davey, th' big boys'll take care o' things down here. All we need do is 'stay put' and keep away from Fort George and all that sickness."

Jane shuddered. Hundreds of the soldiers, including John's regiment, who returned from Canada in May suffered there from malaria and small pox. Her youngest brother, Stephen, from Ballston served as a surgeon.

"Stay put?" David asked.

"What else with all this going on? Ya wanta die of sickness?"

"Nae bither. The British army's gittin' ready. Won't be lang, an' naught ta stop 'em," Sarah nodded at the news, finding deep pleasure in what Yarns revealed after her outrage at the insult of the Declaration. Carleton's preparations to invade the colony, Howe's return from Halifax to Staten Island after his forced evacuation of Boston, and Cornwallis' attack on Charleston in the south on the twentieth encouraged her in thinking that it was only a matter of time before the rebels were completely crushed. "An' who whare ye talkin' ta at Bell's?" she asked for details.

"Ya might be surprised, Sary," Yarns answered without committing himself, sipping from his glass.

"Stop playing cat and mouse, you bastard!" David menaced him.

"David Jones! Dinna spak lik that in my hoose!" Sarah snapped at him. "Gie th' man a chance ta spak!"

"Why should we believe him anyway? He's a consummate liar."

Jane feared that David's temper might prevent them from meeting here. "Leave the man alone," she said bitterly, recoiling at whom she was defending. Ever since she had first met the man, he had taken every opportunity to denigrate her and her family.

"Liar?" Yarns laughed. "Listen, if you were half so spry ta th' talk instead o' holdin' up on that farm o' yars, ya might know what's goin' on, Jones. So my informant is my secret, laddie," Yarns continued to taunt him.

"What do you mean 'stay put' then?" David demanded, barely able to stifle his anger. "What's that supposed to mean?"

"I mean, don't git ideas about *takin' up arms* and flyin' ta Canada, 'cause they're already on their way with a real navy and a lot of soldiers—and I mean *professional* soldiers, not a pack of ragged scarecrows carryin' pop-guns and sticks callin' themselves an army!" Yarns answered slyly. "Carleton doesn't want a lot a corn shuckers like you runnin' at him up there either. He says ta STAY PUT, Jones! Got the message? Or 're ya so hornswaggled in the nuts, ya can't hear no more!"

"If I could only grease the floor with that vermin!" David whispered helplessly as he turned on his heel and left the house.

Jane rushed outside after him.

David stood in the darkness with his fists clenched.

"What are we going to do?" he asked her between clenched teeth as she came up to him.

"What can we do?" she repeated, trying to close her small hand over his fist.

"Nothing! Just sit and wait, if that scumbag is telling the truth."

"Listen, David. If what Yarns says is true, we need not do anything. Carleton will set things right. When order is restored, the Jessups will have their land, you'll have your saw and mill lumber. Can our happiness be far behind? Don't think about Thomas Yarns. Don't do anything rash. We've endured this long," she said hurriedly, trying to sooth him.

"And how much longer!" He spun on his heel and clasped her by the shoulders. "Look at me, Jen. How can I just wait here and do nothing? The inaction is killing me. I am a prisoner on my mother's farm. I can't go anywhere and I must listen to that drunk. How do we know he's even telling the truth? Maybe Carleton is saying the exact opposite. You know what a liar Yarns is."

"I know," she admitted, "but *you* haven't heard anything different. We have nothing to loose by waiting. You can't do anything that might put you in danger. And why should we risk Simsbury! Please, be temperate. We have waited too long."

"And Thomas is going to be married in London in January!" he told her, bitterly contrasting their present unhappiness with his brother's good fortune following on his military career after Woolwich.

"How do you know about Thomas?"

"He wrote Mother. He also says he might be sent over here—oh, what's the use of any of it, good news or bad from him?"

"But we'll be married too!" she said just above a whisper, suddenly very aware that there were still soldiers about the fort and possibly near the house. She didn't give much thought to Thomas' commission bringing him to Colonies with the news of his marriage. "If we don't know the future, we can't despair," she reasoned with him. "So you did not go to Woolwich? What does it matter as long as we are together," she pleaded with him, his news of his brother's happiness, nonetheless, wrenching her. "I am happy for him," she said stoically. "Oh, David, be patient. I love you so." She threw her arms around him and he clasped her tightly.

"I hate myself when I'm like this," he said with his lips against her neck. "What would I do without you?" He kissed her.

"Haste is our greatest enemy, David—" she declared, pushing her head tenderly against his neck and breathing in the hot night with the sounds of soldiers' talking now echoing behind Sarah's house at the fort.

28

September

Thomas Yarns' warning to David not to take up arms in light of Carleton's preparations at first alarmed Jane, for David still fixed on the idea of taking up arms. Yet, did Yarns know something of David's intentions that she didn't know for him to speak to David that way? Sarah had vaguely alluded to her relative's organizing. But hadn't David asked her about Simon Fraser's letter? So why would Yarns speak that way to him? Sarah and Yarns knew something, despite his disclaimer on action. He played upon David's temper. But when she recalled how David had assailed his duplicity and dismissed his warning, she grew calmer as to his intentions.

August saw no open conflict with Sarah Jones. Jane accepted a frosty politeness; John was absent from his farm; and the Committee did not yet try to impress David after his refusal to accept their commission. During the late summer, therefore, the couple enjoyed frequent jaunts along the river with Jane's nieces.

In their hearts, however, how long the lovers' quiet would last distressed them. They isolated themselves and did not speak of events, though they often observed soldiers marching along the river, and clung to the notion that if they didn't speak of the events around them or the future, the future would be kind to them. Sometimes, however, silence made David distant, and Jane grew anxious about him.

A quiet August gave way to early blooming chrysanthemums in the brighter cooler days of September.

Early fall made Jane's love more urgent. Regret for passing summer, mixing with her anticipation of winter, made her the

more passionate, and she resolved to go to Sarah's house early in
the morning before David awoke. The urge came in the evening
after bed. The cool air brought thoughts of him through her
window, and in the pre-dawn freshness she saddled Charlotte, the
depth of the mare's eyes adding oriental excitement to her daring.

Jane stroked the mare's cream-colored mane and pictured her
own flowing hair like strawberries complimenting it. She slipped
the reins, and John's log house, with the dew-flecked maple hanging
over it, fell away behind her. Charlotte's hoofs hardly touched the
road as she flew past the Tuttles' and the neighboring farms.

When Jane reached Sarah's house, she looped the reins through
an iron ring at the back of it, and the damp air followed her inside
the door. Her breathing and the rustle of her petticoat across the
floor brought her to the stairs. She hesitated before Sarah's dark,
haunting pantry, then glided up the stairs and down the hall, and
slipped into David's room. At his bedside, she breathlessly stroked
his face.

"Jane!" he exclaimed, waking.

Her face sank against his neck on his pillow.

"Did you lock the door?" he asked, sitting up. "I don't want
Mother . . ."

She left him abruptly and he didn't finish what he was saying—
On her way back across the room, she slipped out of her petticoat.
Her breathing came in short gasps as September, and that moment
when she always withdrew from him, bloomed within her.

For her, just lying next to him afterward made her complete
enough to imagine preparing his breakfast before he left for his
mill. She inhaled the imaginary perfume of the pine and cedar of
their new house. She smelled it in his room after six years. The
scent was especially sweet since Sarah Jones slept only down the
hall.

David caressed her, as mindful as she was at how her outflanking
his mother added relish to their moment together. "Did Dinah or
Eva see you leave?"

"No, and John's at Fort Independence." She pushed her head
against his cheek, allowing herself his love and her secret triumph

over his mother, so absolutely confirmed by the silence of the house. She shivered, imagining Sarah standing at the open door.

"What's he doing at Independence?"

"They intend to block Carleton on the Lake between Ti and Independence," she answered.

"So, they know about Carleton—it's uncanny what the rebels know about the British."

"It's none of our concern," Jane said.

"Not even if Carleton is successful?" he pressed her.

Talk of Carleton's campaign and John's activity at Independence agitated her. She feared for her brother's safety, and anything could happen with Carleton's advance. She made as though to leave the bed.

"A little longer," he said, clasping her around the waist.

"A little then," she agreed, balancing her desires to stay with the creeping necessity of her leaving. It was too risky for her to have come, especially as David spoke of Carleton and asked about John.

"I have some news . . ." he began.

She stiffened. She never liked it when he said he had "news." She wanted things to remain quiet. Talk of the war upset her.

"Governor Tryon is raising twenty companies of Friends of Government on the quiet from his office in the City. Ebenezer has offered me a lieutenancy and land!" David whispered.

"Land?" she asked, taken by the unexpectedness of the word *land*.

"Ebenezer's dividing twenty-thousand acres among his officers. At least one-thousand on the river for us!"

"But how? The Governor is powerless," she stated.

"But Washington is on the run and Howe controls New York City. When Carleton gets here, we'll have our house and mill!"

She leaned on her elbow and looked at him in disbelief. "Who else did Jessup ask to join him?"

"Solomon and Jonathan."

"But Yarns said in July that Carleton ordered Friends of Government to *stay put*. Those were his words. I remember them."

"Blast Yarns," David answered, passing over him, "we can muster without going anywhere."

"And not be found out?"

"It will be in secret."

"Would it be that easy? You just said yourself that the rebels know everything that's going on. And you promised me you wouldn't take up arms."

"Carleton's coming with a navy and the soldiers Burgoyne brought in the spring. The rebels can't stand up to them. And if we have a chance for land, we should take it, Jane."

Her instincts rose like a covey of startled quail against the idea.

"The rebels might have lost Canada, but they can still fight, David," she protested, the risk of his being discovered shaping in her consciousness. Then, as on past occasions, she seized on Daniel whom she had come to view never took chances, even to her disadvantage.

"Why bring him up? He's staying behind . . ." he confessed in an irritated whisper, his tone nearly conveying that that was best for the invasion.

"He's taking no risk, and there must risk if he's not joining. He would love nothing more than another parcel of Jessup's land."

"But the British *will* win!" he whispered passionately. "And the Committee will detain me now that the mills are closed. When things heat up, the Committee will act," he reasoned. "I must muster with them, land or not. Look, Jen, it's a simple plan: when Schuyler calls up the militias to meet Carleton we'll muster too. And only when Carleton arrives, will we defect. Not before. Carleton will then defeat the rebels and Jessup will honor his promise."

"But, what if Carleton doesn't attack?" she asked, trying to conceive of the plan. "Anything can go wrong, David."

"God, Jen, who is going to stop him? Once he gets under way, he won't be able to stop, but will carry through on his own momentum. And besides, Howe beat Washington on Long Island and he will also march up here. Carleton *must* attack with that kind of support. But say he doesn't attack for some reason. Our Corps will just stay with the rebels, that's all. We have only to pick the right moment to go over." He turned on his side to convince her.

She turned away, wedged between fear, the shock of his disclosure, and the excitement of the possibilities as he explained them. Everything hinged on a moment!

"Besides, I met an agent at Jessup's sent by Sarah's *schoolteacher* in Saratoga. Her cousin is Brigadier Simon Fraser's nephew, and he has authority to raise a corps of rangers. Would you rather me in irons at Esopus like St. Luc and the other detainees if I don't go and that Committee decides to come for me?"

"No, David, of course I don't want that." She then clutched at another objection. "Is Johnson coming with Carleton?" She had made herself clear on his not joining Johnson.

"Don't worry about Johnson," he whispered emphatically, her distinguishing between Johnson and Carleton like trying to separate strands of hair, "he knows us."

"And St. Luc?" The Lakes' Indians at the Cedars made her almost frantic. What he now said about their being *recognized* by Johnson and his Indians presented nightmarish possibilities.

"Hang St. Luc! He's at Esopus . . ." he answered, his voice nearly breaking out of the room.

"Carleton won't bring them?" she asked, seeking reassurance.

"Who knows? Stop thinking about the Indians. This is our chance," he repeated, his excitement ripening to frustration.

"You shouldn't have told me. How can I live with John and Eva knowing this as I do?" Unsure of dissuading him, or how to dissuade him if it was best, she bought precious moments for herself.

"Only a miracle will save the rebels," David stated clearly.

She recoiled. "Don't say that . . ."

"Look, time is short and detention unacceptable. You know that. We have no choice."

"We always have a choice," she said almost vacantly, remembering John's suffering, and how he hadn't given himself a choice either. She couldn't bear John suffering again. Nor could she bear the thought of David being found out and suffering for what he intended to do, nor his suffering at Esopus if he *was* detained. She looked at the wall. The room glowed with sunlight! But if Carleton sailed with his best soldiers and a large navy, why wouldn't his invasion succeed? She now, in desperation as to what to do, found herself arguing the other way. And if the invasion did succeed, they would have nothing to show for it if David didn't join Jessups.

"Are you certain?" she asked. "Oh, I don't know what to think. So much is up to chance, David."

"What isn't, except that the odds are against the rebels. How can they think that they can block Carleton?" He kissed her.

"Oh, God, David, we've waited so long. We do deserve it, don't we?" She pressed her face against his neck, fearing she took a fatal plunge in agreeing. She hung on his words, and sought reassurance in his touch.

"Who deserves it more?"

"We have little, not knowing from day to day—" she continued to convince herself. "—Oh, it will happen, won't it, David? We will have a home, won't we, David, after all this time, even though it frightens me?"

"We will," he answered, brushing her hair with his hand.

"When will you go then?" Suddenly the realization he would actually leave panicked her.

"I don't know—at a moment's notice."

"I must go now. If your mother found us like this . . ." she said, startled by his answer and the light in the room, and almost thinking, if she left him, he couldn't leave her then—they would have to start over, he would have to come to her to say good-bye. But she couldn't leave like this, not knowing when he would be called. The fears and the promise prompted by his request, her agreement, and the fact everything hung on a single event, made her desperate for him. She clutched him to her breast, wanting to live or die in his arms. She needed this moment to hold him. She had to have the memory of him. She pressed herself against him in a way she had never done before urged on by the growing morning and the panic that rippled just beneath her skin—

She lay spent on her side, feeling that no matter what happened now, they had become one, man and wife . . . she had possessed him and nothing on earth could now take him from her.

"I must go," she said softly, growing calm, touching his lips with her fingers, "though it really doesn't matter, if *she* found us . . ." She had consecrated herself, and it brought her peace.

"We'll have it, Jen . . ." he said with warm, satisfied eyes.

She pressed her fingers to his lips. "Yes."

She left the bed and dressed.

They kissed in parting at the door before she slid the latch back, her feeling hollow, yet complete.

—Outside she breathed the cold air. She passed the corner of the house into the gleams of the rising sun on the river. Gaining the road, she looked back to the house. The sun reflected off his window like musket flashes as he waved to her from it.

29

Friday, October 18

Jane stood in the shade twisting her shawl in her fingers with her legs like mop strands from riding the mare. Fear and dread, coupled with the sensation of Charlotte still running, barely allowed her to stand.

The sun had sunk behind the house. The smoke from the chimney flowed over the roof and nearly choked her. She thought she would fling herself into the river rather than face Eva. Desperation and despair devoured her. But she couldn't have stayed at Sarah McNeil's and faced John. What if he had caught David while she was there? How could she have witnessed her brother bringing him into the fort as a prisoner! She had returned immediately.—Yet David's plan had called for Jessup mustering secretly with the militia and then defecting when Carleton appeared! David had told her that, assured her there was little risk. He had told her that as she lay by his side in his bedroom in September!

Near exhaustion, she opened the heavy door.

"Where have you been?" Eva asked searchingly, taking the mint tea, steaming against the orange glow of the fire, off the trivet. "You've been gone all day."

"Out riding," Jane avoided her eyes and took the cup Eva offered her. It rattled on the saucer in her numb fingers. She lifted it to her cold lips. The afternoon wind had gone right through her as she had ridden.

"To the Joneses? You went to the Joneses."

"No . . . ." Jane sat at the table and looked at the knotted log wall. Eva would probe. She wanted to look her sister-in-law in the eyes and blunt her questions, but the ride had taken her strength. She felt as limp as cheese cloth.

"What are you hiding?"

"Nothing."

"You told the Joneses John knew of Jessup's Corps? You betrayed your brother," Eva stated.

Jane turned wearily toward Eva. "And why not? David is my life. Surely you understand. And if John cared, he wouldn't have gone after David. He is not a criminal."

"What did you expect John to do with Carleton breathing down our necks, and the country crawling with armed Tories? John had no choice," Eva gasped in disbelief of her. "How could you overlook the implications of what David intended?"

"They forced him into it," Jane replied, wondering where she would get the strength to contend with Eva.

"Who forced him?"

"That Committee back in July," she stated without force.

"Now he's an *enemy*!" Eva flung her apron on a chair.

"They won't catch him! Certainly not, if John hadn't heard about it in Albany!" Jane said, suddenly charged by the thought of David's capture.

"But John wasn't sure until he saw your face when he told you what the Committee knew. *You* confirmed it, Jane. Your face turned white when John came home."

"He'll never catch David!." she cried desperately, the idea of her being responsible for John's pursuing him tearing at her.

"Oh? He won't catch him?" Eva asked with new weight in her voice, observing her. "So you didn't go to the Joneses after all, but to Edward and warned the lot of them! And what did they pay you, as if they've given you anything, but vain hopes already."

"*You* have land." It slipped out. Her voice quickened like a moth's wing beats.

"*You* sold us out."

Jane stood up. The two women glared at each other like fighting cocks.

"What hope do you have, Eva?" Jane then tried to reason.

"Carleton can't be stopped. He defeated Arnold's navy at Valcour Island five days ago, and now he's at Crown Point."

Eva didn't stop to consider those chances, but pressed her sister-in-law. "We've done what we could for you, Jane, but you took their side. Daniel Jones, Jessup, the lot of them," she numbered them bitterly.

"David has worked like a slave," Jane declared, pushing her teacup from her, "and nothing came of it."

"So, how much *land* did they promise him?"

"Don't ask. We've waited for six years. It's not personal with you and John, Eva. Don't make it sound so." She raised her voice, realizing the military absoluteness now of her's and David's decision. How she wished she could take it back. No amount of land was worth the agony she endured now.

"David has already defected, hasn't he, and you rode to that loyalist McNeil and warned her of John coming after them, didn't you?"

Jane didn't answer. She wouldn't let Eva force her to lie. She had told Auntie, who sent Eve to Pat Smythe who contacted Ebenezer Jessup. Who could she have turned to except Auntie?

"I understand your wanting to warn David. He might have changed his mind, but the whole Corps!"

"I had no choice." She had knocked at his mother's door, and when Sarah Jones' pinched face appeared, she had fled wordlessly, knowing David had left.

"John would have let David go."

"How did I know?"

"You should have trusted him! And what has McNeil ever done, except fill your head with false hopes?" Eva repeated. "Or maybe she fears the Indians will lift her hair, or she'll hang as a traitor if she does nothing for the English. Oh, I won't speak of principles when they lift her hair." Eva's lips trembled.

"St. Luc's in jail!" Jane shot back.

"Jailing him didn't stop the Indians at the Cedars in May!"

"No," Jane answered miserably.

"So, *the scourge* of Esopus' son-in-law, Campbell, leads them."

"Who told you that?"

"John."

"God, Eva, that Committee knows everything!" Could she think of a single time when that Committee hadn't outwitted its enemies, Tryon, the Johnsons, the Mohawks, and now the Jessups?

"Hadn't the Indians even crossed your mind?" Eva asked bitingly. "Yes. They're coming with Campbell, St. Luc's son-in-law. All the Indians from the last war are coming from the Lakes."

"They don't need those Indians!"

"Nor Germans, nor Highlanders to do their fighting either," Eva stated bitterly. "But what else is the Ministry going to do with their riches? God, how they spend blood money, Jane." She twisted her apron in her fingers. Her little girls began to cry. James rubbed his eyes on his mother's petticoat.

"Don't attack me, Eva!"

"You betrayed us!"

"I didn't!"

"That pack of wolves you warned intends to murder us!"

"I love him."

"Then why did you let him join Jessup?"

"I didn't," she answered, weak as a hooked fish with the fight out of her it. Yet how urgently David's voice had fallen on her yesterday, standing with the mare between him and the house. *Carleton's at Chimney Point. The rebels have evacuated Crown Point. Schuyler's mustering the militia at Ti and Independence. I've must go, Jane.*

Oh, no, David! She had dropped her currycomb, fearing she'd never see him again. She faltered, hanging vainly on his arm against the current that threatened to sweep her away.

Carleton's nearly here.

It had been just a couple of weeks ago when she had lain in his arms in his bed at his mother's—

How will I know you're safe? she had gasped.

I'll pick you up at McNeil's when Carleton marches through Edward. This is our chance, Jane. The beginning of our life together—

With his tortured kiss hot on her lips and her eyes swimming, he had slipped away from her into the swirling sunlight.

"You have lusted like Rehoboam after Solomon's corrupt riches!"

Eva's words entered her brain like wooden pegs. "We only wanted to live, Eva," she murmured, her eyes filling with tears with again recalling David's leaving yesterday. And then John had burst upon her this morning saying he knew of Jessup's mustering. She had had to ride to Auntie's to warn David.

"You call your brother's blood on your hands 'a chance at life'?" Eva pursued relentlessly.

"We've harmed no one."

"You sold your honor," Eva insisted, her arms dropping to her sides in despair.

"We love each other!" Jane cried helplessly.

"The yoke isn't heavy enough, but you lay your hand on it too. Lord, in heaven, he can never be forgiven for this."

Jane felt the room close in on her. She half-stumbled to the door.

The night air pressed against her like the sides of a damp grave. How different from this morning when she had gazed at the leaf-strewn ground radiant as a Persian carpet, the air smelling fresh as a clean petticoat. She had agonized over David's leaving before it actually happened yesterday, but had come to accept its brevity so effectively had he assured her of the certainty of Carleton's success. They both had thought that it might take Carleton only a week or two to reduce Ti. But then John had found out about Jessup this morning! She felt again the shock of his intelligence and wrung her hands. What choice had she but to ride to David after John had left in pursuit of him—she had assumed up to now that the Committee didn't know of Jessup's plan—and she couldn't have stood by and watched David rounded up with the rest of Jessup's Corps like so many sheep. But had her warning come in time for him to get over to Carleton at Crown Point? Had he made it?

She had hardly seen the light today, had hardly seen it since David had left . . . except for one moment when she hoped the struggle would end quickly. And she didn't see the light now in the darkness. Only if he would now return to her, come this moment through the woods to her, saying that at the last moment he had changed his mind—if only this night might become day would she know relief. How chill the damp October air!

"Oh, David!" she cried quietly into the night with her back against the cold planking of the door, grieving that she had ever agreed last September to his desperate plan.

30

Monday, October 21

For the next three days, Jane and Eva waited for news of Ti. Each resented the other and hardly spoke. Jane often left the house and watched the other side of the river where dim forms went north, their blue and white coats hardly visible amid the foliage. Across the bay at the mouth of the Sunny Kill, the soldiers also repaired the bridge. Occasionally she heard a shout and the clank of wagons, or saw a soldier carrying his musket when the sun and clear air allowed it. Few soldiers marched on the west side of the river.

In mid afternoon on the third day, with still no news from David or John, a stranger appeared on the shore in front of John's house. Dressed in a shabby brown coat and yellowing gaiters, he carried a bundle. He waved and called, and limped up the hill toward her.

"How far to Edward?"

Jane watched him, hoping he would continue on his way, but he kept coming.

"Five miles!" she pointed north.

He paused and looked at the wheat field and the road where it entered the woods. He glanced thoughtfully at the house.

She approached him and stopped. "Do you have news?" The question came out awkwardly without reference.

"News?" he replied, angling for her meaning.

"Of Ti," she said with a quizzical look, indicating that her question was as obvious as the birds that flew overhead. "The whole Colony is in suspense as to Carleton's success at Ticonderoga."

"Is it . . . oh, I don't know . . ." he played, suggesting only he *might* know of Ti.

"Isn't Carleton invading?" she asked with annoyance. "Surely a man like yourself, traveling, would have heard something."

"Oh, that."

"Well?"

"This Colonel John's place?" He looked closely into her eyes. "It doesn't pay these days for a man to answer sometimes."

"No," she lied, wondering why he wanted to know. "What does who owns this house have to do with whether Carleton succeeded at Ti?"

"You are the one who wants to know." He then began to limp up the slope toward the wheat field.

She watched him. "Wait a moment!" she called, walking after him. "Why do you want to know, if this is Colonel John's house? I mean surely you know something to ask such a question."

The man smiled. "Why do you have to hide the information?"

"I'm hiding nothing. As a matter of fact this is John McCrea's home. But why are you going to Edward? You don't look like a soldier."

The man's eyes narrowed. "I'm going to Edward to see friends."

She leaped at the word 'friends'. "Then you know what's happening, please, tell me—"

"I see you have someone on the other side."

She averted her eyes. "How do I know who you are?" What if he was a Committee spy? But what difference did it make, if she hit a rock in her plunge? She had to know. "With Jessup," she admitted, the name 'Jessup' tightening her throat.

"Jessup's with Johnson from Fairfield County. He's with Carleton. I can tell you that much."

She breathed with second life. "He made it over then!"

"Don't know for sure, but I don't see why not. They had the element of surprise, not the rebels."

"Is it dangerous at Edward?" The idea of going there opened before her like a turn in the river.

"Carleton hasn't arrived yet, but his orders at Crown Point were not to molest anyone. Nine regiments of Foot, too," he let her know. "And Fraser's savages." He spoke with dry pride, as though the name 'Fraser' conveyed special significance, honor, battlefield bravery, success and triumph.

"'Savages'?" She looked with alarm at the woods, imagining Indians dodging among the trees. "St. Luc's son-in-law?" she asked, repeating and hoping to refute Eva about Campbell leading the Lakes' Indians.

"Don't worry about Campbell. He takes his orders from Fraser. Carleton only wanted to use them for defense anyway, but what does it matter. They're under orders."

A frightening picture of red coats interspersed with the tawny bodies of Indians jumped at her. And the man's casual assurances did nothing to ally her fears. "Ti-hasn't-fallen-then?" she stuttered.

"Not yet, but within the week," he stated with bland certainty.

"How do you know that?" she choked with anger, imagining not only David *with* the Indians but, imagining John contending with them as they came over the battlements of Ti.

"It took Carleton two days to take Crown Point after beating Arnold at Valcour Island, and he took Crown Point three days ago. Look, Burgoyne, Philips, Fraser . . ." he ticked their names off on his fingers, "are less than a week from Ticonderoga. You don't think the Yankees can stand up against Generals like them, do you?"

She was caught between being reassured for David's sake, and anxious for her brother. She then thought of David. If he had succeeded in joining Carleton, and she went to Sarah's, her cousin, Simon Fraser, would protect them. And from what this man said, David had probably already reached Carleton. And if Ti fell within the next few days? She would have to be at Sarah's for him. No forts, except Fort Anne, which Polly had described as a barn, lay between Ti and Edward. Carleton's march to Edward, therefore, would take no time at all. She *had* to go to Fort Edward, and the sooner the better to avoid John and the scene she dreaded with him for her warning Sarah about his pursuit of David and Jessup's Corps.

She searched the man's eyes. If he could go to Edward without fear, why couldn't she also go? But what if he was lying or there was a foul up? What if Carleton didn't attack, or what if David had been captured?

"Where are you from?" she tendered, wanting to be more certain of him.

"South of here," he answered vaguely.

"Ballston?" She looked intently into his blue eyes, trying to gauge the metal in his eyes.

"Down that way," he answered without committing himself.

She though of James, William, and Samuel. John had told her a few days ago her other brothers served in Van Schoonhoven's Twelfth Albany Regiment. She didn't want to meet her brothers at Fort Edward. She didn't want to have to lie to them about her intentions. Her other brother, Stephen, ever since spring and the retreat of the Canadian army still cared for the sick at Lake George, and she knew she wouldn't see him.

She pointed across the bay at the rebel soldiers. If this man knew about the British army, he would know about them. "Which soldiers are those," she asked, "the Twelfth Albany?"

"No, the Twelfth, the Thirteenth, and the First New York are at Ti. That ferry still ahead?" he asked.

"Yes," she answered of David's ferry, "though you might have to go to the one nearer the fort. Will Ti fall?" she repeated, focusing on her principle worry.

"What did I say, lass? Ti is doomed! Wait a few days until Edward empties."

"You have friends in Edward," she stated.

"And you're Colonel John's sister, unless his wife. No one's likely to forget hair like yours," he stated without answering or complimenting her.

She wore her hair long. It fell to her heels.

"No need to hide with Carleton on his way." He picked up his bundle and turned to go. "I'll go by the Tuttle's and old man Hilton's place and take Jones' ferry."

"You're in the army . . . ." she declared, offended by his knowledge of the area without answering about himself.

"What makes you think so? You said I was no soldier . . ." he laughed rudely.

Jane flushed.

"You know too much—" She detected a Scottish accent beneath his English surface. "You're Simon Fraser's nephew, and Sarah's cousin. You organized Jessup's Corps," she asserted, boldly risking all on this man being Sarah's other cousin.

He didn't say yes or no, but the indirectness of his reply only served to confirm his identity for her. "I saw you the day your brother came home from Canada. Lot of traffic on the river. You wouldn't have noticed me."

"You followed the army—How does a British soldier hide for five months?" the idea of him on John's heels and then his hiding without being detected aggravated her. Instantly she hated him as the cause for the situation she found herself in.

He only grinned at her, tapped his injured leg, picked up his sack, and began limping up the hill. Then he suddenly stopped. "Teel th' auld woman hallo for me." He then turned away from her and began whistling *Yankee Doodle* as he gained the road.

"The *schoolteacher*," Jane said under her breath. *I knew it all the time,* she thought, taking small satisfaction in his not being a Committee spy.

She turned around and looked at the house. Had Eva seen her talking to the man? What would she tell her? Just a tinker asking directions—but what should she do now? She knew nothing of what was going to happen. But didn't he say that Ti would fall within the week? That Carleton had nine Regiments of Foot? And how would she know, if Ti did fall? And what should she do? Thought of the Indians then rooted her to the ground right there on the side of the hill. Eva had been right about them. And how could she risk going to Sarah's if there were Indians in the woods?

31

Saturday, October 26

Jane took the 'schoolteacher's' advice and waited until the soldiers passed to Ti before herself going to Fort Edward. The day before yesterday the rebels' marching had quickened, as though Carleton was actually threatening Ti. Then yesterday, their numbers had decreased, raising her hopes that she could leave. After the soldiers had passed, she decided to follow after them the next day, to be sure to give them time to march on from Edward for Ti. But would Eva question her absence as she had when she rode to Sarah's to warn David? It scarcely mattered to her now, if David would rescue her.

She rode the mile north to the poplar and willow grove at the narrow part of the river where the Summer Kill entered it on the east bank. Concealed in the grove, she could observe the soldiers marching along the river. As she rode, she noticed the poplars had few leaves and their slender white trunks and branches looked like bones growing from the earth; but the graceful willows held their yellow petticoats against the blue sky.

A redbreast's bright chirping made the grove shimmer, as she dismounted. As she approached them, the willows looked like smudges of yellow powder against the gray maples, but each leaf sparkled like crystal in the early morning frost now that she was beneath them. She walked Charlotte across a patch of grass, leaving her footprints in the frost, and looped the reins over a poplar branch.

The frost began to melt and the dew dropped from the leaves. She took a blanket from behind the saddle. As she held it over her arm, the sun, streaming through the branches, warmed her face and hair. The light made silver columns of the poplars and a palace of the willows. She closed her eyes in the warm, shining quietness of the spot—Breathing the liquid air of the fall morning, she experienced an ecstasy almost beyond bearing: "Oh, for a palace where the length of life grows not. Come back, David," she whispered. At her feet at the edge of the grass, red wild strawberry leaves glistened with dew. Oh, where was he? When would she hold him in her arms again?

The redbreast chirped again through the overhanging branches.

She listened so intently she could have heard an acorn drop on the other side of the river. She pushed the leaves aside and looked— the bright surface of the water cut her eyes like silk. She couldn't see the bridge beyond the mouth of the Summer Kill, but would hear soldiers crossing it when they came. She spread her blanket and sat against a tree. In a few minutes the sounds came—the hoofs and slapping of the planks of the bridge under the wagon wheels—then men's voices encouraging the horses, and the higher call of a boy.

Motionless, she waited for them to appear from behind the trees up the road across from her. She followed the light clanking of a wagon behind the leaves of the trees. The swaying heads of the horses appeared, and then the wagon with the boy on the seat holding the reins. Two soldiers sat on the back of the wagon, smoking pipes. Lean and rangy men followed them, carrying their muskets. The boy's hair took the color of the red leaves. She watched the wagon move steadily along the bank until it passed.

Quiet reined.

Jane sat like a flower caught in a sudden frost. What she saw turned her to ice. The boy's youth blanked out the last eight years and brought her face to face with her own former youth. A purpose, a dream, and a determination: Robbie Yarns drove his wagon to war! Seeing him, filled her with deep and bitter sadness. Emergent and young, each now, though him even more, had opposed and divergent commitments.

Distressed, she stood up, bent the branches back, and looked to see if all of the soldiers had passed. She couldn't, wouldn't, wait another day. She must go to David now. She then snapped the blanket off the ground, and in a moment had her foot in the stirrup.

32

Monday, October 28

Sarah poked at the logs, but the smoke only hung like muslin in the fireplace.

"O' a' nights, nocht a dry log in th' hoose," she declared, straightening up with the lantern light tracing the lines in her round face. "Wad ye fetch same o' those husks, Polly, or we'el hae nae fire for sure."

"There's time, Auntie," Jane remarked, as Polly left the house. She folded a chintz frock.

"Aye, luve, bot we dinna want th' laddies thinkin' th' hoose is desarted."

Sarah poked the logs again to see if the fire had died. She spoke only of seeing her cousin, Simon Fraser.

"We're not in danger . . ." Jane suggested, thinking for the first time now that she was here of the danger she was in if Carleton attacked.

"Na. Ye'll anely hear their brae pipes camin' doon th' heel."

"But so many have gone to Ti!"

Jane guessed, watching them last week, that far more soldiers had gone to Ti this time than had marched to Canada last year. They had answered Schuyler's call like migrating birds. And now that there were none of them left at the fort behind the house, made the night strangely quiet.

"For thir numbers, they canna stand afore English arms. Th' king's army's th' best in th' warld, nocht even considerin' th' rabble hae nae muskets, clothes, nor food. 'Tis nae contest. Ye're an th' winnin' side, lass."

"No more husks for th' fire, grandmother," Polly announced,

coming back through the door with only a half-filled basket under her arm. "My, but it's spooky out there! Even the crickets are laying low."

The cornhusks rustled between Sarah's fingers as she leaned into the fireplace, her fat arms white against the black stones. She exhaled heavily. "'Tis th' lull afore th' race frae Ti bringing Peter back, an' David right behind 'im."

Jane looked at Polly as though her friend sat on the opposite side of a seesaw. They no longer confronted a hypothetical, but the reality of who would go up, and who down in the madness that was about to break upon them.

"Ah, Peter Tearse," Sarah sighed, facing them, "here, hae an apple." She took two from a basket and held them out: "O, th' affairs o' th' heart! Luve hase its ane laws." The women didn't reach for them, so Sarah put them on the table and turned back to the fireplace. Picking up a long match, she bent over, and struck it against the stones, but it didn't light. "Bot nae matter. Peter an' David weel nae fight. Trust me, lassies."

"I'll light th' fire, grandmother."

Polly went across the room to her grandmother and took the match from her and struck it against the stones. The match flared and the husks sprang to life.

Jane picked up an apple. As dark as a strawberry, it reflected yellow flecks of firelight from across the room. She held it like a soothsayer's charm and bit into the thin red skin. How sweet and white!

"If only we knew what was happening and what the Indians are doing," she said more to herself than to the other two women.

"Ah, th' lads weel control 'em," Sarah replied, frowning, as she sat beside her at the table. She then said over her shoulder to Polly, "Yer kin weel mak th' countrie right again." She heaved back around in her chair and touched Jane's hand as she poured herself a glass of whiskey.

Jane's eyes rested on the flames flickering off the black vase in the middle of the table. She had been waiting here for two days and still nothing had happened at Ti! And here alone at night, the Indians might have already surrounded the house for all she knew.

"What's going on?" she asked suddenly. "I don't think I can stand it any longer."

"Dinna worry, yer luve'll came through th' door," Sarah patted her hand, "an' gin he does, we'll be right here awaitin' for im."

"But what if he didn't make it over to Carleton!"

"Patty Smythe wasted nae time gittin' ward ta Ebenezer, lass. I saw him go mysel. Dinna trouble yersel aboot that."

Jane traced a knot in the table—Certainly, if David hadn't reached Carleton, she would have heard by now. Wouldn't John have brought him back here to the Fort?

Outside the window, leaves then scrapped against the glass.

They sat silently.

There was a knock.

"Open't, lass," Sarah directed Polly. "Ye dinna think th' door weel open't itsel, do ye?"

But Polly didn't move from beside her chair. "It might be savages," she said.

"Savages wad be in th' hoose by now. Open't!" her grandmother exclaimed, standing up.

A second knock came.

"Open't it. It maun be news frae Ti!"

Polly then went to the door and opened it to the dim figure of a woman standing outside it.

"Hast Ti fallen, Deborah Freel?" Sarah asked in a rush, pushing away from the table.

"I don't know," Deborah answered, coming into the house, "no one even peeps up there. Everyone's as quiet as owls."

The women looked at each other. Jane stood up from the table. "But surely Mistress Freel . . ." she began before Sarah interrupted her.

"We're askin' o' ward frae Ti. News frae yer husband, Peter," the older woman said.

"I've heard nothing from him, Mistress McNeil," Deborah answered.

"Nothing?" Sarah shook her head. "Thare should be news. An' whare's yer husband?"

"Up with the men at Bell's sittin' in the dark."

"Ah ta hell wi' them lads at Bell's sittin' on thir tush in th' dark, Deborah. 'Tis Ti I want news o'!" Sarah exclaimed, losing patience with her. "But maybe they're waitin' 'til light? They wadna attack at night," she reasoned in reference to Carleton himself, trying to make sense of the situation.

"But they've had all day to do something, grandmother," Polly objected. "That was a grand army comin' down."

"That's right, Sarah, ships covered the whole lower end of Lake Champlain yesterday," Deborah confirmed.

"Yesterday? Th' English lik daylight," Sarah insisted. "An' who cares if ships 're lying aboot. It's fictin' we want."

"Could the numbers of the rebels have turned Carleton around? I've never seen so many rebels," Deborah hazarded, casting for something more logical.

"Na," Sarah repeated with forced certainty. "The English probably canna see in th' dark. Wot's th' guid o' tryin' ta fight ae night?"

Jane imagined the black ships at anchor with John and Peter Tearse waiting on the battlements of Ti above the lake. But where was David? On board a ship, or with rangers and Indians in the woods? She pictured him sitting at a fire watching them paint their faces. Suddenly this room, at the edge of the river, which wound outside the house like a black snake, frightened her. She pressed her fingers against her temples. 'I have nothing to fear out there,' she told herself. Perhaps the rebel soldiers would throw their muskets away. David would then take her in his arms, and they would have the land and house they longed for . . . they would then live among pines and maples where deer would drink at the river. She breathed deeply and fingered the curls on her neck. If the night was the wall of a castle, it tottered before her.

"They're probably having tea together," Polly stated sarcastically. "Peter's probably tellin' Carleton he wasted his time in comin' down here—"

"Ye mean th' rebels might see th' errors o' thir ways," Sarah corrected her granddaughter.

They then heard a sound like a lowing cow outside.

"Was that at yer inn, Deborah?" Sarah asked, going to the door.

The sound filled Jane with dread. She knew cows didn't low in the night. But fighting? Fighting would sound like distant thunder, or low, hollow booming, but from so far off it might sound like a cow lowing. Quiet then fell, and she heard a cat purring outside the house. "Close the door, Auntie."

The old woman closed the door. Then she heard footsteps, and the door shivered instantly behind her. "Deborah!"

"God in Heaven! That's yer Peter, Deborah!" Sarah cried, flinging the door open again.

Jane saw Peter Freel and another man standing behind him in the dark. "What're ya doin' here, woman? Ca'mon home, it's over," Freel shouted angrily as the other man pushed by him.

"Why, Thomas Fraser! Da ye see, lassies, here's my cousin. Th' rebels surrendered wi' oot a shot as I tald ye they wad . . ."

The schoolteacher, Jane met earlier, brushed through the door into the room, his face ashen.

"*Surrendered*?" Freel exclaimed, striking his hat against the doorjamb. "Not on yer life."

"Dinna tell me th' British surrendered, man?" Sarah disputed him as she seized her passing cousin by the arm.

"Carleton's gone," Fraser said soberly to her.

"Nae!" Sarah cried, facing him. "Ye tald me yersel, they'd walk owre th' rebels. That there wadna be a stick o' 'em left standin'."

"The army sailed away hours ago," her relative repeated sharply.

"David!" Jane slumped back into her chair as though struck by a stone.

"Jessup's whole Corps escaped through the woods and sailed off with them for Montreal. The whole damn bunch," he declared through his teeth.

"Wat did they sail awa' for, damn thir souls!" Sarah demanded angrily. "They didna came a' th' way doon here jest ta sail off, man. Are ye daft?"

"The rebels *infested* Ti and Independence," Fraser emphasized.

"Too mony, wi' th' cream o' th' British army lookin' doon thir cannon at 'em, Thomas? Nae, there was anither reason—"

"They came like locusts, woman, thirteen-thousand with cannons on Independence looking down the mouth of the lake at the fleet. They had Carleton like fish in a barrel. Listen to what I'm telling you. You sent them all the right information all right."

"By th' luve o' Jesus. But wad locusts scare off th' King? They jest turned aboot for a bit. They need intelligence, man."

"Do ya think the savages would have left, if the British were comin' back? They sailed away," Freel said, exasperated with Sarah's refusal to accept Carleton had actually sailed away without a fight.

Jane, in shock, looked at the long, reddish cattail spikes arching from the black vase on the table in front of her. "How do you know HE sailed? How do you know anything?" she asked, looking from one to the other of the men.

"All sixty of Jessup's Corps made it to the walls of Crown Point. The savages saved them from capture. *He's* gone, all right, believe me," Thomas Fraser answered, limping over to the fireplace.

The downy heads of the cattails drooped. Jane felt a sharp pain in her breast. "Who almost caught them?" she gasped.

"*Your* brother," Fraser answered, turning and looking at her.

Jane turned her face away.

"Someone warned him about Jessup."

"No," Jane said stubbornly, refusing to even note how Fraser looked for the effect of his words on her.

"Yes. Jessup mustered to Ti. Your brother pursued them. Someone *tipped* Colonel John. He nearly caught every last *one*," Fraser said with cutting precision. "Jessup flew into the arms of the savages and escaped."

She didn't notice Fraser limp out of the room with Freel and Deborah, or hear Sarah say, "He's away ta Canada." She simply stood up from the table, unconsciously touched the ivy pinned in her hair and went out the door where she stood against a pine in the damp air.

A breeze floated over the cold ground. The leaves crackled above her head. Away from the house, flower-like stars carpeted the open sky. A redbreast chirped in the dark. Why had things turned out like this? Why this annulment, her now being caught between John and David and at John's mercy? Bitter tears flowed down her cheeks. "Oh, David, you're gone!" she cried.

She could have hung on, could have faced anything with him with her. But *desertion*? When would she see him again? The earth and air numbed her feet and hands. She wiped her cheeks on her sleeve. And now she must *beg* John's mercy! Polly called to her, but she couldn't answer. She only dimly perceived in the darkness that Polly approached her.

"Jenny, lass, don't take it so hard."

Polly appeared in the dark and put her arm around her.

"I'm lost, Polly." She began to sob. "I can't live without him." The words choked her. She could barely see Polly's face. Her tears flowed as from a spring. "I have no one. Just like that, no one," she said, feebly clicking her fingers.

"You have me."

"I'll rather die than face John and Eva after this," she said.

"No."

"Yes." She pressed her linen against her eyes and looked up into the blackness. Her eyes ached. In a windowless house with neither light nor sound coming through the walls, she was being made to atone for something. Was it for not having prevented David from defecting? Or was it because she had betrayed her own brother?

"I waited for him. I wore my best petticoat for our wedding," she said miserably, lifting the hem of her petticoat in the dark. "And now he won't be coming for me." She clasped Polly tightly in her arms. "He was supposed to come for me. What did I do to deserve this? But you want the same thing, don't you, Polly? You wanted the same thing with Peter. But Peter will come back to you." She stepped back, trying to see Polly's face in the dark.

"Yes, we want th' same thing, lass."

"I' have waited for six years, haven't I, Polly? Haven't I waited that long for David? Tell me, Polly, what am I going to do now?"

"Th' war will end," Polly comforted, "then he will come back."

"But when will it end? How will it end? You don't think that thirteen thousand men will just lay down their arms? Oh, if only Carleton had attacked!" she cried.

"But he didn't, lass."

"I know," Jane replied, suddenly growing calm. "And his turning around like this leaves a draft in my soul."

"Don't say that, lass. You and David—I mean ye're young and th' warld's still open—"

"Open? You mean open like the sky to reveal my ill-fated star? But Peter is safe—and we are friends. Tell me, we are friends, and always will be friends," she began to cry, the stars blinking at her through her tears as she looked at them.

"More than sisters, Jenny McCrea."

"And you will never desert me, will you, no matter what happens, Polly?" She clasped her friend's arms.

"Never, lass," Polly answered, tears coming to her own eyes.

"Whatever happens? Please, say that for me."

"I'll ne'er desert you, Jane."

"We are sisters, aren't we?" She asked, something beginning to snap inside her.

33

November

The first snow, smelling damp and fresh like threshing, came late in the month. Outside her window the flakes rolled in the gray air across the roof; and beyond the field the wind blew them in thin clouds against the swaying pines. The snow sunk through the wheat stubble giving it the appearance of wool.

Jane turned from the window, picked up her mirror and finished pinning her hair before breakfast. She laid the mirror on the table beside the doll at her elbow. She observed the child-like face and sparrow's feather in its hat. The pale blue petticoat, white apron and gray silk robe evoked the delicate plumage of a small bird. Adjusting the robe to expose the petticoat through the apron, she ruffled it to new freshness. When her father gave her this doll, it lived, but, in the somber morning light, it now failed to lift her spirits. The child-like face and adult dress with the apron's worn and yellow fringe opposed one another. Jane pushed the doll to the back of the table.

Picking up the mirror again, she gazed at the abundant folds of her hair, ruddy as fall wheat. In half-profile she couldn't ignore the small wrinkles at the corners of her eyes, nor the faint lines below her nose. She held the doll away from her. Looking at it, she still had time left to her. Carleton would finish what he began—and hadn't Howe recently taken nine thousand prisoners at Fort Washington? Wouldn't his gains shorten the winter? Jane rose from her dressing table and left her room.

In the next room, Eva swung a black pot over the flames and the cover sounded with a dull clank. She frowned at her son when he entered the room wearing his cloak.

"Why do you always want to leave the house when food is served, James?"

He turned back from the door and fussed with little Eva on the floor. As Dinah turned the beds in the loft, the new baby cried. Eva called Dinah for her.

"I'll watch the cooking," Jane said, going to the pot of oatmeal and lifting the cover with her apron. The oats bubbled whitely, and the smoke from the fire brushed her nose. She stirred the oats, and they grew thick and heavy in the water.

"Such a gray morning," Eva noted of the snow flying against the windows. "But it will keep the enemy off our necks."

"A good thing," Jane deflected.

"Yes, after Carleton's pirouette."

The oatmeal turned thickly on the spoon. Jane lifted the pot off the swing arm and brought it to the table. James scowled, while his sister fidgeted behind her bowl.

"Why such a face?" she asked her nephew.

"I want to go outside."

"After eating, your mother said." Jane poured milk over his oatmeal. The boy rested his head on his hand and listlessly turned his oatmeal with his spoon. "It will make you strong," she humored him.

"So I can fight the *Lobsterbacks*?"

"Such spirit for eleven!" Jane said dryly.

She carried the pot back to the fireplace, her nephew's comment about fighting Lobsterbacks prompting her to assess the war. Congress itself had avoided capture by Howe on his march to Philadelphia. And Carleton had left a force at Crown Point and still commanded the lake. It seemed to her that the rebels were on the run and she wondered how long they could hold out. As she hung the pot, the handle pinched her fingers. She dropped the pot on the groove of the arm.

"When will you try to meet your knight again?" Eva asked her. "And by the way, who did you speak to in front of the house before you flew to McNeil's two days later?"

"Someone asking directions," Jane answered indifferently.

"A spy, you mean," Eva commented bitterly.

"Oh, say it, Eva. You've been wanting to ever since Edward," Jane returned sharply not wanting the children to hear their dispute. "Go outside now, James," she countered Eva.

"You left us to burn on this river," Eva accused her as soon as James went out the door.

"John knows the risks. What about him?"

"But he didn't desert us." Eva's eyes were as cold as fieldstone.

"Have you turned my brother against me?"

"He loves his family." Eva's words cut like glass.

"You want to punish me."

"You've done that to yourself already by abetting the enemy and could have been killed for your rashness."

"I have not abetted the enemy, as you call them, Eva. And they would not have harmed women. Carleton said so."

"He did? And how do you know that? That spy told you of course. And you risked your life for Jessup's blood-money on the strength of it without giving any thought as to how Carleton was going to control those Indians," Eva challenged her angrily, handing her baby to Dinah, and bringing homespun to the table. "How different you are from your brother."

"John receives nothing for his service?" Jane returned hotly.

"You tell me." Eva laid the homespun over the table and pinned a pattern to it.

"Congress promises their Colonels eight-hundred acres. Or have you conveniently forgotten that, Eva?"

"The Congress promises land to men who risk their lives for their country. That's the difference."

"And what good would the land do you if John died like almost happened last year in Canada?"

"And you'd rather live with Johnson's fighting crofters? Why can't you see that we are not Scots nor Englishmen any longer—"

"They believe in *Government*," she replied, recalling Abraham Wing correcting James about the English Constitution and the technicality of the Colonies not having representation in Parliament under it.

"That's a weak quibble for the poverty and privilege such government as theirs spawns."

"My father did not condone John's stamp activity. And look how you are made to suffer for it now."

"Nothing comes without cost. And I suppose you're not now suffering with David on the other side?"

Jane didn't reply immediately. She *was* suffering, but she had come to view the Committee as robbers who confiscated people's land, and jailers who put British sympathizers into prison. "I may be suffering, but I'm not stealing."

"And what fiefdom do you stand to lose or gain by what you are suffering?" Eva asked with Dutch sharpness.

"I love him."

"You don't love him for the Country, but the blood-money. Oh, I know you, Jane, to risk your life for it."

"We want a home and family! David got caught up in the circumstances of it, that's all."

Eva dropped her scissors and held out her hands. "Let me see yours. Have his circumstances, as you call them, ever been as hard as this?"

"I helped you in the fields, in the house, and with the babies when you were ill! I don't want to fight with you like this, Eva."

"Yes, you helped me, but you also expected everything to drop into your lap, and, when that didn't happen, you compromised yourself and us."

"But I haven't hurt you. And I am not fighting for them."

"But David is, and you support him. You were going over to the other side. Oh, I should fault myself for not speaking to you when you first came to live with us. You were young then."

"Oh, how much better I feel," Jane said, "but you don't grant me the least of mind and heart. That's the trouble with you Whigs."

Humiliated, she went to the window and looked at the falling snow. If she and David had realized their dreams shortly after setting foot on that shore—but hadn't she spoken her intentions when she had arrived? And what could Eva have said or done to change her purpose? She had not wanted to owe Eva and her brother. And how could David have done anything to change it?

"I'm sorry," she said, sick at heart. How weary she felt as the falling snow weighed her with self-doubt. Wasn't it enough to have lost David? And yet it had just happened. "The times confuse me—" she confessed softly, anguished by isolation. "Maybe you should have said something to me. But events swept over both of us, didn't they? You could never have foreseen this, could you have?"

"It had been a long time coming, Jane. You knew how your brother felt and what he was doing, but you choose not to involve yourself. You put your eggs in David's mother's basket, and listened to that McNeil . . ."

"She's like the mother I never had. You couldn't have been a mother to me, and I had the right of choice. And you can't speak to me now as though I am still eighteen."

"It *could* have been different between us."

"I wasn't one of your children." The words slipped out. Nature had made her a flower of a different hue. She had suffered the bewilderment, the anger, and betrayal that came of it. "It's neither of our faults."

"Will you go again then?"

"You can't ask me that, Eva—" Jane began as she saw John come up the path toward the house. Her lips closed as the door opened. It wasn't cold outside, more wet than cold as the air rushed through the door into the house. She turned and watched her brother lean his musket, looking grotesquely like the long leg of a deer, against the wall. She swallowed hard against seeing him—he had been home only once since Carleton's aborted invasion four weeks ago, and they had not spoken to each other.

"We're leaving Ti, except for a couple of thousand at Independence," her brother said dryly, not offering her nor Eva any other greeting after his long absence. "Washington needs men," he then explained to his wife.

"How can you run from one end of the country to the other?" Jane asked, suddenly wearied by the long anxiety of finally seeing him and now hoping he wouldn't condemn her for what she had done.

She watched him walk wordlessly past her and sit down. He pulled off one of his boots and dropped it on the floor.

"Higson tells me he was a good woodsman. Now he's on the List," he said matter of factly of David.

"What List?" Jane asked, leaving the window. Though John had refused to allow him at the house before he defected, he had not attacked David.

"The 'List of Defaulters'," John answered, pulling off his other boot.

"But David has no land."

"He won't inherit any either."

"But Carleton will return!"

"Probably."

"I don't care who wins!" Jane flung at the wall. "Why torture me? Haven't I suffered enough?"

"More than you deserve," John answered, "but Jessup promised David land. You didn't have to hide it."

"What did you expect?" she cried. "Would you have acted differently, knowing his circumstances and how his mother hates me? If Eva doesn't understand this, certainly you must, John."

"It's a pity you didn't marry when you first arrived. David would have fought for that. He would have had a country to fight for."

Jane turned back to the window and tears formed in her eyes. The bay lay like black pewter plate among white linen hills.

"But I'm not going to attack David," her brother continued. "I only want you to promise me that you won't do it again," he said, his voice as solid as the oak floor.

She touched the glass. It swam in her brimming eyes. How could she know what would happen tomorrow, or next year? How could she forget the terror she had felt at Sarah's that night: the deadly quiet, the black river, her feeling of being abandoned when David sailed away? She wiped her eyes and answered without turning around, wanting something absolute from John.

"Do you care what your soldiers think? Is that why you are asking this of me?"

"No, it is not because of them."

She wanted him to say he asked this of her because he loved her. She had to have him need her, as she needed him, had to know he asked this out of love for her, and for no other reason.

"Because your soldiers might think your sister is a T—" she could barely bring herself to say the word. It stuck in her throat, but she said it, "Tory." Now that she had said it, she wanted him to say the words she knew he must be feeling for her. She wanted him to say he loved her . . .

"I love you, Jane."

Her lips quivered when she heard the words. The bitterness and anguish she felt, how her love for David had become a wall of ice between them, melted. And he said he loved her with Eva hearing it. She turned around and took those short steps toward him. Feeling him strong and responsive, even in the most hopeless of causes, wrung the pain from her—she loved her brother! Her tears fell on his shirt.

"I promise not to wait at Sarah's again," she said, "I do promise you, John. I've got nothing, nothing, if I am not at least your sister."

34

Hogmanay 1777

Jane pressed David's letter in her pocket. "Look up at the North Star on New Year's Eve," he wrote. Two months had passed since his defection before she received this first letter from him. Peter Freel had given it to Polly. He said the risk prevented him from writing sooner. But why, since he only wrote of wanting to come home? "I do not have the heart for dancing or cabrioling on the river at night without you."

The North Star hung in the black sky radiating needles of light through the bitter cold. Jane didn't blink or take her eyes from that shining fantasy which dissolved the sordid tangle of war. One day she might have a new coat with cape and red velvet hood, a scarf of black quilted silk, might even cabriole behind a pair of horses to the sounds of bells, and attend concerts of German and British bands! His mentioning those things filled her with longing, as she stood in front of his mother's house looking skyward with the air like cold gauze on her cheeks. She blinked away her tears and found the glittering Pleiades grouped like dove's eggs in the black sky. In her own winter's shell, she too stood rooted in front of this house, which she had come to despise. But where could she have gone tonight with no one to talk to except Polly?

She scanned the snow-covered river below the hill. The black pines along the opposite bank sparkled in the clear night. A howl came from a distance and it pushed her shivering toward the glowing windows. Her clogs filled with snow. At least Polly knew what she looked at in the cold sky—As she reached the door and lifted the latch, a panting figure ran across the knoll. Alarmed she turned quickly around and saw a musket fire. She pressed against the door. Ghostly figures then appeared on the knoll.

"There, lads!" one of them shouted as their shooting knocked branches from the nearby trees.

"For th' luve o' Jesus!" Sarah McNeil exclaimed, opening the door, nearly causing Jane to fall into the house.

"They're shooting at him!" she cried, pointing to the pursued man.

She watched, stupefied, as the man dodged away from the house and those on the knoll silently moved their priming rods up and down. The man's hollow breathing came across the snow as they took aim again. The muskets flashed across the knoll. The fleeing man's arms flew out and he fell.

"Got him!"

"Rebels," another cursed.

One by one, thinking the man dead, they disappeared over the back of the knoll.

"Leave 'im, lass. Yankees aren't warth th' bother."

"But if he's alive, he'll freeze to death," she protested, leaving the doorway for the fallen man. She picked up his hat when she reached him and noticed blood on the snow.

"Are they gone?" he asked, raising his head.

"Robbie!"

"Tory scum couldn't hit the bottom of a barrel with their muskets in it." He stood and picked up his musket, his face white from the cold.

She started back to the house, expecting him to follow, but he didn't. She turned around. "You want to freeze?"

He came after her and Polly met them at the door.

Inside, Robert unwrapped his scarf and they took off his coat. Sarah pulled him to the table and pushed a tumbler of whiskey at him. "Drink this afore ye git yersel killed an sech a night." Jane unwrapped the rags from his hand and dropped them on the floor. Blood dripped on her petticoat. He swallowed the whiskey and coughed. "Ye shud bring presents an Hogmanay, nocht a hole in yer hand. An' whare's yer fither?"

At the sight of the boy's blood, Sarah Jones turned rigidly away.

"Do you have clean linen, Mistress Jones?" Jane asked, keeping the alkali out of her voice.

"In Canada," Robert answered huskily. "My father's a *flamin' Tory!*"

Sarah's face grew red. "Sech talk, lad!"

"He legged it over with the Jessups' when I was at Stillwater."

Jane again saw Robert driving that wagon on the other side of the river before she had gone to Fort Edward to wait for David. Seeing him again, filled her with longing for David and the anguish that followed Carleton's turn around. But the boy she saw on that wagon, the one who had cut wood for Sarah had grown into a tall, muscular young man.

"Weel, the authorities weel take yer farm, laddie, gin they came pipin' doon this valley."

He looked at his bandaged hand. "Not with me and my brothers fightin', they won't."

"They'll clear ye oot in th' spring. So, mend yer ways gin ye hae th' chance."

"If them Lobsterbacks 're so mighty, how come General Washington licked 'em at Trenton?"

A few days ago on Christmas day, General Washington had defeated Rall's Advanced Corps and took a thousand prisoners. He had Paine's *CRISIS* read to his soldiers to inspire them before the battle. The news of Rall's defeat came as a shock because everyone believed Howe's advance on Philadelphia, through New Jersey, would eliminate Washington. Even the Congress had fled to Baltimore.

"Hessians!" Sarah corrected him. "I suppose ye're a great Indian fighter as weel. Wat're ye gain' ta do gin they came through wantin' ta lift yer hair?"

"Really, Grandmother," Polly said.

"We fought Injuns in the last war."

Sarah turned to the other women. "Listen ta 'im, for th' luve o' Jesus. An' 'im nocht even born yet! Wat do th' rebels expect ta accomplish wi' this laddie's life? One day he cuts my wood, an' th' next he's gettin' himsel shot, an' ready ta tak on th' savages! 'Tis eneugh ta mak a body greet."

Jane wondered about the difference between Polly and Peter, herself and David, even John and Eva. Like Robert, a cross-purpose of flight and pursuit caught all of them—like the Pleiades, they had no more significance than a cluster of coals hissing and steaming in the snow. Luck had saved Robert tonight, but no one knew about tomorrow. She sighed when she thought of David's New Year's Eve letter. She wanted to forget this trouble, but her hopes mattered no more than Robert's. Happiness didn't seem to favor her needs and desires any more than his. The flowers came up and died in the frozen snow-covered earth. The Pleiades didn't move and Orion drew no closer. A gray day always followed a bright one.

"Who chased you?" she asked, feeling suddenly dejected and not expecting a truthful answer from him.

"The scum that burned out Mister Tuttle."

"Where were you going just now?" The burning barn grew vivid in her mind—the smell of burning hay and horseflesh seemed to fill the room.

"Can't tell you where I'm going."

"Why would Tories ambush you on the coldest night of the year?" She noticed a bulge under his shirt. "It has something to do with Fort Independence, doesn't it?" She shuddered when she thought of those men left at Independence after Carleton.

"They're freezing, and I don't like Lobsterbacks, not Pap, nor any one telling me what to do, winter or not. I mean to help *rid* the country of Lobsterbacks," he answered flatly, the whiskey showing.

Papers poked through his shirt. Jane asked to see one and he gave her a broadsheet. "'These are the times that try men's souls'," she read aloud from Paine's *CRISIS*. "You're delivering these?" She had already read a copy of the broadsheet at John's before coming to Sarah Jones'.

"So?"

"And you suppose these will save those freezing men at Independence?" she asked, her tone conveying the hopelessness of his effort. Her thoughts of just moments ago outside of cabrioling in Montreal with David loomed in shocking contrast to the suffering of those freezing men in this weather just north of here.

Robbie stood up and reached for his broadsheets and coat.

"Oh, sit down, Robbie," Polly said, brushing off the broadsheets as of no importance. "You are not going to save those men, and we're not going ta bother wi' yer stuff."

"Don't call me 'Robbie'." He pushed his bleeding hand through the sleeve of his coat.

"Respect your elders, young Yarns," Sarah Jones chastised him from her squeaking rocker.

"Th' lad's jes confus'd," Sarah said.

"No son of mine ever spoke like that."

A rush of resentment seized Jane. Perhaps David himself wasn't cabrioling, but also freezing in some sentry's hut on the river because of his mother.

"Your son left home—and now, he's fixin' to fight us," Robert answered bitterly of David to his mother, wiping the sweat from his face. His reddish-blonde hair curled beneath his hat. He buttoned the broadsheets into his coat and picked up his musket. "I don't want to see neither David nor Solomon," he defied them all, turning and leaving a cold draft behind him as he suddenly went out the door.

"Call 'im bak. He'll *freeze*!" Sarah McNeil immediately protested.

Jane went to the door and opened it. The air cut her face like knives. She tried to call out to Robbie, but the cold choked her. She coughed—Only the moonlight revealed his tracks. He wouldn't come back, even if he heard her. She turned back inside, her fingers burning.

"Wat a fool!"

"I understand him, given his father," Polly sympathized.

"Ta tak up arms against th' King, Polly!" Sarah exclaimed, waddling over toward the fireplace. "Thare's naught worse than lads fictin', even whare fictin's a way o' life. An' for a son ta tak up arms against his fither?"

"It's not going to be a walk-over for all his bluster," Jane said, not caring about Thomas Yarns but rather anticipating the impact of Paine's writing on the resistance. "Carleton didn't walk over, and it's not going to happen next time either." Suddenly the example of those wretched freezing men meant more to her than cannons.

"That's so, Grandmother," Polly agreed, "Carleton didn't turn tail because he wanted a holiday. They gave him his exercise."

"Which side of this 're ye on, Granddaughtir? Or is that Cupid's shot an arrow in yer breast, luve? Nae, matter, luve, tweel tak more than bairns lik Robbie Yarns and luve-struck Yankees ta beat th' British army," her Grandmother laughed.

No doubt Peter had convinced Polly that the rebels had a chance. She had adjusted her opinion since April and meeting Doctor Franklin. But beyond that, Jane read in Carleton's change of heart and Washington's successes a clearer and more painful message.

"Ye forget Washington's rounding up those Germans, Grandmother. These Yankees also fought the French. They're better fighters than you are giving them credit for . . ." Polly retorted.

"Naw. Th' Highlanders an' th' King brought th' French ta thir knees ae Quebec. Came now, lass, th' rebels dinna hae muskets. An' Washington captur'd a lot o' drunken Germans an Christmas day. A pack o' farmers an' boys canna fight seasoned sodgers, lass." Sarah swallowed the remainder of her whiskey.

"And Lexington and Concord, Grandmother? Th' fluke of boys like Robbie Yarns?"

"O' course."

"Breed's Hill, and farmers forcing Howe out of Boston? And those men freezing to death on Independence? We might want it to happen our way, Auntie, but there is something beyond the simple grandeur of the arms of the Empire," Jane added. Sitting here in this room without any male presence somehow gave her a more objective look at the relative strengths of the two sides. The very desperation of the rebels made them formidable.

"Those skirmishes were a freak o' circumstance. Tweel tak a miracle ta beat th' King in his present disposition."

"Then why use Indians?" Jane asked, the very thought of using them offending Nature herself, despite her hope a second British invasion would finally end the fighting and reunite her with David.

"They're bringin' 'em sae th' Pope's people canna tak Canada bak," Sarah countered, re-enforcing, however, the fear of the Indians.

"The demon's out of the bottle and David's with them," Jane cried, looking pointedly at Sarah Jones.

"Yer imagination's gallopin' away wi' ye, lass. David's bringin' th' law bak ta this countrie. Wat's a few savages?"

Jane's fears multiplied. She lost any objectivity she might have had about the conflict. She could never equate Law with Indians, despite Doctor Franklin's assertions. She felt trapped. Her eyes followed the staircase. She walked to the window, drawing the coolness of the floor under her petticoat. She pressed her forehead against the swirl in the center of the glass and inhaled the coolness of the frost on the pane. She burned with resentment, anger, and fear. Where her breath melted the frost, the glass made a green sea of the snow outside.

"Maybe the French will protect us," she reproved the other women, since they all knew that the Congress had sent Doctor Franklin to France before Carleton's aborted invasion.

"The French hate all Englishmen!" Sarah Jones pronounced scornfully. "Franklin and the rebels don't have a prayer getting them to join their side."

"Th' French an' all o' them Popish derfishes ken eneugh nocht ta bak a loosin' horse either," Sarah McNeil added.

"Then why use the French Indians?" Jane retorted, her thoughts swimming in the eerie glow outside. "How cruel to use them after the last war."

"Dinna work yersel up, lass. Hae a dram. Ye worry ta mickle . . ." Sarah put a glass in Jane's hand and touched her forehead with the back of her hand. "Ye're warum. Hast ye somethin'?"

Jane brushed her hand across the window and cooled her

forehead. How nice to dance and cabriole in Montreal, to wear her best petticoats, to meet the wives of the officers, and to dine from silver plate as she had at the Jessups' at Lake Lucerne. She fingered the pearl against her neck and sipped the whiskey. In Montreal under the army's protection, her longing and anguish would vanish—up there she wouldn't have to witness the fates of desperate men, oh, how she wanted to feel the strength and warmth of David's arms around her.

"Oh, David," she whispered against the glass.

"Dinna worry, ye an' David hae yer whole lives ahead o' ye."

"So what about the French Indians?" she persisted, sticking to the older woman like a burr, her eyes focusing on the green hue beyond the glass. That question haunted her—Stories of Indian warfare on the Ohio frontier during the last war still terrified her. And how could she forget Eva's eyes when she said St. Luc's son-in-law led them for Carleton?

"Forgit 'em." Sarah turned away, mistaking the intensity of her gaze for dreamy thoughts of David. "Let our sangs blow owre th' craigs tanite. Th' bluid o' th' Scots runs in yer veins, Jane." She raised her glass and began a reel before the fire, her short heavy figure narrowing the room.

Jane turned and beheld her and her spirits lifted. If her spirits didn't lift, she would surely die this night. Maybe they could have a Hogmanay on the Hudson, there being little else—

"Sing something, Auntie, please," she requested, repressing her desperation. The older woman stood before the fire. "A couple o' sangs o' yer namesake, Jenny McCrea":

> *Comin' through th' rye, poor body*
> *Comin' through th' rye,*
> *She draight a' her petticoatie,*
> *Comin' through the rye.*

> *Jenny's a wat, poor body*
> *Jenny's seldom dry;*
> *She draight a' her petticoatie,*

Comin' through th' rye.
Gin a body kiss a body,
Need a body cry?

Gin a body meet a body
Comin' through th' glen,
Gin a body kiss a body,
Need th' world ken?

"Does that nae cheer ye?"

The woman's eyes sparkled in the lamplight. Jane sipped the smoky whiskey, and the heat from the room enveloped her. The song reminded her of David's first kiss sealing the promise that had brought her up here to Northumberland. "Sing another, please."

Sarah wet her lips and sang as though the words were written on the ceiling.

Within th' bush, her covert nest,
A little linnet fondly prest,
The dew sat chilly an her breast
Sae early in th' morning.
She soon shall see her tender brood,
Th' pride, th' pleasure o' th' wood,
Amang th' fresh green leaves bedewed,
Awake th' early morning.

So thou, dear bird, young Jenny fair!
An tremblin' string or vocal air,
Shall sweetly pay th' tender care
That tents thy early morning.
So thou, sweet rose-bud, young an' gay,
Shall beauteous blaze upon th' day,
An' bless th' parent's evenin' ray
That watched thy early morning.

Young and living under her father's roof, summer mornings

were eternal! Oh, how she yearned to have children! To watch the early morning and to sing to them in the warm and lively fields.

"Sing th' *Highland Lassie*, Grandmother."

> *Nae gentle dames, though e'er sae fair*
> *Shall ever be my nurse's care:*
> *Thir titles a' 're empty show;*
> *Gie me my Highland lassie, O.*

> *Within th' glen sae bushy, O,*
> *Aboon th' plains sae rushy, O,*
> *I set me doon wi' right good-will,*
> *Ta sing my Highland lassie, O.*

> *O, were yon hills an' valley's mine,*
> *Yon palace an' yon garden fine!*
> *Th' warld then th' love should know*
> *I bear my Highland lassie, O.*

> *Bot fickle fortune frowns an me,*
> *And I maun cross th' raging sea;*
> *Bot while my crimson current flow,*
> *I'll love my Highland lassie, O.*

Did David feel she was his Highland lassie? Did he think of her as his palace and gardens fine? Oh, if he did think of her that way, not even Robbie's shooting could now cast a shadow on her desire for the home just a few rods away—nor could Sarah Jones squelch the poetry of its possibility. Sarah then caught her with a song, wedding love and war. As she sang the tears welled in her eyes and trickled down her cheeks.

> *Th' sodger frae th' wars returns,*
> *Th' sailor frae th' main;*
> *Bot I hae parted from my love,*

never ta meet again,
My dear;
Never ta meet again.

Gin day is gane, an' night is came,
An' a' folk bound ta sleep;
I think an him that's far awa',
Th' lee-lang night, an' weep,
My dear;
Th' lee-lang night, an' weep.

The song sank into Jenny's heart. How many nights since Carleton had she wept with longing for David?

"That's done me," Sarah said, blotting her eyes. "'Tis th' time o' year." She walked to the table, half-filled her glass and poured water into it. The water flowed like a benediction, sanctifying Jane's longing:

What dark, solitary, and haunting ballads! She had heard Sarah sing them often, even in David's presence, and they deepened her desire and sharpened her longing. She reached across the table and refilled her own glass and swallowed slowly in sad communion with Sarah widowed, and Polly single. The songs bound her to these women. She licked the liquor from her lips. Polly looked serene in her light gray petticoat, her honey-colored hair softly covering the sides of her face, her lips slightly parted and her eyes half-closed, a thin blue ribbon encircling her hair.

"What comes next?" Polly asked.

Jane lifted her hair from her shoulder.

"Yer hair's as rich as abloomin' field o' clover. 'Tis honey an' strawberries a' owre wi' ye twa lassies. O, ta be young again!" Sarah raised her glass to them, her round face glowing. "Frae oot o' winter ye'll came forth a bloomin'. Lik Demeters we'll summon our daughters an' drink a health ta th' New Year o' seventy-seven—ta th' sound o' th' double pipes an' th' wavin' thyrsus cames th' honey an' th' strawberries."

Jane laughed. Sarah sang again and she and Polly joined her.

> *Should auld acquaintance be forgot,*
> *And never brought to mind?*
> *Should auld acquaintance be forgot'*
> *and days o' lang syne?*

> *For auld lang syne, my dear,*
> *For auld lang syne,*
> *We'll take a cup o' kindness yet,*
> *For auld lang syne.*

> *We twa hae run about the braes,*
> *and pu'd the gowans fine;*
> *But we've wandered mony a weary foot,*
> *Ain' auld lang syne.*

> *We twa hae paidl't i' the burn,*
> *Frae morning sun till dine;*
> *But seas between us braid hae roar'd*
> *Sin' auld lang syne.*

> *And here's a hand, my trusty fiere,*
> *And gie's a hand o' thine;*
> *And we'll take a right guid willie-wraught,*
> *for auld lang syne.*

> *And surely ye'll be your pint-stoup,*
> *And surely I'll be mine;*
> *And we'll take a cup o' kindness yet,*
> *For auld lang syne.*

Jane's feelings came like a spring thaw—she didn't care that Sarah Jones saw her tears. The song made the future unendurable when she realized the incompleteness of the past. Alone, like Persephone, passing from the dark to the light and back to the darkness again, she would walk through the harvest and out again, alone. The utter desolation of such a condition filled her with a strange sense of beauty that threatened to overwhelm her.

"Don't cry, lass," Polly said, touching her arm.

"I haven't cried since October when David sailed away," she lied.

"It goes against me too, when I think o' Peter and this war . . ."

"It's like being caught in a snowdrift."

"Ye're not alone."

The clock, over the fireplace, ticked off the frozen minutes. The door had slammed on her, shutting her out in the cold. She sipped from her glass. "What will happen to Peter?" She had to know how Polly would survive a British victory.

"Grandmother will tell Simon Fraser about him. Peter will never know," Polly answered, tightening her lips.

Jane thought of David's letter coming through her. "What if the rebels catch you?" Thought of it sickened her.

"I'm vera careful."

"What happened to the *schoolteacher*?"

"He went back to Saratoga."

Jane took a small swallow. The whiskey made her toes tingle. She pressed her palms on her knees. "I'll go crazy if I think too much about it, Polly."

Suddenly a rush of cold air came through the room and Louis Cook stood in the doorway. The other two women stopped talking and sat like statues.

"I have Robert Yarns," he said, stepping into the house followed by other Indians who supported Robert. Dressed in skins and wool coats, the Indians loomed as large as bears. Jane gasped at Louis still wearing David's wig.

Frostbitten and exhausted, Robert slumped into a chair. Jane pulled his coat sleeves over his hands and pushed her whiskey glass into his hand. He fumbled with the glass and drank, spilling the whiskey on his cheeks. She gave the bottle to Cook. He drank and passed it to the other Indians. He patted Robert on the shoulder.

"He'll be all right—"

"This man took David and me hunting," Robert explained numbly.

Jane nodded. Of course she should have thought of Cook as an old friend, but she only associated him with painful memories.

Louis pulled his cloak across his shoulders and walked to the door and the other Indians followed him. Their laughter came from outside. Then their silence. Robert moaned and gripped his wrist.

"Hurt, lad?" Polly asked.

"Yeh . . ."

"Ye're lucky ye didna freeze ta death. An' how aboot those savages camin' in lik that!"

"Do those Indians know David?" Sarah Jones asked, finding her voice.

"They're Oneidas, friends of Reverend Kirkland . . ." Robert's eyes were feverish.

"But the one wearing the wig is a slave."

"David sold him that wig," Jane declared.

"What?"

Jane looked away at the dawn, suddenly feeling very sorry for David's mother who in pursuit of her own blind interest had lost the very son she had sought to possess. Then she thought she would never see Louis or David's wig again. How grotesque! And was David suffering? Did *he* ache for her too? She grasped the sill with her fingernails. Pale dawn grew on the snow where the moonlight lay. A small sparrow-like bird landed on the sill, cocked its head, and then fluttered away.

35

March 1777

As sloop-like clouds scudded across the blue sky, pine needles blew like brown darts in the gusting wind outside the window. Jane, Polly, and Content sewed upstairs in the parlor of the tavern. Jane, sitting near the window, sewed a cravat from a piece of blue silk cut from one of her petticoats. "Do you think David will like this?" she asked, holding up the cravat to the other two women.

"I wonder why James hasn't returned from the lake . . ." Content replied with her own concern, looking past Jane's cravat and over the windowsill onto the road. "He is never away this long fishing."

Jane looked at Polly, her eyes conveying how like Content to think only of her own concerns, and folded the silk in her lap. Yet she had been without David for six months! "Do you think a day without James long, Content?" she asked her friend without bitterness, but with only a weary sigh she hoped Content wouldn't miss. How long ago it seemed when David worked here at the Corners, first on the mills, and then alone on the bridge with his hopes resting in the Wing's prosperity and the friendship of Content and James. Yes, it was long ago, and she was a different woman now; and Content was a different woman too. The cares and hopes of young women had passed them. But how comforting it would be if Content would at last acknowledge that she had suffered since the division between James and David and David's defection to Carleton. It didn't matter to her that Content was on the opposite side, like Polly, when it came to her husband. It was only that she wanted Content to feel what she was feeling as a woman because her lover was gone—not a day, but for six months. If her friend, if she could call Content that, would only say something it would relieve her of the isolation of winter and the grief of separation she endured with David's absence. What else was in a friend to do?

"Oh, I am sorry, Jane. I can't begin to know what you have suffered with David's absence."

"I had hoped that you would say that, Content," Jane replied, searching Content's face for the sincerity she had always found lacking in the past, wondering if this was a different person from the selfish young woman who had walked away from her that November day when she stood in the snow near the river bank waiting for David and James to finish their day's work on the bridge. "Are you really sorry."

"Yes, of course, I am—"

"'Of course'?"

"You know what I mean, Jane."

"Maybe I don't know what you mean, Content."

"You have thought me very spoiled by my father, haven't you?"

"I can't deny it," Jane admitted, resisting feeling bitter that James had still worked here and won exemption from the Committee while David had to defect.

"I know what I have been—never as good as you, Jane," Content confessed awkwardly.

"I didn't mean that—"

"But I have felt it often. A woman can only hide from herself for so long. I realize that now when I think of what you have suffered—I mean with David gone, and what led up to it. I don't know whether I could have lived with that and what you are feeling now. I have been very selfish and fortunate—"

"But you lost your first husband."

"Yes, I did, but I was so young and James came so quickly to fill the void Jacob left. I sometimes have to remind myself of that. But you've had no such luck, and I have thought only of myself."

"You think differently about me now? You don't think I was grasping for David—that I was too 'pious' with you?"

"No. I thought that I understood your dreams, and I was jealous of them."

"We have never spoken like this before, have we? But you were only young, Content—and it's not so anymore. I don't feel bitter toward you."

"I know that, Jenny. But you have been affected more by the war than me, and I want you to know I know it. And I think your cravat is beautiful and that David will love it."

Jane touched the younger woman's arm. "Thank you, Content. And we are true friends to that degree," and she gestured toward the window and the gusting wind, "that the war is somehow outside of us."

"Yes."

Footsteps sounded on the stairs and James then entered the room and declared, "A band of Tories and Indians attacked Captain Baldwin on the lake yesterday and took seventeen prisoners."

"James!" Content exclaimed.

Jane averted her glance. How had Content been able to resist her husband's heat?

"Nothing's lower than a stinking Tory coming back with savages! Isn't that right, Jane?" he asked her angrily.

"David wasn't with them! Tell him, 'Tenty. Tell him David wouldn't come back with Indians. You know he wouldn't . . ." Jane replied angrily, turning to Content to come to her defense. "Even Polly knows David better than that."

"Aye, stop jumpin' ta wild conclusions, James!" Polly demanded.

But Jane's imaginings of the Indians racing through the woods outside of Sarah McNeil's, the night she waited for news of David and Carleton, came to life—the helpless cries of women and children here at Corners on their way to William Henry in the last war sounded heavily on the gusting wind outside. But David *hadn't* joined the British out of vengefulness, and it was inconceivable that he would come alone down here with Indians.

"Did they harm families?" she asked bitterly, suggesting to James that he might go on and accuse David of the ultimate sin.

"I don't know, but I do know David's talents in the woods."

"Of course, you know his talents in the woods, James. You were close friends, which is why you rail against him, but you have no right to say that of him."

"Why did he go over then?"

"Must we go into this, Content? Please, tell him to stop."

"David defaulted against his country."

The women didn't reply—James looked at Content, but she was silent. He then left the room.

"Why does he say such things, Content. You know David wouldn't do this—" James' accusation burned into her breast. "And he accuses me—" She folded the cravat. She hated being made to feel suspect and felonious. Eva had made her feel the same way after Hogmanay at David's mother's house when she went there to see Polly and Sarah McNeil, asking her: 'Why are you still associating with that Loyalist? Were you diapered in a tartan? Oh, I would love to see the look on their faces when they hear about Washington's victory over Cornwallis at Princeton.' "You know David," she repeated to both of her friends.

"That doesn't make it less bitter," Content said. "James has never forgiven David."

"What's there to forgive where I am concerned? Why must I feel guilty when all we ever wanted was a home, light and companionship? Are those desires *ignis fatuus?* James basely accuses me! I only want David back. You both know that."

"War does that to men, makes them hard and bitter because they do the fighting," Polly said.

"Excuse me, Polly, but James is not doing the fighting—" Jane corrected her.

"But it is the same with him, Jane. Please, try and understand. He is hardly himself with what's going on—"

"Who is?" Jane agreed. The coldest winter in memory one thousand of the two thousand five hundred soldiers left on Mount Independence after Carleton had frozen to death. Those men would certainly never be the same. The clouds of war were gathering over their heads and events bred a sense of desperation: new officers, Wayne and Van Schaick, had been sent to Ti and Independence;

commissioners were appointed to sell the land of defaulters; Congress had moved back to Philadelphia from Baltimore; and Gates took command of the army from Schuyler—and the attack James reported followed one in February when French Indians took other prisoners on the west shore of Lake Champlain. As though on a mountaintop, Jane watched the storm approach, hoping that the wind might change before it reached her. And though she might pray innocently before it, and try to hide, David's defaulting made her a verbal target, a British sympathizer, if not an enemy. But events frightened her as much as anyone else! So how could she expect that James would act in a civil manner toward her?

"So much for the precious rule of Law that my friend's husband attacks me for something neither I nor David have anything to do with," she said bitterly, nonetheless.

"That changed in his mind when David defaulted," Content said.

"And who brought this on us?" Jane demanded.

"That's obvious," Content said archly.

"But why must I suffer?"

"We're all caught in it. No one knows right from wrong any more," Polly pointed out.

"If I had gone with him, I would have been spared this."

"James doesn't really blame you, Jane."

"David wouldn't have gone, if he had had a chance—"

"Father had to close the mills," Content said, reddening.

"I don't want to say that. We have our own friendship—we have just declared to each other," Jane said, turning her eyes toward the window. She didn't want to rake up what they all knew had happened.

"But you think it?"

"What else can I think? But why think it now?"

"He didn't default because of James," Content said.

"No, he didn't, and you must make him see that."

"But I don't know the reason," Content said. "If you tell me, maybe it will make a difference. I can tell James then."

"I can't tell you, Content—just believe me that it wasn't because of James," she said, knowing that Content would be unable to convince James of anything, and if Content knew the real reason for David's defection it would just make James hate him all the more. Of course it was his desire for land and a home which put him on the other side—and his brother Daniel, his mother, the action of the Committee, and Ebenezer Jessup's offer, 'all these things had made him a skulking Tory,' she wanted to cry out at the walls of the tavern for all to hear.

36

April

The April sunlight, the chirps of red-winged blackbirds and redbreasts, and perfumed-scented air flowed into Jane's room. Not out of bed yet, she could see the sun reflecting warmly off the pastel-hemmed river. And when she opened her eyes she felt transcendent. Her breathing, skin-touch and heartbeat took on the smell, light and sounds coming through her window. As she slipped out of bed and dipped her hands into the basin of water, winter ended for her. The water fell from her hands like a minuet. As she brushed her hair, each long stroke released the scent of flowers, freed the notes of the birds and added color to the trees. She reached for her riding habit and thought of David. Was he putting on his uniform or was he already wearing it and writing her a letter with the birds singing overhead in the trees—or was he shaving . . . She left her room, her domestic imaginings of him increasing her longing for him just as the birds lightened her day.

The sun flooded over the trees across the bay through the front door, filling the house with the clean smell of water and earth as she passed through the house and out the door.

"Eva!"

"Over here!" Eva answered from the clothesline.

Jane's eyes followed the sloping ground to the bay.

"I don't advise riding," Eva said, noticing she wore her riding habit.

"Why?"

After Captain Baldwin's capture last month, Tory resistance had grown. Jane knew that, for even Sarah McNeil had said something "'twas gain' an" up at Sandy Hill and among the other nearby towns she had mentioned. But Jane chose to look unconcerned out onto the bay in response to Eva's question.

"You heard John before he left for Fort George to assist Van Schaick in moving the hospital."

"So much fuss—who's concerned with me, Eva? Neither Tories nor soldiers will have anything to do with me," though last night before falling asleep she had heard voices near the river he suspected were Tories.

"Don't think only of Tories. People aren't considerate of sympathizers."

"My, Eva, do you think anyone cares what I think! Independence for me is old news after last July. What does it matter that the Colony has just declared for itself? I am accustomed to hearing these strong and violent voices. And, as I am John's sister what patriot will harm me? I have nothing to fear between Ballston and Fort George."

Her brothers still continued to serve with Van Schoonhoven's Twelfth Albany Regiment from Ballston after Carleton at Ti—and Stephen still assisted as surgeon at the Lake George hospital. Those were reasons enough for her not to fear that she would be molested as a sympathizer. She didn't need to tell Eva that.

"John worries about you, nonetheless."

"You always said the Whigs had conscience," Jane said pointedly, not distinguishing New York's lawless declaration from the Grant's last January or from the Congress' last July.

"The Tories are arming. Recruiters and spies are infiltrating from Canada. Decent people are edgy and they know you, especially after David's pickle."

"I'll take my chances. I can't be a prisoner here at the house, especially after the winter we've just been through together."

"I suppose the spring day makes it all daffodils for you," Eva consented with a frown.

"Oh, Eva . . ." Jane humored her as she walked on by the clothesline toward the mare.

—As Charlotte walked over the soft ground, the river flowed high with the spring thaw. The land wore light muslin with a green pattern. The gray trunks of birches and poplars breathed winter's cold into the warm air and their leaves unfolded like small pieces of parchment. Jane smelled the cold leaving the earth and felt the mist off the river on her skin. She thought about what Eva had said about Tories organizing and concluded that the British and David would soon be leaving Montreal. With Lake Champlain clear of ice, the navy would sail within the month. She wondered whether David had met Carleton and some of the British officers and their wives.

She approached the grove where she had watched the rebel soldiers on their way to Forts Ticonderoga and Independence last fall. The grove had shimmered with frost then. Now, however, small leaves dotted the blue sky. What possibilities did this change hold out to her? Did it mean that Life was a constant renewal, or only a taunting repetition of blind hopes running down the hourglass? Or did Providence actually preside? Certainly she and David had walked an upward slope . . . At twenty-seven years old she couldn't really decide what Life meant, only that having this thought at this moment filled her with an ambivalence bred of an intense desire for renewal and a dread of the future because she had been disappointed so often.

She smoothed her hair and lifted her face to the sun. The river swished against the bank and the breeze sighed through the branches. A fly buzzed. The world suddenly seemed brighter and larger in spring, and the sky more vast, filling her with a sense of innocence and insignificance that momentarily freed her of any thought whatever except to breath and behold the creation around her. Then a squirrel suddenly began to scold and jerk its tail like a question mark in a nearby tree. She suffered the deflation, and her eyes dropped to the river. Yes, it flowed to Albany, and passed the towns beyond Albany, which she also had passed seven years ago with such hope, before it reached the City. She wanted life to have meaning, not just the privilege Eva accused her of wanting. The river had to mean something. It couldn't be that it just lost itself in the sea. It had to carry something, some force had to draw it forward. And if that was so, then her life had to be like the river too. She wanted David more than anything in life, and her love flowed, like the river, with meaning and purpose toward him. Nothing in Life happened without reason. Hadn't her father always told her that?

She dismounted. This *palace*, where she had sat last fall watching the marching rebels, had neither walls nor roof now in spring, yet the familiar shapes of the trees, the redbreasts and squirrels, and her view of the river brought fall and her watching back to her. This time, however, she would wait for him in summer, and in the afternoon he would come for her. She would wear her hair long, the way he liked it. But how would she explain breaking her promise to John not to wait again for David?

As she sat thinking of what she might say to her brother two figures appeared on the road. She saw them out of the corner of her eye and Charlotte flicked her tail. She looked up when they approached her.

"Hello, Robert."

He stopped and stroked the mare. The boy with him had black hair, long face, and enormous feet that seemed to pull him along. Robert's voice was low and husky. The chestnut geldings they led nipped and pushed their noses at each other and worked their teeth against their bits.

"This here's Jonathan Butterfield over from Massachusetts," Robert greeted her.

"Oh, and what brings him over here?" she asked, not rudely, but coolly because annoyed at having been found sitting here.

"Drawing supplies for the Commissary department. Suspect we can draw up enough lead to pepper the Lobsterbacks and any Injuns they bring along this time."

The other boy had clear quiet blue eyes. In their torn and dirty breeches and shoes with holes in them they looked like tinkers to her.

"You shouldn't hate Indians after January, Robert," she reminded him, thinking that he should know he owed more to Indians than that.

"Louis Cook and those Oneidas aren't French Injuns. French Injuns fightin' alongside the Lobsterbacks aren't worth nothin'."

"Well, driving wagons at Stillwater, you needn't worry about French Indians," she observed dryly, standing up.

"If those painted Frenchies came with Carleton last fall, they'll come again, and you better hope they get no farther than Ti like last time. Your white face ain't goin' ta help you none."

"You are still determined to get yourself killed, aren't you?" She looked from one to the other. "I would have thought that you had learned something by now, Robert."

"But we can fight, can't we, Jonathan?"

"We can shoot at least," Jonathan answered.

"You can't be more than fourteen," she objected.

"Been shootin' since I was ten—if I can hold a shovel full a— , I can hold one a these—" he gestured to the musket slung alongside the saddle of his horse.

"And I suppose that you can shoot better than January, right Robert?" she continued to remind him.

"Skulkers."

"Skulkers or not, you should have more sense than to fight in a man's war."

She reached for her reins, resisting saying more. Talking like this to these two boys unpleasantly diminished her. Arguing the war with Eva, or even Content was one thing, but with a couple of green boys was another. The sun played on her rust-colored hair as she gained the saddle.

"I'm doing my duty. I ain't running from Lobsterbacks," Robert challenged her.

"You're a Yankee," she replied, looking down at him from the saddle.

"I ain't no patent-leathered macaroni with shiny epaulets and a red jacket."

"That's right, Robert."

"Meaning, young man?" Jane demanded, stung by what she took as a reference to David.

"Me and Jonathan don't like being talked down to, much less when painted Frenchies are fixin' to force knives through our hair. Ain't that right, Jonathan?"

Jane flushed. Her sense of grief and betrayal smoldering over the winter after Carleton flashed to the surface. "If you knew anything, Robert—" she began sharply—

"They insulted Mister Hale, and Pap took to his heels. My brothers and me aim to fight."

"Mister Hale spied," she shot back at him at a loss as to how else to stop his talk.

"We will do as well with the same 'regret,' not like that bucket of snakes at Edward," he said hotly for his own part, catching her anger. "A man would understand." He then took the advantage and abruptly pushed by the mare with his horse. "And that will be all to be said about that—"

Burning with humiliation and anger, she watched them walk, ragged as a scarecrows, down the road away from her. Their high-rumped horses seemed to walk on stilts. Without thinking she dug her heels into the mare. In two leaps the mare was at a full run and the wind cut against her face as she lashed out with her riding crop at Robert as she flew by him.

Robert shielded his face from the mud flying from the mare's hooves as Jane flew past him. He stopped and wiped his cheek. He felt like the mare had stung him with her whipping tail. His eyes watered.

Jonathan looked at him. "Nothin' serious. More bleedin' than anything else."

"Jesus, too bad *she* ain't on our side to whip the Injuns for us," Robert laughed, looking at the blood on his hand with odd surprise. He then pulled his shirttail out of his breeches and dabbed his cheek.

"Girls is like that when ya cross 'em," Jonathan said.

"Tories always hit a guy from behind. Colonel John's sister too."

"Why don't he rap her? Serve her right."

They began walking again. Robert shook his head.

"Friends o' my Pap in Fort Edward snookered her."

"You called her a Tory. Think she'll tell her brother?"

"Naw, he chased her macaroni last fall. Legs o' grass. She took the bone out o' him. And a fella that lives with his mother gets slippery and soft, know what I mean?"

"Think she's spyin'?"

Robert scratched his head.

"Her friends at Edward maybe. Aw, huck it, people like that never come to nothin'. What do they know about things anyway. They always have it their way, you know what I mean?"

"Not, exactly, except ya can't trust 'em."

"Yeh. You talk to 'em and look at 'em and nothin's happenin' in their eyes. It's like meetin' up with a polecat at the compost and yer tryin' ta talk him outa lettin' go at ya and he jest stands there pointin' his tail at ya not lettin' on whether he's goin' ta do it to ya or not."

"Yeh, polecats. Their black eyes are jest there lookin' at ya. I know what ya mean, and all the time they're leverin' right there with the trigger between their legs. I seen that. I hate that kind o' thing—lookin' at 'em and not bein' able ta get behind those eyes and into that pointy-head. Yeh, polecats. That's Tories, alright, too. And they carry messages around. And the girls pass messages."

"That McNeil friend o' hers can't carry her tush to the woodpile. Walks like she's luggin' sacks of sand, huffin' and puffin', goin' as fast as a three-legged cow up to her arse in river mud.

"She and my old man were a pair, rollin' out the orders. 'Get the wood, Robert, empty the slops, Robert, do this and that.' But her granddaughter might carry messages. Don't miss nothin' that Polly Hunter. Sharp as a weasel with its nose in the air. She could carry a message. Not tushbags McNeil though—unless there's silver plate, whiskey, or headdresses as high as six story birdhouses in a message."

"Tories all over the place here. Crimus, it's worse than Massachusetts . . ."

"Lots a' skulkers. Come from Montreal and go right down the river to New York to suck up to Howe. You Grants people scoutin' through here all the time lookin' for 'em. How'd you get over here anyway? You would a been better off stayin' in Williamstown."

"Naw. We're jest pushin' the stuff over from there, but I didn't expect ta get bushwhacked in Salem—crimus. And only bringin' a wagon from Arlington ta Edward, too. Just made it over the side before hoofing it to Edward."

"I got ta hand it to you. I only saw Carleton's coattails up at Ti. Took it into his head to sail back up when he seen us all there waitin' for 'im."

"Well, I'm suppos'd ta drive wagons and cows ta Stillwater ta Schuyler. They're stackin' for the army there."

"Yeh, got to get ready for Johnny and his painted Frenchies this summer."

"Mess o' Tories at Salem, huh?"

"Suspect you met some Munros and Ramseys. More o' that highland trash like McNeil. Like ta hang out in the bushes and take a guy from behind. But them are left overs from Carleton—most o' 'em already hoofed it over. That how you got your face scratched?"

"Prickers from divin' into the woods. Run like a hare," Jonathan laughed.

"And with feet like yours? You must a been walkin' on the treetops with them feet. But, Jesus, you know about Tory scum now, I reckon."

"You bet, Robert. But what was she sayin' about January to ya. Didya meet Injuns?"

"Sort a. Same thing as you mostly." Robert stopped and held out his hand and pointed at the puckered spot in his palm. He turned his hand over. "Come out the other side. Skulkers tried to nail me. I lay like dead in the snow in front of her—out lookin' at the stars when I come through with readin'."

Jonathan whistled.

"Can still shoot though. Happened near her macaroni's house. She brought me in." They walked on in silence.

"But what about the Injuns?"

"Ah, some local Injuns I knew found me in the snow after I left the house. Lost my way, you know. I was cold. But ca'mon, let's get outa here," he said, bringing up the reins and jumping up on his horse. "Race ya down ta the ferry." Clods of earth flew up behind them as they raced each other down the road.

Charlotte nibbled the grass above the river. The river had a dark leaden hue. A cloud passed and Jane drew her jacket closer, then leaned over and flicked the mud from the hem of her petticoat. The road followed the river like a muddy gash. She then saw the boys come flying out of the woods below her along the road, their long arms and coattails flying above their horses' racing bodies. She watched them stream along the road, their hats pushed flat by the wind. She watched them indifferently, her anger having left her as quickly as it erupted. She preferred to imagine the bright uniforms of soldiers, their muskets and swords gleaming in the summer sun, their groomed horses, the officers' wives following in their carriages after them, rather than give any further thought to young Yarns . . .

Did it even really matter what happened to those boys when the army came? Death held no terror for Robert, even though she had tried to tell him—and how often had she awakened in the morning with the weight of her own father's death in her soul? She alone knew the absoluteness of death. The iron-gray branches of the maple swing-tree and the grief-becalmed swing her father pushed her on summer evenings confirmed it. When she remembered his beard and level eyes, or when he said, gently touching her face, 'Your mother's eyes and hair', spoken sadly as though to her mother on a distant shore, Death came to her in slow degrees. When he died he took the life of the swing-tree with him; he took the features of his face and his words with him into the cold earth. He left and never returned: 'He was a good man, Jane,' his friend, Wheeler Case, had said to her at his funeral. 'He's in a better place.' Suddenly a young girl stepped on the threshold of life. What did young Robert Yarns know of the terror of death and its emptiness? No, she really couldn't think about him.

She then started down the slope toward the road. How often on such a spring day had she and David walked together? and she hadn't heard from him since January!

The mare's hoofs sunk into the ground and made sucking sounds in the muddy bank as she crossed the road to the river before returning home. She let the mare drink, but then she lifted her head. Peter Freel came from behind some low bushes in a skiff! Jane's heart leaped.

Freel's oars clanked and he lurched toward the bow of the boat when he came up to her. His foot touched the bank. "Waitin' for something?" he asked coolly, reaching into his pocket and pulling out a handkerchief to wipe his face. "Lucky I found you. Skinners all over the place."

"Give me the letter," she said breathlessly, certain he carried one.

"Letter?" Freel asked.

"Listen, there's no one here to see you and you gave the last one to Polly. Let me have it, please."

Freel walked toward her and brushed Charlotte's withers with his hand as he slipped the letter up to her. He then returned to his skiff, smiling through his brown teeth.

Jane pushed the letter into the folds of her petticoat and urged Charlotte up over the bank.

Montreal April 20, 1777

Dear Jenny, no doubt you wonder about me. I am safe and trust this letter finds you well. In February word came the rebels won a battle at Trenton, & in March we learned of their preparations at Ti. It is not, however, likely to do them much good as the king's cousin, General Burgoyne, is expected back from England next month to take command of the army from Carleton. Members of Parliament will join the expedition to restore government. Preparations for the expedition have started, and we will be together again, soon. Simon Fraser will command the Light Corps including Jessup's, like last year. Tell Sarah McNeil I met her cousin. Everyone expects the war to end. Confidence is high. Lady Harriet Ackland, Baroness Von Reidesel, etc., will accompany the expedition. Dear, Jen, know that I love you and miss you sorely, but don't worry about me.

No more at present—but believe me, I'm yours aff'tly till death.
David.

ps. Thomas was married in January and he will be coming
with Burgoyne!

Jane turned the letter over. A hundred questions raced through her mind: how well did he know Simon Fraser, had he met the Baron, where had he met the Baroness and Lady Harriet? They expected General Burgoyne back from England, and his brother, Thomas, would be coming with him? Did that mean that David had met the General before he had left for England? Did any of the people David mentioned know him by sight, by name? And Burgoyne was the king's cousin and Members of Parliament were joining the expedition! And when had he heard from his brother? His last words when he parted from her that day she was brushing the mare rang in her ears: *Jenny, this is our chance.* That their trials would soon end made her giddy—no more delayed hopes! She floated like a bird on an updraft. He wrote on the twentieth, the very day the Colony declared its Independence. She saw a new life, free of innuendo, insult, and uncertainty, open like the sky before her. At last, summer would end her anguish.

She looked riverward for Freel for him to take a reply back with him, but the man was gone. Only the sun lay on the quiet river making David's letter like the balm of spring—but nothing had matured yet, which like the season simply promised to emerge to ripeness. And David had spoken of only plans and intentions. But what more was there? He spoke of restoration really, the best people would re-establish the accustomed ways. The Continent that had been repeatedly heated and chilled by war and chaos would finally grow calm. His brother's, Thomas', marriage and commission in the army offered a prospect of stability and an example to her and David. Wasn't David right to have defected? Hadn't they both really followed their intuitions in re-embracing the parental bonds? His letter redeemed her and promised to calm the raw spirit of the country. What she had been subjected to up to now seemed only a temporary aberration. She had been right all along in resisting the eruptions of the times.

She turned Charlotte back up the road toward John's house now confident in meeting Eva because she alone knew what was about to occur. Against this knowledge Eva's words and actions now seemed like a kind of puppetry little knowing that the strings that held her up were about to be severed. So anguished had she been over these months by being trapped among people close to her who insisted on shaming her for what David had done, she gave little thought to the personal suffering this would cause Eva in her turn.

37

May

As she bent over, Jane cupped one of the scarlet tulips in her hand and turned it towards the sun. She had forgotten about planting these bulbs early in the fall, but now these flowers popped up like little soldiers affirming the promise held out in David's letter.

She heard John's boots squeak on the threshold behind her as he came out of the house. He paused behind her and she knew that he watched her. She was struck by the sad geometry of his distance from her while she stood among the scarlet ranks of her planting.

"Beautiful," he said, coming forward.

"Aren't they?" she answered, releasing the tulip and observing him in his blue jacket and white breeches.

"They are the color of your hair. Perhaps Schuyler knew that when he gave them to me."

"How does such an aloof man know about the color of my hair?" she asked with surprise.

"You're out riding along the river. Everyone knows the color of your hair, Jen."

"Did he say that?"

"He said, 'I have some tulips, Colonel. Give them to your sister to plant. They are the color of her hair.'"

"Were you embarrassed? Does he know about David?"

"I don't know. I didn't ask him. He only knows that you are my sister, I think. It's nothing to be concerned about. I'd be flattered."

"It was considerate of him. And I guess I am flattered," she said blushing with the light playing in her blue eyes. And of course she was flattered to have been noticed by such a man. But where had he seen her? "But I would have asked where he saw me."

"He's been to Edward. Perhaps he saw you at McNeil's or you might have even seen him on the river and not known him, in which he case he might have noticed you. Certainly you made an impression on him."

"I don't recall seeing him. No, I have never seen him—" but how would she have known him unless up close? Except for Robbie Yarns, the soldiers had all come to look alike to her. "I only saw his Albany house from the boat when I first came up."

"Perhaps he saw you on the boat then?"

"I only saw his daughters on the lawn in their white hats," she laughed.

"I'll ask him, if you like." John then looked out over the bay.

"That's not necessary, John." The war and what these tulips foretold made the information about when General Schuyler had seen her gratuitous and inappropriate.

"Must you leave?" she asked, following his glance down to the shore where several soldiers waited for him.

He pointed across the bay to a line of bateaux moving slowly down river. "Yes, I must go. The Congress has ordered the First New York to Saratoga, as I told you. That's them there, and I must join Deerborn up at Ti," he answered, then noticed as an afterthought, "Stephen hasn't come yet?"

Jane shook her head. She had been out here waiting for Stephen herself. He was being detailed to Saratoga, too. He had promised them he would stop at the house on his way. It would be the first time she had seen Stephen since he had been sent to the Fort George hospital a year ago after the Canadian retreat. But why had the Congress ordered the First New York from Ti when they defended Ti against Carleton last fall? Did this mean Burgoyne wasn't marching? "Don't you expect the British?" she asked.

John smiled. "Yes, of course, we do. Burgoyne arrived in Quebec two weeks ago."

"So why is the Congress withdrawing the First New York to Saratoga?"

"That's military intelligence," John laughed.

"John!"

"I didn't mean anything by that," he said. "It's a fair question."

The day after she had received David's letter, General Gordon from Ballston had captured forty Tories defecting to Canada on the first of May. William and James had been with him. There had never been any family secrets kept from her because her brothers favored the Congress.

"But you haven't heard about Edward Jessup? How he jumped the falls up at Lucerne and escaped to Canada? You might even know the gorge, having visited up there. The Indians from Canada are alerting the Tories to Burgoyne's coming."

"No, I do not know the gorge, John. And I am not privy. But Edward's escape means forfeiture of his land, doesn't it?" she asked, fully knowing that John knew what that meant to her and David if Burgoyne failed.

"That's what it means. Forfeiture. Jessups were covering the odds both ways when Edward stayed behind. Now it's all open. They've laid all their cards face up."

"What else haven't you told me?" she asked, unable to keep the bitterness out of her voice.

"You don't know then?" he asked, genuinely surprised.

"Here at the house, how could I know anything?"

"You haven't heard from David? He doesn't write you?"

"Not about these things," she said. "—But even if he did, what use would it be to me?" she asked by way of admitting the truth he suspected in what David's letters to her contained.

"They also captured James Higson yesterday on his way fishing to Lake George."

"They!"

"Tories. Just like Baldwin," he added.

"What a croquet!" she exclaimed of the detention and ambuscade which marked the struggle.

"Yes, it's a war without rules—which reminds me, Congress paroled St. Luc too."

"Were those his Indians at the Jessups'?"

"Don't know. We didn't catch them."

"And James?"

"They took him to Montreal."

She immediately imagined David affronting him. She knew he had no love for James. She then thought of Content and how she had told her David wouldn't do what James had accused the Tories of in their treatment of Baldwin. "What could they possibly gain by taking James?" she asked, shocked.

"Nothing, except terrorizing the country. Part of the plan is to terrify the countryside."

"But how can the Congress possibly win? How can you prevail with a handful of soldiers at Ti and no hope of the French joining you?" She spoke clearly from exasperation.

John reacted calmly to her. "I know it looks meaningless to you. And maybe even hopeless for us. But we'll have soldiers by fall, Jen, and Johnny can't resist a sideshow."

"Meaning?"

"We'll entertain him along the way."

"You speak in riddles, John. But it really doesn't matter because it's us women—Content, Eva, and me—that suffer what's happening."

"I can't deny it," he admitted. "But the men suffer, too. I don't need to remind you of the suffering and our loses at Independence last winter."

"Nor of the Canadian campaign either," she chipped in shortly, "but we're the ones left behind." Her mind swam with Edward Jessup's flight, St. Luc's parole, James Higson's capture, and John's stratagems. She wanted Burgoyne to finish it. The specter of Carleton's armada sailing away merged with Schuyler's ghost co-coordinating streams of wagons and supplies up and down the valley. Her only hope of sanity and salvation lay among the tulips at the hem of her petticoat.

"Those soldiers going to Saratoga is a Schuyler trick," she said half-aloud with a gesture of her hand.

"We must beat Johnny before Albany . . ."

"How can you be so cool, John?"

"I'm not cool, except it has always been war here. War with the French, war among the Indians before the French and the English ever planted us here, and now war with the English themselves. If I appear cool, it's because we hope to put an end to it all—*somehow* put an end to it all," he said with quiet conviction.

"At Saratoga? That's where you hope to end it? And so the maneuvering has begun! How long will it take?" she cried, unable to fathom what he meant about there always being war here—

"At Saratoga, perhaps, but the longer it takes, the better. We will fight from Ti *to* Saratoga. And don't you attempt anything foolish, Jane," he said directly.

"That's what really gives you heat, doesn't it, John?"

"I told you I love you—it's not the men and stop thinking it."

"I promised you," she rejoined, feeling she had hit him unfairly. She knew that he loved her.

"I trust you then."

"You don't need to say it . . . But I don't think the British army will comply with your plan. They'll come straight away, surely you know that."

"Is that what David wrote?"

"Yes." There was no keeping anything from him.

"I thought so. But we know what he doesn't know. Burgoyne will not come straight away, but will chase us," he corrected her. "As General Washington has observed, Burgoyne is a general of detachments."

Washington's name raised goose bumps on her neck. A year ago last August, Howe had nearly cornered him on Long Island, but, with his back to the East River, his Gloucester fishermen had ferried his army from Brooklyn across the river to the City in a night fog. Washington was the fox Howe could not catch. But would the General divide his army? Would the rebels succeed in dragging the affair out over the summer? And what would she do? If she couldn't wait for David at Sarah McNeil's as she had done with Carleton, then she must go to Albany with Eva and the children.

"And if General Burgoyne does not detach?"

"But he *will*—that's how he fought in Spain. And we will fight and retreat to entice him—like Washington did when he retreated across the East River and then later across the Hudson only to win victories in New Jersey at Trenton and Princeton. Burgoyne *will* detach!"

The tulips brushed against her petticoat as she turned away from her brother. Thought of Washington iced her spirit. He succeeded beyond all understanding given the repeated odds against him.

"You must think Providence favors you." What else could she call it?

"'God helps those who help themselves,' I think is the expression. But there is no doubt that there is a spirit in the men and in our Cause. Practically speaking, the French will enter the war, if we whip Burgoyne. I must leave now. I have to say goodbye, Jane."

"And if Providence favors you, where does that leave me?" she asked out of love, pity, and resignation.

He clasped her gently by the shoulders, wordlessly cupped her face in his hands and kissed her. "It is beyond any telling what the future holds for any of us," he then said.

She then watched him walk away from her down to the water's edge to his soldiers. She lifted her hand to him in parting as his boat worked its way out onto the bright May bay.

38

June

As the ferry neared the bank, Jane gripped Charlotte's bridle and spoke to the ferryman. As she stood on the ferry in the light breeze, her knees felt weak. She regretted making the trip, but she could not turn back now.

"Ten Broech's militia and New Hampshire lads," the ferryman answered her as to their regiments.

The soldiers streamed along the road as the ferry slid against the bank. They looked at her as the boat touched. Charlotte's hoofs sounded on the planking as Jane and the other passengers walked off the ferry.

The soldiers stepped aside and large hands came forward for the mare. Jane released her grip on the bridle and walked ahead. Men carrying muskets ebbed around her.

"I'll take her."

Robert Yarns stood behind her holding the mare's reins. Glancing at him, she adjusted her hat, which she had adorned with a turkey feather she had found on the ride up. As he held the mare, she slipped her foot into the stirrup and rose to the saddle. The young man leaned on his musket and gazed up at her. He wore his tri-corner cocked to the side. His yellow-red hair curled up to the sides of it. His coarse shirt, open at the neck, seemed to hang on him.

"Let go, Robbie," she said.

But soldiers swirled around her—how could she think it was going to be easy to go to Fort Edward and on to Kingsbury with so many soldiers marching to Ti and people going to the polls to elect their new governor now that Tryon was out of the Colony and the Assembly was in the hands of the Congress?

"I'll lead you," Robbie said.

"Kingsbury . . ." she acquiesced almost inaudibly.

"We're goin' to Ti ta join St. Clair and his Continentals," he informed her over his shoulder.

Robert didn't exactly have the air of a gentleman, but there was something seasoned about him, something in his eyes and in the way he handled Charlotte's bridle which made him seem older to her—"Not driving wagons?" she asked, as they joined the stream of men.

"No." He lifted his musket. "Aim to shoot this. Fight back," he smiled, touching the light red line on his cheek.

The soldiers swirling around them at the ferry thinned as they gained distance from the landing. Their marching filled her ears. The soldiers had patches on their clothes, torn shirts, red, brown, and black hair. The river looked like a gray shawl beyond the trees.

"You were rude to me," she found herself replying to the way he touched the scar on his cheek.

"Daniel is in Kingsbury . . ." he volunteered, seemingly unconcerned as to why she struck him.

"Yes." She then dropped the matter of her striking him.

Jane had received a disturbing invitation from Deborah saying that Content was visiting her. Normally Content would have written to her herself, Jane thought She guessed, however, that Content wanted to see her out of concern for her husband.

"Tories captured James Higson, you know."

"I heard," she admitted, struck by the coincidence of his mentioning just what she was thinking of—

"Something personal, I would say, like Richardson murdering old Mister Parks at the Corners for his title papers."

She couldn't argue with him. John had told her that Richardson had murdered the old man. It wasn't difficult to imagine the Wings' shock at the murder of one of their neighbors. John himself worried about his family when he was absent from the farm.

"Richardson shot the old man's son on his own doorstep, too."

"Who captured James, Robbie?"

Robert shook his head. "Does it matter except Tories?"

The reins shook in her hands.

"David's not one of them," she asserted huskily.

"I can't say the same for Pap," he replied under his breath.

She didn't comment. She had no liking for Thomas Yarns, and his son's dislike of his father didn't surprise her. She was more concerned about Burgoyne and Robbie's reaction to him. John had told her that Oneida and Tuscarora scouts had brought the news that Indians from Montreal accompanied Burgoyne and that he was encamped on the Bouquet River twenty-two miles north of Crown Point. Such news had to frighten Robert. "Are you frightened yet, Robert?"

"Naw."

His answer touched her oddly. Though he irritated her, his facing battle and possible death moved her. He must know he could not walk away from this game. His 'Naw' sounded like a strange 'good-bye.'

"Least, we're havin' our elections before Johnny gets here."

His youth and naiveté about elections bespoke his innocence. How could he knowingly walk toward the end of his world like this?

"Don't elections presume too much with the army just north of here?" she probed him.

"Naw, it gives us somethin' to fight over," he answered, making dying sound frivolous. She had witnessed Eva's passion, had listened to Abraham's reasonings about unity and the rule of law, had heard John speak coolly of strategy, but she had never witnessed such casual innocence and clarity of purpose. He shocked, baffled, and humbled her.

They reached the clearing behind the fort and, as the line of soldiers continued, Robert stopped at the fork in the road. In his own way he seemed almost beautiful to her in the matter of fact way he said, "Camp's over there." He had a lightly tanned, clear skin with just the stubborn beginnings of a man's stubble on his face. And he had deep brown eyes. He was too young to go to war!

She wanted to say that to him—she didn't want him to leave her like this. She had known him too long. Tears welled in her eyes when she allowed him to walk on without saying anything to him in parting, his legs slightly bowed, his hat cocked off to the side, walking away from her in his youth with his musket.

"I'll be going on!" she called after him.

He turned and waved in a familiar way like a younger brother, then disappeared among the other soldiers.

Jane rode on to Sarah McNeil's through the dust churned up by the marching men and the wheels of their wagons. She tasted the grit of the road on her lips and teeth.

When she approached Sarah's log house, she noticed how Sarah's roses, tied with faded red ribbon, arched against the logs of the house. Flies buzzed in the low eaves over the doorway and smoke curled from the chimney. But the house seemed deserted.

She dismounted and walked to the door and opened it. The house was as dark as a cave.

"Auntie!"

Jane closed the door behind her and looked out at the passing soldiers on the road. The talk of others of them filtered back down the hill through the trees. She looked for Robert, but didn't see him. Of course, Sarah and Polly hadn't known she was coming because she hadn't had time since receiving Deborah's note to send them one of her own—perhaps they had gone to Argyle for the day to see the Allens? She decided to wait for a few minutes on the chance they would return.

The house faced northeast, and the sun filled the yard. Cool riding up from the ferry along the road under the trees, the June sun now was intense. She took off her hat and laid it in her lap. She stroked the turkey feather absently while two soldiers observed her as they passed the house. She had no doubt Robert would tell John, if he met him, that he had seen her.

She watched more of the soldiers walk up the road toward Ti. There were a lot of soldiers marching, but not nearly so many as had gone to meet Carleton in the fall. They didn't seem to be in any hurry either. Probably because Burgoyne was coming slowly.

It had taken him five weeks to reach the Bouquet River, halfway between Edward and Montreal. And at his present rate, he wouldn't arrive down here until sometime in July, she thought. A fly buzzed and she brushed it from her face. She then wiped her forehead—though a month still separated her from David, greater numbers of rebels soldiers had indeed opposed Carleton. But hadn't John said that the longer it took Burgoyne to get here the better, and that they would have the soldiers they needed for their defense by fall? Thought of his strategy made her uneasy. And she was accomplishing nothing by waiting here. She gazed at the rising hills. The pine at the top of the second boldly embraced the air with its branches. A pair of redbreasts wafted across the yard. She might wait all day and Auntie and Polly might never return. She put her hat back on and turned Charlotte around before mounting.

Jane then cantered beneath the cool trees and slowed to a walk at the top of the first hill. At the second hill, near the spring, soldiers leaned against the great pine she and David knew so well, while others filled their water bottles at the spring. Sunlight twinkled faintly in the spring as it flowed from the rocks and under the logs across the road. Flowing down the hill, it echoed in the woods. But it was not a pretty song for her now.

"I'd bet on that mare in the quarter mile. Where'd you find her?" one of the soldiers, leaning against the tree, asked her as she approached the spring.

"My brother bought her in Albany," Jane answered, unable to ride by without being rude.

"You're Colonel John's sister," another observed.

"Yes," she flushed. It made her uneasy that these soldiers knew who she was—but John was right. She rode often, and the men would look.

"He knows horses."

"Seen you ride along the river." The man had pleasant eyes and kindly voice. He was older than the others, yet tall and angular like them. "My daughters would like a little mare like yours."

"How old are your daughters?" she asked.

"Thirteen and fourteen. What's the mare's name?"

"Charlotte . . ." Jane hesitated.

"Pretty name."

"Honors the King's mare, right enough," a younger soldier near the tree remarked.

The older man laughed. "They celebrated the King's birthday in Montreal on the fourth—used the celebration to send Johnny off down to us too."

"I named her seven years ago," Jane explained, "before any of this." She avoided looking at the younger soldier.

"Seems a long time, don't it, lads? Seven years?" the younger soldier asked the others. "We been fightin' a long time, it seems . . ."

"Are you New Hamsphire men?" she asked, recalling the ferryman's comment on where these soldiers were from—

"Yep. Been at it since Breed's Hill."

"How about that mare's name, she can't change it now, can she, lads?" the older soldier intervened, humoring them. He picked up his water bottles. "Change comes of itself, I reckon, lads."

"I guess so, Pop—especially if a man stands long enough in one place. Things will jest change right around him."

Jane took the opportunity the older man offered her and stepped the mare over the corduroy bridge. There was something brittle in the younger men she didn't like.

"Take care . . ." the older man said.

She waved to him from behind and cantered half-mile up the road to Sandy Hill where she passed more soldiers. She didn't look at them or at the houses she passed. She didn't care. These poor farmers now soldiering ploughed the land and lived in log houses. She pictured their overworked wives overwhelmed by children. How else could she expect such men to behave if they thought they were fighting for their lives and homes? But hadn't they brought this war upon themselves? Yet the contrast between them and their lives with her familiar imaginings of parks with cultivated gardens beneath high stone walls and large white houses with long drives to columned porches and carriage houses—and men with powdered wigs, and women in elegant clothes sitting in gazebos—disturbed her. The war in this respect was clearly between farmers and gentlemen. These rough-looking and reckless men marching to Ti would meet uniformed men on horseback, bagpipes and bands, women in carriages. Stemming from her concern for her own family, she was inclined to dismiss them reflecting that that older man should have remained at home to care for his daughters, instead of marching to Ti.

She came to the Kingsbury crossroads and observed in a glance Daniel's house on the corner among the maples and pines. Its wide white-trimmed windows looked in a proprietary way onto the road. And there was Content's carriage in front of the house.

She dismounted and tied the mare to a wooden post. Just as she knocked on the door a bluejay shrieked in the branches of the pine overhanging the doorstep. There was no answer so she walked in—

The hallway was cool. She walked into the parlor. But it was empty!

"You received my note, Jane!" Deborah exclaimed, seeing her as she came into the room.

"You sounded urgent."

Deborah took her hat.

"Look at your hair. Not a strand of grey. And I'll be white by next year!"

"Where are your appointments?" Jane asked of the missing furniture.

"You are not half as shocked as I am, Jane." Deborah looked as though she was about to cry. "A Lieutenant gave us slips of paper for them last fall. And he took all our hay and grain. Imagine! And Daniel says the mills will be next . . ." she almost sobbed.

"But they took Abraham's mills a year ago. Wasn't that enough for them?" Somehow, too, she had never thought that the war would touch Daniel so accustomed was she in thinking that he would take care of himself.

"Where's Content?"

"Just let her talk." Deborah took her hands.

"What?"

Content then rushed into the room.

"'Tenty!" Jane exclaimed, taken back by her rush.

"Don't touch me!" Content snapped.

"Oh, Content, don't. Jane has come to see you . . . Oh, where's Daniel?" Deborah cried, leaving the room.

Content shook. "You must make him stop!"

"Stop who?"

"David!"

"What about him?" Jane's hand came up to her neck.

"Don't believe her," Daniel said, coming into the room. "She's half—crazed."

"William Robards doesn't lie, Daniel!" Content shouted angrily.

"Shush . . ." Daniel waved his hands at her. "Do you want every rebel on the road to hear you? Come into the kitchen."

In the kitchen, Daniel wiped his glasses and focused on his sister-in-law. "Now, tell Jane what you heard," he instructed Content.

"William Robards escaped from Montreal. He told father David and Ebenezer Jessup taunted and beat him, Andrew Fuller, and James, just the way they beat Captain Baldwin last April. That's what William Robards said, Daniel! And you told me last March that David wouldn't do anything like this, Jane, and I believed you."

"You must be mistaken. David wouldn't do that," Jane recoiled.

"He did! He guarded and beat James. William Robards isn't a liar."

Jane felt sick. She had had the same vague fear of what David might do to James when John told her in May that James had been taken to Montreal by Tories. And she again remembered the Kingsbury bonfire when the two men had nearly come to blows.

"Why is he guarding *my husband?*" Content demanded of Daniel. "You are his brother. Make David stop." She turned on Jane. "Make him stop, Jane!"

"It's baseless slander . . ." she stuttered.

"You know he hated James for getting Jacob's position at the mill. You denied it in March, but it's true, Jane."

"No, he doesn't hate him."

"He does!"

"It's your fault," Jane struck out at Daniel. "You shut David out and poisoned your mother against us!"

"I didn't," Daniel sprang up from his chair.

"You did. It's all your fault!

"No. David didn't need the money nor the land."

"What?"

"You dig your spurs into me without knowing a thing, Jane McCrea."

"What?"

"It was for his own good."

"You mean denying him property and earning his way with his new saw was for his own good? And if that was for his own good, then your losing all your furniture and your mills is for your own good, too. Your hypocrisy has appalled me all these years Daniel!"

"Listen, Jane, why does mother coddle him?"

"I don't care about her. She's miserable, and she'll suffer for it just as we have.—Besides, Daniel, she doesn't coddle him, she possesses him!"

"For God's sake, Jane, he'll be rich when he's forty."

"Rich at forty? What does that mean to us after what you have done, and what he is facing because of it?"

"His father was a Junker killed in the French war. My mother receives money from his family as long as he lives with her. When he's forty he'll inherit a fortune," Daniel said angrily. "Now you know."

"I don't care."

"But David does."

"What do you mean?"

"He knows all about this!"

"I don't believe you."

"It's true."

"And why wouldn't he tell me?"

"Because he wanted to make it on his own and look where it's landed him."

"And that's why you resisted him and denied us both and poisoned his mother? You actually hated him for that!" she charged him, the last seven years of disappointment and frustration erupting with in her. If she hated Daniel before this for his miserliness, she despised him now for it.

"He's the son of mother's lover. Mother never gave a thing to the rest of us," Daniel exploded in his own defense. "Don't blame me, blame our mother."

"So you wrung him dry, and made us wait for seven years?" she cried, outrage boiling within her. She turned her back on him and the tears burned her eyes. "What kind of a family do you have that would do such things to each other? What do I care about your mother's lovers—any of them!" It now became suddenly clear why David wouldn't confront his mother about the tinker on that cold January day when she had ridden over to see him. She raised her hand to her head feeling faint, vaguely hearing what was said behind her.

"What are you going to do?" Content demanded of him.

"Ebenezer put David up to it, probably ordered him to do it after Edward ran out," Daniel continued to defend himself. "But, Jesus, it doesn't matter one way or the other. David's with Burgoyne."

"But what about James!"

Daniel sat down. "I'll have him released when Burgoyne gets here," he said, resigned to having to do something.

"How will you do that?" Content continued to pursue her brother-in-law.

"Yes, how, after steering him toward the Jessups! You watched him take up with them while you stayed behind. Of course, you would have liked him to join the rebels and take your mills. And of course, every penny your mother received for him went into land you own—" Jane burst out, turning around and confronting him again.

"How are you going to get him out?" Content almost shrieked.

"So help me, if you breathe a word of this, I'm a dead man," Daniel said to both of them. "I'm Burgoyne's supply officer, and I have influence."

"For once you might use your influence for some good, Daniel, for all you've told us." Jane bit her lip not knowing whether Daniel could do anything for James or not. And for hers and David's part, what did she care if David was to inherit a fortune? It would come too late to help them. And she couldn't fault herself for loving him regardless of what some distant future promised them. But he had kept this patrimony from her—yet how important was that? Perhaps he had felt ashamed knowing what they both knew about his mother's infidelity behind the barn that fall; knowing what they both knew about why she had slandered her that miserable Christmas. For all of that, though, nothing could excuse the way Daniel had treated David, nothing excused the desperation he had engendered in him which had brought them to this pass— "And is that all, Daniel? Have you told us everything?" she asked.

"It will be each for himself when Burgoyne comes," he said simply.

"Yes, of course, just as it was before all this which makes it all so meaningless—"

"Don't put such a cast on it, Jane," Deborah nearly pleaded with her. "Look at us. The rebels have taken everything!" Her graying hair bespoke the truth of what she said.

"And if General Burgoyne succeeds, you'll have your wealth back again, and not be the wiser for having lost it."

"And you never aspired to these things, Jane McCrea?" Daniel challenged her. "You can't tell me that."

"Perhaps I did aspire to them, Daniel. Perhaps I still do. But I never tried to deny them to others as you have done. Perhaps we all shall pay. At least I admit it and have felt the guilt that comes of wanting to possess—I felt it up at the Jessups when they celebrated their Patent. I luxuriated in their wealth and felt the shame of it. No matter how rich you are Daniel, you will never be free of the guilt that comes of it when others are denied it. You see, I can speak this way to you because this is what I have been made to feel by you and I'm not even a rebel."

"And what do you think the rebels want, if not property too?"

She nodded in agreement, but added, unaccountably thinking

of Robert Yarns, "and something even greater, none of us will ever know because there is no chance now to change—the die has been cast."—Though she had a faint perception of it, if only because of what Daniel had done to her. "I'll take my hat now, Deborah."

39

July

After learning at Daniel's of David's alleged treatment of James Higson, Jane received a second letter from David a few days later written from the Bouquet River. Coming on the heels of Content's allegation, it filled her with dismay because General Burgoyne's Proclamation to the countryside issued the same day from the same camp contradicted its contents. With the army on the march, David's letter advised her to go to Sarah McNeil's for safety, but Burgoyne's Proclamation urged people to stay in their homes.

David hadn't even mentioned Indians in his letter, but Burgoyne chillingly had: 'I have but to give stretch to the Indian forces under my direction . . . to overtake the harden'd Enemies of Great Britain and America . . . wherever they lurk.' What was she to do? Time was running short. On June thirtieth, Brigadier General Simon Fraser had crossed Lake Champlain to Three Mile Point, and on July first the army had embarked from Crown Point to Ticonderoga, the same day General Schuyler passed on the river to Fort Edward with two thousand militia. And John had just told her, stopping by the house, that Burgoyne was only a mile and a half from Ti and attack was imminent—

During the first week in July she agonized over what to do. Would she actually be safer at Sarah McNeil's because her cousin, Simon, commanded the Indians? And what of her promise to John not to go there and wait in the line of march again like she had with Carleton? Her mind raced. But if John himself was at Edward, would he mind half so much if he could see her nearby? Undecided, she waited for news of Burgoyne's attack on Ti, as if news of it would help her make up her mind, after all, she reasoned since

Ticonderoga was thirty miles from Edward she could go and return without being in danger. On the spur, she decided to go to Edward.

But when she arrived she found the road clogged with horses, wagons and rebel soldiers and Sarah gesturing wildly to her from her yard. The older woman's face was boiling from the heat and excitement.

"Ti fell twa days ago, lass! The British Navy dogg'd these rebels to Skenesborough where they fired their bateaux," she shouted, half stumbling toward the mare.

"What!" Jane exclaimed. "I haven't heard a word about Ti." Suddenly she felt she had made a terrible miscalculation in coming.

"It's true, lass, the rebels evacuated Ti and burned their boats in th' wee hours this morning. They marched all night," Polly confirmed, following her grandmother.

"I jes tauld her, Polly," Sarah interrupted her impatiently. "I want ta ken what ye learned from Peter. Did Johnny get th' whole lot o' em?"

"No, Grandmother, the others fled across th' lake into th' Grants."

"Sae, wat's keepin' th' army frae camin' an th' heels o' these?" Sarah demanded, jerking her arm toward the road and the retreating rebels.

"Colonel Long in the rear at Fort Anne is covering this retreat." Polly took off her bonnet.

"Sae, that's thir arse? Colonel Long ae that chicken hoose Fort Anne?"

"Aye, Fort Anne, Grandmother," Polly repeated.

"Gaw, ye'd think they' pull in thir shirttails an' hoof it ta Albany wi' th' whole British army climbin' up thir baks! Bot, nae, they got ta piddle aroond in this heat. My, bot 'tis hot!" Sarah exclaimed.

"Go back to the house, Grandmother, before ye collapse. Ye're soakin'." Polly urged her.

"Th' whole rebel army's an th' run an' we're in th' middle o' it. I tauld ye 'twad be a walk through. Weel, camon, lass, ye jest canna stand oot in th' sun, and ye canna gae bak wi' a' them rebels cloggin' th' road," Sarah pronounced, before starting back to the house.

Jane dismounted and walked the mare across the yard to the house. In the shade of the house standing by the mare she then watched the soldiers continuing to come down the road toward the fort. How could she leave now even if she wanted to? There were hundreds of rebel soldiers on the road! She then suddenly thought of David.

"Where is *he*?" she asked Polly.

"I didn't think ta ask Peter, but he must be either followin' these wretches, or chasin' those across th' lake," Polly answered.

"Across the lake?" Jane asked.

"Aye, inta the Grants," Polly clarified.

"Oh, no," Jane murmured, recalling John saying Burgoyne could not resist a 'sideshow', "they shouldn't do that . . ." But maybe David would come straight to Edward and not pursue across the lake, she thought desperately.

"Burgoyne weel stop ae Skenesborough ta git himsel thegither, if th' Navy's thare. Dinna worry, lass. Ye'll see yer luve in nae time."

"And what makes you say that?" Jane turned on her—

"If th' rebels 're runnin' they'll keep runnin', dinna mind that, lass, and wot canna run weel be muster'd in for th' prison ships in the City arter they came through."

"Ah, a bless'd sight. I tauld ye, lass, th' rebels 're nae match for th' King. An' leuk, half o' these call themsels Scots! Bot nae New Englander's a Scot, if he's frae Ulster. They're a pack o' Irishmen th' whole length o' th' Connecticut River," Sarah said contemptuously. "Jes think, th' British drew cannons up Sugar Loaf Hill o'er lookin' auld fort Ticonderoga. Lik fish in a barrel, wi th' heavy guns pointin' doon an 'em, th' rebels scrambl'd oot of th' fort ae nite! Didna I tell ye nocht ta fool wi' th' king's army wi' thir superior engineerin'? Wada been th' same last fall wi Carleton ta, if that yellow-skirted bird hadna turned tail. Eve, dinna stand thare gin a body's dyin' o' th' heat!" she shouted at her black woman who stood in the doorway. "Hangin' an th' door, as if she's n'er seen a sodger."

"Have you seen John? Is he here? I don't want him to see me."
Jane moved toward the door of the house. She needed time to
collect her thoughts.

"Ah, dinna worry mickle aboot 'im. He hase a' he can do wi'
that rascal Schuyler practicin' same desperate prank given thir
present situation," Sarah said, gesturing disdainfully at the fort
behind the house.

Leaning back against the house in deeper shadow, Jane grew
calmer. As she watched the soldiers take off their packs and unhitch
their horses from the wagons and set up tents amid the stragglers,
which still came down the road, she tried to assess her situation.

"How long have they been retreating?"

"All morning. Add this mob to what Schuyler and yer brother
brought with him must total a couple of thousand men," Polly
answered.

"Campin' under our windows!" Sarah said with disgust.

"But what am I going to do, not knowing where David is?"

"Ye canna dae a thing, lass, except hae same nosh an' watch th'
circus."

"The circus?" But she was desperate to know of David. She
couldn't eat at a time like this. Was he in the Grants? Simon Fraser
had crossed the lake a week ago. She knew that already. Had David
gone with him, or was he on his way to Fort Anne only eight miles
away? Her heart leaped when she thought he might be at Fort Anne.

"Aye, 'tis a circus right eneugh. Dae ye hear that?" the old
woman asked, cocking her head in the direction of the hill.

In the distance Jane heard sounds like the breaking of sticks.

"What is that?" she asked.

"Th' sounds o' rabbit-hunting!" Sarah laughed. "Now camon
in for a bite." She then got up off her chair and heaved herself
through the door.

The firing intensified, then tapered off. Jane stood there holding
her breath as though she listened to a bizarre threnody in her
honor. The sound filled her with horror.

"Come into th' house and eat, lass," Polly urged her. "That's
likely ta go on for some time—"

But Jane continued to stand there like a statue, listening. Then the shooting abruptly ended. She waited. Polly took her by the arm and then closed the door after them.

Jane tripped over a chair in the dark.

"Keep th' door open, Polly. Forgit aboot th' bluidy flies . . ." her grandmother scolded.

Jane stood in the dark. Shapes appeared. She grasped a chair. Polly passed her like a shadow to the other side of the table.

"Dinna be surpris'd, if th' lads came through taday wi' that shootin' up th' road. 'Tis a wee reel 'afore th' real festivities and yer reunion wi' yer luve, lass," Sarah said across the room to Jane.

"Are we safe here?" Jane asked, feeling like she had entered a tomb.

Sarah's bulk loomed up from the floor as she approached the table. "O' course, lass. Safe as kittens in a hayrick. Didna ye read Burgoyne's Proclamation?"

"Yes, I read it," Jane answered, touching her side with the realization that she should have stayed back in Northumberland. "He said for people to stay in their homes. I shouldn't have come."

"Nonsense, lass. An' whare 're we, except hame? Yer safe here right eneugh."

"And what about Peter?" Polly asked. "What will happen to him when the army marches through? They can't stay at the fort."

"O' course nae. He maun fend for himsel lik th' ither rebels. Arter it's a' owre, we'll see ta 'im. I'll spak ta Simon aboot 'im. Dinna worry, Polly."

"And the Indians?" The more the room lightened, the darker Jane's thoughts became. "Have you thought of them?"

"O' course, dae ye think Simon wad let savages loose, gin he kens we're awaitin' for 'im?"

"Has he written you, Auntie?" Jane pursued her, though she could hardly see Sarah's face.

"Ye tauld me David met 'im. Ye tauld me David met Simon, didna ye, lass? An' as that's th' case, Simon kens whare we are."

Jane's eyes adjusted to the dark room. "So we have nothing to fear then?"

"Th' Proclamation stated Burgoyne wad use 'em against th' rebels—'th' hardn'd enemies of Great Britain an' America.' Ye read that, didna we, lass? Nae man in his right mind wad use savages against innocent people, ye ken that. Sodgers, aye, bot inhabitants, nae."

But what was Sarah saying? Had she written her cousin or not? Yet Polly had passed information to Carleton about the soldiers at Ti last fall, and Daniel served as Burgoyne's supply officer. And wasn't the whole area sympathetic? Many in Sandy Hill, Argyle, and Salem sympathized with Government. That reassured her more than Sarah's indefiniteness about writing her cousin. Yet had *she* written him?

"Did you write him?" she asked directly.

"O' course, gin I was in New York."

"New York?" she asked in disbelief.

"Aye, I received a letter frae him aboot wanting land up here."

"Then he still thinks you're in New York!" Jane exclaimed.

For a moment, Sarah was silent. She then spoke up. "'Tis sae. That is he must ken whare we are wi' his meetin' David. An' sartinly th' Jessups 're nae sae daft as nae ta tell him aboot thir neighbors. An wad Simon question them? Aye. Wat sort o' an army do ye think is camin'? A crowd o' pumpkin eaters wi' barley chaff for brains? Burgoyne's nae swallowtail lik Carleton. 'Tis th' finest army e'er ta put foot ta leather. Did ye see 'em run frae Ti? An' Burgoyne's settin' up a reunion wi' Howe in Albany. They'll cut New York awa' frae th' Grants, an' gin that hoppens th' rebels weel melt bak ta thir farms. Ye'll then hae yer weddin' in Albany. As for th' savages, ye maun ken, lass, 'tis a proper body o' men which weel n'er allow savages ta harm onyone. Nae hounds 're again' ta be set lose, as lang as a Highlander or a king's sodger draws breath. Sae why, gin th' countrie's aboot ta be delivered frae these wretches, 're ye actin' lik a bird wi' th' weegies? Wave th' Proclamation, if ye see 'em camin'. Wave it high."

Jane sank onto a chair. She had always assumed Simon Fraser knew Sarah lived at Edward—and hadn't David advised her to come here? His advisement gave her more reassurance than Sarah's circumlocutions. It meant that he was coming for her—yet, how did she know that he wasn't this moment in the Grants? Finally, she didn't know what to think of her situation, except that John himself was still at the fort at her back and the rebel soldiers outside the house offered protection from the Indians.

As she sat there with her elbows on the table unable to eat what Sarah pushed in front of her, she slipped into a deepening gloom and answered the other women absently in monosyllables. At last, taking Polly by the arm, she roused herself and left the house—

What she saw outside wrenched her. Groaning men were being littered down the road. Jane recoiled. The incongruous strains of "Yankee Doodle" then came after the wounded from beneath the trees farther up the road.

"This must be the results o' Fort Anne we heard earlier," Polly observed, without cynicism. "Judging by the sound o' it Colonel Long must hae been successful in stoppin' th' pursuit."

Soldiers in their blue coats with white facings escorting a prisoner marched into view. Jane sank against the side of the house. "There's John," she said. "He's seen me."

"What can he do, lass? Pay him no mind."

But Jane immediately saw the annoyance on John's face when he saw her. He broke from his men and walked across the yard to her. "Surprised to see you here, Jen," he said coming up to her. "It would be safer for you back with Eva and the children. You, too, Polly. You and your grandmother should get ready to leave. Hasn't Peter spoken to you about leaving?"

"No, Colonel. Tho' I suspect he will—" Polly answered.

"I hadn't heard anything of Ti, John, and thought I could get back home, Ti being so far from here," Jane explained, knowing by his tone and Polly's presence he wouldn't force the issue of her promise to him here.

John nodded—not approving exactly, but indicating he understood her intention and accepted it. He then turned and pointed to the prisoner being marched passed them. "That Captain of the Ninth Regiment is one of Fraser's Advanced Corps. Too bad

Colonel Long's men ran out of powder. He would have taken the whole regiment."

Jane took the news like a blow. David's first letter had mentioned that Jessups' Corps served under Fraser! Before she could speak, a soldier appeared beside John.

"Colonel, that Captain says Fraser, the Hessians, the Tories and savages have gone after St. Clair across the lake. Fraser was already on the other side before we evacuated Ti. Francis' and Warner's New Englanders are in the rear with the sick."

Jane froze.

"Any Tories with Hill at Fort Anne, Standish?" John asked, himself interested in where David was detailed.

"Few, if any," the Private answered before leaving them.

"Now you know, Jen," John said, turning to her.

"He's across the lake, isn't he?"

"Yes," he confirmed. "He has to be across in the Grants."

"I'll leave in the morning then." She looked blankly at the ground, her eyes as dry as roadside stones. What would become of him in the company of savages, pursuing desperate Yankees?

"You could have spared yourself this, Jen."

"I had to know." The sun blinded her.

"You saw what Long did to the Ninth—I told you Burgoyne would pursue."

"Yes."

"You can't do him any good here."

"Was Standish with Colonel Long?" she asked, thinking that maybe there *was* a chance that David was with Hill at Fort Anne.

"Yes, and Robbie Yarns."

"Robbie?"

"Haven't seen him—not everyone's in—" John looked toward the soldiers still coming down the road.

"No, I haven't seen him either," she said.

"All right. I trust you'll do what's safe. Polly—" John tipped his hat, then turned and left them.

"What 're ye goin' ta do, lass," Polly asked her, "knowin' he's on th' other side o' th' lake?"

"I don't know . . ." Jane mumbled as though she was left floating in a bog.

"Then stay here for th' night an' see what happens—there's not likely ta be anything more here after th' dustin' this lot gave Hill."

—That night the three women sat outside the house. Campfires played among the trees across the road smothering the scent of the pines with smoke. Voices, the clanking of pots, crickets and the croaking of frogs by the river echoed in the night. The rasping of stone on iron mingled with the crickets. The campfires flickered behind the forms of soldiers. Jane felt like a shade sitting in the eerie darkness. No news had yet reached them from the Grants on the success of Fraser's pursuit of St. Clair.

"Lik insects sharpenin' thir jaws on thir bluidy stanes. Suppose these Beezelbubs think they maun use axes!" Sarah whispered under her breath.

"Ye should be more respectful of the Yankees, Grandmother. They are men. They're not devils," Polly declared.

"'Tis luve that spaks for ye, Bonnie Polly."

"It's what I've seen, Grandmother."

"Aye, an' I've seen it taa, an' 'tis th' folly o' men. If I had th' say o' th' action oot thare I'd send these lads bak ta thir wives and wee 'uns. War's nae proper sport for lads. Thir's same evil in them tho' ta do it—thir's evil in ony kind o' fictin'."

"John said there is a spirit in the men. Eva even sees the hand of Providence in it," Jane said, rubbing her arms.

"An' I ask how Providence can prosper wi' bloodshed? I ask ye that, lass. Providence means Peace, nae war wi' men killin' each ither."

"How can we know?"

"Ah, 'tis common sense. Th' deil maks men refractory."

"But as we sit here there must be some purpose in it. Nothing happens without purpose, Auntie."

"Then why are yer twa lads an opposite sides? Whare is th' purpose in that, I ask? Even luve can be controverted by th' deil. If it is nae that, then I canna mak sense o' it."

"There are certain things beyond our understanding, Grandmother."

"I understand it right eneugh, Bonnie Polly. Ye gat a countrie here that's taa big for gaiters—"

Jane felt Polly touch her arm and she looked up to see John approaching them through the darkness. She then noticed Peter's light hair against the glow of the night fires.

"The Generals invite you to the fort," Peter said without any introduction.

"Aye, they maun be feelin' th' loneliness o' this spooky evenin', Peter Tearse," Sarah said to him half-aloud. The women then rose silently and followed the men across the yard to the fort.

Schuyler's mansion and the dreams it silently evoked in Jane only eerily contrasted to the present catacomb-like gloom of the fort as she approached its walls, as high as hillsides.

And why did Schuyler and Arnold want to see them? Did they suspect Sarah and Polly, or did they want to reassure them that they were in no danger? She couldn't refuse Schuyler's invitation with John on his staff, nor could Polly refuse because of Peter being Arnold's Adjutant. But would Schuyler question her about David? Would Sarah give her away? And what would she say to Schuyler, if he questioned her about her tulips, if he remembered giving them to John?

They walked across the courtyard, shaped like a clothes iron, to the barracks where a guard opened a door.

A short man blocked the light at the far end of the room. His voice died away as they entered. A table in the middle of the room offered sherry and coffee.

"Colonel!" the short man addressed John.

John's introduction and the man's replies came like mummery, as Jane observed Schuyler, the man she heard so much of, the man whose daughters she saw on their lawn from the bateau when first coming to Northumberland. She studied him. He wore epaulets and a high collar. He had a long Dutch face, close-set eyes, and the bearing of a patrician with an impatient nature.

General Arnold was short, straight and wore his hair in a queue.

His epaulets, a white cravat, and sharp gray eyes contrasted his flamboyance with Schuyler's reserve.

"Congratulations on yer heroic defense at Valcour Island, General Arnold," Polly praised him.

Did she praise him because Peter was his Adjutant, or because she sincerely admired his defense that saved the army from pursuit after Quebec, which gave Carleton a taste of the resistance he would meet at Ti? Jane wondered.

"The lads fought like lions," Arnold said, raising his eyebrows.

"Eneugh ta turn Carleton aboot," Sarah added, scarcely concealing her disapproval.

"General Schuyler's lads at Ti and Independence take the credit for showing Carleton this end of the lake," Arnold corrected her, indicating by his look he immediately guessed her other thoughts.

"Scottish?" General Schuyler also observed of Sarah's accent.

"A Yorker frae Inverness, ye maun say," Sarah side stepped, only too aware of Peter and which side the Highlanders and other Scottish immigrants from the Meadows had taken in the conflict.

Schuyler accepted her claim with a mild nod as he appraised her from a height.

Jane heard innocuous words addressed to her, but she saw in General Schuyler's eyes a mixed reflection of her own seven-year anguish, longing and waiting—on the surface he embodied afternoon leisure, an elegant home, and graceful daughters. But those cool blue eyes, which epitomized elegance, also expressed that daring and resourcefulness that had turned Carleton back and separated her from David. She gazed at him, hearing, but not hearing his words aware that if anyone could look through her he could.

"And how have the tulips faired, Miss McCrea?" she heard him ask her.

"They are beautiful, General, and I thank you for them." How strange of him to have given her the emblems of her hopes—those scarlet flowers mustered in front of John's imaging her desires *in lieu* of the real thing such a short distance to the north!

"They are from Amsterdam. And your brother is a good officer, and you have such lovely hair—"

"Jane's visiting up here, General," John answered for her.

"I see—"

"I so admired your Albany home, General Schuyler," Jane said, unable to restrain her praise of the 'Pastures' even as she blushed with his compliment.

"The lovely 'Pastures'! But how cold in winter on that hill! Albany suits my wife and daughters, better, however."

"Yes, of course," Jane said, "and you have another . . ."

"At Saratoga, yes, where I would spend my life, if it wasn't for this," he indicated pleasantly with a flourish of his hand at the barracks.

"Yes . . ." she agreed, thinking how different life would have treated her, too, if this man had employed David.

A knock then came at the door and she lost Schuyler's attention.

"Pardon, General, but we took heavy losses at Hubbardton in the Grants this morning—Hale's Second New Hampshire surrendered, and Francis was killed," a voice came over the threshold.

"Francis killed!" Arnold exclaimed, rushing toward the man. "Surely you must be mistaken."

"No, General. Reidesel prevented Francis from turning Fraser's flank."

"And St. Clair?"

"In Castleton with the main body. He only heard the battle."

"And Fraser?" Schuyler asked quickly.

"A fifth of his force killed and wounded—"

Jane's knees began to tremble. Polly held her elbow.

"Has St. Clair left Castleton?"

"For Stillwater."

"He did nothing!"

"Only heard the shooting."

"But Castleton's just south of Hubbardton!"

There was silence.

"Jesus!" Arnold swore, "St. Clair should have assisted."

"Let's go, lass," Polly said, "they hae nae interest in us now."

"Ladies, Colonel . . ." Schuyler said by way of apology as they went toward the door.

Jane felt her knees begin to buckle. 'Heavy losses . . . a fifth of Fraser's force killed and wounded.'

"It'll take them a week to get here," Schuyler said, his form blocking the lantern light from the table as the women walked toward the door.

But what of David? 'Francis killed!' As Jane fumbled for her shawl it slipped over the side of the chair. She leaned over for it. The shadows of the talking men brushed over her.

"Burgoyne will re-group at Skenesborough."

"This way, lass."

"We need time to get St. Clair here, Colonel McCrea . . ."

Could she reach Skenesborough?

"Take the militia up Wood Creek and fell the trees, Colonel . . ."

She and David could flee to Montreal, if she could reach him at Skenesborough.

"and block Burgoyne's march."

Polly ushered her out the door.

"Burgoyne will have to wait for Fraser to get back from Hubbardton before he advances."

The words fell behind the door as they gained the entrance of the fort. Outside, the rasping of axes had ceased. The rebel soldiers were packing in the dark. Their knives and axes gleamed in the firelight. How could she reach Skenesborough?

The three women made their way out of the fort and onto the road. Jane half-stumbled up the road, regained her footing in the dark, and then bumped against the taut line stretching into the road from a half-illuminated tent. She looked inside as she half-fell passed it.

"No!" she cried, seeing his pale face and the empty sleeve folded over his chest.

"Come on, lass," Polly said, trying to take her arm.

"'Tis nae time for loiterin'," Sarah urged as well.

Jane stood there as soldiers passed them. She gently pulled her arm from Polly's grasp and put her hand on his cool forehead. She whispered to him, even touched his eyelids with her fingertips.

"Yes," she answered vacantly, not knowing, for a moment, who she looked at. A surgeon approached her from the back of the tent. "Where did this happen?" she asked him.

"Fort Anne. He couldn't take the shock of the amputation . . . do you know him?"

"Yes, I know him . . ." she began to sob, realizing now just how completely she knew him as she brushed her fingers over the scar on his cheek. The tears welled in her eyes and fell from her chin onto Robbie's sleeve. "Yes . . . I know him . . . he was only a boy!"

40

The sight of Robbie Yarns convinced Jane that she should return to Northumberland—his cruel death and the sight of war sickened her. And John promised to send word to her if he learned anything of David. There was no point in her staying at Sarah McNeil's, and hadn't she received David's second letter from Freel at home? Wouldn't she hear from him there again?

Back at Northumberland with Eva as she waited from one day to the next, Jane kept hearing the news of Hubbardton through Schuyler's open door, kept seeing Robert's pale face, and imagined what might have befallen David. Guilt seized her for not having kept him from defecting and for having struck Robert with her riding crop. She imagined she saw her own life in David's motionless body on the battlefield of Hubbardton and kept thinking that the white scar her riding crop had left on Robert's cheek somehow sealed her own fate. Somehow Robbie's death and the dangers David faced seemed the last statements on the series of disappointments and disasters the last seven years had brought her. She experienced shame and regret, even came to envy the young man his sacrifice and began to question whether she and David had failed each other, concluding that no one would mourn either of them if he was killed in battle or if she happened to die by some fluke of chance. Such thoughts intensified her longing for David even as she despaired of her own future.

As Jane waited, she watched families flee to Albany—far more people than she suspected favored the Congress' cause, or were they only fleeing the Indians? She watched women and children across the bay on their bateaux; flatboats loaded with sheep and horses; and canvas-covered skiffs high like icebergs in the July sunlight. And when Eva filled sacks with dishes and linen, she thought if she didn't go with her, she must face alone what came. Filled with anxiety for David, guilt and remorse, and fearing desertion, she rode along the river looking for Freel bearing David's letter.

Finally, on the thirteenth, five days after returning from Edward, Freel appeared south of the island a mile from John's house. She rode into the river and snatched the letter from him before he reached shore, then dug in her heels and broke the seal on the bank.

David had escaped destruction' at Hubbardton! "Oh, Lord!" she cried, her eyes flying across the page. He repeated that the army would march to Edward, and that she should go to Sarah's again! But how could she face soldiers and the aftermath of battle again! His request opened the door of a tomb! And what of John?

Jane reined the mare toward Freel's boat.

"Where is he? Where's the army?"

"Skenesborough!" Freel called across the narrow beach.

"Skenesborough!" She glanced at the letter, "—David wrote on Friday, the eleventh. Today is Sunday."

"Fraser joined up from Hubbardton only yesterday. Johnny's got ta git his army together and clear the road first. Build bridges . . ."

"Bridges!" she exclaimed.

Then she recalled that Schuyler's militia had left five days before, on the eighth, to fell trees and block the creek. She remembered him ordering John to do it when news of Hubbardton came to the fort that unforgettable night. John had left the next morning, Tuesday, with his soldiers carrying their axes.

"I don't know why Johnny's comin' the creek way, unless to celebrate his victory at Hubbardton."

"Victory, with so many of Fraser's force killed and wounded? If Burgoyne has many more victories like Hubbardton, he won't have any army left."

"Well, let's hope that was a fluke."

"And so how long will it take to come by way of the creek?"

"At least two weeks. Fraser started building the road today. But they should have come down Lake George like always. They'll git nothin' but trouble comin' the creek way. It's a swamp. They'll have ta build forty bridges which will give the rebels time ta git ta Edward. St. Clair's Continentals, seventeen hundred of them, plus six hundred others come up from Peekskill yesterday. Even more gatherin' at Saratoga." Freel rummaged in his pocket and waved a paper. "Here's Schuyler's proclamation warnin' people not ta go over ta Johnny, and askin' for more men and supplies for Edward. While Johnny's buildin' that road, th' rebels are gatherin' their army!"

"Did you see David?"

"He's workin' on the road. Got his letter from Ramsey in Munro's bateau service."

"His letter's dated the eleventh. They'll march in a few days," Jane declared, wanting to negate Freel on how long it would take the army.

"They're startin' the road today. David probably didn't know about it when he wrote. He'll tug' branches, swat black flies, and build bridges for two weeks." Freel laughed at the effort. "You'd think Johnny would fight rather than build a highway though all that muck to Fort Anne. If he has an army left once he gits here, we might see something. Yep, he'll stay at Skenesborough a couple o' weeks until that road's done, though he might float some cannons down Lake George."

"A couple of weeks! Where did Ramsey see David?"

"On the road. Any message for him?"

David had not known about the Wood Creek road when he wrote three days ago, she thought, her mind racing. Thought of John felling those trees tortured her. Lord, it was happening just as he said it would—and it would take two weeks. The longer it took Burgoyne to move his army the better, he had said. She wheeled the mare around.

"It will take two weeks then for them to reach Edward?" she repeated.

"At least two weeks, if they're lucky."

"I'll wait . . ." she called to him, the idea of having to wait another two weeks nearly crushing her.

Freel nodded and pushed off; his oars flapped low on the water.

Jane rode up the road. How could she wait for two weeks at Sarah McNeil's? How could David expect it of her knowing, as he must, that the rebels held the fort? Hadn't she risked enough going there twice already?

She halted the mare. The sun reflected harshly off his letter as she read it again. He insisted she *not* go to Albany with Eva, "but stay at Sarah's where I will join you."

She refolded the letter. How could he ask her to wait there when he didn't know when he would arrive? She would have to go against that tide of refugees she had been watching and risk being swallowed by Schuyler's army at Edward. And what if John saw her? She couldn't face him again. And what if there was a battle? Even assuming she got to Edward and waited for David to come for her, he mentioned nothing of marriage. And he had known why his mother had stalled their marriage—and she knew why he hadn't mentioned his circumstances to her. Had any of that changed? Thought of his inheritance at forty sickened her. Did he expect her to wait thirteen years more? But she *had* to be with him! But wasn't it more reasonable for her to remain here in Northumberland certain of his safety now, or even go to Albany with Eva where he would find her after Schuyler surrendered? She should have told Freel that. She *couldn't* risk going to Edward again. But *did* David have a plan? He seemed definite the war would end: "I think this year, as the rebels cannot hold out and will see their error." But they had waited seven years already! Certainly he could wait a little longer and find her in Albany. "Oh, God," she whispered in despair at returning to Edward.

But as she rode back to John's and passed the wheat field, she began to think differently of the situation. The high wheat, like a green sea, recalling her first wild ride on Charlotte, spoke to her. The earth needed a sowing hand and she needed to wait for David at Sarah's. The sun kissing the wheat *demanded* she wait for him— he would come for her and they then would marry and have their family. Nothing else mattered. She had jumped to only negative possibilities back there at the river. Only the timing was crucial.

One picked strawberries before the redbreasts ate them. This wheat needed the husbandman, the sunset an appreciative heart, the crickets a listener, and she needed David. He wanted what she wanted. But the danger? David undoubtedly knew Simon Fraser, the other officers and their wives. Inevitability and propriety accompanied his request, didn't they? Oh, to be in his arms again, to hear his whisper, feel his touch, his strong hands, to kiss the wrinkles on his neck, and follow the curve of his nose with her finger. She ached for his touch, that surrender, yearned to perfume his desire and possess him. *Aff'tly till death. David Jones.* She would give her life to him. She could endure the rebel soldiers at Edward, if he *would* only come for her. Death meant nothing compared to that expectation.

Her fingers tightened on the reins. Who would stop her? She need only lift the reins. The dust would settle behind her—then her heart sank. Her strength fluttered from her grip. Night would fall. John and those felled trees blocked the way. And what of her promise to her brother not to go to Sarah's? Despairing as to what to do, she continued riding on to the house.

When she arrived at the house, James was tugging at one end of a black trunk trying to skid it through the doorway into the house. She pushed on the trunk with him and found Eva sitting in the bare room at the table with quill and parchment. Jane touched the folds of her own pocket containing David's letter.

"When will you leave, Eva?"

Jane took off her bonnet and sat opposite her sister-in-law, her eyes resting on Eva's curled and precise script. At first the name Beekman had meant little to her. Eva had never discussed her family and she had assumed that her sister-in-law was without property like herself. But when she had returned from Sarah's on the seventh, Eva had questioned her, while holding her father's promise in her hand! It was then that she learned what a large landowner her father was. Seeing her replying to her father now undoubtedly planning her arrival in Albany filled her with bitterness. She then looked at the yellow cat on the cool flagstones of the hearth and resentment, at the definiteness of Eva's plans in the form of her father's letter on the table beside her own, in contrast to her own indecision, welled up in her. Her fingers trembled as she spoke. "And what of your principles?"

"My family changes nothing," Eva answered her.

"Then I must pack," Jane stated, wanting to make Eva feel mean in her security.

"If my father didn't have property, we would go elsewhere, Jane," Eva said, her quill briefly scratching the parchment. "Do you regret David's defection?"

"You know his family," she answered, weary of thinking of how property had determined what his family had done to them.

"I tried to tell you," Eva replied, unexpectedly reaching out for her hand.

Jane stood up, refusing to be touched.

"His family compromised us. I thought we had a choice," she stated bluntly. Who could have foreseen seven years of deferred hope and such opposing interests, David serving the British, and she and Eva in flight because of it?

"We all have choices."

"I never had a choice," Jane said, rubbing her hand on the table, not wanting now to deny Eva anything about the way she felt because there was no point in hiding anything any longer— she even strangely now only wanted to give to Eva as they talked— yes, giving defined her wanting, and property made giving possible. Yet that had compromised her—so what choice had she ever had? If property meant giving, she wouldn't deny that she wanted it, if that was the way it was going to be. "You've witnessed my ambitions and distress, Eva. You have seen my dreams dashed."

"We *still* have choices, Jane."

"Needs. You mean we still have needs."

"You don't hate me, or the children, or John then?"

"How can I hate you given what you are facing? I only grieve for what *I* have lost and wasted . . ." Jane answered without self-pity.

"We will prevail—" Eva noted coolly, "But for yourself was it the young Yarns boy? You were sick about him when you came back from Edward . . ."

"Partly." Jane shuddered, remembering Robbie's amputated arm and his scar. "He gave so much, I had no idea of . . . to give one's life for something like that makes any other kind of wanting almost pointless."

"He sacrificed—don't blame yourself."

"Somehow, I can't help it. I feel responsible somehow—" She didn't know why she felt responsible for what had happened to Robert; she just felt some unexplainable guilt for what had happened to him. "But I can't change. Things have gone too far for me."

"Oh, Jane!" Eva clasped her hands.

"I'm not like you, Eva!" She exclaimed. "The surgeon didn't even know Robbie's name. You can't ask me to give like that. I have gone too far—everything is at risk for me. I can't reverse the last seven years. I can't change what all this means to me after the loss of my father, my plans with David, or my living like this here with you and how we have fought with each other. I can't surrender the past eight years of my life." Yet, she needed strength and purpose, needed correct desire, needed somehow for Eva to understand this. But no one spoke for her, or understood her desire. How could Eva ask her to choose now with David only a few miles away?

Jane looked out the window with distance in her eyes. She so wanted to see a celestial pasture stretching above the wheat, but the small glass framed emptiness, not Zion, above it.

"You should pack then, regardless of what you might be thinking now. At least at this critical moment, you should be practical. I have already packed," Eva stated, fearing Jane was on the verge of some desperate action. "You must leave with me and let events take care of themselves. The choice is made for you."

41

13 July

The tiny doll, looking as though it could speak and had an important message to give her, lay in late afternoon in the trunk on top of her clothes. Jane observed the clothes that had inspired her childhood. And so what did the doll say now? 'We are the stuff as dreams are made on, and our little life is rounded with a sleep.'

Jane breathed the words, sat on the trunk where the doll slept and gazed through the window. How that line of poetry, now coming from the doll, had inspired her, imbuing the Hudson River with the possibilities of Eden. And how curious David's millwork had fit Ferdinand's stacking logs, except that the tempest had engulfed them and David had had to flee the island and Prospero's rule proved uncertain. Now, through the window, the graceful willows lining the river of the island hardly raised her spirits as they drooped in the summer heat. Without hope in life, enchantment died, making life indeed a small troubled sleep. She had believed in the happy ending, her dreams becoming reality, which had proved, however, only a poet's and a young girl's wishful thinking.

She rested her elbows on her knees and her face in her hands. Her hair fell over her arms. What a mistake, she thought, blindly led by a doll, and trapped by a poem, which now only testified to her present loneliness.

The day wore on to sunset, and night fell. Jane didn't leave her room, but lay on her bed and looked at the log rafters. She didn't close her eyes when the room became dark.

"Coming to supper, Jane?" Eva called to her.

"No."

Visions, accompanied by singing crickets, played against the darkness: David worked on the road with uniformed men, and John felled trees not far ahead of him. Jane passively watched her imaginings on her bed, saw the coming battles, fire and smoke, and the Indians coming through the woods. She fled, and David became a distant, yet immediate dream, strangely out of time and place. Or she stayed and David came with the soldiers in their scarlet uniforms, her *tulips*, vivid in the sunlight against the green leaves of the trees. Or she stayed and the Indians found her: 'I have but to give stretch to the Indian forces under my direction . . . ' She closed her eyes, and turned over and pulled up the counterpane, her imagining making a tomb of the room.

She must apprehend things and stop dreaming, must face the fact the British employed Indians. Burgoyne had made that clear. Coming from St. Regis, Lake of Two Mountains, and Kahnawake, they had fought at Hubbardton where so many soldiers had died—but her imagining couldn't penetrate what had happened at Hubbardton.

Jane listened beyond the door of her room and the house, gaining small comfort in knowing that Eva and the children slept. The darkness terrified her. The crickets sounded like little drums, the owl's hoot like a human voice. Gradually the summer night grew full, ebbed and flowed with the half-heard sounds of running. Finally, it all fell away and she slept:

> *. . . she walked at night towards John's house. Strangely lit up with a grand porch and people surrounding it, crashing and loud noises came from inside it. She watched dragon-like shadows breathing fire beneath the trees. How strange not to see the maple tree hanging over the house! But this was John's house with its heavy cedar shakes and logs at the corners. Yet, Brant looked at her from the porch, his feathers and cape and his gold link-chain glowing in the darkness. And Sir Guy Johnson stood there too in pulsating emerald! She called out in her sleep, "David!"*

"Jane," Eva said gently, clasping her shoulder. "You're dreaming."

Jane sat up, brushed her hair back and rubbed her eyes. Her dream retreated just out of reach into the gloom of the night.

"I fell asleep."

"I'll get you some water."

A faint light reappeared in the doorway when Eva returned and the water splashed into her basin. Jane took off her petticoat and hung it over her chair.

"What time is it?" she asked.

"Three o'clock."

"I'm packed, Eva," she disclosed, reaching for her nightgown on the hook by the door. It wasn't there, so she felt for it in the trunk, touching the doll.

"Want this left open?" Eva asked at the door.

"No, it's all right," Jane answered, lying back on the bed and wiping her forehead with the end of her sheet. The heat rose from the back of her neck to her cheeks and forehead. David would protect her. She sighed in the cool night air as it wafted off the river and through her window. The war would end in a year—the Congress *must* submit. Afterwards, they would reunite, she consoled herself.

In the morning with the sun spread on the bay, yellow flowers bloomed across the hill. A fish jumped, and a boat moved insect-like on the far river, fluttering in the white of women's petticoats. Jane picked up the wash basket, heavy as last night's dream, and carried it to the clothesline. Except to dry these clothes, the women only awaited the boat John was sending to them to take them to Albany.

As Jane hung the clothes, her eyes drifted to the field and the woods beyond. She wondered if it was possible to break her estrangement with Sarah Jones. Surely the woman wanted news of her son, if David hadn't written—and if she brought her news of him, perhaps his mother would relent toward her, seeing she herself desired to forget the past. But how could she, herself, forget Sarah's money and how she had used her son for it? Yet, if she could bridge their estrangement that would be best for the future—she and his mother might even wait for David together if the desirability of it arose—Jane then finished hanging the clothes and left for Sarah Jones' farm.

Standing before Sarah Jones' door Jane knocked a second time. When she was about to turn away, the door opened and Sarah Jones stood there. How thin and tired she looked!

"I thought you would want news," Jane said to her.

The heavy smell of rum permeated the airless house as Sarah opened the door to her. Inside the house she motioned her to a chair with a nod and an imperious gesture before sitting across from Jane.

"And why wouldn't I be alone with my sons gone?" Sarah replied indifferently.

"I received a letter from David yesterday."

"He hasn't written *me*," Sarah then commented, receiving this news like an injury.

"Perhaps he wanted me to tell you what he wrote," Jane offered.

"Did he say that?"

"No, but I haven't visited you because . . ." She thought she would tell her why she hadn't visited but twice since the new year as a way of reaching her.

"That David wrote you is all I need to know," Sarah interrupted her, sculpting her words from ice.

"David is coming to Edward," Jane said precisely.

"Why doesn't he write *me* and tell *me* that? Is his heart so shallow for his mother that he dips his quill in a thimble?"

"I assumed he wrote you."

"You assumed! And what does he say *you* should do?"

"Wait at Sarah's for him," Jane answered, drawing back against the chair at the woman's hardness.

"And *me*! Did he tell you to come here?" Sarah's eyes gleamed like knifepoints.

Jane colored. "He did not tell me to come," she said evenly, feeling the heat beginning to rise to her cheeks.

"A *neat* crochet! And with all this," Sarah opened her palms to the house, "not a word to his mother in nine months. And you'll wait at McNeil's. Sit and wait in her hut with no consideration whatever for me."

"But that's why I have come. I thought . . ." Jane grew hot, Sarah's rebuke threatening to choke her. "You speak of consideration . . ." but she held back what she knew of her dead lover and the money she had been receiving against the increasingly remote possibility something might be salvaged with this woman.

"Consideration!" Sarah nearly screamed.

"Do you feel in danger?" Jane asked sharply, unable to quell her own sudden anger.

"Who knows what the rebels might do with my sons fighting them? But that's no concern of yours as the sister of a rebel Colonel."

Jane bristled, all thought of reconciliation vanishing. "Would you feel safer with me here?" Her tone was like a knife stroke.

"God knows I've grown seven sons," Sarah answered, repudiating any suggestion she valued her. "After all I've done for David, he doesn't write . . ."

"After all you've done!"

"I've given my life."

"He slighted you?"

"Tell me, since you know him so much better." Sarah's voice crackled in the room as she stood up. "Would he want me to throw myself on McNeil's protection too? Or wait here for the rebels to burn me out? A fine choice!"

"You used him!" Jane shouted. "That's why you refused to let him marry me."

"Yes!"

"The money you received! And if he won't write you, it's because you used him and slandered me," Jane cried.

"You're shameless!"

"You spread lies about me while you and Daniel used him. And you used me to get him up to this house! Now you have no one."

"You turned him against me. Oh, to have such thankless children." Sarah unlocked her heart and let the sharp-beaked nestlings fly out.

"You now reap what you sowed."

"He *deserted* me!" Sarah cried in self-pity.

"I have no pity for you."

"You encouraged him," Sarah glared.

"You forced him over!"

"Get out!"

"Face what you've done to your son. You are a wretched woman and no mother to a son."

Sarah put her hands to her face. "He loves me," she repeated, "now I told you to get out!"

"You tried to turn him against me, but he knows you . . ." Jane hurled at her, standing up unable to check the flow of her bitterness accumulated over the last seven years. "You abridged him all these years. Where does such meanness come from?"

"I was put here to spike your desire, Jane McCrea, and you'll never have him," Sarah hissed, her arms shaking as she gripped her chair.

"And the British will win, and you will still lose him as he is lost to you now!" Jane exclaimed, seeing a final choice in David's not having written his mother.

"And *you* want the rebels to burn every Tory house from here to Albany! *You* want this house to go up in smoke because you couldn't have that heap of rotting lumber out on the knoll. But he won't marry you! I know my son."

"He will marry me, and you will burn in hell for what you have done. He's coming for me! Understand that, Sarah Jones. He is coming for me!" Jane shouted, flinging herself at the door.

"He will not come for you. You will never see him again, you shameless tart!"

Jane ran from the house. She caught Charlotte's reins up in her hands and flung herself up on the mare. She leaned forward in the saddle. "Oh, David!" If the mare now plunged into the river, it would soothe her agony! Jane let the mare go, and the mare streaked down the driveway onto the road.

Far up the road Jane walked through the scrub overlooking the river. The brush snatched at her petticoat. She had dismounted and now let the mare wander away on her own. Maybe the rebels *would* burn Sarah out, she grieved bitterly. David knew his mother's deceit. And if only he would marry her! She couldn't lose him now. But how hopeless were two armies separating her from him! Her mind and heart were aflame as she walked aimlessly across the hill.

"What shall I do?" she cried bitterly, her tears hot on her cheeks. She couldn't go to McNeil's. She had already packed to go with Eva. And her humiliation because of James Higson and Content kept her from finding sanctuary at the Wings'. She had only David's appeal and his mother's undying hatred. And how could she keep this from Eva?

She came to a stone and sat on it. Holding her knees and swaying, she looked distractedly at the grass. She lifted her head expecting to see neither the river nor the sky. Her father had spoken of Providence. He had taught her every creature had its destiny— Destiny! If she ever needed her father's faith, she needed it now— *"Oh, Father!"* she cried. If only she had his consoling words— "Providence and God have denied me, why am I sent from hope to hope looking for a husband and for the children I never bore?" She rested her head in her hands—

—Time passed and then she looked up. Near her Louis Cook held Charlotte. Jane lifted her sleeve to her face. He handed the reins to her where she sat. She took them from him.

"David is with the Redcoats," Cook stated with uplifted eyebrows.

"Yes, he is," she confirmed miserably.

The Indian nodded, taking in her grief. His long, straight black hair clung to the back of his neck. "And the Yarns boy fought for the Bostonians," he said sadly, spanning the river. "And the Johnsons sent Reverend Kirkland away from the Oneidas."

"Will you fight the Johnsons because of it?" Jane asked.

"Hen."

"Why?"

"Because both of them have spoken in twisted shapes."

"Is Atsitsina with you?"

"Hen. He's an Oneida Indian now."

"And is Johnson with Burgoyne?" Jane asked, fearing the futility of her past attempts of keeping David from joining them.

Cook shook his head. "No, Johnson will be coming with St. Leger down the Mohawk River in another month to link up with Johnnie Redcoat. Johnson and Brant have been recruiting at St. Regis. My brothers might join them, though I told them not to fight," he laughed shortly. "It is a grave mistake for them to join the Redcoats. There are too many Bostonians, and they will have it their way in this war."

"Then you will not meet David, but St. Leger? You will not fight against my husband?"

"I may meet St. Leger, and who is to say I will not meet David also?"

"What do you mean?"

"The Indians with the Redcoats at the head of the lake come from Montreal. I will meet my friend, Thomas Williams, from Kahnawake," Louis smiled faintly. Then his lips became cold. "Or I will see our old 'friends' from the Lakes—Le Grand Sauteur, Matchekewis, Akewaugehetauso—the famous Charles Langlade—and St. Luc La Corne, or . . ." he stopped, "names you do not know, but old 'friends' from the last war who fought for the French."

Louis, speaking of the "thousands" of Indians of Burgoyne's Proclamation, chilled her. Her arms dropped to her sides and she let go of the reins. "The French Indians," she murmured.

"Hen, three days away. And so you must go home," he said, as if commenting on a bird that flew over. "It is not safe here for you."

Jane picked up the reins, stood up, and walked obediently to beside the mare. When she gained the saddle she saw other Indians down the road waiting for Louis. She recognized Atsitsina. The irony of his meeting his own people in war after coming from the Lakes stung her. How had even that Indian been spared? "Those are Oneidas and Tuscaroras, aren't they? The same that brought Robbie back in winter, and they will help Schuyler and the rebels, won't they?" she asked of the other Indians with Atsitsina. "And why?"

"For the same reason the Johnsons and the Mohawks are on the other side. In this war it is brother against brother because they want to fight for the father of the Bostonians. We have never had such close relations to the King as the Mohawks."

"Louis," she said as he began walking away.

He turned around and walked back to her and waited for her to speak.

She didn't know how to ask him, but she knew somehow that they would probably never meet again, and there was something she needed to know about his black skin.

"Were you a slave, is that it?" His blackness would contravene the King and explain why he was fighting.

He smiled. "My father was a slave. He lived with the 'Benakis."

"So you are an Indian and the son of a slave. You Indians don't have slaves and so you believe in *freedom*, too, like the rebels?" she asked awkwardly, trying desperately to find some common ground with him.

"We Indians do not have slaves, except through war we own our prisoners. The 'Bostonians' are like us," he answered with a wry smile, "which is one reason we 'younger brothers' will fight by the side of the Bostonians."

"What do you mean you own prisoners? How can you own prisoners, if you don't own slaves?"

"Only that a warrior owns the prisoner he captures. The prisoner belongs to him because he has forfeited his life on being captured. So no other warrior may take him away from his captor, except that the warrior who captured him would kill the prisoner. That is the way among us Indians—this is the way we fight. You cannot take a prisoner from another warrior is all I mean. We do not own slaves," he repeated.

"And so what have you done with David's wig?" she asked, superstitiously feeling somehow that Louis owning David's wig might make him think he had a prior claim to fight and capture David in battle.

"Sold it to a Johnson Mohawk Indian."

"So his wig meant nothing to you?"

"No."

"And where are you going now?" she finally questioned.

"To receive my old friends from the Lakes coming with the Redcoats," he laughed, "I have yet an old game of *baggatiway* to finish with those Indians from the Lakes."

"You will not fight against David then! Promise me you will not."

"He sold me his wig, and I let go of it. I have no need to *coup* his real hair. No, I will not fight against your husband, but call to him to throw down his musket because you wait for him."

Jane then watched Cook walk back down the hill relieved that at least this one man would not turn his hand against David.

42

Jane and Eva anxiously waited for the next two days for the bateau to take them to Albany. The bateau would arrive the twenty-second or twenty-third, Tuesday or Wednesday. She and Eva could breathe for a moment, but only long enough to watch the people flee from the Corners, Argyle, Salem, and even Kingsbury. Boats on the river and wagons loaded with furniture, woolens, clocks, mirrors, and kitchen pots streamed south on the other side of the river along the road. Women walked beside the wagons, children rode and the horses pulled, a steady stream of refugees paralleled the flow of the river . . .

In late afternoon, they watched the exodus. The bay, flat and cheerless between shadow and light, depressed time itself. "Look at what the Pope's troops, the minions of Hell, are causing. Now they come again," Eva said of how fear of the Indians emptied the countryside as she refolded John's letter. He had confirmed what Louis Cook had told Jane about the expected arrival of the French Indians. They were with Burgoyne's army. The rebels had already skirmished with them somewhere near Kingsbury. The rebels had also evacuated and destroyed Fort George. The British would finish the road and clear the creek between Skenesborough and Fort Anne in a week. A thin shadow, like the black hem of a gray petticoat, began to appear on the shore below them.

Jane fingered the large bun of her hair. The sight of so many people fleeing brought home to her the reality of an Indian attack. She couldn't dispute Eva about the people's fear of the Indians. She no longer saw meaning in what occurred—the British use of Indians made her as cynical and angry as Eva.

Clear yellow light washed the opposite shore. The shadow in

front of the two women widened to a broad black ribbon as a cloud drifted across the summer sky.

"Those Ottawas and Winnebagos drank English blood on Langlade's doorstep at Michilimackinac on your thirteenth birthday," Eva said to drive the point home about the people's fear of the Indians.

A breeze made ripples offshore and shadow blackened the bay. They could still hear people moving, but they couldn't see them. Jane didn't care whether Eva knew or not about Sarah Jones.

"David's mother said she would never allow him to marry me," she offered, however, rubbing a mosquito bite on her finger.

"No sensible man would ask a woman to marry him under these circumstances, anyway—but if David really loves you, I wouldn't be too concerned about his mother. I thought that you had settled that between you some years ago."

Jane smiled weakly. She deferred to Eva's common sense.

Yet when would Freel again appear with a letter from David?

* * *

Near dark the following day, Sunday, after sitting by the river with Eva in the late afternoon, and after not finding Freel along the river during the day, Jane again encountered the schoolteacher, Thomas Fraser. But this time instead of meeting him by chance at the shore of the bay in front of the house, she came upon him on the road. He had detoured beyond the wheat field and was coming through the woods. Not recognizing her, he jumped off the road as she rode toward home. She hadn't seen him since the night he had brought the news to Sarah McNeil's that Carleton had sailed back to Montreal.

"That mare steps so quiet one would think she had leather on her hoofs," he remarked sourly as she approached him in the semi-darkness.

Meeting him made her stomach flutter. His appearance at this time made Burgoyne's approach seem almost ominous given what happened with Carleton. Yet, how close was the army? And hadn't

Burgoyne already reversed Carleton's ill success of last fall at Ti? Wasn't victory certain? Why then did his appearance make her so anxious?

"How long before Burgoyne reaches Edward?" she asked quickly should he try to leave her.

"A couple of weeks for Johnny to reach Albany," but he stated unhurriedly, dropping his haversack on the road.

Jane leaned toward him in the faint light. "But I didn't ask about Albany, but Edward."

"Are you going to try again?" His voice suddenly became hushed.

"Not like Carleton!" she protested.

Fraser shook his head. "Carleton came in October, too late in the season. If he had come in July, he would have attacked Ti. But the army's beyond Ti now, and no rebels are going to stop Johnny from reaching Albany. They're all in the fields. Johnny's got an army and the rebels don't. Johnny should be at Edward toward the end of the week."

Jane felt momentarily reassured. What Fraser said agreed with John's letter of yesterday saying that the Congress would not have soldiers enough to meet Burgoyne until later in the season. And if Burgoyne moved quickly, the rebels couldn't muster in great numbers against him. But it had taken Burgoyne almost three months to come this far! How could she be sure that he would reach Edward at the end of the week?

"And work on the road?" she asked anxiously, "that might take longer than you think. The longer it takes to finish the road, the worse the army's chances."

"No. Only a day or two more to finish the road."

"I have had no news. Not anything."

"The army will march in a day or two, I tell you, for all of Burgoyne's stupidity in building that road. Relax."

"How can I relax after the last time when you were so sure?"

"Burgoyne has lost valuable time, no doubt. The army should be fighting, not engineering. That kind of effort uses up supplies and weakens the men—*but* it will turn out all right. You can count on it this time."

"You told me that last time," she repeated, wanting him to continue to correct for her what went wrong with Carleton.

"No one could have predicted what Carleton did," he answered sharply, "no one expected those numbers at Ti and Independence." He exhibited the same heat at Sarah's that night. "But at least it set the stage for this . . ." he said technically. "Burgoyne won't fail, though, for his blunders up to now. He has a 'Spanish' reputation to protect."

"You still say that after Hubbardton? He should never have crossed the lake."

"Well, he did cross the lake, and the rebels lost heavily too for him doing so."

"But they can regroup and fight again," she found herself echoing John.

"You sound like a strategist."

"My brother is a Colonel, remember?" she asked bitterly, not only because what John had predicted was coming true, but because this man before her had given her false hopes.

"And so what are *you* going to do, if you have all the answers? The same as last time, fly up to Sarah's?"

"I probably shouldn't ask you to advise me after last fall," she continued, unable to keep the censure from her voice.

Fraser dismissed her skepticism. "Have you read the Proclamation?"

"Yes, I have read it, and what the General says about the Indians is not very comforting . . ."

"Then stay at your brother's house. Howe's coming up from New York and St. Leger will be marching down the Mohawk valley. Between the three of them they'll split New England away from New York. Stay put like the General writes. If you don't want me to advise you, listen to him."

"But you have no high opinion of Burgoyne by the way you talk, and last time you advised me to go . . ."

"It's different now. Ti has already fallen, and the army's on land and motion. Carleton never left his ships. Burgoyne has accomplished that much, if you don't believe anything else. And what's at Edward to stop Burgoyne? Oh, the rebels will skirmish, maybe all the way to Albany; but they won't stop the army, and you don't want to be caught in the sniping."

"And what about Sarah and Polly? Won't they be in danger? What have you advised them to do?"

"They'll be all right if they stay inside the cabin and hang a white flag on the door."

"A white flag? Do the French Indians know what a white flag means?" she almost laughed in disbelief.

Fraser shrugged his shoulders.

"A white flag is not much protection," she said.

The General's Proclamation, her promise to John, having received no other letter from David, and now the unpredictability of the Indians all proscribed her not going to Sarah's. She knew that only too well. Yet, perversely, David's mother compelled her to go. Jane's indecision cut her like knives. But what if Simon Fraser knew his cousin was waiting for him? She returned to that old question as though she still sought safe anchorage there.

"Does he know where Sarah lives?"

"Sarah sends information, doesn't she?"

"And so have you sent information. *You* must have said something to him, if Sarah hasn't," Jane sought double assurance. "Haven't you ever spoken of Sarah to Simon?"

"Simon knows," was all Fraser answered.

"Then I would be safe there! Then you advise me to go!" She wanted him to make up his mind. His indecision nettled her and made her suspect that maybe things wouldn't go right for all his assurances to the contrary. After all, why should she trust this man's judgment after what happened last time with Carleton?

"Your going up there or not is for you to decide. Go, if you want." Fraser looked down at the dark road.

"You have doubts," Jane asserted, leaning over the mare's neck. "You contradict yourself."

"You'll be safe if the Indians don't get their hands on rum. What more do you want me to tell you?"

"Oh, God," she whispered, "why did they bring them? You are as uncertain about what might happen as I am."

"St. Luc whipped them up is all I can tell you. Burgoyne couldn't leave them in Canada with those Frenchies in his rear without an army to protect the country."

"Then the army fears those Indians too. Why didn't the King promise them something? Are the Colonies more important than a few trinkets to the Indians?"

"You don't understand. The rebels brought this on themselves."

"But the whole countryside is beginning to flee to Albany! How can you expect to win the people by employing Indians?" she protested by blaming him personally.

"The War Department and the Ministry make our alliances. Burgoyne didn't want them, I tell you."

"Carleton brought them too. You can't deny that. The British have been trying to get the Indians into this all along. Admit it, Thomas." Jane used his name for the first time.

"Carleton's different," he avoided.

"How different?"

"I was his secretary and I know the man," he disclosed.

"His secretary? How does that change St. Luc hating all of us?"

"He hates Burgoyne too."

"That's what I mean. Then why did he bring the Indians into this? My brother told me the Congress tried to keep the Iroquois, especially, neutral. But the Johnsons—it was the Johnsons and Brant, wasn't it?"

"Unfortunately, yes" he admitted without revealing the truth that the Ministry had also been hot on Carleton bringing in the Lakes Indians as well as the Iroquois from the very beginning. "But I must go. It's so dark now, I can hardly see—"

"Where are you going?"

"Fort Anne. The army has already arrived there." He picked up his haversack. "Good luck and don't forget the white flag." Fraser then abruptly walked on—only his silhouette could faintly be seen in the remaining light that fell on the road between the trees.

John's house looked deserted when Jane arrived back there—

only the faintest light came from the small north window. The house was as bare as a barracks.

A child's voice floated up the hill. Eva and little Eva, hardly visible, were sitting on the grass by the water. Lightening bugs flickered in the warm clover-perfumed night and a fish jumped offshore.

Jane had often sat down there by the water after David had left her. She would let the night caress her before sleep, or else she bathed in the spirit of the night and in the miles of rich earth and the flowing river before she met him. The night and the land, like wine, made one a little crazy with desire. Let them come with their hautboys, pipes, and scarlet uniforms, their white wigs and gleaming swords, fine clothes and horses, mahogany carriages and silver goblets. Let them water the ground with their blood and the blood of their savages as long as it wasn't David's blood! The night had made her indifferent to how the conflict ended except that she and David would finally be together!

Jane noticed Dinah's petticoat in the dark. It reminded her of the white flag Fraser said for her to tell Sarah to hang on her door. She handed Dinah the reins and suddenly compelled to know her adjustment in the face of the coming conflict asked her, "Are you leaving, Dinah?"

"Why o' course," the black woman answered.

Dinah's direction surprised her. But Dinah had opinions—had she forgotten her speaking of John buying her freedom that cold January night when she had first read Paine and argued with Eva?

"We never talked before, Dinah."

"I told you two years ago yer brother means to see th' country independent. He wants freedom for us black people too. And black men fight alongside th' Yankee's, 'cause I seen them. I seen them from th' City along this river. Tho' they can't go back now with Mister Howe there. Us black people 're not so blind we can't see what this means. Ye've no cause ta fight Missus Eva. Go tell her you'll leave wi' us," Dinah said abruptly, leading the mare into the darkness, the mare's tail whipping the night.

Jane walked down the hill. What else could she have expected Dinah to say to her?

As she sat next to Eva a sudden light popping in the distance sounded like rain falling on dry leaves.

"Want to sit in Auntie's lap?" Jane asked her niece, the firing sending a shiver up her spine.

"What's that sound, Auntie Jane?" Little Eva asked, leaving her mother's arms and coming to Jane's lap.

Jane stroked the child's hair.

"The music of independence," Eva answered for her of the distant musket fire.

"I want it over," Jane simply said for herself, thinking it not like music at all, but more like hail beating against an upturned kettle. Yet she unconsciously touched the cameo, a pursed blood red rose on a pearl face, against her neck and looped her hair with her fingers onto her shoulders. Why must Eva, this night of all nights when the bateau was expected at any moment, speak of independence? Couldn't she just have let their talk of yesterday afternoon about the Indians putting a panic into the people suffice as an understanding between them? Eva's talk of independence nearly provoked her into speaking of General Howe's and St. Leger's approach. But Dinah's short speech and Eva's hopes also saddened her, for she loved them despite their struggle. She didn't have the heart to tell her of Howe and St. Leger. And how could she tell them that they hung like hummingbirds over an impossible nectar when her own future was in doubt? As she beheld Eva, the first rays of the moon caught her sister-in-law's yellow hair.

"You'll speak of Providence next," Jane said, "but it will take a miracle for what you want to happen, Eva." As undecided as she herself was she couldn't, nonetheless, give up hope that Burgoyne would succeed where Carleton had failed.

"Don't you know?"

"Know what?"

"That God's a Whig!" Eva declared.

Jane laughed and, turning the cameo in her fingers, fixed her eyes on the moon. "How like you, Eva!" But awe of this night and the haunting exchange of musketry in the distance conspired against levity "—It's beyond imagining what God is." She rubbed the satin air of the night on her arms and thought that a January window with a candle behind it looked like the mist that veiled this moon. A light breeze pushed the mosquitoes over the water. And how sad and glorious—almost like a requiem—the sound of shooting now made the night.

"Words can't describe the pain of birth," Eva observed of the same sounds of musketry.

"If Providence had it differently, I would stand vestal to you and worship your intent as the mother of a nation, Eva; but God hasn't willed it. Everything is against it. A grand army is about to break upon us."

As Jane spoke, she wondered whether Eva would remember what she now said to her. She brushed her hand over the light heads of the clover and plucked one and pushed it through a buttonhole in her blouse. Nights like this were hymns. As the breeze played through her hair, she had a claim equal before God to Eva's when it came to happiness and children, didn't she? Wasn't her promise as a future wife and mother equal to Eva's?

The shooting grew louder.

"I find little romance in this war, Jane McCrea," Eva said softly, "only a religious purpose."

"Your faith overwhelms me, Eva," Jane replied, awe itself compelling her to speak. "You always cast things in the largest terms."

"And why shouldn't I when my husband and your brother has risked and is risking his life for his country? Besides 'they', the grand army you speak of, are at Fort Anne." Eva stood up. The child left Jane's arms. "And we will burn the wheat this year. We will scorch the earth for Burgoyne's 'victory' banquet . . ."

"Yes, they are at Fort Anne and what a celebration," Jane replied unhappily, looking up at her sister-in-law with sorrowful eyes because she knew that this brief exchange only distanced them from each other the more and that Providence could only favor one of them.

43

It was Wednesday when Jane again met Freel on the river. The soldiers of Congress had begun retreating on Monday. Jane's words came like wing-beats, for she and Eva also expected John's boat.

"Where is David now?"

The seal on his letter demanded breaking, but Freel had to explain to her. He spoke quickly, eager to leave.

"At Fort Anne on his way ta Daniel's. I'm ta meet him there tomorrow. The rebels are burning Fort Edward and fighting broke out in Kingsbury this morning. You got ta answer that," he gestured impatiently at David's letter.

"Fighting this morning? At Daniel's?"

"Yes, at the crossroads."

"When will David reach Edward?" She broke the seal.

"Friday or Saturday. Sunday at the latest. The rebels 're evacuatin' the fort."

The last line of David's note shouted at her: *BE AT SARAH'S. WILL BE MARRIED ON THE SABBATH.*

"Tell him, I'll wait."

She watched Freel step into his boat as soldiers appeared on the opposite bank of the river. They walked with a leaden regularity toward Saratoga.

Jane turned the mare and broke into a run. If only the bateau John was sending wouldn't arrive until tomorrow!

And the bateau did not come that evening as the two women waited within the house where Eva sewed a pair of James' breeches, and Jane glanced at her trunk in the corner of the room and thought of what she should take and how to open her leaving for Edward with Eva. She had to speak now while Dinah drew water at the well.

"I'll say good-bye to Sarah and Polly tomorrow," she informed Eva matter-of-factly, keeping any suggestion of her excitement out of her voice.

"Tomorrow? But it's dangerous. Fort Edward is being evacuated," Eva replied with surprise as she pushed the needle, pulled the stitch, and broke and knotted the thread.

"Not more than for Sarah and Polly. There is still time to say good-bye to them."

"They should leave too. It is hard to understand why they would want to stay. Unless . . ." Eva paused.

"Peter is there . . ." Jane quickly interjected, not wanting to answer Eva's awkward questions.

"When will you return then?"

"Tomorrow afternoon."

"And if you miss the boat? What should I tell John?"

"I'll see it coming as I ride along the river. I will shout over to them."

"But you might miss it." Eva folded the breeches in her lap. "Why are those two staying?"

"Does it matter, if I'm just going to say good-bye?"

"They're waiting for Burgoyne, aren't they? Sarah McNeil's connected with them."

"They've no place to go."

"No, I don't mean that. She's tied to them. And you have received a letter from David like last time, haven't you?"

Jane hesitated. "Yes." It was fruitless to try to evade Eva.

"Where is he?"

"At Fort Anne." She left out his going to Daniel's.

"What do you intend to do? Wait for him again even though you promised your brother not to?"

"You heard me promise him, Eva. Why would I go back on my promise? You don't trust me, do you?"

"Should I, Jane?"

"Of course you should."

"I want to, and you don't know what will happen if you go to them now."

"I'll go and return quickly. There won't be any danger in that."

"There is always danger. The Indians are out in front. At any moment the eclipse could happen. It's foolhardy. Even that McNeil and Polly should leave. Even if they know someone on the other side, there's no telling what the Indians will do," Eva repeated more emphatically. "We care about you, Jane. That should be obvious to you And John would never forgive me if I didn't speak against your going at this time like this."

"I'll leave early in the morning and return in the afternoon. There is no danger, Eva. The road is alive with soldiers—they would be the only danger if there was any at all—"

Jane turned away from her and went to her room to retire for the night effectively closing the subject. The more Eva talked the harder it was to resist her arguments.

Jane turned back the counterpane and undressed. She lay on her bed and tried to anticipate tomorrow. Not knowing what awaited her filled her with disquiet and she fell asleep and dreamed about what would happen:

—The air, rich and light as French pastry, intoxicated her. Jane knew the people by their *eclat des grandeurs,* snowy wigs, scarlet coats, flowing satins, damasks and lawns. She wore a white tulip-like petticoat and her hair in a cadogan in thick red club turned under in a loop and tied around the middle with blue silk and a pompon of white roses.

My darling.

She knew he couldn't resist touching her arm or the light needlepoint at her elbow. The women introduced themselves and then passed, their eyes bespeaking charm and love of ease. Across the meadow by the river soldiers paraded. She lifted the loop of her hair with the back of her fingers and the sunlight smiled on her lips.

I'm dreaming, she said.

No. You are not dreaming, Mistress Jones.

David raised her hand to his lips. He wore a large, black butterfly-like bow behind his neck and adjusted the blue crepe under his chin. For a moment she viewed the wedding as though through silk gauze: tall well-groomed horses seemed to float on the grass to the popping of champagne corks and the spirited music of the band under the elms of Schuyler's house. In his bagwig and long blue and white coat with shining buckles on his shoes, the sun a melody on his face, she raised her eyes to David and felt the completeness of her new name.

A couple introduced themselves: he in red frock and striped waistcoat with laced-edged shirt ruffle, and she in round hat, her hair flowing over her tight-waisted jacket which sloped away to pleated frills and yellow petticoat. A redbreast and a canary had alighted in the garden. The lady said she had never seen such abundant hair as hers—then they walked toward the tables on the grass near the river.

The General comes.

She hardly noticed the General's escort fall away in her blush.

Charmed. La fleur de la jeunesse! The General said, lifting her hand. *I understand your eagerness, Lieutenant, to claim such a flower.*

Jenny, don't do it'

Two soldiers held John near the river.

John's all right, Jen. David's voice was dry and soft. He took her by the arm.

Let my brother go! she appealed to the General.

Burgoyne frowned. *Let the Rebel go.* He turned back to her. *Pleased?*

Don't let them hurt him, David. Her voice quivered.

Meet your new friends, David said, indicating other people for her to meet.

But where are Auntie and Polly? She wanted people she knew near her.

Haven't seen them since Edward, David answered languidly.

Jane glanced toward the house at the soldiers. People held tall-stemmed glasses of honey at the red linen-covered tables. A man in blue rode a black horse up from the river.

Red linen is so festive, dear. A woman with striking black hair said to her, gripping her hand with the strength of a man. *'A lovely garden wedding!'*

You hurt me!

Jane pulled her hand back as though pricked by a thorn. The woman held the open brooch with its gleaming pin. David kissed her bleeding palm.

She bumped against the General.

Come, my flower, let's drink some champagne. The blue rider's black horse punctuated the solemn strains of the band. *We have come from Canada for your wedding and here's the minister.* The mounted clergyman wore a round black hat and feather. A long sword hung from his white sash, and he had the Bible in his hand. *'Not every woman has a military wedding conducted by Monsieur Langlade.'* Except for his sword and the blue coat, he looked a little like her father. The silver basin on the table gleamed. She tried to pull away.

Oh, father!

Jane turned in her bed in the faint dawn through the window. She lay there breathing heavily staring into the dark room. Her door then opened and Eva stood with a light.

"The bateau has arrived, Jane."

"I'm not going," Jane mumbled.

"But the British are near Edward. We must leave now." Eva's voice rang in the room. "You can't go to say good-bye now either. It is certainly too dangerous."

"I can't go with you," Jane answered, numb from her nightmare.

"Jane, listen!" The children crowded in the doorway around Eva.

"I told you last night, I fear nothing." Her dream urged her from bed, and she lifted her light chintz frock and black callamink petticoat from her trunk.

"Listen to reason. Think of the danger," Eva declared. "And why that petticoat?"

Jane shut out Eva's words and slipped out of her nightgown. She was running from the soldiers who waited for them outside the house as much as to her wedding. She buttoned her blouse and brushed her hair.

Eva then left the room.

David had written of marriage on Sunday. It was her last chance. She had to escape now! She drew on her frock and pinned her hat. Her traveling bag hung from her shoulder. Dawn spread over the floor when she left her room.

"What shall I tell John?" Eva demanded.

"That I've gone to say good-bye." She stood poised on the edge of some finality.

"It looks as though you are dressed for some *festivity*," Eva observed archly.

"No," Jane diffused as she crossed the room to the door, "I am wearing only what's appropriate."

"As for some Sabbath outing?" Eva called to her as Jane left the house.

In the cool morning air in full view of the soldiers who waited at the shore near the bateau, Jane bridled and saddled the mare. Before gaining the saddle Eva's comment on some 'festivity' re-triggered her dream. Feeling faint, she laid her head against the saddle. But no, she could not stay. She had to leave.

"I'll wait as long as I can for you," Eva called to her from the open door. "I didn't hear what you said about *not* going with us. Remember that."

Behind her mother through the door the sun brightened little Eva's face. The child held her mother's petticoat. Jane walked back to them and slipped by her sister-in-law and kissed the child . . . .

"I must do it, Eva," she declared looking up at her, not contradicting whether she was just going to say good-bye or going with her on the bateau.

Later, the water bubbled like champagne as the ferry drifted on the current toward the landing. Free at last of waiting, indecision and fear, divided feelings and the uncertainty of meeting David, an imperative surged through Jane as she measured the opaque depths beneath the rocking boat. Her father, David, the British officers and their wives impelled her forward. And not the least was David's mother! But the dread of her dream. Her father wearing a sword. John's cry. Her callamink petticoat on the top of her trunk, rather than the blue one!

She turned against the railing and looked north: smoke blackened the sky over the bateaux that came toward the ferry. She couldn't take her eyes from those black clouds.

Why should the black smoke, obscuring the sky, transfix her so when she was flying to her lover? The lapping of the river against the side of the ferry recalled his touch and the warmth of his kisses. They had become one that day while his mother had slept. He had belonged to her from that moment. She knew possession—making love had made them whole.

The trees on the bank cast shadows over the water as the ferry drew against the landing.

"They're leavin' nothin' for Johnny," the ferryman said, pushing his weight against the pole, reminding her of Eva's comment on the rebels burning the wheat. Congress would scorch the earth to deny the British food. How desperate a sacrifice! But the same necessity that made them do it, which drove the horses and the wagons and produced the rattle of chains and the grating of iron-hooped wheels on the road, also urged her flight.

She led the mare off the ferry and spoke to some soldiers.

"Has Colonel McCrea passed?"

Bearded men spoke.

"Hours ago."

The men, with their oxen and wagons of flour and bags of gunpowder, continued on their way.

She had not seen John. The way was now open to Sarah's and her marriage by the army chaplain on Sunday! A burning fort as a backdrop to her wedding mattered less to her than presenting David's mother with a *fait accompli*. After the army entered Albany, she and David would have Jessup's land, the mill and their home. Hope buoyed her. After ten months, David would come to Sarah's and take her away.

Beyond the wet stretch near the fort the stream of men and wagons ahead of her entered the shaded road. Smoke billowed from the mounds of the fort. Soldiers were priming their muskets, filling powder horns, and smoking pipes among their tents.

Sarah came out of the house as Jane rode up to it. Squinting into the sun the older woman pointed at the soldiers on the road. "'Th' rear guard tidying up th' ashes o' th' fort. Arnold's somewhare aboot. I dinna think ye'd came, lass—an' in yer elegant petticoat, nae less."

"I've received word from David! My wedding is Sunday!" Jane said excitedly.

"Bless ye, lass! Gin did ye git ward frae im?"

"Peter Freel brought me a letter yesterday."

"I wisht Polly was here ta hear't, bot she's gane ta th' Allens. An Sunday, ye say?"

"Yes, and a military wedding!"

"Aye! A double triumph! Polly weel be yer bridesmaid, an' I'll gie ye awa' lik yer mither. Polly has left tho'. Peter was atryin' ta git us inta th' boats. Did ye brang ony ither clothes wi' ye?"

"No. Eva thinks I'm returning. I've only come to say goodbye, she thinks."

"Aye. That's guid. Shud keep yer brither frae bein' ta suspicious."

Jane dismounted and hitched the mare. Too excited to sit and smelling the roses against the side of the house, she stood there looking up the road toward the hill.

"Where's the army now? Freel said there was fighting at Kingsbury . . ."

"Aye, that's wat I heard ta. Bot they're a couple o' hours march in Kingsbury wi' thir baggage an' a hundred rebels lurkin' in th' woods. Weel tak th' whole army a couple o' days, at least, ta git hir."

"Peter Freel told me David was going to Daniel's. He could come today then!"

"Naw. David wadna came wi'oot th' army, and Freel says th' army's floatin cannons doon Lake George. Tho' I dinna ken why they need cannons wi' th' fort in ruins. Th' smallest pop-guns wad tak these scarecrows."

"There will be fighting here then!" Jane exclaimed. Suddenly Eva's warning became very real.

"Nocht if th' rebels tak ta thir boats which it leuks lik they're doin'. Tho' maybe thare weel be same fictin' in th' woods afore th' rebels git thir arses inta th' boats," Sarah reconsidered.

"When is Polly returning from Argyle?"

"Sunday. Peter shud be awa' by then. She didna want a scene wi' im."

Soldiers walked toward the hill. She wondered how David could reach her with them here. She recognized one of them. "There will be fighting if they are marching that way."

"Those 're 'pickets'."

"Won't they prevent David from coming? How much simpler it was last fall with no soldiers at the fort."

"Th' rebels weel fly lik starlings, dinna worry. Yer dreams 're aboot ta came trew arter a' this time."

"That's Lieutenant Van Vecten," Jane reminded her. "He doesn't strike me as a man who will fly."

"Oh, aye, he weel hae ta watch oot for himsel! Ye'll hae nae problem wi'im. There weel be nae more o' him doggin' yer steps like he used ta do."

"Have you seen Thomas?"

"Ye mean that schoolteacher cousin o' mine?" Sarah laughed. "Nae, he's wi' his men."

"I wish I knew how David is going to get through." Circumstance linked him with the way Thomas Fraser had tried to evade her questions about the Indians.

"Damn th' savages, lass," Sarah guffawed.

"Burgoyne's Proclamation mentioned them."

"Ta scare th' rebels."

"What a romance!" Jane said pathetically. "They're like dragons stalking my distress."

"Dinna worry, th' General weel preside owre yer weddin'. I a'ways told ye, ye think ta much aboot th' savages."

"But you don't know them—if you were born in this country you would know them."

"Ah!" Sarah waved her hand.

"Don't mock me, Auntie . . ."

"I'm not, lass. 'Tis jest yer taa skittish."

"And where are the rebels retreating to, Saratoga?" So frightened of the Indians was she that she almost wished the rebels would not retreat. Yet, if they did not retreat John would come after her.

"I heard 'em talkin' aboot gain' ta Summer Kill across frae yer brither's hoose."

Jane pictured the encampment across the bay from the house. But why there? John wouldn't have been far behind the arrival of the bateau then. Eva had probably already told him that she had left. But why had Polly left Peter? Sarah had said it was because Peter was trying to force them to leave.

"If there wasn't any danger then why would Peter try to make you leave?"

"He's a sodger—an' spakin' o' th' deil—"

Peter came across the yard toward them.

"Does John know you've come up here, Jane?" he asked.

"I've come to say good-bye," she evaded. He stood before her like a blue heron. His light blonde hair reminded her of the crest of a tall bird standing in the shallows of the river looking for fish.

"The Indians will reach Kingsbury tomorrow. We've already skirmished with them. I'll take you to the kill tomorrow."

"A bateau came for Eva and the family this morning," she deflected. "John knows where I am and is not disturbed."

"That's the boat you and Polly should have boarded, Sarah," he said pointedly to the older woman, not replying to Jane's assertion whether or not John would be disturbed knowing she was here.

"I caudna leave wi'oot Polly, now cauld I, Peter Tearse?"

"We'll evacuate by Sunday. It's only Thursday. There's still time," he said. "But it was foolish of her to leave like that. The Indians have a way of getting into the woods."

"Polly weel be awright, Peter Tearse. Ye said yersel we hae 'til Sunday," Sarah countered him.

"Not in the woods," he contradicted her flatly.

There was a long silence. The two women dropped their eyes. Smoke continued to billow from the fort behind the house. Peter then turned on his heel and left them.

That night Polly's safety in the woods preyed upon Sarah, and the following day she began to drink heavily. In the evening she had wild qualms.

"We gat ta git oot, lass!" Her whiskey breath fogged the room, and the house pulsated with crickets. "I canna tak it wi' th' sodgers shoutin' orders an' changin' th' guard, an' savages behind evera tree!" She sat heavily, her thick accent clinging like burdocks to the rafters.

"Please, Auntie, it will soon end."

The syllables of her appeal rose like blind birds in the dim room. Sarah's drink-inspired fears filled every crevice of the house. Jane was on the verge of rushing outside.

"Th' place crawls wi' adders, th' vera trees scare me ta death," Sarah moaned in her chair.

"But it's like the Highlands . . ." Jane reminded her.

"A wilderness fit anely for savages an' rebels, ye mean. Nae matter where I leuk I see savages an' hear th' wolves howlin'."

Sarah's white bonnet bobbed in the firelight. She reached across the table and poured another drink. "God hase forsaken America wi' th' red deils camin' for us. I can see 'em camin' through th' woods an thir bellies." The howling of a wolf pierced the cabin, raising goose bumps on Jane's arm. "Hear't! Why did I ever came ta this Godforsaken countrie?" Sarah stood up, her sticky breath melting in the room. "I'll ne'er go ootside again! Bot 'tis sae hot in here!"

"Take off your bonnet, Auntie. And remember you told me not to fear? Why are you this way then?"

"Ah, dinna question me, lass!"

Sarah then went to the door, but drew back when the wolf howled again. She whirled heavily around and threw her bonnet on the table. "Leuk, my bloomin' bonnet's e'en alive!" She shrank back away from the table and cried, "O, forgie me, lass, 'tis th' drink an' bein' wi'oot Polly that's maks me act this way." She clutched Jane's arm. "Forgie me, please," she pleaded, "anely Polly keeps me right. Wat weel became o' me wi'oot her? I'm anely a string o' puddin' wi'oot her, jes' food for th' worms."

"She will return tomorrow."

"Bot remember wat Peter Tearse said aboot th' woods an' th' savages? I'll wake in th' night wi' my e'es open thinkin' o' wat Peter said, an' then fall bak ta sleep an' wake wi' my head hollow as thunder. An' th' fear o' wat he said weel still be stuck in my brain as afore I slept." She struck her glass on the table. "Do ye really think thare's nae danger frae th' savages? Do ye think Polly weel be awright wi' th' Allens? Do ye think she'll hae nae trouble gittin' bak ta us?"

"She'll be all right, Auntie. Please sit down. You've no need to worry." But the half-crazed woman was raising her own fears again. And the howling of the wolf raised goose bumps on her neck.

"Bot I can smell th' deils." Sarah's eyes turned toward the rafters. "An' I ken ye can smell 'em taa, lass—" Her eyes opened wide as she turned to Jane. "'Tis lik th' English ta conjure up th' forces o' th' deil against thir ane people! God, they're a cruel race, even th' rebels didna desarve sech policy. Th' King butcherin' his ane children. An' my pore Polly in th' woods! If God's above, let 'im guide that wee bairn, I rais'd gin my ane daughter died in my arms. O, sweet Catherine, God rest yer soul that ye dinna witness this blasphemy against yer mither an' yer wee bairn. O, that Bonnie Prince Charlie hadst beat 'em inta th' sea at Culloden. An' my ane cousin, Simon, himsel leadin' th' deils! Wat hoppen'd ta th' Scots ta sacrifice thir ane children lik this; ta lead th' vera savages that slaughter'd our kinsmen in th' last war? I dinna need ta teel ye aboot wat hoppen'd ae th' Corners or Fort William Henry gin St. Luc tipp'd th' bucket for the deils ta drink bluid oot 'o, do I, lass? Lassies' shoes an' petticoats were left hangin' by th' savages on th' bushes alang th' road arter they were through mutilatin' 'em—Aye, 'twas a' those Lake savages wi' St. Luc and M. Langlade, the vera ones that handed the shot ta Braddock and th' rebel General Washington gin he was a boy in th' last war—" She focused on Jane with Druid intensity.

The name of Langlade inflamed the remains of Jane's dream. He was the rider on the black horse. The man from Canada who had come to marry her and David.

"Tak me ae my ward, lass, 'tis lanely here. Bot I'm thankful ye're wi' me. I caudna tak it by th' Styx wi' oot ye," Sarah said, gesturing at the wall of the house toward the river.

"Auntie . . ." Jane felt she would suffocate if she didn't get to the door.

"Stay, lass," Sarah held her with an iron grip, "maybe yer brither's oot thare. 'Tis a meanness beyond comprehension ta leave me now wi' my mind ajumble wi' leapin' savages!"

"I'm not going anywhere. And John is down river, isn't he? He can't come for me. You have nothing to fear." Jane turned her head and gasped for breath.

"Dinna go oot."

"I can't go anywhere else!" Jane cried, trapped.

"Stay wi' me then."

"But I need air! Let me go, Auntie!"

"Nae! Ne'er, lass!"

"Let me go!" She pulled from Sarah's grip.

"Th' rebels weel git ye. Stay hir, I say. Th' English weel slaughter 'em a'."

"Stop, Sarah!" Jane cried, pulling free and standing.

Sarah slumped back into a chair. "Go then, lass, I canna haud ye," she whimpered, rubbing her red eyes with her palms.

Gasping for breath and pulling at her collar, Jane flung open the door and stumbled out into the warm July night leaving Sarah's moaning behind her. What if Sarah continued like this for another two days?

When Jane got outside and away from the house she looked up. The stars burned through the black spaces between the treetops. Through the thin smoke from the fort, shadowy forms sat near small fires. It was hardly the scene of rescue she had imagined. She caught her breath.

"Jane."

She looked into the night. Oh, why must Peter come to torment her now? But maybe he could help her—"Sarah's in a bad way, Peter," she said desperately.

"She and Polly should have left with the others. I told you that this afternoon."

"Then why didn't you keep Polly here?"

"I didn't think she would do it," he answered flatly.

"Is it really so dangerous then that you could take the chance of not talking to her and seeing her go like that?" She wondered how he could see her in the dark, dressed in her black petticoat.

"What was I to do, put them both in irons and throw them on the bateau? Yes, it is dangerous. The Indians have been scalping all the way down from Montreal."

Jane noticed how he looked off into the night.

"Go get her then. What's preventing you?"

"Only time and the fact that I would be court-martialed if I left my post."

"Do you fear a court-martial more than what might happen to Polly?"

"You don't mean that, Jane."

"No, I suppose I don't."

"But *you* must leave. John will demand it when he finds out that you're still here."

"And so when are *you* leaving if John demands it of me?"

"After Polly returns. I expect on Saturday. She will have no reason to stay away longer than that."

"Then I'll wait too," Jane said. "We're both in the same pickle."

"Oh?"

Jane drew away from him. It had slipped off her tongue. "I mean we are both waiting on the bateau."

"No. You're waiting for David."

"Please, I am not waiting for David. I don't even know where he is—I told you I only came to say good-bye to Sarah and Polly, and Polly's not here yet."

"Have it your way then," he said unconvinced. "Can you convince the old woman to leave if Polly's not back?"

"She won't leave without her." She knew it was no longer important if Peter knew of Simon Fraser and Sarah. "How long have you known about Sarah?"

"From the beginning. But you must leave, Jane. We can't protect you."

"That chills me."

"I'm hiding nothing."

"It doesn't look good for you either."

"The Redcoats underestimate us, and there's a spirit in the men."

"Even with Howe and St. Leger on their way?"

"So, you know?—But they'll pay the price," Peter said firmly.

"And so will you pay for not having married Polly before this."

"I don't believe in Greek weddings."

"Greek weddings? I come here of my own free will."

"Do you, Jane? I'm not convinced of that."

"Meaning?"

"You haven't told me the truth. I know your situation. Polly has told me about his mother. You are waiting for David."

"Well, you know more than I do then." His intelligence insulted her when she herself had decided to come here only this morning. She was annoyed and insulted that Polly had mentioned this to him. "How can you speak of me when your own future stands so nakedly before you?" she asked with an edge to her voice, though not wanting ragged edges with him. "You imply David is some Achilles."

"Who can think of weddings at a time like this? I am only saying, if you are going to get thick with me, Jane, that Polly should not have gone to Argyle. If you are waiting for David, that's your own business."

"It's too late now for anything else."

"No, it's not too late, and you know you'll hear from John."

Yes, she thought, if she heard from him she knew what he would say to her. She was about to say that when Sarah broke from the house.

"Jane, lass! 'Re ye oot thare?"

Sarah's round form swayed in the doorway.

"I'll know what to say to John," she said, touching her neck. "And I hope you'll say nothing to him. For your part Polly should return soon too. That should be enough for you, except for Sarah." She turned away from Peter and walked back to the house. As resentful of him as she felt she also experienced a strange relief in his knowing what Sarah Jones had intended for her. She had concealed this sore in her breast for too long.

That night Eve and her children in the loft, Sarah's snoring, soldiers talking outside, and the unfamiliar room kept Jane from sleeping. The shadowed rafters gave no clue as to when John might write or where David was. Her uncertainty underscored her rashness in coming and threatened her with panic as she lay in the dark. But that the end of the war neared helped calm her. She *had* to hear from David tomorrow, Saturday. Freel *had* to bring a letter from him. She breathed to calm her beating heart and fell asleep before dawn.

But soon after Jane fell asleep Sarah awakened her from across the room. The older woman rolled on her bed in the faint light of the window above her.

"'Re ye awake, lass? I've gat a horse's thirst, an' a throbbin' in my head ta shake Beezelbub frae 'is cake o' ice!" Sarah sat up on the edge of her bed with her head in her hands her bonnet ribbons hanging to her elbows. "Wad ye go for water?" she moaned, pointing pitifully to the bucket beside the hearth.

Jane rose from her couch, picked up the bucket and left the house.

Outside redbreasts lightened the road ahead of her. She paid no attention to the soldiers as the bucket swayed from her elbow. The badly rutted road had seen the Canadian campaign of 'seventy-five, the retreat in 'seventy-six, the reinforcement of Ti and Independence last fall, and the Congress' retreat this spring and summer. Burgoyne would add to the rotting leather and canvas, broken bottles, and split boards which littered it. No longer the serene walk she once knew, a puckered scar ran between exposed rocks and gullies to the top of the hill. Though the morning air relieved her somewhat, the condition of the road and Sarah's illness depressed her.

When she approached the spring she found pickets standing guard near it. She walked to the spring. Its moss-lapped sides were eroded, but it still gurgled beneath the arching pine and flowed under the broken corduroy road. She dipped her bucket not glancing at nor minding the soldiers—then a musket fired ahead up the road from her. She quickly righted the bucket.

"Don't dally—"

Lieutenant Van Vecten, hidden by the trees, had walked over to her from a nearby blockhouse.

"I won't, Lieutenant," she replied shortly, startled by the musket shot.

"We've seen Indians this morning," he informed her.

"What Indians?" The tips of her fingers suddenly felt numb.

"French Indians, flying like birds ahead of Johnny. We'll be leaving Edward tomorrow."

"And what do you suggest?"

"That you be on the bateau."

"Isn't that presumptuous of you, Lieutenant." But she was too tired to argue with the man.

"Not where your life is concerned, Miss McCrea," he answered.

Jane thanked him for his news and picked up her bucket and left him, the small stones of the road hard under her clogs. Her heels striking the road, she had a glimpse of the sky between the overhanging branches of the trees. Imagining Indians flying above the branches quickened her steps.

At Sarah's she bumped the door open with her elbow. What darkness and the stale smell of whiskey! How close after the sun and morning air! It made her almost ill to enter the house, but she did enter it and set the bucket next to Sarah's bed.

The sick woman rolled on the edge of the bed and plunged her cup into the bucket. "—Wat did ye see, lass?"

"Lieutenant Van Vecten and some others," Jane answered, avoiding mentioning Indians.

"How mony? One-hundred and fifty?" Water dripped from the older woman's hands.

"I don't know. Some soldiers by the spring were the only ones that I saw."

"Arnold's leavin', by th' leuks o' it. Saw 'im packing his trunk wi' papers while ye was awa'—"

"Van Vecten said they would leave tomorrow."

"Sae ye'll hear frae David today for sartin. Nae savages up thare? Ye didna see ony savages did ye?"

"No." Jane feared the shock of telling her what Van Vecten had said to her about seeing them.

"O, my head! O, for a cup o' tea!" Sarah looked at her with imploring red eyes. Then she seemed to rally herself. "Drunk or nocht, we maun address th' prospect o' savages."

"They're up there," Jane then admitted, unable to kept the intelligence of them to herself.

"Wat! Maybe we can git doon here," Sarah bellowed, lurching to the root cellar and pulling up the trap door. "Bot how am I ta git my fat arse doon thare!" she cried, mortified by the impossibility of it. "'Twad be lik squeezin' a turnip inta a cup," she cried pathetically. "Leuk ae them stair." She dropped the door and looked at the loft. "Bot how ta git up thare?."

"David will have a plan." If it came to hiding in the rootcellar, Jane had seen Sarah down there before.

"Ah, th' savages weel busy themsels wi' th' rebels onyway," Sarah said half-aloud. "Wat wad they want wi' a mourning dove lik me, onyway?"

"We can leave with the soldiers tomorrow," Jane suggested, thinking they ought to do it.

"Yankees? Nae! Came an, let's lite this fire an' hae tea—" but Sarah imagined Indians like painted Bedlam inmates on their way to a hellish circus. "Eve, git same wood!" she shouted, bowling toward the door.

Jane followed the black woman out of the house. The midmorning air had turned soft in the hot sun. Her eyes involuntarily crossed to Freel's inn. It looked deserted. She had not seen Deborah these two days. At the entrance to the smoldering fort General Arnold still read his papers. Jane stepped back from the corner of the house to the door.

"I'm going to water the mare," she said to Sarah. If Arnold saw her it was unlikely he would intercept her. He had his mind on more important concerns than what she might be doing.

"Awright, lass." Sarah nearly stumbled from the door in the bright light. Jane watched her, holding her head, make her way to a chair under the roses.

Jane crossed the road. The mare wasn't moving, but standing there in the open spot off to the side of the fort with her head down. Jane immediately saw in the knot above her hooves that Charlotte had hobbled herself with the tether line. Reaching the mare, she tugged at the rope twisted around the mare's fetlocks. Two soldiers, seeing her struggle, came over to assist her.

One of the men worked his knife into the rope. Jane remembered the other soldier as the one who had spoken to John when Colonel Long had brought in that British captain after the battle of Fort Anne three weeks ago. He was thin and of medium height.

"You're Colonel John's sister," he said to her. "I'm Private Sam Standish from Fellow's regiment. This is Lieutenant Palmer—"

"I remember you at James' wedding in Ballston the summer of 'seventy," Lieutenant Palmer said, holding the cut rope. "A mighty fine wedding."

"Yes," Jane said, "is James here?" She dreaded seeing him or any of her brothers here.

"No, he's not here, but at Stillwater with the Twelfth. We're the Fourteenth." Lieutenant Palmer then tossed the cut knot into the bushes.

"Thank you. I would not have been able to free her myself," she said taking Charlotte's halter.

"Indians up at Kingsbury, you know—the Lobsterbacks are right behind them."

"Yes, I know. Lieutenant Van Vecten said you would be leaving soon." Jane then led the mare away.

As the mare drank down at the river behind Sarah's house the water dripping from her chin made circles on the quiet surface and Jane grew calmer in the sunlight. Of course Palmer and Standish feared the Indians. But what should defenseless women fear from them? She seized on Doctor Franklin's description of the Indians and what she knew of them through Louis Cook to balance her own terror of them. She had many hours to wait for David and she had to make up her mind that she had nothing to fear from the Indians. She had to have faith that she had nothing to fear from them, she told herself. There was reason in all happenings. What she did was no exception. She must trust Providence to shield her. She couldn't let her imagination wander like Sarah's. After watering the mare Jane returned to Sarah's and the day wore on—

By evening David had still not written, and Jane and Sarah listened to the evening and to the soldiers talking as they relieved the picket guard up the road. Jane strained to hear some other sound in the night. Perhaps David might be close bye; perhaps he might try to call to her. But, except for some soldiers' isolated words, stillness lay like a fog upon the night.

"Ne're saw it sae quiet. 'Tis spooky," Sarah said, pulling her bonnet strings and loosening a button on her blouse.

"The British must be very close," Jane replied in a hushed voice barely being able to make out Sarah's face in the dark.

"Why not came doon the river behind th' hoose an' tak 'em by surprise? If I was commandin' th' army I'd hae my rangers all through these woods."

"Be practical, Auntie. David would send Freel first."

"Maybe th' rebels intercept'd 'im."

"How does David know I'm even here unless Freel tells him?" Then Jane thought she heard an oar clank near the house down by the river so suggestible had the night made her.

"Savages! Do ye see ony paper?" Sarah whispered, pushing her arm over Jane's as she sat in the chair next to her.

"Paper?"

"White paper o' friends o' government. Th' rebels wear sprigs o' evergreen in thir hats."

"Shush . . ." The sounds ceased and the minutes wore away— Jane, nonetheless, continued to listen hoping that David would come for her tonight.

—But he didn't come, and lack of sleep forced the two women to their beds for the night.

Saturday morning fewer soldiers seemed to remain at the fort.

And only a few rods down river from the house, where a stream drained the low ground behind the fort, two loaded bateaux leaned against the slow black current. Across the river from where Jane watered the mare again, the island's treetops were bathed in the sunlight. Yet Jane felt cold in the quiet woods.

Then Charlotte's hoofs sucked in the mud up the slope to the house. As Jane rounded the woodshed crockery seemed to break inside Sarah's house; or was the sound more like stones against the side of a barn? Fighting beyond the hill? Jane stood in the shade, listening. Was David coming? Was he fighting his way toward her? The reins felt like whalebone between her fingers.

A hand touched her shoulder.

"John has written. The first bateau is ready." Peter Tearse handed her a note and it slipped between her fingers. The firing ceased.

'Come immediately,' it read. The blood rushed to her face as she hurried into Sarah's house to reply. As long as he wrote and didn't come for her she still had a chance of reuniting with David! At the dark table inside Sarah's house the quill squeaked across the parchment.

Outside Jane handed her reply to Peter. "When will the second bateau leave?" she asked.

"Go with the General now," Peter answered, evading her question about the second bateau.

"The second one, Peter. I am not speaking of General Arnold." There was a note of panic in her voice.

"At the last minute."

"Monday then?" she guessed. If Monday, she would need to answer John a second time should he write again. David had to come before Monday.

"Your reply to him says Monday?"

"Yes," she lied.

She then watched Peter walk away, the distant sound of musketry making her almost serene. How long had it taken her to realize she had nothing to fear? Just those shots and Peter Tearse's sudden appearance with John's demand!

A flick of white across the road and Deborah Freel was waving to her from the door of her inn. Jane immediately crossed to her.

Deborah backed into the house, swinging the door open behind her as Jane approached the inn.

"Come in, Jane. I've baked some bread." Deborah's eyes darted at the road before she closed the door. "Peter's here!" she exclaimed breathlessly, taking Jane to the end of the dark hall where Freel stood. The three of them then went into the kitchen.

"It took some doin' gettin' back last night with th' rebels in the woods," Freel said.

"Please," Jane asked quickly, extending her hand for the letter she knew he must have with him.

"Don't ya wanta know about him?"

"Where did you see him!"

"At Daniel's with Solomon. They say to stay at the inn tonight."

"Let me have his letter . . ."

"On the table."

Jane fumbled under the table linen at her elbow. As she read, her face turned white. She leaned against the table. Her voice sounded as though she was choking on smoke. "Tell him, I approve—"

"You'll stay then?"

"Yes," she answered softly, barely conscious of leaving the inn.

And what would she tell Sarah? That she must stay at the inn because of John?

But Sarah was alarmed when Jane told her that she was to stay at the inn. Yet, reassuring her that she would return in the morning helped to calm the woman's fears somewhat. Then another note from John in the afternoon convinced Sarah that Jane's staying at the inn was best. Jane then answered John that she would return by the bateau tomorrow morning, Sunday. She tried to keep David's letter from Sarah, but Sarah pressed her.

"How's he camin' luve?"

Jane walked to the small north window. The declining light held her in gray suspension.

"A simple escort, Auntie!" she whispered, pressing her palms hard against the windowsill.

"Escort!" Sarah flicked at the word like a strange insect.

"I'm to be taken to Chaplain Bruendel," Jane amplified with wide staring eyes.

"I dinna ken th' name Bruendel, lass. O' course evera army hase its chaplain. Ye mean a guard o' honor wi' drums an' pipes?" Sarah came to the table which separated them.

"Just the thing for a country lass," Jane said, wringing her hands. "I must clean my petticoat, my hair . . ." her fingers brushed her hair.

"Bot wat's wrang, lass?" Sarah asked, seeing Jane's pallor in the window light.

Jane averted her face. "I have no jewelry."

"I hae baubles." Sarah walked over and took her arm. "Wat aboot th' escort?" Her words fell heavy and joyless as stone. "I dinna fear stayin' alane wi' Eve an' th' bairns, an' see th' wisdom o' yer stayin' ae Deborah's for th' nite, bot ye're nae tellin' me somethin', lass."

Jane tried to make her words dance in the dark room, but they broke like porcelain at her feet.

"He's sending Indians."

"Wat! Savages!"

"The rebels have marked him!" Jane cried with anguish.

"Bot that's trew o' ony sodger."

"It's the only way!" she cried out again.

Sarah turned away to a corner of the room and fumbled in a chest.

"Aye, some jewelry ta wear," she mumbled absently as a sleepwalker hardly understanding what she had heard, "for th' occasion." She re-crossed the room and raised a gold pendant to Jane's neck. The chain dripped from her fingers in the meager light of the window. "It taks th' color o' yer hair."

The gold strawberry lay like a large tear in Jane's palm. "But I can't, Auntie . . ." her voice trailed off with the gold strawberry gleaming mistily in the mirror against her black bodice and her red hair.

"Won't th' chaplain Bruendel gie ye a fine military weddin'? 'Tis bonnie, this strawberry pendant," Sarah said near tears herself, apprehending the reality of Jane's disclosure about the Indians.

"Perhaps, I might conceal it under my blouse."

Jane loosened a button of her bodice and felt the strawberry cold as death between her breasts.

"Ye canna conceal yer ruddy hair, nor th' blush an yer cheek which spaks o' th' Scots, Jane McCrea!"

"I'm not to be sacrificed! It frightens me to wear this outside my bodice," Jane exclaimed, recoiling.

"O, *hang* th' savages!" Sarah declared with sudden Celtic fervor at the chance of Jane displaying her jewelry to the officers who would receive her. "Ye're lik my ane daughtir ta wear th' piece for a' ta see!"

"You would sacrifice me with this around my neck? Remember yesterday and your fear of Polly and the Indians!"

"'Twas th' whiskey. Bot, if ye're set against th' piece, 'tis awright wi' me," Sarah said more meekly, taking back the pendant. "I luve ye, lass. 'Twas anely thinkin' o' th' occasion." Sarah withdrew into the shadows. "Ye can do worse than be marri'd by the chaplain," she nearly whined, strung between her fear and her pride of show as she closed the lid of the chest.

Jane sighed when the clasp snapped, then wrung her hands and looked distractedly into a corner of the room. Her deferred Eden bloomed on the other side of a yawning abyss!

"How can he ask it of me? I pleaded with him not to join the Johnsons. I told him no . . . . Has he forgotten Braddock, or William Henry? Must I deliver myself to them? I am no Ephigenia!" Her words cut her throat like glass.

"We maun do't," Sarah answered stoically, resigned to whatever offered, the fight seemingly going out of her completely in the face of the looming inevitability of events. "We a' walk in th' valley o' th' shadow o' death. 'Tis wat maks us pure an' haly. Th' guid Laird guides yer steps ta Paradise. Oh, God, lass, I ken 'tis time ta put yersel inta th' hands o' th' Almighty." She then woefully clasped her hands in the dark.

"But I'm not pure . . ." Jane cried. "Have I acted meanly towards John or Eva, or towards David's family? Why must I shrink from the cup of my wedding? Tell me, before I die!" She held out her hands to the woman in horror and supplication.

"'Tis anely a scheme ta git ye owre. Think o' yer weddin' an' th' life afterwards. If I had th' same prospect, I wad dance an th' road. Gat ahauld o' yersel, Jane. David's on 'is way." Sarah shook Jane's arm, telling herself, as well as Jane, that this would end well.

"We'll go together then, won't we, Auntie—like mother and daughter? You'll give me away, speak for me?" Jane wiped her eyes and glanced upon the floor to get her balance.

"Aye, we weel go thegither." Sarah set crystal glasses on the table and filled them with red wine. "Here a libation. I drink ta yer luve and health, lass—an' anither for Polly."

Sarah's passive acquiescence gave Jane some rare unintelligible strength. The warm, dry wine on her lips made her moment of horror awesome and even beautiful. She experienced a strange quietness, almost like the hand of Providence upon her, and her fears retreated. She thought she could even hear the gallop of David's horse.

"Now for scanes afore ye go. 'Tis dusk, an ye maun hauld ta David's advisement lest we find oursels trundl'd off doon river by yer brither." Sarah put down her glass and took Jane to her bosom. "Lang ago I larned gin ta stop strugglin'. Th' hand o' th' Laird 'tis owre us now. 'Tis in th' request."

Jane's tears fell on the older woman's shoulder, and without a word she left the house.

A few minutes later Deborah opened the door to Jane's light knock. When it closed behind them, Deborah whispered, "Your room is ready."

The two women went up the narrow stairs, their petticoats brushing the walls, the stairs creaking like an old footbridge. Warm from the wine at Sarah's, Jane didn't think of the Indians. She thought only that, 'The lot is cast into the lap, but the decision is wholly from the Lord.' The redbreasts chirped, if one was happy or sad.

Deborah opened the door to one of her front rooms. The curtained window overlooked the road, and a candle gleamed on a night table. A decanted bottle of perfume and the candle adorned a single red rose in a black vase. Deborah fluffed the bed high and fresh and folded towels on it. A bathing tub occupied a corner of the room. Deborah's attention touched Jane as she laid her shawl on the back of a chair.

"Jane, this is the night before your wedding. Sherry is in the cabinet. I'll pour your bath."

The candle flickered in the wetness of Jane's eyes.

Above the tear-shaped leaves, the petals of the rose scented her fingertips. The petals had the moist texture of butterfly wings. Jane slipped the ribbon from her hair, and her hair fell rose-colored, long and fulsome down her shoulders and back. She hung the ribbon in a black loop on the chair. The sherry welled lightly from the bottom of her glass.

Deborah brought in steaming water. Steam feathered the surface within the tub.

Jane slipped out of her petticoat and laid her clothes across the chair. She looped her hair over her shoulder. If she had ever dreamed of Heaven on earth—palaces with eternal springs and summers, and four-in-hand to take her where she wished to go—it couldn't equal the delight of this bath.

She leaned against the inside of the tub and the water reaffirmed her femininity, cleansing her, imbuing her with acceptance, making her femaleness sacred. She no longer sought to belong, whole of body with full breasts, hips and thighs veiled by her streaming hair, she offered herself in marriage, gave her womanhood for new life: the dark July clouds reflected on the river in gray and black agate as she made her way to him, the water parting and falling towards her, his taking her in his arms, her feeling as weightless as a rose on the water, 'thy rod and thy staff, they comfort me . . . ', she had felt his urgency in the river, that Prelude, daring herself, only to swim back with yearning in her strokes, leaning into them, reluctantly pulling herself to the shore. And then there came her surrender in his bed . . . and after tomorrow, they would no longer steal moments together, for she would only need to yield to his gentle touch.

She stood up in the cool water and squeezed the wetness from her hair. It hung soft and damp between her breasts and against her thighs.

She walked to the table and the perfume cooled her skin. She dried her hair with the towel.

After putting on her nightgown, she brushed her hair, full and soft as silkweed—brushed it back from her forehead and down the back, from the sides of her head to the back, curving it, mane-like, fertile, long and full. When she felt it clean and cool she sprinkled perfume on her brush—her hair took the scent and highlights of the rose, its enchanting red, and velvet petals.

She folded the counterpane back and smoothed the sheets, and, with a last sip of sherry, sweet as strawberries on her lips, extinguished the candle. She then parted the curtains and the cool summer night, sweet with pine, billowed into the room. The cool air lay darkly on the road glowing moistly in the soldiers' small fires near the fort. Overhead, pearl stars studded the velvet sky. Alone and sequestered with the sherry tingling in her veins, breathing the night air, she experienced a rare excitement. Silence carried the tinkling of the stars—as if a princess in some remote castle, she expected her knight. She had only to call softly for the owls to fly, or for a nightingale to land on his saddle. Had he known how she waited for him, he would, she knew, come up the stairs this instant.

In the morning, the windowsill brimmed with yellow light. Jane looked out. Dew darkened the road, and the grass between the forks glistened. The room had cooled, but the sun, flooding it, promised a hot day.

She brushed her hair and each stroke reminded her of the excitement she had felt leaving Lamington—as now, new life beckoned her forward, determined the steps she was taking.

Jane laid the brush on the table and as she dressed and looked out the window, the last seven years of waiting seemed to vanish.

Her petticoat hugged her hips and waist, and her bodice lifted her breasts as she buttoned it. She took the black ribbon and brought it under her hair, retying it at the top of her head, lifting her hair from her neck. She brushed her hair again and pinned the rose in it.

She then left the room, her callamink petticoat brushing the staircase like falling leaves.

At the foot of the stairs and down the hall children prattled in the kitchen. Jane opened the door. She thought her whisper would carry through the walls of the inn to the outside.

"I'm leaving now, Deborah."

"How lovely you look, Jane McCrea!"

"I will be married today."

"Yes, and in the sight of God—but the soldiers are on picket duty!"

"The soldiers are on picket duty, but I'm ready . . ." Jane said, suddenly feeling Deborah's anxiety.

"But you must eat before you leave," Deborah insisted, turning back to her stove.

"But if they should come . . ." Jane stayed her arm.

"Just some biscuits, then." Deborah wrapped several in a napkin and took Jane's wrist.

Jane stood full bosomed and erect in her black petticoat with its embroidered hem and white ruffled blouse under her chintz frock with the rose in her flaming hair. "It's not like any other day," she prayed aloud, accepting the biscuits like an offering.

Outside, the honeysuckle and pine evoked the incense in her father's church and the grass sparkled. When Jane saw soldiers standing under the trees on her left as she crossed the road, she almost expected to hear the marching boots of the British.

When she reached Sarah's door, Sarah opened it before Jane even touched the latch.

"Did they see ye, lass?" Sarah asked her in a hushed voice.

"Only those soldiers over there," Jane nodded.

"We'll sit ootside ta show nothin's amiss then."

"There is nothing amiss, Auntie." Jane turned from the

doorway, also wishing to stay outside. Looking up the road, she wondered when the escort would come . . .

Sarah pushed from the doorway, her foot hitting the ground heavily. "Deborah gave ye pastry."

"Biscuits, yes."

Sarah pulled a chair away from the house and Jane sat down next to her.

The scent of roses filled the air—For no reason, Jane's heart began to beat wildly and she felt faint. She put the small bundle of biscuits on the ground beside her chair. She wanted to make small talk, wanted to put the words into proper order and fashion the day. Would they come for her now, an hour from now, this afternoon?

"Look at my hands, Auntie . . ." she said, turning up her glistening perspiring palms.

"Polly hast ta git here first," Sarah said as though Polly's coming would dry Jane's palms. Sarah then took out her sewing, drew the threat up smoothly and hooked the needle through the cloth. Her short fingers worked the needle back and forth. "Polly weel came wi' us ta meet Simon." Small patches of light appeared under the trees as the sun climbed. "Remember ae th' Jessups gin I tauld ye ta wait? Now David's camin' wi' Generals, thir ladies, an' th' pick o' th' aristocracy in thir bright coats. Tell me thare's no reward for waitin', Jane McCrea."

"You foresaw it all, Auntie," Jane smiled, thought of her wedding making her light-headed.

"Frae th' very first." Sarah's face broke into happy lines.

"Has Peter left yet?"

"Arter ye went ta Freel's he took ta his bateau wi' Arnold. I tauld 'im ye went hame, bot he didna believe me. 'Tis jest as weel he's nocht here gin th' army cames. I wadna want 'im ta git killed."

Jane brushed her perspiring palms on her petticoat and breathed deeply. She didn't doubt Peter would soon marry Polly regardless of what happened.

Soldiers, joking as they passed, went up the road toward the hill.

"Them fellows might git a scatterin' afore they came bak—" Sarah said, piqued by their levity. Others soldiers followed them.

"Don't say that, Auntie!" Jane recognized Lieutenant Palmer among them.

"Who cares for thir brazen leuks?" Sarah's needle gleamed and disappeared into the cloth.

"All the same . . ." Jane began, as musket shots, hard and sharp, not flat and hollow like before, came from the hill. Her breathing suddenly stopped and she rose from her chair. Shots splattered through the trees followed by hoarse yelling and more shooting—then the woods in front of the house erupted with running rebel soldiers. They ran down the road and from the bushes near the river. Jane's legs turned to sand as they rushed by her toward the fort. Then she saw them: painted, rushing and jumping after the soldiers! And they saw her. They leaped and jumped and holding hands rushed toward her.

Sarah pushed by Jane into the house. Jane's petticoat caught on the door latch as she followed after Sarah.

"Git in!" Sarah shrieked, halfway into the root cellar. With her foot on the step, Jane grasped the trap door behind her. Sarah's arm flew up against Eve's efforts to get in after them with her children. "Nae!" Sarah screamed, disappearing into the opening with Jane stumbling behind her, the door coming down behind her head.

Jane huddled in the dark with her breathing bursting her lungs. Why had the Indians rushed upon them like that? Why was she huddled in this dark hole like a frightened animal? She should have been led by the hand through the sunlight to the sounds of redbreasts, flutes, and hautboys in her ears.

Sarah trembled against her.

Then the trap door suddenly flew open.

"*Friends! Friends!*" Sarah cried, as the Indians pulled the two women from the root cellar.

Outside on the road other Indians flew by the two women. One of them carried Sarah's mirror. Jane looked into the older woman's eyes.

"There maun be a mistak, lass!" Sarah cried to her, her face as white as linen. She put up her hand as though to ward off a blow and reached for Jane.

"Auntie!" Jane cried, unable to grasp Sarah's hand as she was pulled away from her. "Where are they taking you?"

"We maun git ta my cousin, we maun git ta 'im!" Sarah shrieked back at her, as the Indians half-carried her up the road away from Jane.

In the iron grasp of another Indian's hand over her arm, Jane stumbled and tripped on her petticoat after Sarah.

Out of breath when she reached the pine, Jane saw Sarah's petticoat on the ground at the side of the road ahead of her. She then glimpsed Sarah's bonneted head moving down the road among the trees when the Indians who had half-dragged her up the hill stopped at the spring.

Jane caught her breath. Lieutenants Palmer and Van Vecten lay dead, face down where the spring flowed over the side of the road. Private Standish stood near the tree with his arms tied and with blood on his shoe. Indians stood by the pine. She heard flat and distant firing back at the fort. She looked for Sarah, but now only heard the older woman's coughing far down the road. Private Standish stood ten feet from her—Jane tried to scream after Sarah, but her cry stuck in her throat.

Jane stood there in a frozen daze; she felt almost as though she was sitting back in Eva's frozen house that January with Paine's pamphlet calling for independence on her lap. She had no feeling in her right hand. She scarcely breathed as she looked at the trees, the Indians around her, and the dead soldiers on the side of the road. Her eyes rested on Standish's face as he stood only a short distance from her. His face was expressionless, but she saw his recognition of her in his eyes.

Then she saw a group of Indians running down the road toward her. She watched them come. She wondered what they were running toward. They came like wolves, their eyes upon her. They rushed upon her. She drew back from them—they rushed by her and at the Indian who held her. Rifle butts then thudded on flesh as the

Indian released his grip on her arm. They were fighting over her!
She gasped. Stepping back, her hand jerked involuntarily to her
throat. Louis Cook's words cried out at her: 'The warrior owns his
prisoner!' Her head turned as she watched them struggle over her.
She glanced again at Standish. Then the man who had pulled her
from the root cellar sprang away from the other Indians and
suddenly turned on her—he leveled his musket at her breast. She
looked down at the hollow, narrow and harsh barrel of the musket.
It looked like an odd fireplace iron about to speak to her about her
life going by her now. "No—" she groaned, turning her face away
as the barrel flashed in her eyes, making her oddly float over the
spring to David where he sat on the roots of the pine, the spring
flowing near his boots, and where she finally sighed to him, 'Your
hair is as crimson as the anemone. Are you pausing from the hunt,
leaving Aphrodite in her winged car high above to join me here,
David? I am Jenny with the red hair, your gift from God . . . '

'Jenny, let me draw your soul within my lips and drink your
love,' she heard him breathe, taking her in his arms and pressing
his lips to hers . . . .

44

Sunday July 27

As Jane was leaving Freel's in the morning, David waited on the steps of Daniel's house. Tortured by lack of news following his decision to send the Winnebagos for her after Thomas Williams had refused him, he had not slept.

"What's happening, for God's sake?" he mumbled aloud, on the verge of running down the road for her himself. Surely the Winnebagos should have returned by now!

As he looked through the gray morning mist a group of Indians and the man who sent the Winnebagos came toward the house.

"Langlade!" he called to the man, leaving the steps and meeting the group. "Any news?"

The short balding man put his hands on his hips "—I've heard nothing," he answered in his French and Indian accent. "The Bostonians have their pickets out."

David focused on the man's moccasins in the faint light. Of course, the rebels would post pickets after their skirmishing here at Daniel's yesterday. "Send these, too, then . . ." he said impulsively, indicating the Indians with Langlade. "What's three pounds fifteen shillings? I'll buy them all rum . . ."

Langlade cocked his head and shrugged his shoulders—it didn't matter to him, if this Lieutenant paid. His Indians had received no rewards on this expedition. Burgoyne would only pay for live prisoners, unless his Ottawas brought him the scalps of dead men. How unlike the French the English were! Langlade spoke quickly in Ottawa and gestured to David.

David looked among the stoic faces of the Indians. They would be needed if fighting broke out down there at Edward. The

Winnebagos could decoy the rebels, while the Ottawas brought her across the lines. But was he assessing the situation correctly? Were impulse and desperation dictating to him? For a moment he was confused as what to decide.

But the Ottawas grunted and left. And Langlade nodded to him and walked away. It was decided. Done!

Doubt instantly seized him. As the Ottawas faded into the mist, David turned after them. "Bring her back safely!" he shouted after them in a desperate afterthought, his words echoing hollowly in his own ears. How could he have forgotten Thomas Williams' injunction not to use Indians! But he couldn't stop them now.

Feeling as though a rock had fallen on him, David returned to the steps and pressed his forehead against the doorjamb. Why had the Ottawas appeared like that? He groaned in the doorway and turned his face away from the yard where the Tory rangers were lighting their cooking fires.

"Why are you shouting?" Solomon asked him, coming to the threshold behind him.

David's eyes wandered over the yard. Thin curtains of smoke wafted beneath the pines. "That half-breed, Langlade—" he half-answered sickly.

"What about him?"

"His Ottawas just left . . ." David's voice fell off. The sun burst through the trees making Greek pillars of the smoke.

"Why Ottawas after Winnebagos? I thought we had agreed."

"I know!" he snapped back, recalling the dangers Williams had warned him of in sending any Indians at all. "But something's happened and she's not back yet—and I thought two bands might be better . . ." he blurted out, desperation forcing him to admit responsibility for sending the Ottawas. "God! I should have sent her with Deborah to the Wings." He struck his knuckles against the door and lurched off the steps to the large pine in front of the house. The Tories' fires in the yard raised the bile in his throat. And sight of Freel standing on the road waiting for the expected British regiments entered in his ribs like a knife.

"We can't do anything now. Do the Ottawas know about the

Winnebagos?" Solomon asked. "Did you tell them there was already a band out, should they meet them?"

"I don't know what *he* said to them," David groaned, "but, they're on the same side."

Solomon shook his head. How could anyone tell? The two tribes might fight over her. "So you said nothing to them about the Winnebagos?"

"No," David choked.

"Relax. There's nothing you can do now. I'll get breakfast." Solomon scratched his chin and re-entered the house.

"Or *made* her go to Albany with John, anything, but this!" David shouted, sick at heart, at the empty doorway.

In the yard, he poked the nearly lifeless coals with a stick to cook what Solomon brought from the house. He thought bitterly about Williams, and his own stupidity in pinning his hopes on him. So what, if he knew these woods, or if his grandmother told him 'to prevent, if possible, the massacre of defenseless women and children.' But wasn't that why he first asked him to go for her? Yet the rebels had resisted every inch of ground, and he should never have agreed to Solomon's plan of using them. But he had jumped at the plan himself: wrote Jane from Skenesborough to go to Edward! Even Thomas had thought it was a good idea. The possibility of extricating her from Edward had made the quill quiver in his hand. Yet after Freel had taken his letter, Williams had refused: *You've come to conquer the country. If you succeed you'll have your white squaw: she is now safe, and to attempt to take her by force by our Indians may endanger her life, as there may be a skirmish . . . so she had better remain where she is now.* An so why had he done it? Because after the winter in Montreal and the battle of Hubbardton two weeks ago, he feared he would never see her again! Desperation had driven him to it, he had had no choice, but Langlade. Now, God only knew what would happen with two bands of Indians out there, and the rebels spoiling for a fight.

He gathered needles and twigs. His arms shook as he threw them on the coals, making smoke. As he was about to return to the house in giving up quickly re-kindling the fire, the needles suddenly fluttered like birds.

He stood there mesmerized by the flames and recalled how an evening fire had made bluebirds of her eyes and a sunset of her hair. He heard again the crickets' music, the owls' echoes, and the bass' splash on the moonlit river. Lying on the bank beneath the purple pines they had spoken of children, their home, and a mill. Jane's hair, softer than merino, had covered his naked chest. He had gathered it to his lips. When she wore it long, it was as smooth as milk, yet fresh as water. In the firelight it was either the color of ripe strawberries or the golden-red of autumn leaves. And her hair smelled like roses! And he never tired of stroking it. And how she would laugh, 'Would you still love me without it, David?' How desire tormented him now as then. His mouth against her ear, he would drink the scent of her hair.

Standing by the flames, he also relived that moment after her father's death when she spoke to him in the strawberry field in Lamington. As she had kneeled among the plants, he had realized that the 'sister' next door had become a woman. His throat had tightened, and he melted into the ground. Her hair lay like red silk over her back and shoulders. No longer the awkward girl he had grown up with, flowers sprang under her feet—her arms, bare below her elbows, were as fine as marble to the ends of her fingers. And she had sung as she had picked the berries and looked at him with eyes as blue as the eggs of redbreasts.

David. She had purred.

When you asked me to come, I . . .

She touched her hair. Her eyes had pearl-like depth.

You are going north . . . .

You want to go too? he could scarcely stand; his heart had thumped like a drum.

Yes, her eyes answered, revealing not a stream to measure, but a river to chart.

They had walked along the Peapack afterwards, the light deepening her eyes to a green-blue. The crinoline of her petticoat had pressed against his legs. He had followed her, drunk with desire. He stood at a warm spring wanting to drown there. And how he had worked on mills and bridges, given in to his mother to save her income from his father's family believing his inheritance would save them in the end—and how desolate Montreal had been without her. It was then he had realized waiting for her was worse than death!

"Be patient," Solomon said of his staring vacantly at the invisible flames dancing in the morning sunlight. He then kneeled and skewered some beef on a rod and placed it over the fire making the fat hiss.

"I can't eat any of that." David surfaced from his memories. If only they had stayed on the Peapack, he thought with a groan.

"You must eat something," Solomon insisted, filling a cup with tea for him.

"Drink?" Yarns asked, appearing from behind the house and pushing a jug against his elbow.

David's chest tightened. Yarns' hat, pushed up over his forehead, revealed a bandana of white skin above his eyebrows. Yarns swayed, his grin revealing two dark upper teeth in a face of gray stubble.

David elbowed the jug away.

"We're marching." Yarns declared, pushing between the brothers to the fire.

"Get away from me!" David shouted.

"But we're so close ta good ole Edward, Davey, lad, and ya'll be meetin' yar luve," Yarns drawled.

David clenched his fists.

"I told ya ta marry her," Yarns continued drunkenly. "But you sent Injuns—"

Hollow musket fire then came from down the road.

David jumped to his feet.

"It's nothing," Solomon said calmly. But he cocked his head in that direction. There was then another volley of musketry.

"Don't count on it bein' nothin', Solomon, whare Injuns are consarned, right Davey? And didn't I tell ya ta marry her?" Yarns turned to him.

"I'll put a ball through you!" he threatened, gripping his musket.

"Now, camon, Davey!" the man exclaimed, shrinking back away from him. "Ya wouldn't hit a friend, not right here."

"David, the army's here, and there's brother Thomas with them," Solomon intervened, pointing.

The Twenty-Fourth in their red coats with white lace, willow green facing and red and green stripes were schooling like tropical fish at the crossroads. David's anger, boiling like pitch after eight months of Yarns, subsided when he saw the soldiers and his brother, and saw that Yarns had left.

"God help him, if he's with us when we advance . . ."

"Forget about him. Look, there's Fraser too." The Brigadier rode his white horse at the head of the marching Twenty-Fourth.

David had difficulty looking at the man. Fraser's brilliance at once incriminated him for the stupidity of what he had just done while, given the Brigadier's near disaster at Hubbardton, a cloud seemed to hang over the man which filled David with foreboding. Yet Fraser *was* resolute and daring. He was the most respected officer in the army. He had taught the English light infantry to flight on the fly like the rebels, and his infantry was the cream of Burgoyne's army—and he *did* succeed in everything he attempted. And yet, for all his daring genius, his swift pursuit of the rebels to Hubbardton, with the remnants of this very regiment schooling before him, had nearly ended in disaster! The Twenty-Fourth had lost its commanding officer, Major Grant, and a fifth of its men when it attacked Warner's Green Mountain Boys on the other side of Sucker Brook—even the Twenty-Ninth and the Thirty-Fourth commanded by Balcarres suffered the same losses from Francis' Eleventh Massachusetts who repulsed their three assaults on the hill. A cloud of doom hung over Fraser which would have engulfed him at Hubbardton, if Reidesel's Jagers hadn't arrived to save his left from being driven in by Francis. But didn't that mean the man had luck?

David kept his face turned away from the Brigadier. The coincidence of his being Sarah McNeil's cousin, and that he had

asked Jane to wait there for him filled him with mixed hope and
dread. He didn't know which side of the face of fate would be
shown him, and he feared looking at Fraser.

The assembly drum then sounded and two other regiments
appeared down the road. He looked at them and the sunlight
flashing off their bayonets and new rifles. Events could change
quickly—when it seemed the Advanced Corps was lost at
Hubbardton, fate had turned against the rebels and, instead of
himself or Fraser scythed down like wheat by rebel bullets, it was
Francis who lay dead on the hill, and it was the victorious British
officers who read his papers and took his watch, knowing how
close—within a wing beat—Francis had come to wiping them all
out! If fate favored the army, fate would have to give him Jane. The
gray clouds over the green hills of Hubbardton had mysteriously
propelled him south to her.

He let his eyes then fall on Fraser. How bold he was; how clear
were his blue eyes; how compassionate he had been toward his
wounded at Hubbardton when he knew he had to leave them
behind when necessity drove him through Castleton to
Skenesborough to rejoin Burgoyne. Yet, how those wounded men
left on the hill at Hubbardton for ten days until they could be
littered back to Skenesborough had suffered. David didn't want to
think about it—he couldn't think of Fraser in any one way. He was
like the smudged globe of a lit lantern, a dark kind of light. And
his hopes for Jane now emitted a dark kind of light. God, why had
he sent those Indians.

Ottawas, Sacs, Fox, Menomenies, Winnebagos, Sioux,
Chippewas, St. Regis and Kahnawake Mohawks were now
gathering across the road in front of Daniel's. He had sent these
very Indians for her . . . . The ones she had protested to him of—
the French Indians from the Lakes! And there, St. Luc, paroled
from Esopus, stood with his second, Langlade, and his lieutenant
and nephew, Gautier de Vierville, and Pierre Queret, Amable de
Gere, called the La Rose, Louis Hamelin . . . all the French and
Indians who had defeated Braddock. And hadn't Sarah filled Jane's
ears with William Henry, Louisburg and Quebec? He now imagined

how Jane had reacted when she received his note telling her to wait and that he was sending Indians for her. But fate *had* urged his daring decision when Williams refused him. Something outside him had made him call upon the Indians, and made him think of them as his 'Jagers' at the critical moment to bring her safely to him; and if he had waived in the grips of destiny, fate might have refused him! Whether he had acted from daring or desperation, success had to crown his plan just as it had crowned Fraser's pursuit and final successful encounter with the rebels at Hubbardton. The pattern had been set for him, and, like it or not now, he had been caught in it.

"Don't block the way, Lieutenant. Join your Corps."

A cavalryman's stirrup caught his belt buckle as the man rode by him. A knot of officers, including Fraser, his nephew, Captain Alexander Fraser, and Majors Ackland and Balcarres entered the house. The red-striped Fifty-Third paraded behind the Twenty-Fourth.

"Come on, David," Solomon said to him, "you can't just stand here."

David followed Solomon and his other brothers, Jonathan, John, and Dunham. His legs bore him along as though he was dreaming of walking. He asked about his brother Thomas with the same blank indifference.

"Where is Thomas?"

"Returned to the artillery in the rear."

When David and his brothers reached the road and joined Jessup's Corps, lethargy seized him. Nerves before the advance, his anguish at having heard nothing of the Indians' mission, the hot sun and the dust stirred up by the soldiers' boots, it didn't matter, the effect was the same: he just stood there on the road feeling that an enormous pressure on his head, shoulders and chest was pressing him into the very road. But what did a few farmers' grisly scalps taken by the Winnebagos and the Ottawas along the way matter? They had gone for his beloved and chaplain Bruendel had blessed the undertaking in agreeing to marry them—didn't he have faith? Weren't Solomon and Thomas going to stand by him? He hadn't gone to Woolwich, but why should he have gone there if the military effect of Thomas rank and uniform was the same with Thomas at his side? Oh, what did it matter? Only, where was Jenny? he asked himself as the hot July sun beat down on him.

As he struggled to keep his head up and his eyes open in the hot sun and dust of the road, the coyote cries of returning warriors echoed from across the field where the Indians assembled.

"Who are *they*? What are those shouts?" Solomon asked, catching David's shoulder, inferring these might be their Indians who were re-entering the camp.

David broke from the ranks and looked beyond Ebenezer's Tory rangers to the house where the cries seemed to come from. He then saw Indians enter Daniel's house and heard a woman's high-pitched cries break across the heads of the soldiers. "Oh, God!" he shouted, lunging past Solomon and flying across the road to the house where he burst through the hall into the parlor.

"'WHY DID YE SEND YER MURTHERIN' SAVAGES ARTER US!" Sarah McNeil shrieked breathlessly as she stood half-dressed in her torn chemise in the faint light against the black fireplace.

"I thought you were in New York City, Cousin," Fraser addressed her. "Get her clothes!" he boomed to his orderly.

David lurched toward her, looking frantically for Jane among the officers and Indians. "Where's Jenny!" he shouted at her.

"Camin' arter me, David, wi' th' savages," Sarah cried, grasping his shirt and pressing her face against him.

"Where is she!" He turned like a blind man from her not seeing or hearing her. Then he wheeled back around to her again and saw her pointing. David gasped. "But I did not send him!" he cried, his eyes adjusting to the dark room. "I didn't send any of you!" He spun on his heel and clutched Sarah's arm and pointed at another Indian. "There, that man brought you, Sarah. And where's the other woman?" he demanded, throwing himself on a Winnebago of the first band whom he recognized.

"Th' lassie was behind me . . ." Sarah repeated from behind him. "And whare's Polly?" she sobbed, her face wrinkling uncontrollably. The orderly then draped a coat over her. "Polly was wi' Eva, David . . ."

Her cousin, Simon, shook his head and put his hand on her heaving shoulder. "'Tis a conquered country and we must wink at these things," he pronounced stoically.

"Wink! Who'd a thoght ye'd brang savages, Simon!" Sarah wailed back at him. "Hir we ware waitin' for ye, an' a pack o' deils descend upon us. How caud ye brang savages, gin ye're tryin' ta free th' countrie? Hae ye nae remembrance o' th' last war, man? If ye thoght ta win th' countrie, ye lost it now! An' ye call yersels civilized. O, man, wat hoppen'd ta Jenny? I'll scald yer very skin wi' my tears, man, if onythin' hast hoppen'd ta hir!"

A cloud passed outside and the room darkened. Choking, David addressed the Indian he recognized. "Where's Langlade!" he demanded of him, before seeing Langlade himself in the doorway behind the Indian. "Where is she?" He rushed over to him.

Langlade merely stepped aside and another Winnebago came through the doorway bearing a black ribbon and rose attached to what looked like the roan tail of a horse.

David's head jerked back, and the black strawberry stenciling near the ceiling over the door to the parlor blurred as he looked at it. He raised his arms from the elbows and took the familiar weight of her hair into his hands.

"Better one die than two nations quarrel," the Winnebago said in broken English.

David raised her hair to his lips and smelled the rose still in it . . . .

EPILOGUE

1777-1790

As news of Jane's death shot through the army, Solomon kept David from recovering her body. "No one's to leave camp until Burgoyne arrives in camp," he told him, trying to read eyes as cloudy as bottom water.

But the brothers didn't have long to wait, for Burgoyne arrived that night, Sunday, July 27, and ordered a council with the Indians for the next day.

The shade of Montcalm hung over the council. When called to stand forward the Winnebago warrior bore himself as a man who had committed no offense. Wiser warriors answered for him: he had feared a counter attack from the Bostonians from the fort after capturing the woman; the Ottawas had intercepted him and challenged his possession of her near the spring, and she had died to end the quarrel. He did not know she was the white man's squaw. The young warrior, for his part, made no apology, but an older warrior said of him: "He is a rising young warrior. We Indians regret the death of the red-haired woman."

But the General feared other murders. He knew what effect such killings would have on the spirit of the rebels and on those against the war in England.

"I enjoined you in May on the Bouquet River that no payment would be given except for live prisoners and the scalps of slain soldiers. This man will hang!"

"These Winnebagos joined you only eleven days ago," St Luc protested, rising to his feet, "and you didn't repeat your injunction at Skenesborough. If you hang this Indian, the rest of them will desert you and waste the country from here to Montreal."

Burgoyne observed his old French enemy, well aware of St. Luc's resentment of the Americans after their alleged treatment of him at Esopus when he declared, on his release two months ago to Governor Tryon, the necessity of loosing the savages on the frontiers of "these rascals to terrify them; necessary to do this summer to finish the war which they had started." He would never forget his injuries from "these beggars, *les miserables Rebels. Qu'il faut brutalizer les affaires.*" And St. Luc, serving without commission, had not honored his parole not to take up arms against the rebels. A thorn in the General's throat, he had worked the Indians to white heat before the expedition. He would have wasted Canada himself with no British army to prevent it . . . . And so, did David Jones himself hire the Indians? the General asked.

"Did you hire them, Lieutenant?"

"No," David answered, feeling close to death. He had *not* hired them to take her life. His mind swam in the hot morning as he held the pouch containing her hair and the black ribbon she had worn as he answered the question put to him in council. And what did it matter, if Burgoyne's orderly officer had already entered in the army records, "Lieutenant David Jones' account for money paid for an Indian pilot to go for Intelligence . . . Three pounds, fifteen Shillings," the price of a barrel of rum, to prove his testimony false? He lied now to salve his grief, to save the honor of the army, and to protect Sarah McNeil's listing in the army's records as a Loyalist Ranger; just as he denied the army's chaplain, Bruendel, had agreed to marry them, despite what Burgoyne later wrote to the rebel general Gates in early September that 'Two chiefs . . . had brought her off for the purpose of security, not violence to her person." He would pay the price of honor to preserve the power of princes.

The General swallowed hard. What good would it do to hang this Indian? It was a heinous act, but he had no choice but to capitulate to them, St. Luc, and to the Ministry responsible for raising the Indians. Let Jones blame them in not saying that he had hired them, notwithstanding his own later contradiction in writing Gates. So the warrior went free.

The Indians had no booty, no English milk, and no payment for scalps. What war valued the enemy's life over the warrior's? They took no towns, brought back no women to re-populate their wasted villages! "Let the English war among themselves," they counseled the following day before one thousand of them took the trails back to Canada.

And so Burgoyne's dwindling army marched, and David searched for his beloved. He looked for her body near the spring beneath the pine he knew so well. He stood on the bank of the sloping road and saw where she fell in her blood on the leaves . . .

A boy from Sandy Hill saw him standing there on the hill near the spring and the pine . . .

"Jane McCrea," the boy said, approaching him, using her name as though he knew her, "was buried yesterday south of the fort next to Lieutenant Van Vecten. Mistress Bell placed a cap over her wounds . . ." the youth's voice echoed as clear as a mourning bell.

"What was she wearing?" David half-sobbed, his heart like twigs as he felt her shape on the leaves with his hands.

"A black petticoat. The Indians cut off the bottom of her frock. She was dressed for her wedding, we were told. They pollarded her, Mister," the boy said, wondering at how the man stroked the leaves.

David found the soft earth of the twin graves off the road south of the fort. He sat with his head in his hands and wept over the mounded earth.

"Bury her hair here, David. Let her rest. Let the chaplain say the words," Solomon tried to console him. But he couldn't reach David in his grief, and the army marched through Edward without them.

The two brothers stopped at their mother's farm, and David gazed upon the knoll and the flowering nightshade near the stone outcropping where he and Jane had planned to build their house. He gazed at the black mildewed lumber of their future home.

"I can't see her," he said of his mother, the tears splashing in his eyes.

But Sarah Jones had heard the news, and she demanded that they give up their commissions.

"We can't," Solomon said for both of them.

Sarah Jones looked vainly for the light in David's eyes. His expression by the door left her speechless. "Davey!" she cried as he left the house.

The brothers rejoined the army, and for two months Solomon explained to David what occurred. It was like speaking to a figure carved of wood:

The rebels had scorched the countryside and driven off the cattle from here to Albany. The army weakened for lack of food. The horses couldn't draw the wagons and cannons . . .

Word has come that the rebels have turned St. Leger back at Fort Stanwix . . . The Oneidas and Tuscaroras—and Cook— remember him? Were at Oriskany . . . do you hear me, David?

"The army grows desperate. Burgoyne still listens to Skene, but instead of advising a road through a marsh, he now advises sending the Germans, our Corps, and what remains of St. Luc's Indians to Bennington for forage and fresh horses . . . ."

"What month is it?" David only asked vacantly.

"August."

"Only August? How come she hasn't come yet? Oh, where is my Jenny with the red hair? Oh, wait a few days, Solomon," David said darkly, suddenly foreseeing the outcome of Bennington through the veils of his grief, "and only those few Indians will survive Bennington."

"And so how many lost at Bennington?" he asked with an odd curiosity a few days later, as he observed the river flowing to its inevitable end in the sea. It wasn't a river any more, only a cold dark flowing of his own life's blood.

"All nine-hundred of them were lost, except for St. Luc's Indians as you forecast. It was Warner and Stark again. But worse than Breed's Hill this time."

"Oh, Warner and Stark?" David welcomed the names of Warner and Stark as though they had been pistol shots to the brain. He regretted he hadn't fallen to Warner at Hubbardton. It was a cruel fate to have only his jacket riddled with bullet holes.

"You should have heard St. Luc berate Burgoyne for not sending reinforcements."

"Oh? I should have? And what good would reinforcements have done our cursed countrymen? Who might be worth reinforcing among them? Our Corps? I know about reinforcements in this war . . ., see how I've been reinforced. She is always with me." David touched the pouch tenderly.

"But the Yankees tied them to their horses and dragged them through every town . . ."

David laughed bitterly. "I wish they had done that to me. I might have met John. He might have saved me with a musket ball, or sent me to the Simsbury mines in Connecticut with the others who have betrayed their nation," he said, his mind wandering. "He should have sent me to Jen. I should have been her husband beneath the ground, not some rebel soldier."

"You don't understand. Burgoyne won't let this abuse of prisoners go," Solomon said.

"No, of course not. He'll sound the alarm like a cuckoo," David replied emptily, alluding to Burgoyne's protest to Gates. "And Gates will reply stirring the horror and conscience of the nation . . ." as he did in early September:

> that the savages of America should, in their warfare, mangle and scalp the unhappy prisoners who fall into their hands is neither new nor extraordinary, but that the famous Lieutenant General Burgoyne, in whom the fine gentleman is united with the soldier and scholar, should hire the savages of America to scalp Europeans, and the descendants of Europeans; nay more, that he should pay the price for each scalp so barbarously taken, is more than will be believed in Europe, until authenticated facts shall, in every gazette, confirm the truth of the horrid tale.
>
> Miss M'Crea, a young lady, lovely to the sight, of virtuous character, and amiable disposition, engaged to an officer of your army, was, with other women and children, taken out of a house near Fort Edward, carried into the woods, and there scalped and mangled in a most shocking manner. Two parents with their six children, were all treated

with the same inhumanity, while quietly resting in their once happy and peaceful dwelling. The miserable fate of Miss M'Crea was particularly aggravated, by being dressed to receive her promised husband; but met her murderer employed by you. Upwards of one hundred men, women and children, have perished by the hands of the ruffians to whom, it is asserted, you have paid the price of blood.

"Now Jane's murder is in every gazette, on every tongue, in every ballad!" he cried with sudden passion. "But let them come from every town and hamlet! Let them skewer me on their pitchforks and tear at me with their scythes for what I've done to her! That Indian pollarded my love, the boy told me! My Jenny with the flowing hair *pollarded* like some tree."

Speechless, Solomon observed his brother. His heart turned in his chest. But how true of Gates' publicly throwing her death at Burgoyne. His writing publicly of Jane's death had raised the countryside against the army! Washington had even dispatched Morgan's Riflemen from the south to meet them—they ran all the way without wagons or horses . . . . And where was Howe after St. Leger had been turned back? Gone to Philadelphia! The rebels then had stopped the vaunted three-pronged attack to separate New York from New England! The grand design conjured up by the Ministry smoking calabashes in London had turned the soul of a Continent against them.

Through the smoke and fire of Freeman's Farm, David saw Louis Cook and Atsitsina, and Morgan's Riflemen who never missed . . . and here Burgoyne had only gone out to test their line, "A reconnaissance," leaving fifteen hundred of his best soldiers dead on the meadow! David groaned for her as the glory of the British army lay dying in the moonlit field where the wolves fed upon them . . . . and he groaned for her as his own brother, Thomas, pride of the artillery, lay dead on the field! And what a walkover these rebels would be. "The war cannot last," he himself had even written to her.

And the army staggered after Freeman's Farm, and with it the surviving Jones brothers staggered, their strength together with the army's drained way from hunger, exposure, exhaustion . . .

In October, the army retreated, but the thousands of militiamen, responding to Jane's murder, choked off the roads, and the army was forced to perch miserably behind the jumbled protection of the mounds of Bemis Heights.

"We're all going to die here like Jane and Thomas, unless we get out," Solomon said gravely.

"I want to stay and die with her. My brother is not enough. I can't leave her here alone. What is David Jones without Jenny McCrea?"

The sky poured forth musket lead and cannon balls. Arnold attacked, "Come on, lads!" and broke the Germans. Morgan's Riflemen shot the crupper from under Fraser's horse's tail. "They've marked you, General!" his men shouted at the Brigadier. "A soldier does not turn his back," came the Brigadier's reply before a second shot took him out of his saddle.

The next day they carried the dead Brigadier to the top of the hill to his open grave and Bruendel's voice, like a nightingale's, was lost in the rebel cannonade which followed them. Fraser wedded Death too! Unable to retreat, the army died on Bemis Heights. Saratoga! David choked on this harvest of death so near the yawning lawns of Schuyler's estate which Jane admired, so near the flowing river they made love by in the moonlight, so far away from where she lay in the earth beside Van Vecten.

Burgoyne received Gates' terms.

"We must leave. The rebels will kill us, if we're on the roll," Solomon said to him.

"I'll be closer to her if they take me. They will tie me to the tail of a horse. I will wear the tail of a horse from the back of my head."

"Listen, David. Burgoyne's surrendering on the seventeenth. We have little time."

"I don't care . . . I want John to put a bullet here," David replied, pointing to his heart.

"Burgoyne gives us three days to get to Canada. You're leaving with me before dawn," Solomon insisted.

David looked into the fire, finding it easy not to hear Solomon. Canada? Williams, the Indian sitting next to him, lived there. Canada was *his* home. His own home was where Jane lay.

"St. Luc and his Indians have already left. It will rain all night. We've got to get out before morning."

David didn't notice Solomon look into the dark woods. If Solomon allowed it, he would have thrust his hands into the ashes of the fire, the ashes of his heart, and rub his once passionate dreams into his face, dying where he sat.

"The Americans have fighting spirit," Thomas Williams said to him.

The Indian's words chilled him. "Yes, they have fighting spirit. How can it be otherwise with her blood in their veins?" But the Indian meant no harm, he admired their kind of prowess, though if he only knew how he spoke from the grave! Yes, he had fought for the British and knew white men's war, knew spirited and rangy men could and did defeat a grand army, and he knew he would miss nothing he didn't already know when the English would smash their rifles in impotent rage when they stacked them in surrender to the rebels. So humiliated were they, so unlike real men they couldn't bear the shame of being watched by their conquerors and must have it stipulated that no Yankee would see them surrender! Such smallness of heart didn't deserve a Continent. Yes, the rebels fought better, and if he had fought alongside them, he would have fought better and won too, would have worked the same hills, built mills on the same river, breathed the same air, threshed the same wheat and loved his Jane whose life, given his strange husbandry, helped birth a nation! His countrymen had defeated him; he had defeated himself in his pride.

If he had listened to Thomas Williams, Jenny would still be alive . . . . If he himself had listened to her cries, he *himself* would be alive. She had told him that this was not an Indian war. The pain in his chest filled his eyes with tears. He had sent the dragons she had feared all along. They had pollarded her, the boy said! Slaughtered her and ripped her hair off like a wig. Pollarded! That tender face and those eyes; that fair skin laid to the bone by the knife—"N-o-o—"

"Listen to me, David . . ." Solomon said, seeing his brother's tears streaming down his face in the firelight turn the dirt on his boots to mud.

That Indian had pollarded that head! He couldn't speak, she blocked his tongue. He would never find his way through the woods in the dark. He was a dead man.

—Even after his mother had joined him and Solomon in Augusta Township in Canada, he continued to grieve for Jane and wished himself in the grave beside her, the pollarded woman who helped give victory to the rebels at Saratoga; and he grieved upon the French who entered the war because of her and Saratoga. His Jane had been more powerful than Franklin! He brooded when even the Elder Pitt had spoken in Parliament of her death, turning even the English against their war. Yes, Lord Suffolk's condoning using Indians against the Americans, "to use all the means that God and nature had put into our hands" to put down the rebellion, had prompted Pitt's outcry against the horror of it:

> I am astonished, shocked to hear such principles expressed;
> to hear them avowed in this house or even this country. My lords,
> I did not intend to encroach again on your attention, but I
> cannot repress my indignation. I feel myself impelled to speak.
> My lords, we are called upon as members of this house, as
> Christians, to protest against such horrible barbarity. That God
> and nature had put into our hands! what ideas of God and
> nature that noble lord may entertain I know not, but I know
> that such detestable principles are equally abhorrent to religion
> and humanity. What, to attribute the sacred sanction of God
> and nature to the massacres of the Indian scalping knife! to the
> cannibal savage, torturing, murdering, devouring, drinking
> the blood of his mangled victims! such notions shock every precept
> of morality, every feeling of humanity, every sentiment of honour.
> These abominable principles and this more abominable avowal
> of them, demand the most decisive indignation. I call upon that

right reverend and his most learned bench to vindicate the religion of their God, to support the justice of their country. I call upon the bishops to interpose the unsullied sanctity of their ermine, to save us from this pollution. I call upon the honour of your lordships, to reverence the dignity of your ancestors, and to maintain your own. I call upon the spirit and humanity of my country, to vindicate the national character. I invoke the genius of the constitution. From the tapestry that adorns these walls, the immortal ancestor of this noble lord, frowns with indignation at the disgrace of this country. In vain did he defend the liberty, and establish the religion of Britain against the tyranny of Rome, if these worse than popish cruelties and inquisitorial practices are endured among us. To send forth the merciless cannibal for blood!—against whom? Your protestant brethren— to lay waste their country, to desolate their dwellings, and extirpate their race and name, by the aid and instrumentality of these horrible hell-hounds of war! Spain can no longer boast preeminence of barbarity. She armed herself with blood-hounds to extirpate the wretched natives of Mexico, but we more ruthless, loose these dogs of war against our own countrymen in America, endeared to us by every tie that should sanctify humanity. My lords, I solemnly call upon your lordships, and upon every order of men in the state, to stamp upon this infamous procedure the indelible stigma of the public abhorrence. More particularly I call upon the holy prelates of our religion to do away with this iniquity; let them perform lustration to purify their country from this deep and deadly sin. My lords, I am old and weak, and at present unable to say more, but my feelings and indignation were too strong to have said less. I could not have slept this night in my bed, nor reposed my head upon my pillow, without giving this vent to my eternal abhorrence of such enormous and preposterous principles.

The Indians! He himself and the British were responsible for what they had done! God and nature had recoiled at this war, and Jane had atoned for the horrors of it. Her election—*Pollarded!*

We Indians suffer from you white people. We struggle for our own survival . . . The Great Spirit has chastened you.

Thomas' words fell upon his ears like bloody rain. He had advised against sending Indians—he knew what war had done to his people. So why hadn't he, too, listened to his grandmother on protecting women and children? Had his grandmother's warning come from her own father's pulpit at Deerfield? What divinity had guided her fateful admonition to her grandson?

David brooded when he explored the Ottawa for the British army after fleeing to Canada. By the river with his back against a tree and the broadsheet of Pitt's speech on his lap, he remembered how Jane wished that summer day in Ballston to honeymoon in London—

'And where would you like to be married?"

'Albany,' she had answered, holding the thin crystal of the wine glass between her fingers and kissing him with wine on her lips.

And our honeymoon?

London, she had answered with the virginal lustrative grace of a woman of promise and hope, her eyes the color of the eggs of redbreasts.

David cried at finding her example on Pitt's lips and learning the French Court spoke of it! He took his finger off the trigger and he leaned against the tree wishing to die, but appalled death would only erase his precious knowledge of her that day they lay together in his mother's house—

He brooded on the news drifting to Canada of the battles of Kaskaskia, Vincenes, Chillicothe, King's Mountain, Cowpens, Guilford Courthouse—and finally he brooded on Yorktown, the Peace of Paris and the ratification of American Independence in 'eighty-four—

He grieved how his intended bride had wedded a nation. His tears scalded his cheeks and ate away his heart—

But he didn't think of Daniel and Deborah and their two-thousand acre loss, how as sutler and sutler's wife with their two children they drew provisions until the end of the war at Isle Aux Nois before settling in Elizebethtown—

And he gave little thought to the memory of his brother,

Thomas, killed among the artillerymen at Freeman's Farm, who at one time couldn't be spoken of because of Golden Hill—

And he didn't think of Polly Hunter and Peter Tearse who refused to let the war prevent their marrying seven weeks after Jane's death prior to Freeman's Farm; nor did he think of the new house they built for themselves in Fort Edward in 'eighty; nor that Sarah McNeil lived with them—

Nor did he think of the Jessups' lost property and their failure in England to convince the King to recompense them for their loss . . .

Nor of the Johnsons who continued to fight a bloody frontier war in New York against the Americans dooming themselves and the Iroquois to the futile British cause until Sir Guy became Superintendent of Indian Affairs in Canada at the end of the war, having finally lost his influence among the displaced Mohawks—

Nor did he think of Freel who had carried his messages to her, and his drawing provisions for Deborah and their children at St. Jean's sur Richelieu; who became an officer in the Loyalist Rangers in 'eighty-three; and who returned to Edward after the war to look for his property without leaving a record as to his success—

Nor of Content Wing and James Higson reunited through Daniel's efforts before the war's end to rebuild and prosper together with the whole Wing family—

Nor of Thomas Williams who had sat next to him by the fire and who had escaped with him from Bemis Heights that cold and rainy October morning before the army surrendered at Saratoga; who continued to serve the British until the war ended, after which he traveled to Massachusetts to renew his family ties through his grandmother, Eunice Williams, of Deerfield—

Nor of Louis Cook to whom he sold his wig, who with his Oneidas and Tuscaroras fought 'like Bull dogs' at Saratoga after Oriskany; who the Congress, at Schuyler's bidding, was made Lieutenant Colonel for his service—

Nor, and least of all, did he think of Yarns who returned to Kingsbury after the war to reclaim the land his sons worked, only to be run out of town like a common thief never to be seen again—

Nor did he think of John, for, if he had thought of him, he might have known he would not have agreed to publicizing Jane's death for the grief and humiliation it had caused him—and Wheeler Case would not have written those poems and ballads about her which had whipped the people to such resistance—had Burgoyne not first charged Gates with rebel cruelty toward the Tory prisoners at Bennington.

Nor did he think of Eva, the mother of Jane's nephews and nieces, though he felt her death in 'eighty the same year the Tories torched John's farm, forcing him to rebuild in Salem where he remarried and became First Clerk of Washington County after the war . . . (though David would have mourned had he learned John and his new wife, Eleanor McNaughton, named their first daughter after his sister:

John heard the baby's cries. They accompanied the fluttering of a sparrow in the roadside dust outside the window. He thought of General Washington's remarks as a fitting eulogy for his sister when he wrote in August of 'seventy-seven in response to Burgoyne's Proclamation:

> Harassed as we are by unrelenting persecution, obliged by every tie to repel violence by force, urged by self-preservation to exert the strength which Providence has given us to defend our natural rights against the aggressor; we appeal to the hearts of all mankind for the justice of our cause; its event we submit to Him who speaks the fate of nations, in humble confidence that as his omniscient eye taketh note even of the sparrow that falleth to the ground, so He will not withdraw his countenance from a people who humbly array themselves under his banner in defence of the noblest principles with which He hath adorned humanity.

God's omniscient eye had noted that sparrow that fell.

The woman helping in Eleanor's delivery—Dinah now living with her husband—came into the room behind him, and the sparrow flew away.

"A little girl, Colonel."

John turned from the window and the flitting sparrow and beheld the red-haired baby. He took her in his arms. "We'll name her 'Jane' in memory of my sister," he said.)

No, he wouldn't think of John because as he, David Jones, walked the long and empty wilderness of the Ottawa in his broken surveyor's step, his cheeks furrowed, his heart rutted with grief, he thought only of his Jenny, until that day in seventeen-ninety when, with her name still on his parched lips, sudden death finally brought him *peace* at the age of forty.

BIBLIOGRAPHY

Anburey, T. WITH BURGOYNE FROM QUEBEC. Toronto: MacMillan of Canada, 1963.

_____. TRAVELS THROUGH THE INTERIOR PARTS OF AMERICA. 2 Vols. 1789.

Becker, J. P. SEXAGENARY. Munsell, 1866.

Bevier, A. G. THE INDIANS: OR NARRATIVES OF MASSACRES AND DEPREDATIONS ON ThE FRONTIER. Roundout: Town of Wawarsing, 1975, reprint of 1846 edition.

Boyland, B.R. BENEDICT ARNOLD THE DARK EAGLE. New York: W.W. Norton, 1973.

Briaddy, Katherine Q. YE OLD DAYS, A HISTORY OF BURNT HILLS-BALLSTON LAKE. Ballston Spa: The Journal Press, 1974.

Brown, Lloyd, A., and Peckham, Howard, H. edits. THE REVOLUTIONARY WAR JOURNALS OF HENRY DEARBORN, 1775-1783. New York: Da Capo Press, 1971.

Brown, W. THE GOOD AMERICANS. New York: William Morrow and Co., Inc., 1969.

Burgoyne, General John. A STATE OF THE EXPEDITION FROM CANADA, AS LAID BEFORE THE HOUSE OF COMMONS. J. Almon,1780.

Carleton to Lord Dartmouth, Letter dated Nov. 20th, 1775, Public Archives of Canada.

COLDEN PAPERS.

Commager, N.S., and Morris, R.B. THE SPIRIT OF 'SEVENTY-SIX Vol 1. Indianapolis: Bobbs-Merrill Co., Inc., 1958.

Dann, John C. ed. THE REVOLUTION REMEMBERED— EYEWITNESS ACCOUNTS OF THE WAR OF INDEPENDENCE. Chicago: University of Chicago Press, 1977.

Digby, Lieutenant William. THE BRITISH INVASION FROM THE NORTH. Digby's Journal of the Campaigns of Generals Carleton and Burgoyne from Canada, 1776-1777. New York: Da Capo Press, 1970.

DOCUMENTS RELATING TO THE COLONIAL HISTORY OF NEW YORK.

Egly, T.W., Jr. HISTORY OF THE FIRST NEW YORK REGIMENT, 1775-1783. Hampton: Peter E. Randall, Pub., 1981.

Dunham, Sarah M. Letter, Kingsbury, October 20, 1843. Fort Edward Historical Society.

Dupuy, Colonel Ernest R, "THE BATTLE OF HUBBARDTON, A CRITICAL ANALYSIS," Prepared for the State of Vermont Board of Historic Sites, December 1960.

Fitch, Asa, Dr. Winston Adler, ed. AS WE WERE.

_____. HISTORY OF THE TOWN OF SALEM (Salem: The Salem Press, 1927.)

_____. THEIR OWN VOICES, ORAL ACCOUNTS OF EARLY SETTLERS IN WASHINGTON COUNTRY, COLLECTED BY DR. ASA FITCH, ed. Winston Adler. Interlaken, 1983).

Flick, A. C. THE AMERICAN REVOLUTION IN NEW YORK. Port Washington: Ira J. Freedman, Inc, 1926.

"Gen. Fraser's Account of Burgoyne's Campaign on Lake Champlain and the Battle of Hubbardton," Stevens' Facsimiles, Vol XVI, No. 1571.

Gerlach, D.R. PHILIP SCHUYLER AND THE AMERICAN REVOLUTION IN NEW YORK 17331777. Lincoln: University of Nebraska Press, 1964.

GLENS FALLS POST STAR articles on the Wing Family: 1 /25/ 83; 1/11 /33; 1/12/33; 9/3/37.

Goodrich, John E., ed. THE STATE OF VERMONT—ROLLS OF THE SOLDIERS IN THE REVOLUTIONARY WAR, 1775 to 1783. Rutland: The Tuttle Co., 1904.

Graymont, Barbara. THE IROQUOIS IN THE AMERICAN REVOLUTION. Syracuse: University of Syracuse Press, 1972.

Hadden, Lt. James M. HADDEN'S JOURNAL AND ORDERLY BOOKS. Freeport: Books for Libraries Press, 1 884, 1970.

HALDIMAND PAPERS, LOYALIST VOLUMES, PUBLIC ARCHIVES LIST OF LOYALISTS. Ms Group 21, Vol B 166, 167. The National Archives of Canada, Ottawa.

Henry, Alexander. ATTACK AT MICHILIMACKINAC. Mackinac Island, Michigan: Trikraft, Inc., 1978.

Hill, William H. OLD FORT EDWARD. Fort Edward: Privately Printed, 1929.

HISTOIRE DES GRANDES FAMILLES FRANCOIS DU CANADA.

Holden, A. W. A HISTORY OF THE TOWN OF QUEENSBURY. Albany: Munsell, 1874.

Howson, Gerald. BURGOYNE OF SARATOGA. Times Books.

JOURNAL DES VOYAGE DE M. STAINT LUC DE LA CORNE, ECR. DANS LE NAVIRE L'AUGUSTE, EN l'AN 1761.

Langguth, A.J. PATRIOTS—THE MEN WHO STARTED THE AMERICAN REVOLUTION. New York: Simon and Schuster, 1988.

Lossing, Benson L. THE LIFE AND TIMES OF PHILIP SCHUYLER, Vols I & II. New York: Da Capo Press, 1973.

_____. THE PICTQRIAL FIELD-BOOK OF THE REVOLUTION, Vol 1. Freeport: Books for Libraries Press.

Lt. JAMES MOODY'S NARRATIVE OF HIS EXERTIONS AND SUFFERINGS. NEW YORK TIMES and Arno Press, 1968.

MacDonald, Judge H.S. "The U.E. Loyalists of the Old Johnstown District," Ontario Historical Society, Papers and Records, Vol Xll. Toronto: Published by the Society, 1914.

Marshall, John. THE LIFE OF GEORGE WASHINGTON, Vols. l & II. New York: Walton Books Co., 1930.

Martin, J.P. PRiVATE YANKEE DOODLE. Boston: Little, Brown and Co., 1962.

Mathews, H.C. FRONTIER SPIES. Fort Myers: Ace Press, 1971.

McKean, Rev. Samuel, address delivered Friday August 3, 1877, FORD EDWARD GAZETTE on the anniversary of the death of Jane McCrea, July 27, 1777.

MEMORIAL BIOGRAPHIES OF THE NEW ENGLAND HISTORIC GENEOLOGICAL SOCiETY, Vol lil, 1856-1859. Boston: Published by the Society, 1883.

MUSTER ROLL OF CAPTAIN EBENEZER JESUPS COMAPANY OF LOYAL AMERICANS FROM THE PROVINCE OF NEW YORK, at Point Claire, 24 January 1777: Xerox of the original.

Naudain, Florence A, "Colonial Corinth (Jessup's Landing)—A Bicentennial Cameo of the Jessups and Their World during Our Revolution," ms. copy from Mr. Arthur Eggleston, Corinth Historian, 1976.

Neilsen, Charles. AN ORIGINAL ACCOUNT OF . . . BURGOYNE'S CAMPAIGN. Munsell, 1844.

Pound, Arthur, and Richard E. Day. JOHNSON OF THE MOHAWKS. MacMillan, 1930.

Reid, Arthur. REMINISCENCES OF THE REVOLUTION, OR, LE LOUP'S BLOODY TRAIL FROM SALEM TO FORT EDWARD. Utica, 1859.

Riedesel, Major-General Friedrich von. MEMOIRS, LETTERS & Journals, ed. Max von Eelking, trans. W. L. Stone. Munsell, and Arno reprint, 1886.

Roberts, James A., comptroller. NEW YORK IN THE REVOLUTION AS COLONY AND STATE. Albany: Press of Brandow Printing Co., second edition, 1898.

Saffell. RECORDS OF THE REVOLUTIONARY WAR. Baltimore: Genealogical Pub. Co., 1969.

Scheer, George F., and Hugh F. Rankin. REBELS & REDCOATS. Mentor Book, 1957.

Smith, H.P., ed. HISTORY OF WARREN COUNTY. Syracuse: D. Mason & Co.,1885.

Society for Historical Research Journal, Vol 26, pp 140-44 including letters between General Burgoyne to his officers including General Gates during the expedition to the Colony of New York in 1777.

Sparks Mss., "Journal Traveling Notes for Historical Research, 1829-31. Houghton Library, Harvard.

Stanely, Lieutenant Colonel F. FOR WANT OF A HORSE. Sackville, New Brunswick: Tribune Press, 1961.

Stone, William L. THE CAMPAIGN OF LIEUT. GEN. JOHN BURGOYNE, AND THE EXPEDITION OF LIEUT. COL. BARRY ST. LEGER. Albany: Munsell, 1877.

_____. THE LIFE OF JOSEPH BRANT-THAYENDANAGEA Albany: Munsell, 1838.

Stuart, E. Rae, M.A., "Jessup's Rangers as a Factor in Loyalist Settlement," The Ontario Department of Public Records and Archives, 1961.

"Sylvester's Saratoga and Kayadrossera. An Historical Address Delivered at Saratoga, July 4, 1876."

TANGUAY'S DICTIONAIRE GENEALOGIQUE DES FAMILLES CANDIENNES.

Tasse, Joseph, Mrs. Fairchild Dean, trans. "Memoir of Charles Langlade, Wisconsin State Historical Society, Vol 11.

Thatcher, James. MILITARY JOURNAL OF THE REVOLUTION. Hartford: Hurlbert, Williams & Co., 1862.

Thomas, Lester St. John. TIMBER, TANNERY AND TOURISTS. Lake Lucerne: the Committee on Publication of Local History, 1979.

Van Doren, Honeyman, A. "The Indian Massacre of Jane McCrea in 1777," SOMERSET COUNTY HISTORICAL QUARTERLY, Vol. 7, No 4. Somerviile, October 1918.

Van Tyne, Claude H. THE LOYALISTS IN THE AMERICAN REVOLUTION, 1902.

WHITEHALL TIMES, 8/22/1877.

Willett, Colonel Marinus. NARRATIVE. Arno Reprint.

Williams, Eleazer. THE LIFE OF TEHORAGWANEGEN, ALIAS THOMAS WILLIAMS, CHIEF OF THE KAHNAWAKEH TRIBE OF INDIANS IN CANADA. Albany: Munsell, 1859.

Wilson, D. THE LIFE OF JANE McCREA WITH AN ACCOUNT OF BURGOYNE'S EXPEDITION IN 1777. New York: Baker, Godwin & Co., Printers, 1853.

Wing, Halsey McKie. "Reminiscences," typed mss. dated Sept. 15,1917. Glens Falls Crandall Library.

53177698R00231

Made in the USA
Lexington, KY
24 June 2016